MENTORSHIP/METHODOLOGY

MENTORSHIP/METHODOLOGY

Reflections, Praxis, Futures

EDITED BY
**LEIGH GRUWELL
CHARLES N. LESH**

UTAH STATE UNIVERSITY PRESS
Logan

© 2024 by University Press of Colorado

Published by Utah State University Press
An imprint of University Press of Colorado
1580 North Logan Street, Suite 660
PMB 39883
Denver, Colorado 80203-1942

All rights reserved

 The University Press of Colorado is a proud member of the Association of University Presses.

The University Press of Colorado is a cooperative publishing enterprise supported, in part, by Adams State University, Colorado State University, Fort Lewis College, Metropolitan State University of Denver, University of Alaska Fairbanks, University of Colorado, University of Denver, University of Northern Colorado, University of Wyoming, Utah State University, and Western Colorado University.

ISBN: 978-1-64642-580-8 (hardcover)
ISBN: 978-1-64642-581-5 (paperback)
ISBN: 978-1-64642-582-2 (ebook)
https://doi.org/10.7330/9781646425822

Library of Congress Cataloging-in-Publication Data

Names: Gruwell, Leigh, editor. | Lesh, Charles N., editor.
Title: Mentorship/methodology : reflections, praxis, futures / edited by Leigh Gruwell, Charles N. Lesh.
Description: Logan : Utah State University Press, [2024] | Includes bibliographical references and index.
Identifiers: LCCN 2023033380 (print) | LCCN 2023033381 (ebook) | ISBN 9781646425808 (hardcover) | ISBN 9781646425815 (paperback) | ISBN 9781646425822 (ebook)
Subjects: LCSH: English language—Rhetoric—Study and teaching (Higher)—Methodology. | Writing centers—Methodology. | Mentoring—Study and teaching (Higher) | Methodology—Study and teaching (Higher) | Mentoring in education.
Classification: LCC PE1404 .M457 2024 (print) | LCC PE1404 (ebook) | DDC 808/.0420711—dc23/eng/20240105
LC record available at https://lccn.loc.gov/2023033380
LC ebook record available at https://lccn.loc.gov/2023033381

Cover art: © Shutterstock/Wall to Wall

CONTENTS

List of Illustrations   vii

Introduction: "At the Slash"   3

PART 1: MAKING SPACE AT THE SLASH

1. Embodying Cultural Rhetorics Methodology through Mentorship
   Elise Dixon, Trixie Smith, and Malea Powell   25

2. The Twilight of the Methodology Course, or How I Learned to Tell the Tale and Leave It
   Brad Lucas   41

3. Gentefying or Gentrifying? Mentoring Up to Code on the Methodological Block
   Eric A. House, Kelly Medina-López, and Kellie Sharp-Hoskins   57

4. The Legacy of Care: Origins and Expectations of Mentoring in Writing Center Methodologies
   Devon Fitzgerald Ralston   73

PART 2: SUSTAINABILITY AT THE SLASH

5. Building Research Trajectories through Mutual Multigenerational Mentoring in Writing Program Assessment
   Gregory J. Palermo, Qianqian Zhang-Wu, Devon Skyler Regan, and Mya Poe   91

6. Expanding the WAC Network: The Cross-Institutional Mentoring Project
   Alisa Russell and Thomas Polk   109

7. Professionalizing Mentorship: The New Ethos of Academic Publishing
   Jessica Clements and John Pell   127

8. Slow Mentorship: A Feminist Methodology for Un/Becoming
   Lesley Erin Bartlett, Jessica Rivera-Mueller, and Sandra L. Tarabochia   145

PART 3: METHODOLOGICAL INNOVATIONS: BRIDGING THE SLASH

9. Who Mentors the Mentors? How Writing Center Pedagogy, Labor, and Administrator Status Impact Methodologies
   Elizabeth Geib Chavin and Beth A. Towle   163

10. Rethinking Mentorship through Institutional Ethnography and Writing Center Pedagogy: Mapping Up to Engage in Transformative Work
    Anna Sicari   181

11. Connecting Roles and Purposes in Undergraduate Embedded Mentoring
    Keaton Kirkpatrick   197

PART 4: COMPLICATING THE SLASH: FUTURES IN MENTORSHIP/METHODOLOGY

12. Leaky Bodies and Connective Tissues: A Cripped Metho-Epistemology of Mentoring
    Leslie R. Anglesey and Melissa Nicolas   217

13. Testimonio as a Methodology for Examining Marginalized Experiences with Mentorship
    Michelle Flahive   235

14. A Post-Arrival Mentorship That's Not a Mentorship: Mediated Discourse Theory and the Ecological Approach to Learning over Time and Place
    Aurora Matzke and John Paul Tassoni   252

Acknowledgments   271
Index   273
About the Authors   291

ILLUSTRATIONS

FIGURE

3.1. Hand-painted sign, "Disculpe Las Molestias, esto es una Revolución"   64

TABLES

2.1. Early 2000s views of historical periods in rhetoric and composition   50
4.1. Toward more deliberate mentoring practices   86
11.1. Experience and training of combined course faculty and mentors   205
11.2. Frequency of roles used by combined course mentors in their classroom interactions   210

MENTORSHIP/METHODOLOGY

Introduction
"AT THE SLASH"

Leigh Gruwell and Charles N. Lesh

We can trace the motivation for this edited collection to a specific moment. Or rather, we can trace it to a place: a basement room in a convention center in Kansas City. We suspect some of you were in Kansas City at the time too, in 2018 for the Conference on College Composition and Communication (CCCC). *Languaging. Laboring. Transforming.* And like many of you, before the conference started, we sat down and decided which panels we'd like to attend, together or separately.

As two pre-tenure faculty members in rhetoric and composition at Auburn University, we had recently been in talks with administration on adding a methodology course to our graduate curriculum.[1] "Graduate students in writing studies *need* a methods course," we would tell anyone who might listen. And finally, they did listen. As a member of the Graduate Studies Committee, Leigh was tasked with drafting a proposal and justification for the seminar, and if our faculty up-voted the curricular addition, she would go on to teach its first offering.

Back in 2018, our goal at CCCC was to attend as many panels on methods and methodology as we could, in an attempt to develop our own approach and to articulate the importance of methodological training in writing studies to folks outside the field.[2] This is what brought us to the small, brightly lit basement room for a roundtable session titled Preparing Graduate Students for Research.[3] Exactly what we needed. And based on the attendance of the panel, it was also what a lot of others in our field needed. The room was packed, standing room only, by the time the first speaker started introductions.

During this engaging and informative session, panelists shared a variety of anecdotes, curricula, and course designs intended to communicate and model methodological thinking to emerging researchers. As we listened to these reflections, as we filled our notebooks with ideas, we began to see a link, however implicit, emerging between methodology and *mentorship*: that how we know and come to know things about writing—that is, methodology—is constitutively tied up in who we know and how we know them—that is, our performances of mentorship. As we left the room and ascended the stairs to another session, we decided that, in our own work at Auburn, we had to start locating our thinking on methodology at this intersection with mentorship.

Over coffee later that day, we began thinking about our own experiences and histories at that intersection. While the methods course Charlie took at Northeastern University during his doctoral work was surely important, the actual critical orientation he developed in his ethnographic work with graffiti writers grew more directly out of the relationships he had with faculty members who guided his project and, maybe especially, the community members who participated in it. Both groups—faculty and community partners—directly mentored him through the rhythms of the research process. It was in those mentoring spaces where he developed what Jeff Grabill (2012) has called a research stance, his own "position or set of beliefs and obligations that shape how one acts as a researcher" (211).

Likewise, Leigh recalled how her dissertation research on feminist rhetorics in digital communities was shaped by the mentorship she'd benefitted from at Miami University. She'd purposefully chosen to work with faculty members with expertise in feminist methodologies, but soon found that the values that drove her advisors' research also informed their approach to mentorship. That is, the "care, collaboration, dialogue, ethics, mutual respect, and hope" (Enoch, Jack, and Glenn 2019, 12–3) that define feminist methodologies were foundational to the relationships she formed with her mentors and, accordingly, the research that resulted from those relationships.

In retelling these experiences, we began to position mentorship as a primary location from which new approaches to research surface (or fail to surface), where new methodologies emerge (or fail to emerge). In other words, we began to see mentorship, through the research it nourishes, *as the location where the future of our field is invented, or where the past is reproduced.* In this initial conversation, we began to articulate some key questions that drove our decision to undertake this edited collection: What is the relationship between mentorship and methodology, and how can we make that relationship more visible? How can our methodological work change what counts as mentorship, and how might our diverse performances of mentorship (re)invent our methodologies? How are methodologies shaped, diversified, or constrained by mentoring relationships? What does this intersection, between mentorship *and* methodology, mean for current and future work in writing studies?

Fast-forward a few years and through a few conference panels of our own on the subject, and here we are, still thinking about that *"and"*: mentorship *and* methodology. These conversations laid the foundation for our earliest articulation of this project and its primary provocation: that mentorship plays a central role in the production of innovative and potentially more equitable approaches to research, a sensitivity to the how and why of research integral to pushing the field in new and progressive directions. If we are to understand mentorship in this way, we must acknowledge and make visible mentoring arrangements performed across a variety of institutional, disciplinary, and community contexts. We hold strong to these convictions. The aforementioned course proposal was ultimately approved. Leigh taught the first offering of that course in fall 2020, and Charlie taught it in fall 2022. In this and other work, we find ourselves positioning these two core disciplinary terms in tandem.

Or it might be more accurate to say that we find ourselves positioning them *always already* in tandem. That is, as we began to compile and edit this collection of essays, we began to rethink the "and" in our initial formulation. At the beginning of this project, we saw ourselves bringing two distinct but clearly related conversations in writing studies into generative contact. Here is mentorship. Here is methodology. Now we have mentorship and methodology. But then we started to actually build this project. We read and we wrote. We called for proposals and reviewed chapters. We collected and edited the essays in the collection you now hold. In this process, we began to wonder if what we were really trying to do was bring two terms, with discernible boundaries, into contact and conversation. Rather, it began to feel like what we were trying to do was make visible their already convergent, mutually constitutive natures.

As we discussed this project, with each other and with colleagues, we found ourselves defaulting to "mentorship/methodology," with the slash performing its more convergent function. In the slash, we hope to signal dialectic interplay, definitions contingent on contact. Rather than separating these two terms, we see the slash signaling the productive overlaps, tensions, and encounters that exist between them. We've come to see this project and the essays that comprise it as not bringing two discrete concepts together but rather inhabiting and theorizing the spaces where they are already colliding. At the slash, we've come to embrace a way of thinking: that in writing studies there is no methodology without mentorship and no mentorship without methodology. And once this interdependence is articulated, a revised set of questions arises: Where have current arrangements of mentorship/methodology taken our field? Where do these points of intersection exist? In performance and practice? In theory? In research? What image of our field do they produce? Who and what do they serve? How can we revise them? And how can we better articulate, and write about, these spaces—like our own experiences above—where mentorship and methodology collide in productive disciplinary work?

We are certainly not the first people in writing studies to recognize the transcendent power of mentorship, how it moves between and affects other spaces of disciplinarity. As one instructive example, in "Mentoring as Mosaic: Life as Guerilla Theater," Lynn Z. Bloom (2007) offers the image of the mosaic to demonstrate the way that mentoring can color the entirety of our curricular and extracurricular lives. She catalogs the ways we

> can experience the mosaic of mentorship, acquiring the elements of what we need to know and do to survive, even prevail, in professional situations. In real life, these invariably leech into the person, but to keep the metaphor intact let's imagine straight, precise edges rather than the blurs and blots of an Impressionist painting. When the pieces are assembled and adjusted to fit the contours of our individual personalities and our particular work, the mosaic delineates a professional portrait that is like no other. (87)

We find Bloom's metaphor of the mosaic to be generative. The disparate components of the mosaic, the roles we've taken on and perform, appear chaotic when viewed up close. Yet with the privilege of distance, they form a coherent, legible pattern. And still, as Bloom herself notes, the clear boundaries between these parts are illusory, creating a false sense of separation, of discrete things *brought together*. Mentorship *and* methodology. In reality, these simultaneous parts of our identities—researcher, teacher, mentor, mentee, and so on—swirl together, existing within the "blurs and blots" of everyday life. This collection attempts to capture those messy moments, to theorize what it means when our work as researchers, mentors, and mentees collides in the production, revision, and reproduction of our field and our roles within it.

We dwell on the slash here, with all its "blurs and blots," because we think that a more explicit interrogation of the ways that mentorship and methodology collide in productive or unproductive ways is increasingly urgent. In the slash, we see a space in which an exclusionary status quo is maintained or, potentially, where a more equitable future is imagined. It can be either, but it can't be both. Conditions in writing studies have prompted recent disciplinary reckoning around issues of identity-, race-, gender-, and class-based inequities in our field that have long been swept under institutional rugs. As we discuss in more detail below, many of the most important conversations on mentorship and methodology revolve around issues of identity, exclusion, and justice.

For example, in a recent symposium in *Rhetoric Review*, Ersula Ore, Kim Wieser, and Christina V. Cedillo (2021) bring together a range of "counternarratives that tell how these particular BIPOC scholars size up and subvert an oppressive system to find the nurturance and community they need to succeed in often hostile spaces" (208). While distinct, the narratives that comprise this special issue share common features, the editors note, often linked by the various permutations of inequity found within academic spaces. Mentorship becomes central to any effort to mitigate these challenges, to the extent that they can even be mitigated in settler institutions like academia. "Mentorship and community-building," as Ore, Wieser, and Cedillo powerfully put it, "are central to this work—and to keeping BIPOC in the academy" (209).

Black and women of color feminists in writing studies and beyond have been especially incisive in their arguments about how mentorship is crucial to undermining the racist, sexist hierarchies of academia. bell hooks (1994) has written extensively about the radical potential of teaching and service, seeing the mentorship practices implicit in both as critical to building a more inclusive and just academy. Such work not only creates spaces that value racialized identities but is essential to sustaining academia itself (29–30). Closer to our disciplinary home in writing studies, Carmen Kynard (2020) has repeatedly highlighted the stark "ontological absence of Black women" (18) that marks the field, and argues that an equity-oriented model of mentorship needs to go beyond simply "teaching young Black faculty the rules of the academy" and instead must be "about centering Black thought and Black life in people's lives at the academy" (18). What Kynard, hooks, and many other Black and women of color feminists (Hull, Shelton, and Mckoy 2019; Ribero and Arellano 2019; Scott et al. 2021) teach us is that mentorship *is* methodology, and that both must focus on racial justice. If not, we rob each of its transformative potential.

Embedded within these conversations about mentorship, methodology, and identity is a question of that slash, the ways that mentorship in all its forms—formal or informal, radical or conservative, institutional or community, ad hoc or sustained, vertical or horizontal—(re)produces different patterns of disciplinarity and disciplinary research. In the slash, then, we find both the perpetuation of harmful systems of exclusion and the potential for change, for more equitable forms of mentorship and research to mutually nourish each other and move our field toward more inclusive practices. Attending to the slash, making it more visible, presents significant opportunities to support and cultivate diverse ways of knowing and being in writing studies, something that many of the chapters in this collection articulate in local and global ways.

As two white, cis-het, recently tenured professors, we recognize that we are hardly the people to do this work alone. We also recognize that inhabiting these and other subject positions of privilege while attempting to do this work requires attention to the relationship between editing and identity. How can we ensure that our curation of this conversation doesn't solely include experiences that reflect our own? Of course, this question is never answered in an entirely satisfactory way. We suspect any reader who has ever edited a collection of their own feels this tension. Still, this question motivated us, and continues to motivate us, to have conversations with each other, with mentors, and with editors on equity- and justice-oriented approaches to collection creation. It's not enough, we learned, simply to identify our own subject positions in the introduction, note how they likely limited the perspectives found in the book, and move on. Rather, we have to interrogate those positions and our own editing practices, and actively work to mitigate their limiting potential. We also have to recognize that this mitigation can never be entirely successful.

A more equitable field begins, in part, with editing practices that include intentional discussions of who has access to collections, where the call for proposals (CFP) circulates, and how the contributors are mentored through the publication process. In their work on "inclusion activism" in editing practices, Blewett et al. (2018) write, "If we want equitable representation in our scholarship and in our field at large, we have to create the conditions to make it happen" (275). This involved us in two initial ways: the CFP and its circulation. In the CFP, we included language that signaled not only our interest in publishing diverse perspectives on mentorship and methodology but also our belief that any collection on the subject without those perspectives would fail to capture the field as it currently stands. To prompt this sort of inclusion, we also paid particular attention to how we circulated the CFP: to larger, discipline-wide venues (WPA-L, for example), but also to graduate-student specific venues, individual SIGs, and social media. This intentionality, we hoped, would ensure a diversity of perspectives and voices, particularly from communities historically underrepresented in our disciplinary venues. As we made these editorial and circulatory decisions, we did so with the explicit intention of crafting our collection in a way that "builds upon the diversity that has historically marked our field's teachers and classrooms, but not our published scholarship"

(Selfe, Villanueva, and Parks 2017). While we have undoubtedly fallen short of this goal, we do believe it is worth making these choices explicit as we continue to strive toward more equitable editing, mentoring, and research practices.

These behind-the-scenes conversations are a manifestation of the larger hope we have for the collection. In the aforementioned symposium issue, Ore, Wieser, and Cedillo (2021) offer thoughts on what allies might do in mentorship spaces given the enduring inequities in the academy:

> It means offering mentorship to your BIPOC students and colleagues with the understanding that many of us navigate the academy all by ourselves, minus the structural support that we are assumed to have had and that many of our privileged colleagues did. It means trusting your students and colleagues and refusing to silence or ignore their grievances because they are not part of your experience or could potentially "cause trouble." But it also means admitting that "many pockets of bigotry, intolerance and repugnant elitism" exist, and fighting to keep them out of our classrooms, organizations, and institutions (see Brooks). It means being upfront with mentees about what they should expect from whom—who is safe and who is not—and speaking up and taking action when abusers strike. It means centering the needs of the most vulnerable in our academic communities, including students, adjuncts, and staff.

Our hope, realized in part by this collection, is that locating these conversations at the intersection of methodology and mentorship might promote some of this work—that in the exploration of the moments and spaces where these two concepts collide, we might begin to make visible more ethical mentoring spaces and more ethical methodologies that, taken together, might push the field in more equitable, and even radical, directions.

It is a lofty hope. But in the essays collected here, we find glimpses into projects that begin to perform this convergence in productive ways. In the remainder of this introduction, we offer some framing thoughts for those chapters. We consider how our field has theorized and studied mentorship, how we've theorized and studied methodology, and the stakes of theorizing and studying their intersections. We conclude with a brief overview of the chapters in this collection.

MENTORSHIP *AND* METHODOLOGY: A SHORT LITERATURE REVIEW

Writing studies has regularly sought to interrogate where our methodologies emerge, including the positionalities and relationships that inevitably inform our methodological commitments (Banks, Cox, and Dadas 2019; Fleckenstein et al. 2008; Powell and Takayoshi 2003; Sullivan and Porter 1997). Central to these conditions are the mentoring relationships that produce and bind members of our field. Despite this disciplinary history of reflecting on and refining models of mentorship (Ballif, Davis, and Mountford 2008; Bloom 2007; Eble and Gaillet 2008; Okawa 2002), existing scholarship on mentoring rarely addresses how often it directly informs and is informed by methodology, while scholarship on methodology doesn't typically acknowledge its relationship to mentorship. Here, then, we trace how the field has taken up these two terms—mentorship and methodology—separately, noting how the slash we see as connecting them has been implicit, if unexamined, all along.

Mentorship

Mentorship has always been foundational to writing studies, which has decades worth of scholarship devoted to exploring varied structures, effects, and practices of mentorship. Scholars have shared personal stories of mentorship (Bloom 2007; Horner 2008), seeking to understand how mentorship changes across specific institutional locations such as writing programs (Denny 2010; Meeks and Hult 1998; Moore 2018) and graduate education (Clary-Lemon and Roen 2008; Kameen 1995; Madden 2020; Turner et al. 2017). Collaborative scholarship also dominates mentorship research, as differing configurations of mentorship relationships reflect on, theorize, and model their experiences making knowledge together (Browdy et al. 2021; Gindlesparger and Ryan 2016; Rodrigo et al. 2014). Taken together, this scholarship evidences the field's long-standing interest in making mentorship visible as well as its belief that mentorship is essential to professional (and often to personal) success. Yet, our understandings of mentorship have evolved alongside the field itself: as writing studies matures into a fully fledged discipline, discussions of mentorship have expanded from uncritical lore to examinations of how mentorship functions as a prerequisite for a healthy, sustainable discipline.

While this abundance of research all agrees on the importance of mentorship, it also continually highlights the frustrating institutional invisibility of mentorship work. Indeed, some scholars point to the implicit but durable assumed connection between mentorship and teaching to explain why the intellectual and emotional labor of mentorship is so often overlooked (Clary-Lemon and Roen 2008; Day et al. 2013; Rodrigo et al. 2014). If mentorship is simply an extension of teaching duties, traditional thinking goes, then it deserves no special recognition or support within departments or institutions more widely. Frequently this dynamic is especially amplified for scholars of color (particularly women), who often find themselves assuming large mentorship responsibilities without formal recognition or resources (Kynard 2020; Mullings and Mukherjee 2018; Ore, Weiser, and Cedillo 2021). One solution to this persistent problem, suggest Day et al. (2013), is to simply recategorize mentorship: rather than seeing it as teaching or service, we should instead see it as scholarship. "Like editorial and curatorial work," they explain, "mentoring advances scholarship in the field, forging relationships among scholars that make possible new and potentially innovative work and allowing voices to be heard that might otherwise remain silent" (202). We agree that positioning mentorship as intellectual work is crucial, not just to ensure appropriate credit in annual reviews and for tenure and promotion but also to highlight how foundational mentorship is to a diverse range of disciplinary knowledge-making practices. Supporting mentorship, in other words, supports methodological advancement, perhaps most especially for underrepresented scholars.

Many writing studies scholars have made this case bluntly, framing mentorship as a matter of survival for those who have not traditionally been welcomed into the academy. Feminist scholars especially have been vocal in arguing for the importance of diverse approaches to mentorship attuned to the needs of women, often in explicit opposition to traditional, hierarchical models of mentorship (Balliff, Davis, and Mountford 2008; Fishman and Lunsford 2008; Morris, Rule, and LaVecchia 2020). Feminist mentorship tends to advocate more collaborative, egalitarian approaches such as "mentoring networks" (Eble and Gaillet 2019), "feminist comentoring" (Godbee and Novotny 2013), and "horizontal mentoring" (VanHaitsma and Ceraso 2017). Mentorship, in these configurations, is a political act that seeks to recognize and support the many (sometimes competing) aspects of women's identities so that they may better navigate and even undo the exclusionary structures of academia.

Advocates have also extended these discussions of mentorship-as-survival to explore mentorship's potential to support racial and ethnic minorities including Black and Latinx scholars in the academy. In one notably early example of such an approach to mentorship, Gail Y. Okawa's (2002) *CCC* article "Diving for Pearls" argues for "the need for better support systems for scholars of color," noting that mentorship in this context is necessarily an "activist practice" that "is critical to the survival and success of graduate students and junior faculty of color in the academic culture" (509). More recent scholarship echoes and amplifies

Okawa's call to see mentorship as necessary to the survival of BIPOC scholars. Ore, Weiser, and Cedillo (2021) explain that "because universities were not created for BIPOC and we were never intended to succeed in those spaces" (208), mentorship is critical to ensuring BIPOC scholars can "create spaces where we *do* belong" (209). Even when BIPOC scholars are able to create such spaces, many are still faced with the realities of navigating primarily or exclusively white environments (such as graduate programs), having to rely on white mentors who believe that they "do not have to push for change so long as they offer advice or simply warn those under their care" (Garcia et al. 2021, 55). Indeed, writes Kynard (2015), BIPOC scholars must learn to navigate "a field whose central knowledge-making industry—both its journals and the processes of selecting its editors—reproduces racist logics" (3). Thus, while mentorship can be liberatory, a means of reshaping the academy to eliminate the kind of exploitative or demeaning relationships that can silence or exclude BIPOC and other marginalized scholars, it (especially in its most uncritical formations) can also be fraught for those scholars who must rely on often regressive mentorship relationships based on raced hierarchies in order to ensure access to the academy.

Shannon Madden (2020) echoes this concern in her introduction to the edited collection *Learning from the Lived Experiences of Graduate Student Writers*, arguing that "traditional" approaches to mentorship can risk stifling scholarly and methodological advancement: when graduate mentorship is limited to "learn[ing] to perform research by carrying out faculty study designs," we risk not just privileging "certain ways of knowing" but ultimately the stifling of "writers from marginalized identity groups, as well as the future of knowledge across fields" (16). Mentorship, then, is powerful in both its progressive and conservative forms: while on the one hand it can serve as a gatekeeping mechanism, it also has the potential to reshape scholarly practice in writing studies by validating the embodied knowledge-making of scholars who have traditionally been excluded from disciplinary conversations. Mentoring that acknowledges or makes space for different, traditionally underrepresented or excluded epistemological positions can ultimately create a more inclusive academy as well as more just theories of writing and rhetoric.

Methodology

Methodologies are the larger epistemic commitments that guide how a researcher understands processes of knowledge-making, including decisions about specific methods. Feminist methodologies, for example, tend to emphasize reciprocity, reflexivity, and social justice–based outcomes for participants (Kirsch 1999; McKee and Porter 2010; Powell and Takayoshi 2003). These values would thus shape how a researcher selects or performs specific research practices such as interviews or participant representation. Because methodologies determine *how* we know, they are also critical factors in *what* we can know. Methodological decisions, that is, are rhetorical decisions. For this reason, writing studies scholars have long encouraged researchers to examine how one's positionality might shape their epistemological claims, invoking metaphors like "orientation" (Banks, Cox, and Dadas 2019), "ecology" (Fleckenstein et al. 2008) or even "messiness" (Rickly 2007) to highlight the reality that research is not a neutral, distanced event but instead emerges from the unique and complex networks of identity, body, and relationality that define every research project.

From this perspective, knowledge-making is embodied, situated, and located; we do not know beyond our bodies and the relationships we form both within and outside academia. It is a process of forging, sustaining, or troubling our connections with other knowers, perhaps particularly those we might consider mentors. In one notable study, for example, Takayoshi, Tomlinson, and Castillo (2012) surveyed researchers in writing studies to better understand how they made methodological decisions. They found that "82% of participants identified experiential knowledge as the source of their methodological choices" (108). Their participants also suggested that one important source for generating research questions/methods is "connecting with esteemed and intellectually stimulating colleagues" (111). In other words, researchers make methodological choices based on their experiences and their relationships. As Jennifer Clary-Lemon (2018) puts it, "Our research and chosen methodologies [function] as part of a network of intersubjective human relations," inextricable from "other flows of information, complementary ways of knowing, and interrelationships" (208). In this collection, we seek to highlight the fleshy relations that govern our research's visibility, as we believe doing so can invite not just new methodologies but new ways of being and relating to one another.

Recognizing the ways in which methodology emerges from our varied embodied subject positions necessitates deep reflection. An important part of this process, writes Jacqueline Jones Royster (2000), is "an acknowledgement of passionate attachments," which asks the researcher "to specify attachments, to recognize who has produced the knowledge, what the bases of it are, what the material circumstances of its production entail, what consequences or implications are suggested by its existence, and for whom the consequences and implications hold true" (280). Understanding our many "passionate attachments"—including who we make knowledge with and for—will, in many cases, require a reimagining of our methodologies, as we may need to employ "a broader, sometimes different range of techniques in garnering evidence and in analyzing and interpreting evidence" (251). Royster (2003) emphasizes that this work is fundamentally generative, so that "a different sense of the [disciplinary] landscape can be made visible, can be deemed valuable, and can become instructive in the re-envisioning of what constitutes knowledge" (161).

Thus, acknowledging from whom and where our methodologies spring is explicitly antiracist and decolonial. In their book *Race, Rhetoric, and Research Methods*, Lockett et al. (2021) explain how racism "affects how we design research, what we claim is the truth about what we observe, how we learn, our decision-making, and ultimately who we will communicate with and who we will try to become" (17). Our methodological choices will necessarily reflect the racist assumptions and biases that undergird all facets of contemporary life, including our disciplinary work. As Ruiz (2021) explains in her solo-authored chapter in the same book, such "epistemological racism" continues to mark even the field's so-called critical methodologies, such as feminist methodologies, which "are embedded in traditions of Whiteness and Western oriented epistemologies" (39). One way to uncover these racist and colonial legacies, we believe, lies in unpacking the contexts from which our methodologies emerge, including the exclusionary structures and practices that continue to dominate the field.

As we hope to have made clear, we recognize a capacious and multi-sited approach to mentorship, one that values but exceeds traditional graduate student-faculty advisor relationships. Likewise, we also embrace an expansive rendering of methodology, recognizing its ability to articulate not just our research practice but all of our academic labor, including teaching, service, and mentorship. The slash that unites these terms thus invites similarly generative approaches to knowing and being within writing studies.

Mentorship/Methodology

It is at this intersection between how we know and who we know that we locate the work of this collection and, ultimately, our hopes for it. As we've said, we believe that spaces of mentorship/methodology can counter instances of epistemic injustice—what Beth Godbee (2017) describes as "harm done to people in their capacities as knowers" (207). Yet these spaces can also perpetuate harm. We hope, then, that in emphasizing spaces at the slash, we see them for what they are: spaces of potential, of either maintaining the status quo and the discipline's complicity in systems of domination, or of radical chance, where we might counter that complicity and project new ways of knowing. Because we recognize how our privileges limit our capacities to perform this work, we believe the conversation at the slash must be multi-vocal, must contain a diverse cacophony of voices pushing the slash in productive directions. The four parts that comprise this collection reflect that sometimes harmonious, sometimes dissonant, chorus.

Each chapter in part 1, "Making Space at the Slash," invites readers into the production of the new spaces required for this work, the critical practices implied in this type of slash work. To start us off, Elise Dixon, Trixie Smith, and Malea Powell consider how the spaces of graduate mentorship, particularly during dissertation writing stages, might be informed by the principles of cultural rhetorics. This type of responsive, even radical, mentorship reflective of larger methodological criticality challenges existing models of graduate student training, where graduate students are mentored into the field's methodologies. In his chapter, Brad Lucas likewise describes the futility of these types of generalized, one-size-fits-all spaces of methodological mentoring. Blending personal history with disciplinary currents, Lucas challenges us to think beyond the methods seminar toward something like mentoring methodologies: structures of training that move beyond exclusionary surveys toward more hyper-local, justice-oriented training. To understand this (re)production of core disciplinary spaces, we need new vocabularies. Eric A. House, Kelly Medina-López, and Kellie Sharp-Hoskins offer language to understand this type of spatial work. Building on feminist work by Black, Indigenous, and women of the global majority (BIWGM), House, Medina-López, and Sharp-Hoskins argue that we need new spaces of methodology and mentoring "that do not dispossess, bypass, or whitewash students' (home) language, literacies, and embodied expertise." To that end, these authors offer "gentefying" as an alternative to the ways our disciplinary block is and continues to be gentrified. This takes work, and Devon Fitzgerald Ralston provides a glimpse into some of what that might look like. Drawing on autoethnographic narrative and histories of writing centers, Ralston argues for a deliberate centering of mentorship in writing center work, to think of mentoring "as a methodology, one that is deliberate and focused and one that can be flexible and evolving as we open spaces for previously underrepresented voices."

In all of this work, we see how the slash can open up new spaces for disciplinary work, both new work to be done and structures to be built.

As this collection acknowledges the need for the production of these new spaces at the slash, it likewise acknowledges the need to consider the sustainability of these spaces, their ability to survive within increasingly unstable institutional landscapes. The chapters that comprise part 2, "Sustainability at the Slash," theorize and document programs designed to flexibly and sustainably continue the mentoring work of methodology, and the methodological work of mentorship, albeit on different scales and in different ways. For example, Gregory J. Palermo, Qianqian Zhang-Wu, Devon Skyler Regan, and Mya Poe describe a cross-generational assessment project at Northeastern University designed to both mentor future generations on the crucial, but often overlooked, assessment practice of writing program administration and make assessment work there more responsive to the school's international population. This blending of the local and global—to build mentoring spaces at once responsive to local conditions and broader disciplinary needs—is a current we see running through this section. In their chapter, Alisa Russell and Thomas Polk describe the experiences of graduate students and faculty inhabiting larger disciplinary spaces of mentoring: the Cross-Institutional Mentoring Program (CIMP). In pairing graduate students and new faculty with more experienced Writing Across the Curriculum (WAC) scholar-practitioners, the CIMP provides the authors a context to study the ways WAC methodologies, broadly defined, are circulated and transmitted within the field. Jessica Clements and John Pell likewise seek to render visible what is often invisible in our field, namely paths toward academic publication. Drawing on a rich archive of social media posts on the topic of publication and on their own experiences as editors at *Present Tense*, Pell and Clements survey more ethical and, frankly, more productive methodologies for publication mentorship. Lesley Erin Bartlett, Jessica Rivera-Mueller, Sandra L. Tarabochia's chapter again demonstrates the diversity of these spaces at the slash and that sustainable mentorship/methodology work requires us to theorize mentoring spaces that stand outside of hierarchical, neoliberal models. In introducing "slow mentorship" in the context of an informal writing group, these authors give name to many of the sustainability practices we see at the slash, a mentorship practice that is "holistic and counter-cultural, that values 'excess,' identity work, and agency."

Part 3, "Methodological Innovations: Bridging the Slash," asks readers to consider the varied methodologies we might adapt to study, theorize, and improve mentorship across the discipline. The chapters in this section all underscore the need for intentional, if flexible, methodologies for understanding mentorship, ultimately demonstrating that an impoverished view of one is an impoverished view of both. Elizabeth Geib Chavin and Beth A. Towle offer an exploration of how labor practices within writing centers have shaped methodologies within writing center studies, ultimately advocating for additional investment in methodologies specifically focused on decolonizing writing center spaces, practices, and scholarship. Also located within the disciplinary location of writing center studies, Anna Sicari's chapter provides three case studies to argue for the value of institutional ethnography as a methodology for studying—and improving—mentorship. At the same time, Sicari draws attention to how responsive writing center mentorship practices can make institutional ethnography methodologies more attentive to the specific needs of marginalized identities. Finally, Keaton Kirkpatrick presents the results of a mixed-methods study of a course-embedded undergraduate mentorship model. Not only does Kirkpatrick highlight the value of this specific approach to undergraduate mentorship, but his chapter also demonstrates the importance of methodological diversity when studying mentorship.

We conclude the collection with part 4, "Complicating the Slash: Futures in Mentorship/Methodology." The chapters here work intentionally to expand and even in some cases undo the slash that we imagine holding mentorship/methodology together. Together, they invite readers to critically examine the narratives, bodies, and experiences we rely on to understand how we learn and do within the discipline. Leslie R. Anglesey and Melissa Nicholas introduce "leaky" as a metaphor to describe the ways in which our messy, imperfect bodies inevitably inform our ways of knowing and relating to one another. Using an approach informed by disabilities studies, Anglesey and Nicholas argue that their "cripped version of mentoring" can create spaces for similarly expansive, embodied, cripped methodologies. Michelle Flahive's chapter follows, serving as both a model of and an argument for *testimonio*, a methodology for understanding how lived experiences shape knowledge claims. Examining her own experiences as a Latina graduate student navigating a predominantly white institution (PWI), Flahive makes a compelling claim for *testimonio*'s potential to not only highlight how knowing is tied to bodies tangled in systems of power but to counter larger epistemic injustices. To close the collection, Aurora Matzke and John Paul Tassoni present what we see as a productively oppositional understanding of mentorship/methodology, one that counters many of the commonplaces that ground the rest of the chapters. They rely on mediated discourse theory to explore the ecological nature of learning and becoming together, complicating (and even refusing) traditional mentorship narratives in the process.

The cases, illustrations, and reflections readers will find here traverse our disciplinary landscape: from writing centers to faculty offices, from homespaces to lecture halls, from writing groups to cross-institutional networks, to spaces beyond and in between. As they move, they cast mentorship/methodology in sometimes quite different ways. There are palpable tensions, discrepancies, and differences: an instructively muddled mosaic, perhaps, to return to Bloom's (2007) metaphor. But read together, they produce mentorship/methodology as an important and urgent disciplinary location, a place where we can take stock of the work we've done and haven't done, the work we're doing and the work we must do. This collection attempts to capture and theorize those messy moments when our work as researchers, mentors, and mentees collides in the production, revision, and reproduction of our field and our roles within it.

NOTES

1. We've chosen to use the term "pre-tenure" to describe our positions, but we wish to call attention to the difficulties of naming institutional locations, especially in the context of mentorship relationships. Language like "mentor/mentee," "expert/novice," or "early-/late-career" can imply problematic hierarchies that don't often reflect the varied subject positions within academia. Nor does this language necessarily reflect the expansive approaches to mentorship this collection presents. We asked authors to be attentive to the politics inherent in and enacted by these terms; that is, we asked them to be intentional and critical with the language they use to describe institutional positions. We'd like to thank one of our anonymous reviewers for bringing this to our attention. We also encourage readers to reflect on the ways our disciplinary vernacular can undermine the creation of new relationships within institutional structures.
2. Our department at Auburn University is integrated, with faculty and undergraduate/graduate students from literature, technical and professional communication, creative writing, and rhetoric and composition. In this introduction, we use writing studies to speak to the broader field that includes rhetoric and composition as well as technical and professional communication, although readers will notice that authors across this collection have chosen to use a variety of names for the field.
3. Our thanks to roundtable participants Keith Grant-Davie, Elizabeth Keller, Breeanne Matheson, Kate Pantelides, Rebecca Rickly, Nancy Small, and Eric Stephens for their work on this panel.

REFERENCES

Ballif, Michelle D., Diane Davis, and Roxanne Mountford. 2008. *Women's Ways of Making It in Rhetoric and Composition*. New York: Routledge.

Banks, William P., Matthew B. Cox, and Caroline Dadas, eds. 2019. *Re/orienting Writing Studies: Queer Methods, Queer Projects*. Logan: Utah State University Press.
Blewett, Kelly, Christina M. LaVecchia, Laura R. Micciche, and Janine Morris. 2018. "Editing as Inclusion Activism." *College English* 81, no. 4 (March): 273–296.
Bloom, Lynn Z. 2007. "Mentoring as Mosaic: Life as Guerilla Theater." *Composition Studies* 35, no. 2 (Fall): 87–99.
Browdy, Ronisha, Esther Milu, Victor del Hierro, and Laura Gonzales. 2021. "From Cohort to Family: Coalitional Stories of Love and Survivance." *Composition Studies* 49, no. 2 (Summer): 14–30.
Clary-Lemon, Jennifer. 2018. "Serendology, Methodipity: Research, Invention, and the Choric Rhetorician." In *Serendipity in Rhetoric, Writing, and Literacy Research*, edited by Maureen Daly Goggin and Peter N. Goggin, 205–218. Logan: Utah State University Press.
Clary-Lemon, Jennifer, and Duane Roen. 2008. "Webs of Mentoring in Graduate School." In *Stories of Mentoring: Theory and Practice*, edited by Michelle Eble and Lynée Lewis Gaillet, 178–192. West Lafayette, IN: Parlor Press.
Day, Michael, Susan H. Delagrange, Mike Palmquist, Michael A. Pemberton, and Janice R. Walker. 2013. "What We Really Value: Redefining Scholarly Engagement in Tenure and Promotion Protocols." *College Composition and Communication* 65, no. 1 (September): 185–208.
Denny, Harry C. 2010. *Facing the Center: Toward an Identity Politics of One-to-One Mentoring*. Logan: Utah State University Press.
Eble, Michelle, and Lynée Lewis Gaillet, eds. 2008. *Stories of Mentoring: Theory and Practice*. West Lafayette, IN: Parlor Press.
Eble, Michelle, and Lynée Lewis Gaillet. 2019. "Re-inscribing Mentoring." In *Retellings: Opportunities for Feminist Research in Rhetoric and Composition Studies*, edited by Jessica Enoch and Jordynn Jack, 283–303. West Lafayette, IN: Parlor Press.
Enoch, Jessica, Jordynn Jack, and Cheryl Glenn. 2019. "Introduction: The Endless Opportunities for Feminist Research." In *Retellings: Opportunities for Feminist Research in Rhetoric and Composition Studies*, edited by Jessica Enoch and Jordynn Jack, 3–15. West Lafayette, IN: Parlor Press.
Fishman, Jenn, and Andrea Lunsford. 2008. "Educating Jane." In *Stories of Mentoring: Theory and Practice*, edited by Michelle Eble and Lynée Lewis Gaillet, 18–32. West Lafayette, IN: Parlor Press.
Fleckenstein, Kristie S., Clay Spinuzzi, Rebecca J. Rickly, and Carole Clark Papper. 2008. "The Importance of Harmony: An Ecological Metaphor for Writing Research." *College Composition and Communication* 60, no. 2 (December): 388–419.
Garcia, Christine, Les Hutchinson Campos, Genevieve García de Müeller, and Christina V. Cedillo. 2021. "'It's Not You. You Belong Here.' A Latinx Conversation on Mentorship and Belonging in the Academy." *Composition Studies* 49, no. 2 (Summer): 53–69.
Gindlesparger, Kathryn, and Holly Ryan. 2016. "Feminist Fissures: Navigating Conflict in Mentoring Relationships." *Peitho* 19, no. 1 (Fall/Winter): 54–70.
Godbee, Beth. 2017. "Writing Up: How Assertions of Epistemic Rights Counter Epistemic Injustice." *College English* 79, no. 6 (July): 593–618.
Godbee, Beth, and Julia C. Novotny. 2013. "Asserting the Write to Belong: Feminist CoMentoring among Graduate Student Women." *Feminist Teacher* 23 (3): 177–195.
Grabill, Jeffrey. 2012. "Community Based Research and the Importance of a Research Stance." In *Writing Studies Research in Practice*, edited by Lee Nickoson and Mary P. Sheridan, 210–219. Carbondale: Southern Illinois University Press.
hooks, bell. 1994. *Teaching to Transgress*. New York: Routledge.
Horner, Winifred Bryan. 2008. "On Mentoring." In *Stories of Mentoring: Theory and Practice*, edited by Michelle Eble and Lynée Lewis Gaillet, 14–17. West Lafayette, IN: Parlor Press.

Hull, Brittany, Cecilia D. Shelton, and Temptaous Mckoy. 2019. "Dressed but Not Tryin' to Impress: Black Women Deconstructing 'Professional' Dress." *Journal of Multimodal Rhetorics* 3 (1). http://journalofmultimodalrhetorics.com/3-2-hull-shelton-mckoy.

Kameen, Paul. 1995. "Studying Professionally: Pedagogical Relationships at the Graduate Level." *College English* 57, no. 4 (February): 448–460.

Kirsch, Gesa. 1999. *Ethical Dilemmas in Feminist Research: The Politics of Location, Interpretation, and Publication.* Albany: State University of New York Press.

Kynard, Carmen. 2015. "Teaching while Black: Witnessing and Countering Disciplinary Whiteness, Racial Violence, and University Race-Management." *Literacy in Composition Studies* 3 (1): 1–20.

Kynard, Carmen. 2020. "'All I Need Is One Mic': A Black Feminist Community Meditation on the Work, the Job, and the Hustle (and Why So Many of Yall Confuse This Stuff)." *Community Literacy Journal* 14 (2): 5–24.

Lockett, Alexandria L., Iris D. Ruiz, James Chase Sanchez, and Christopher Carter. 2021. *Race, Rhetoric, and Research Methods.* Fort Collins, CO: WAC Clearinghouse.

Madden, Shannon. 2020. "Introduction: Valuing Lived Experiences and Community Mentorship." In *Learning from the Lived Experiences of Graduate Student Writers*, edited by Shannon Madden, Michele Eodice, Kristen T. Edwards, and Alexandria Lockett, 3–31. Logan: Utah State University Press.

McKee, Heidi A., and James E. Porter. 2010. "Rhetorica Online: Feminist Research Practices in Cyberspace." In *Rhetorica in Motion: Feminist Methods and Methodologies*, edited by Eileen K. Schell and K. J. Rawson, 152–171. Pittsburgh, PA: University of Pittsburgh Press.

Meeks, Lynn, and Christine Hult. 1998. "A Comentoring Model of Administration." *WPA: Writing Program Administration* 21, nos. 2–3 (Spring): 9–22.

Moore, Cindy. 2018. "Mentoring WPAs for the Long Term: The Promise of Mindfulness." *WPA: Writing Program Administration* 42, no. 1 (Fall): 89–106.

Morris, Janine, Hannah J. Rule, and Christina M. LaVecchia. 2020. "Writing Groups as Feminist Practice." *Peitho* 22, no. 3 (Spring). https://cfshrc.org/article/writing-groups-as-feminist-practice/.

Mullings, Beverley, and Sanjukta Mukherjee. 2018. "Reflections on Mentoring as Decolonial, Transnational, Feminist Praxis." *Gender, Place and Culture* 25 (10): 1405–1422.

Okawa, Gail Y. 2002. "Diving for Pearls: Mentoring as Cultural and Activist Practice among Academics of Color." *College Composition and Communication* 53, no. 3 (February): 507–532.

Ore, Ersula, Kim Wieser, and Christina V. Cedillo. 2021. "Symposium: Diversity Is Not Enough: Mentorship and Community-Building as Antiracist Praxis." *Rhetoric Review* 40 (3): 207–256.

Powell, Katrina M., and Pamela Takayoshi. 2003. "Accepting Roles Created for Us: The Ethics of Reciprocity." *College Composition and Communication* 54, no. 3 (February): 394–422.

Ribero, Ana Milena, and Sonia C. Arellano. 2019. "Advocating Comadrismo: A Feminist Mentoring Approach for Latinas in Rhetoric and Composition." *Peitho* 21 (2): 334–356.

Rickly, Rebecca. 2007. "Messy Contexts: Research as a Rhetorical Situation." In *Digital Writing Research*, edited by Heidi A. McKee and Danielle Nicole DeVoss, 377–397. New York: Hampton Press.

Rodrigo, Shelley, Susan Miller-Cochran, and Duane Roen, with Elaine Jolayemi, Cheri Lemieux Spigel, and Catrina Mitchum. 2014. "DIY Mentoring: Developing Personal Learning Networks." *Enculturation*, April 7, 2014. https://www.enculturation.net/diy mentoring.

Royster, Jacqueline Jones. 2000. *Traces of a Stream: Literacy and Social Change among African American Women.* Pittsburgh, PA: University of Pittsburgh Press.

Royster, Jacqueline Jones. 2003. "Disciplinary Landscaping, or Contemporary Challenges in the History of Rhetoric." *Philosophy and Rhetoric* 36 (2): 148–167.

Ruiz, Iris D. 2021. "Critiquing the Critical: The Politics of Race and Coloniality in Rhetoric, Composition, and Writing Studies Research Traditions." In *Race, Rhetoric, and Research Methods*, edited by Alexandria L. Lockett, Iris D. Ruiz, James Chase Sanchez, and Christopher Carter, 39–79. Fort Collins, CO: WAC Clearinghouse.

Scott, La-Toya, Kimberly Williams, Andrea N. Baldwin, and Laura Gonzales. 2021. "On Testimony, Bridges and Rhetoric." *Peitho* 23 (4). https://cfshrc.org/article/on-testimony-bridges-and-rhetoric/.

Selfe, Cynthia, Victor Villanueva, and Steve Parks. 2017. "Generating the Field: The Role of Editors in Disciplinary Formation." *Composition Studies*, no. 17.

Sullivan, Patricia, and James E. Porter. 1997. *Opening Spaces: Writing Technologies and Critical Research Practices*. Greenwich, CT: Ablex Publishing.

Takayoshi, Pamela, Elizabeth Tomlinson, and Jennifer Castillo. 2012. "The Construction of Research Problems and Methods." In *Practicing Research in Writing Studies*, edited by Katrina M. Powell and Pamela Takayoshi, 97–121. New York: Hampton Press.

Turner, Heather Noel, Minh-Tam Nguyen, Beth Keller, Donnie Johnson Sackey, Jim Ridolfo, Stacey Pigg, Benjamin Lauren, Liza Potts, Bill Hart-Davidson, and Jeff Grabill. 2017. "WIDE Research Center as an Incubator for Graduate Student Experience." *Journal of Technical Writing and Communication* 47, no. 2 (April): 130–150.

VanHaitsma, Pamela, and Steph Ceraso. 2017. "'Making It' in the Academy through Horizontal Mentoring." *Peitho* 19, no. 2 (Spring/Summer): 210–233.

PART 1

Making Space at the Slash

1
EMBODYING CULTURAL RHETORICS METHODOLOGY THROUGH MENTORSHIP

Elise Dixon, Trixie Smith, and Malea Powell

After completing my comprehensive PhD exams, I (Elise) knew I wanted to write about a concept I had come to understand through my exam process: the idea that when cultures, organizations, and communities make things together, the process of making helps to shape and build their world. In my exams, I had defined the concept as "making as world-making." I knew I wanted to articulate this concept in my dissertation through a queer lens, but I wasn't sure how. When I submitted my first dissertation idea to my advisor, Trixie, my plan was to think about making as world-making through archival research, focusing on the worlds that could be created through zine-making. I didn't want to interview anyone, because, if I'm honest with myself, I didn't want to go through the trouble of having this "making as world-making" concept challenged by outside forces. I wanted to use my concept and apply it to something else.

Of course, Trixie wouldn't have it. Or, rather, Trixie listened to my idea intently, asked good questions, leaned back in her chair as I explained my idea, and didn't provide a concrete answer about whether she thought my plan was good or not. She only asked me to keep thinking and said she would too.

A few days later, as I finished up my shift in the writing center that Trixie directs, she approached me with an idea: "I know you want to look at making, but I think you should consider a community that makes. In your exam you discussed Sistrum, Lansing Women's Chorus and the Lesbian Avengers. What if you thought about one of these organizations? I know you liked learning about the Lesbian Avengers in our queer rhetorics course. What if you interviewed members of the Avengers?" It wasn't my original plan, so I took a few days to think about the possibility. Working with the Lesbian Avengers—an activist organization originating in New York City and coming to prominence in the early 1990s—seemed daunting. I didn't know who to get in touch with or how, and I was intimidated by working with lesbian activists as a bisexual woman married to a man. I wasn't sure that I would be welcome, and I liked the perceived comfort and anonymity of archival research.

Still, I trusted Trixie to guide me. A few days later, I caught up with her. "Ok, what should I do first? I think I need to read more theories on making," I suggested.

She shook her head. "I think you need to read way more about the Lesbian Avengers. You've read enough theory for now; learn the community."

And she was right. For the remainder of my time preparing, researching, interviewing, and writing, I found myself completely unlearning the concept of "making as world-making" as I had originally understood it. My participants—particularly Chanelle and Maxine—challenged me to see the concept of making in their own terms, terms that were distinctly lesbian (when I originally had planned to discuss the concept as queer), collaborative, and much more nebulous and intangible. My research participants, in other words, taught *me* everything I know about making as world-making. They made the world, and my responsibility was to listen.

This is what cultural rhetorics work looks like—recognizing that we have more to learn than we have to teach, that we do our best creating when we begin with listening, when our mentors start from a place of listening too.

* * *

In this chapter, we (Elise, Trixie, and Malea) discuss how a cultural rhetorics methodology impacts mentorship of graduate students, especially through the dissertation-writing process. Drawing from our personal experiences, we—one recent PhD graduate (Elise) and two members of her dissertation committee (Trixie and Malea)—discuss how embodying a cultural rhetorics methodology means deviating from traditionally Western modes of dissertation mentorship. In particular, we will describe three key cultural rhetorics tenets—decolonial practice, relationality, and storying—that inform our methodological priorities, and therefore our relationships, to one another as mentors and mentee. Thus, we focus on our embodied practices of cultural rhetorics through working to relinquish power in mentor/mentee relationships, learning with and alongside research participants as well as each other, and encouraging methodological flexibility. Further, we argue that cultural rhetorics methodology is engaged *through* and *in* the mentorship process of a cultural rhetorics dissertation, which further models for a mentee how to engage cultural rhetorics methodologies in their own work.

Scholars of cultural rhetorics "investigate and understand meaning-making as it is situated in specific cultural communities"—the project of cultural rhetorics emphasizes that "cultural communities engage in their own sets of theories and practices that scholars can learn (from) alongside these communities" (Powell et al. 2014). Thus, cultural rhetorics scholars understand that theoretical frameworks cannot be separated from the practices of the communities. For example,

> using Burke's pentad to understand North American indigenous practices of powwow dancing would not fall within current cultural rhetorics practice. Building a theoretical and rhetorical frame from the specific tribal and intertribal practices of powwow dancing, looking at how different indigenous cultures' stories, beliefs, and traditions inform that shared rhetorical practice *could* fall within current cultural rhetorics practice. (Bratta and Powell 2016)

Working from an understanding that all rhetoric is cultural and all cultures are rhetorical does not simply shift how a person *thinks* about research but also shifts a person's practice of doing that research. Just as cultural rhetorics research means working to relinquish power over research participants, cultural rhetorics mentoring means working to relinquish power over a mentee. This work is hard, especially when a mentee is still in the learning stages and looking for answers or a "right way" to do research.

Cultural rhetorics methodologies are often flexible and can shift depending on the study, the researcher, and the community participants. A cultural rhetorics methodology is similarly interested in how "scholarly practices attune to methodological fit," as House, Medina-López, and Sharp-Hoskins discuss in this collection. A cultural rhetorics methodological priority means mentoring researchers to learn *from* and *alongside* their research participants, indicating that neither the researcher nor their mentor is the expert on the cultural community—the research participants *in that community* are the experts. Mentorship derived from cultural-rhetorics values centers the stories of the research participants as both practices and theories. In essence, "we can learn from the stories we tell and re-tell what we do with cultural communities and the experiences of working with those communities. Those research stories are data for analysis" (Mukavetz 2014). Those research stories are also models for learning from communities. Therefore, mentorship from a cultural rhetorics standpoint is about encouraging methodological flexibility, perhaps by being willing to change one's methods to meet the needs or wishes of participants, growing in understanding alongside participants, asking participants what they need, and honoring those needs even when it means changing strategies, to name a few examples. One way to encourage this practice is by modeling that same flexibility in one's mentorship. Cultural rhetorics mentorship seeks to actively avoid imposing a particular theoretical or methodological lens on a community and its practices and instead seeks to support researchers as they learn from a community what theories and practices are valued in that community. In turn, modeling this flexibility as a mentor can help the mentee reflect that same openness in their methodologies.

Doing this work in an academic system that does not support this model can be met with great institutional resistance. This work can be seen as too hands-off, not rigorous, or unfocused by those accustomed to Western research practices. However, cultural rhetorics is rigorous *because* of its flexibility and attendance to participants; it asks the research to both value and engage daily with these methodologies as a way of seeing and being in the world. Indeed, it is "at the space of embodied practices of the scholar—and not simply the scholar's attitude—that cultural rhetorics connects those who study it *and* those who live it" (Bratta and Powell 2016). In this chapter, we will illustrate the complexities of cultural rhetorics methodology as we experienced it in our own embodied mentorship relationships and practices. We will also provide reflection and advice for others engaged in re-orienting their own methodological mentorship practices. In some parts of this chapter, we'll name ourselves as individual writers directly while at other times leave the reader to understand our messaging as a collective voice.

DECOLONIALITY

To start, cultural rhetorics draws upon decoloniality as a means to de-link from colonial understandings of what "counts" as knowledge, as meaning-making, as theory. According to the Cultural Rhetorics Theory Lab (CRTL),

> Communities are made up of people, with real lived experiences and lives at stake. As members of this rhet/comp community, we are invested in actively creating and sustaining a visible space considerate of relational and complex histories of rhetoric. We've learned this from decolonial scholars who enact practices within their communities to not only survive colonialism, but create a place for present and future generations to engage with their traditions. (Powell et al. 2014)

If, as the CRTL asserts, part of the work of decolonial scholars is to create space for us to think about knowledge as always connected to and generated through relationships with others, we might consider how colonial approaches would be about top-down hierarchical productions and receptions of knowledge. In essence, colonial approaches to knowledge production would look something like Freire's (1968) banking model of education, in which a person with a knowledge set imparts that knowledge upon a docile collection of seemingly empty vessels of human understanding. This model is often reified in both the classroom *and* through colonial mentorship models in which mentors essentially replicate themselves through imposing their own methodological values upon their mentees. Coloniality relies on this model in order for those in power to maintain it through the production of the same knowledge; we see this most frequently in our education system that bases itself on Western European thought beginning from the Renaissance to today.

Modernity and colonialism are tied together through history, where a Western understanding of the world became the most valid way of being. According to Walter Mignolo (2011),

> modernity is a complex narrative whose point of origin was Europe; a narrative that built Western civilization by celebrating its achievements while hiding at the same time its darker side, "coloniality." Coloniality, in other words, is constitutive of modernity—there is no modernity without coloniality. (2–3)

Modernity gains its power from the narratives of progress and achievement, all of which are filtered through an understanding of capitalism as the main means to "progress." In a university setting, modernity-coloniality often makes itself visible through power inequities where certain Western schools of thought are privileged over non-Western ways of knowing and doing, if non-Western ways of knowledge-making are even acknowledged.

We also see modernity/coloniality through the university's compliance with the systemic oppression of minoritized faculty and students: sweeping scandals under the rug, underpaying and abusing contingent and adjunct faculty, and developing gatekeeping methods designed to keep marginalized people and their perspectives marginalized. In a mentee/mentor relationship, we might see modernity/coloniality manifested in egregious ways, like an advisor taking advantage of graduate or undergraduate student labor, or in more subtle ways, like an advisor imposing their own theoretical framework on an advisee's work without listening to the advisee's ideas or offering other choices or guidance.

Colonial advising models like this can then be reproduced or replicated by the mentee in their research or community-engaged space, which further reproduces the system.

If coloniality/modernity is rooted in the assumption that Western thought and its colonial underpinnings are The Best Way to make a society function, then the mission of decoloniality is to acknowledge that there are indeed options other than coloniality, modernity, capitalism, and Western notions of linear progress. According to Mignolo (2011),

> the defining features of decolonial options is the *analytic* of the construction, transformation, and sustenance of racism and patriarchy that created the conditions to build and control a structure of knowledge, either grounded on the word of God or the word of Reason and Truth. . . . The decolonial option starts from the analytic assumption that such hierarchies are constructed . . . and specifically that they have been constructed in the very process of building the idea of Western civilization and modernity. (xv–xvi)

In particular, Mignolo's understanding that hierarchical knowledges are socially constructed is of the utmost importance to cultural rhetorics scholars.

Like most disciplines, rhetoric and composition has a canon of classical rhetorical scholarship rooted in Greek and Roman rhetoricians—their work is often taught to graduate students explicitly (and usually undergraduates more subtly through concepts like ethos, pathos, logos) as foundational—that is, as the (only) starting point of human meaning-making as it can be valued today. A decolonial cultural rhetorical approach would be to dismantle this understanding by acknowledging other important forms of knowledge creation and meaning-making beyond and alongside the traditional Western canon. In essence, "decoloniality, therefore, means both the analytic task of unveiling the logic of coloniality and the prospective task of contributing to build a world in which many worlds will coexist" (Mignolo 2011, 54). A cultural rhetorics approach to knowledge is to see it as relational (created and ever-existing through relationships with others and the world around us), constellated (non-hierarchical and non-linear), and always rooted in people and the stories we tell each other. Rather than thinking of rhetoric as *only* a product of the work of ancient Greek and Roman philosophers, cultural rhetorics allows for other additional origin points of meaning-making alongside the Western canon.

Western and colonial understandings of knowledge and meaning-making in rhetoric and composition have evolved over time to especially rely on specific values, such as an adherence to Standard Academic

English, privileging text over other forms of meaning-making (like oral traditions, crafting, beadwork, etc.), and asserting that there is one specific way to formulate a text (think thesis-driven essays, etc.). A decolonial approach to rhetoric and composition allows scholars to see those values as an option alongside other potential forms of meaning-making and to see the damage that can be caused when we overly rely on Western frameworks to study and define non-Western ways of thinking, storying, and creating.

It is difficult to fully divorce oneself from coloniality when we exist in a system where modern/colonial ways of being are privileged over all others. Academics in the United States—such as the three of us—are always already operating inside a colonial structure because the university itself is deeply connected to coloniality/modernity. For example, the three of us met and worked together at Michigan State University, the first land-grant institution in the United States, which resides on land ceded in the Treaty of Saginaw in 1819. Michigan State, like all universities occupying Indigenous lands, is always operating from a colonial framework, as the university itself exists because of settler colonialism, and then reifies Western modernity consistently (as most, if not all, universities do) through the reproduction of Western thought and values, often, in part, through mentorship models that reify colonial methodologies.

For all of these reasons, working from a decolonial approach within a university system may look like small, seemingly insignificant (inter)actions—storying, listening, and working. However, everyday actions of individual actors within a larger system can "bring to light the clandestine forms taken by the dispersed, tactical, and makeshift creativity of groups or individuals already caught in the nets of the 'discipline'" (de Certeau 1980, xiv–xv). In essence, while the institution itself may be built on colonialism, individuals within that system are still able to undermine it in small ways through daily, individual decolonial acts. According to de Certeau (1980), "the more a power grows, the less it can allow itself to mobilize part of its means in the service of deception. . . . Power is bound by its very visibility. In contrast, trickery is possible for the weak, and often it is his only possibility" (37). Precisely because academic institutions are often large, all-encompassing systems, faculty and students alike (as weaker members) can move relatively freely as individuals using tactics of subversion. Tactics, according to de Certeau (1980), can comprise "clever tricks of the 'weak' within the order established by the 'strong,' an art of putting one over on the adversary on his own turf, hunter's tricks, maneuverable, polymorph mobilities, jubilant, poetic, and warlike discoveries" (40). Decolonial approaches within an academic discipline may be seen in subversive acts of teaching, writing, small and large forms of protest, daily interactions among varying communities of practice within a department or discipline, and, of course, through mentorship.

In our discipline (rhetoric and composition), a decolonial approach to research may look like many things. Starting from a methodological perspective, research in a university setting often centers around and values objectivity or distance in both quantitative and qualitative research. Linda Tuhiwai Smith (2021) explains, "In [imperial Western] research the concept of distance is most important as it implies a neutrality and objectivity on behalf of the researcher. Distance is measurable. What it has come to stand for is objectivity, which is not measurable to quite the same extent" (56). A decolonial approach to methodology would recognize that objectivity itself is an imperialistic Western concept rooted in Classical and Enlightenment philosophies, as well as academic ideas of disciplines/disciplining (65–66). Methodological approaches are human constructions themselves and, therefore, imbued with the values of whatever community developed the methodological approach.

From a colonial framework, knowledge exists "to be discovered, extracted, appropriated, and distributed" (Smith 2021, 58), with the story stripped away. In rhetoric and writing research, such means of research were often reflected in the positivistic studies of cognitive development in the 1970s and 1980s and have since burgeoned criticism that led to the social turn of the 1990s. The social turn reflected an understanding of the importance of attending to identity and the cultural, political, and linguistic systems often attached to identity. Since the social turn, cultural rhetorics scholars have continued to argue that if "we proceed from the already-voiced assumption that all rhetoric is a product of cultural systems and that all cultures are rhetorical, . . . understanding the specificity of the bodies and subjectivities engaged in those practices must be central" (Bratta and Powell 2016). To attend to bodies and subjectivities is also to attend to the cultures and stories connected to those bodies and subjectivities; to take this further, one must understand the layered and relational makeup of the community one is studying or working alongside. Attending to the values and cultures of a community, and understanding a community's storying of itself, are integral to honoring one's relationships to their participants and to the relationships created through writing and rhetoric research, especially for those who aim to do cultural rhetorics work within the field.

In Elise's dissertation, a decolonial approach to her specific research was to make sure that she did not impose her own specific lens to the work of the activists she interviewed, members of the Lesbian Avengers, an activist organization most prominent in the early 1990s. From the construction of emails to her participants to the transcribing of their interviews, she worked to maintain transparency, ask for their feedback, and negotiate their multiple (sometimes conflicting) interpretations of various events, and changed her work to reflect that. She submitted each chapter draft to all participants and made any and all changes they suggested. She aimed to treat them as the experts of their experiences that they are and to place herself in relationship to them as a learner of their expertise (rather than the other way around).

Similarly, a decolonial approach to the mentor/mentee research relationship meant maintaining transparency, asking for feedback, negotiating the research and writing process, and viewing/treating the mentee as the expert of her own project and her own goals (not unlike the building of a "methodological homeplace" in House, Medina-López, and Sharp-Hoskins's chapter in this collection). To work in close proximity with a mentee, while paying attention to their embodied experiences throughout the project, can be a complicated process that can be misread by others who don't operate in this way, particularly folks who are not approaching the research relationship from an Indigenous, queer, or feminist lens (as we all were). This recognition of being humans working with other humans is particularly important, as we all worked to maintain relationships across the committee and the research, worked to decolonize the dissertation writing process, and held space for each other's stories as well as the participants' stories, while also bringing with us the stories of previous mentor/mentee relationships rooted in cultural-rhetorics values and methods. For example, Elise was pregnant throughout her dissertation-writing process; her first conversations with Trixie about the Lesbian Avengers were right after she discovered she was pregnant and consequently all writing check-ins began with health checks and talks about parenthood.

In order to do this work, we all relied on each other to best maintain this kind of decolonial orientation to the research, the writing, and the mentorship. It is important to note here that decolonial mentorship looks very similar to decolonial research: rather than telling Elise what to do and how to do it, Trixie and Malea repeatedly asked Elise about how she might approach certain situations, provided mentor texts of other doctoral students who engaged in similar research, and then assumed that what had been taught over the years had provided Elise enough information to process the work on her own. In essence, the decolonial approach to doctoral research mentorship was to put faith in the foundation that had been built through coursework, comprehensive exams, and our many conversations in and outside of the institutional setting. Trixie and Malea wanted to model for Elise what she might choose to do with her research participants and their stories. Indeed, it is the methodology, the process, that is actually the important piece of the mentoring relationship. If the mentee continues to work with the same community or moves on to other communities and questions, it is the process that will stick with them, so they need to learn from the process—what works, what doesn't—so they continue to grow and become good mentors to the mentees they will work with.

STORY

Cultural rhetorics operates from the understanding that stories are crucial parts of our cultures, regardless of what cultures we align ourselves with or come from. We see story as a practice, theory, and methodology. Few in academia see storytelling as intellectually rigorous, but often that is because they are simply using other words to describe what is actually, in fact, story. Anecdotes are powerful rhetorical tools used to build common ground with an audience. Narratives are often stories with a different name. All of our research tells a story of some kind or another, and we rely on stories to understand our collective past and make sense of our collective future, both in and outside of academia. According to Thomas King (2008), "the truth about stories is, that's all that we are" (2). However, often when we think about stories, we limit ourselves to an understanding of story as easy, uncomplicated, or undemanding. Rather, a cultural rhetorics orientation sees the complications of holding space for multiple stories, including stories of pain and stories that contradict each other. Indeed, "the practice of story doesn't always feel good, and the stories produced in that practice aren't always happy celebrations of our community's accomplishments" (Powell et al. 2014, act 2, scene 3). Attending to stories in cultural rhetorics work often means holding space for conflicting stories, making room for counterstories, or trying to understand the multiple truths that can be derived from the same story (i.e., constellating the stories), and all of this is incredibly difficult and rigorous work when done ethically and with the care that cultural rhetorics asks for.

Frequently, cultural rhetorics research is qualitative in nature and focuses on interviews or story-sharing of specific communities, where the researcher interviews or has conversations with the community members as experts of their experiences. Cultural rhetorics methodologies strive to derive an understanding of that specific community's theory or theories and practices without placing an outside theoretical lens of meaning upon the community. Some examples of that work might include Andrea Riley Mukavetz's (2014) research with the Little Traverse Bay Band, Marilee Brooks-Gillies's (2013) work with craft communities, or Maria Novotny's (2017) involvement with the Art of Infertility organization. In each of these women's projects, the community members' understanding of the world was privileged over the researcher's, derived from the intentional work of building reciprocal and ethical relationships between researchers and participants. Additionally, in each of these projects, story was a central part of the meaning-making process for both researcher and participants, in ways that can feel both positive and negative for all.

Cultural rhetorics mentorship is often centered around how best to engage with and treat participants' stories with respect and care, especially for a doctoral student whose first foray into cultural rhetorics research is the dissertation. In our case, Elise's dissertation examined the sometimes conflicting stories of four different members of the Lesbian Avengers. Often, the stories of two lesbian avengers were not just conflicting but in direct tension with one another. In one specific instance, when Elise emailed a chapter draft to her participant, Maxine, she took issue with a great deal of the story told by another member. Elise worked to include everyone's story, while being careful to make sure to explain that each person's story was their own truth—there was no way to dial anything down to what "really happened." Elise relied heavily on Trixie's advice for how to navigate the tension among members. Rather than provide specific concrete advice to Elise, Trixie offered a listening ear and referred her back to the power of holding space for multiple stories. She also asked lots of questions about how the stories could be constelled and put into conversation with each other and with other material items that related to/represented the Lesbian Avengers' past actions and stories. In the end, Elise Dixon (2020) concluded one dissertation chapter as follows:

> This chapter was a struggle for me as I worked to illustrate how the Lesbian Avengers came apart through the voices of four different people with four different perspectives. In discussing the un-making of the organization, I am also engaging in a re-making of sorts as I piece together these fragments of stories. Sharing this re-making with the participants of this study has meant being open to their expertise over the situation, while also attempting to constellate everyone's story even as they conflict with one another. I am extremely grateful to Maxine, Sarah, Kelly and Chanelle's patience with me and guidance in the writing of this chapter in particular. (116)

Cultural rhetorics mentorship is sometimes about paying attention to the story that the researcher might be telling themselves about how to do research. Additionally, it may be about attending to past stories about how research should be conducted or used, and then making those stories—and their inadequacies—clear to the mentee. Mentors and mentees are engaged in an act of storying not just the dissertation being written but the process of compiling, researching, and writing. Attending to past stories that the academic institution has told about how research can and should be done, as well as to the stories of who has been damaged by those methods, is critical to the work of cultural rhetorics mentorship and methodology.

RELATIONALITY

As mentioned previously, another important tenant of cultural rhetorics research, and thus cultural rhetorics mentorship, is the idea of relationality. In *Research Is Ceremony: Indigenous Research Methods*, Shawn Wilson (2008) concludes that relationality sums up the entire Indigenous research paradigm he is explaining, because relationality, or relationships, is a part of all of the elements of the model he shares:

> Just as the components of the paradigm are related, the components themselves all have to do with relationships. The ontology and epistemology are based upon a process of relationships that form a mutual reality. The axiology and methodology are based upon maintaining accountability to these relationships. . . . An Indigenous research paradigm is relational and maintains relational accountability. (70–71)

Mukavetz (2014) further illuminates Wilson's claim by adding that as researchers—and we would add as mentors and mentees—it is up to us "to further develop a language that articulates the interconnectedness of these concepts" (113). She adds that it is through the practices of relationality, "respect, reciprocity, and accountability," that we are able to ethically and responsibly "cultivate and maintain the relationships we form with people, spaces, land, and the Universe" (113).

One method of practicing this relationality is explained by John Gagnon and Maria Novotny (2020) through the idea of "research as care." In response to their own efforts to prioritize relationality while conducting research in communities where women had experienced various kinds of trauma, they propose a methodological tool kit that "not only cares for the stories [that] are told when collecting participant narratives" but also cares about the "embodied being of [the] participants" through "a series of ethical checkpoints" and the idea of "shared ownership" (72). This negotiation of story and meaning cultivates and maintains relations, honoring the gifts of story, time, and relationships. It is also this negotiation that gives real meaning and truth to the research, to the stories that are often to be shared in other communities, contexts, and venues, which necessitates great care and accountability.

As illustrated above, in order to maintain her relationships with four different lesbian avengers, Elise had to find ways to respect the different, conflicting stories she was being told. She also had to balance the stories being told in this moment with the existing artifacts, which included handbooks, films, memoirs, flyers, pamphlets, and other paraphernalia. In fact, being very clear about the relationships among these various stories, including their histories and points of documentation, became a way of responsibly and care-fully navigating and sharing the varying stories.

I (Trixie) remember Elise sitting in my office, asking me what she should do as she summarized conflicting stories as well as feedback from some of her community members. It was clear that Maxine, one of the founders of the Lesbian Avengers and one of the community members most invested in a relationship with Elise and the dissertation she was writing, had become the outside mentor-reader for the project and that it was of the utmost importance to maintain this relationship. But it was Elise's relationship with the community and with Maxine, and not mine, so it was my job at that point to ask the hard questions; questions designed to model looking at the stories from all sides; questions that would help Elise place the stories side by side, even when in tension, but give them equal voice and say in the story; questions that would help her constellate the whole of the stories being presented. This was the only way for me to maintain my relationship with my mentee, Elise, and for her to maintain relationships with her community members.

Wilson (2008) explains that "we are accountable to ourselves, the community, our environment or cosmos as a whole, and also to the idea or topics we are researching. We have all of these relationships that we need to uphold" (106). Cox et al. (2021) in "Embodiment, Relationality, and Constellation: A Cultural Rhetorics Story of Doctoral Writing" talk about one method of upholding all of these relationships through reciprocity—the action of holding oneself accountable to not only participants or community members but also to those in the academy where one is working—as either graduate students or faculty members. They write, "We see reciprocity as anchored in care; care for each other, care for our participants and communities, care for our audiences, and in the instance of doctoral writing care for our committees and colleagues. . . . We want to be respectful of and accountable to our participant communities while also being respectful and accountable to our disciplinary field(s) and readers" (156). It is in this way that we constellate across and stay attuned to all our relationships.

ADVICE

In this final section, we offer some suggestions for both mentees and mentors doing cultural rhetorics work. Rather than offering specific and detailed guidelines for doing cultural rhetorics work, we aim for our stories told above to provide some key examples of how cultural rhetorics mentorship and methodology can be enacted on a daily basis. Therefore, these bulleted lists are intended as guidelines and suggestions for cultural rhetorics doctoral writing. Just as Trixie and Malea worked carefully to give space to Elise as she made her own way through her dissertation work, we offer these bullet points as lessons that have been helpful to us, rather than as rote rules to follow when engaging in cultural rhetorics work.

For mentees:

- Recognize that cultural rhetorics methodology is a lived practice that spans beyond your theorizing or writing. It is lived and breathed in the relationships you build.
- Understand the most important work you do in academia is relationship-building.
- Ask lots of questions, of your mentors, your participants, your cohort members who are also working through their dissertations.
- Reflect on your process throughout each stage of your work. Sometimes the work you do in your dissertation is not the end but a means to a fuller understanding of methodology / methods / cultural rhetorics.
- Be ready to forgive yourself for mistakes and move on.
- Be aware of your committee members' own relationships to each other, to you, to your work, and to the field.
- Be mindful that many of your peers will NOT be in these kinds of mentoring relationships, which might cause stress, anxiety, or conflict as you move through your milestones and processes.
- Remember that there is room for reciprocity in your mentor/mentee relationship. When you can, find ways to extend the generosity your mentor has extended to you.

For mentors:

- Ask your mentees what they need, treating them as the experts of their own lives and learning.
- Take care of/with your mentee. Remember that you are in relationship with the mentee and need to pay attention to them as human beings and not just as researchers. The relationship should last much longer than the research project or topic.
- Hold space for your mentees to make mistakes, backtrack, start again (repeat).
- Be prepared to listen to and hold onto, in confidence, the stories your mentee will collect and (re)tell; you will need to help them sift through the stories for meaning(s) and help them hear what is not being said.
- Ask lots of questions (genuine questions) designed to help them think about what they are learning and how they are sharing it in their writing, presentations, and so on. Since we are not experts on their communities, we have to trust them to know their communities, but we also have to push their critical thinking through dialogue and questioning.
- Pay attention to what you can learn from your mentee, not just what you have to offer them. Good mentoring relationships are reciprocal (yes, we're back to reciprocity and relationality).
- Be honest with mentees about the process—both of producing milestone components, such as exams and dissertations, and of engaging with those milestones in ways that are useful to the mentee and the community they are working with, even though these milestones weren't necessarily designed to accommodate such relationships.
- Be honest with yourself about the capacities and limits of your energy—make those opportunities and boundaries clear to the mentee.
- Be mindful of your colleagues and of their perceptions about what mentoring in this way looks like—too often, CR mentoring and relationality get written off as being "friends" with a mentee instead of serving as an "authority figure" for them. Colleagues will mistake this as not being "rigorous" with mentees and their work. While this is patently untrue, knowing how to respond to this kind of assumption in your relationships with your colleagues can be helpful for how they envision and interact with your mentee's work, as well as with you.

CONCLUSION

After sending my completed dissertation to all participants, I (Elise) received an email from Chanelle. She wrote, "I haven't read every word of the dissertation yet, but read quite a bit. And I want to thank you for your focus on the Lesbian Avengers, the making, the un-making, the remembered and the partially remembered, the told and the untold, but not forgotten." I read her words to me over and over. It's one thing to complete a dissertation, pass the defense and get the PhD; it's another to have your work affirmed and appreciated by the very people who helped to make it possible. This email, among other correspondence with my participants, was a product of the careful labor of cultural rhetorics work, of the many conversations I had had with my mentors over the course of years. In the end, in many ways, this email from Chanelle meant more to me than the day I was first called "Doctor." It exemplified to me the true value of cultural rhetorics work, of the relationships that had been made through the process. It evidenced a truth that cultural rhetorics mentors had shown me: relationships are always the most important part.

REFERENCES

Bratta, Phil, and Malea Powell. 2016. "Introduction to the Special Issue: Entering the Cultural Rhetorics Conversations." *Enculturation: A Journal of Rhetoric, Writing, and Culture* 21.

Brooks-Gillies, Marilee. 2013. "Crafting Place: Rhetorical Practices of the Everyday." PhD diss., Michigan State University. ProQuest.

Cox, Matt, Elise Dixon, Katie Manthey, Maria Novotny, Rachel Robinson, and Trixie G. Smith. 2021. "Embodiment, Relationality, and Constellation: A Cultural Rhetorics Story of Doctoral Writing." *Re-imagining Doctoral Writing*, edited by Cecile Badenhorst, Brittany Amell, and James Burford. Denver, CO: WAC Clearinghouse.

de Certeau, Michel. 1980. *The Practice of Everyday Life*. Berkeley: University of California Press.

Dixon, Elise. 2020. "Making as World-Making: What the Lesbian Avengers Can Teach about Communal Composing, Agency, and World-Building." PhD diss., Michigan State University.

Freire, Paulo. 1968. *Pedagogy of the Oppressed*. Philadelphia, PA: Routledge.

Gagnon, John T., and Maria Novotny. 2020. "Revisiting Research as Care: A Call to Decolonize Narratives of Trauma." *Rhetoric Review* 39 (4): 486–501.

King, Thomas. 2008. *The Truth about Stories: A Native Narrative*. Minneapolis: University of Minnesota Press.

Mignolo, Walter. 2011. *The Darker Side of Western Modernity: Global Futures, Decolonial Options*. Durham, NC: Duke University Press.

Mukavetz, Andrea Riley. 2014. "Towards a Cultural Rhetorics Methodology: Making Research Matter with Multi-Generational Women from the Little Traverse Bay Band." *Rhetoric, Professional Communication and Globalization* 5 (1): 108–125.

Novotny, Maria. 2017. "The Art of Infertility: A Community Project Rhetorically Conceiving Failed Fertility." PhD diss., Michigan State University.

Powell, Malea, Daisy Levy, Andrea Riley-Mukavetz, Marilee Brooks-Gillies, Maria Novotny, and Jennifer Fisch-Ferguson. 2014. "Our Story Begins Here: Constellating Cultural Rhetorics." *Enculturation: A Journal of Rhetoric, Writing, and Culture* 25.

Smith, Linda Tuhiwai. 2021. *Decolonizing Methodologies: Research and Indigenous Peoples*. London: Zed Books.

Wilson, Shawn. 2008. *Research Is Ceremony: Indigenous Research Narratives*. Black Point, Nova Scotia: Fernwood.

2
THE TWILIGHT OF THE METHODOLOGY COURSE, OR HOW I LEARNED TO TELL THE TALE AND LEAVE IT

Brad Lucas

As Noam Chomsky noted in 2000, "In any field that has significant intellectual content, you don't teach methodology. You just watch people doing it and participate with them in doing it." Two decades ago, that assertion both troubled and inspired me; at the time, I was being mentored into the field while writing a dissertation on its methodology stories, observing my mentor teach those stories to us novice researchers. I aspired to, and later would, do similar mentoring while teaching those stories in my own graduate methodology courses. In this essay, I draw on my mentoring and methodology stories while arguing for eliminating the graduate-level "introduction to methods" course for more mindful, inclusive research mentoring structures. In doing so, I take up Rebecca Rickly and Kelli Cargile Cook's (2017) charge to "challenge the very infrastructure in our research culture" and "be more transparent in our representation of research and our methods for teaching graduate students to conduct it" (119). After all, graduate-level mentoring is, in varying degrees, inextricable from knowledge production.

My story is inspired as a *festschrift* to my mentor, Jane Detweiler, who guided me through the discipline and my dissertation, a meta-investigation of the histories of research in rhetoric and composition. I explore her methodology mentoring beyond the classroom and how I sought to replicate it in my own program by teaching several iterations of "the methods seminar" while mentoring doctoral students through their dissertations, institutional review boards (IRB), professional development, and a dwindling job market. Along the way, I take up the importance of singular mentoring moments, the value of time and presence, and the vital role of decolonial and antiracist perspectives. This is a parallel story about the field's emerging identity and self-awareness—and my own.

https://doi.org/10.7330/9781646425822.c002

As the field maneuvered to establish itself as a discipline, the "methods course" initially provided curricular presence and highlighted specialized practices beyond literary study, anchored in books like those of Lauer and Asher (1988), Kirsch and Sullivan (1992), and MacNealy (1999)—and illustrated through various research reports serving as "mentor texts" offering models for understanding methodological diversity and putting it into practice. A generation later, research scholars embraced an ecological model that accounted for the "mess" inherent in the work (Fleckenstein et al. 2008) while new directions emerged through edited collections (Nickoson and Sheridan 2012; Powell and Takayoshi 2012), queer methodologies (Banks, Cox, and Dadas 2019), and decolonial stances (Chilisa 2012; Patel 2016) alongside Indigenous perspectives (Smith 2012; Wilson 2008) contributing to a rising awareness that, as Tukufu Zuberi and Eduardo Bonilla-Silva (2008) have it, "the more researchers deny the connection of White logic to methods of research the more entangled they become in the morass of justifying the legacy of White supremacy" (19). These vital advances make the stark Western whiteness of a one-size-fits-all survey course in methodology untenable—and, I argue, position research mentoring instead as the preferred path. Put simply, in preserving a survey approach there is a risk of upholding white supremacist legacy structures, but we can mobilize our inherited mentoring methodologies to structure new relationships and orientations that account for comparable equity, complexity, and difference for the future.

I. MYSTERIES UNLOCKED: FIRST STEPS INTO THE DISCIPLINE

In recounting my mentoring experiences alongside advances in the discipline, I recognize the risk of "majoritarian storytelling," which Tara J. Yosso (2006) defines as "a method of recounting the experiences and perspectives of those with racial and social privilege" (9). I present here the majoritarian storytelling I experienced—and for years embraced—for the purposes of contrast, highlighting the learning experiences and legacy narratives that later needed to be corrected, or unlearned, for better understanding of methodology and mentoring. As Frankie Condon (2012) writes, "if white participation in the production of resisting stories of racialized experience is to be meaningful, the stories we tell and the manner of their production must be conceived of as opportunities to learn, to revise, and to reconstruct in order to more fully represent, one hopes, increasingly nuanced understandings" (37). I share this story not in some attempt to transcend my privilege as a cisgender white heterosexual male—or absolve myself of complicity in the systems that permitted me to succeed in graduate school and secure a place in the academy. As Michelle Flahive (this volume) argues, white faculty must be willing to engage in discussions of whiteness and white supremacy in predominantly white institutions (PWIs). I hope to do some of this work here by sharing what I (un)learned as I constructed a new perspective, attempting to reimagine and revise my understanding of meaningful graduate education—and focusing on individual mentoring that foregrounds student perspectives and orientations (and decenters replication or decades-old experiences like my own).

Like many others, I began my PhD studies without a clear sense of what I was getting into. Having completed an MA in literature, I learned about this "emerging field" of rhetoric and composition after realizing that I wanted more confidence in my writing pedagogy. At Texas State University, I had my first real conversation about the field with Jaime Armin Mejía, who pointed me to the Conference on College Composition and Communication (CCCC) and some of the nation's top PhD programs, helping me see a future for myself in writing studies. Although I had not studied with him, he treated me to a long advising session—a pivotal mentoring moment—that gave me direction, perspective, and inspiration. In the decades since, I have valued his advice and kept vivid that experience, *for even one mentoring moment can help a student discover the field, imagine possibilities, and find a way.* Many other mentors have shaped my journey, but this story focuses on how my dissertation advisor, Jane, became the primary mentor in my career and—not coincidentally—how methodology was, and is, central to that relationship.

I began my doctoral work with a vaguely stated interest in the "intersections of literature and rhetoric," but I honestly didn't have a research focus. As a PWI, the University of Nevada did not pose racial obstacles for me in terms of access to the predominantly white faculty. It was not a question of whether I would find mentorship but how the relationships would eventually form. Any talk about mentoring back then was informal and anecdotal, with no program-based mentoring structures, and "the dissertation committee" was the primary focus. I quickly learned from other graduate students that I should find an advisor and assemble a committee, and that those people would determine my fate. I wasn't savvy enough to seek out a mentor when I arrived on campus (Goldsmith, Komlos, and Gold 2001, 49), although I felt comfortable stopping by faculty office hours. I knew that "publish or perish" was real, and some of my peers urged me to follow the publication trail and choose an advisor accordingly. Around that time, Janice Lauer (1997) affirmed such a mentoring role as "crucial to help individuals map their paths through a department's requirements and make decisions about whether, when, and where to publish . . . gaining the depth and expertise necessary for research and, ultimately, publication" (231). The logic was fairly simple: the faculty who published the most would guide us through the mysteries of getting published, and if they directed your dissertation, they could pave your way to the PhD and a tenured position.

The count-the-publications method of advisor-mentor selection was unquestionable for some students, and accepted begrudgingly by others, but it typically precluded faculty at the junior ranks. Goldsmith, Komlos, and Gold (2001) interrogate and confirm this sometimes unavoidable dilemma: "Should a student aim intentionally to work with the professor who has the highest professional profile? . . . If I were really pinned down and forced to answer the question, I'd say yes—all other things being equal, pick someone with a high professional profile" (48). The notion of "picking" an advisor seemed impossible without a research plan, yet the drive to find one early on was palpable. The narrow focus on productivity *initially* prevented me from considering early-career or new faculty—although they had been my best mentors.

In my second year of coursework, I took Jane's seminar, Rhetorical Text Interpretation, which brought me to genre, narratology, textual analysis, qualitative research, and writing in the disciplines. Her Research in Rhetoric and Composition seminar followed the program's methods course. Everything about the discipline then crystallized for me, as Jane led us through the widely accepted "formation story" of the field through its research narratives, its landscape of methods, and the broader concerns around publication and the profession. While individual scholars were named, even praised, for their contributions, the focus allowed us to "do like" rather than "be like" them: a replication of methods rather than individuals. However, we typically did not acknowledge that the field's whiteness positioned most of us as *already like them* in a replication queue of perspectives and orientations, carrying out similar work for similar ends.

We learned majoritarian stories. We learned about the power dynamics between literature studies and rhetoric and composition through scholars like Susan Miller (1991) and the adoption of methods from other disciplines—and questioning of rigor—coming from Stephen North. We saw the discipline's growth tethered to its research identity and productivity, tracing its mid-1960s emergence to Janet Emig's case-study research and other process studies in the 1970s, later supplanted (or supplemented) by cognitive-process models in the 1980s and then in the 1990s qualitative approaches informed by postmodern and poststructuralist perspectives. We learned a cast of characters and a story to be told—and various ways to plot it. I dutifully aligned and oriented my own scholarly growth with these concerns, defining myself not just through the methods but the figures who fought for it: a tale of white Western knowledge, power, and domain struggles anchored in the economics of scholarly productivity.

It was a field scrapping its way into disciplinary independence, tearing loose from the literary and embracing a university's full range of methodologies for endless vistas of rhetoric and writing—and it echoed my own unfolding "coming of age" story. We learned not only how methods worked but where they came from and how their results were evaluated. We learned about the editing and publishing mechanisms for judging research, and over time, the mysteries of scholarly publication seemed to unlock themselves (without "high profile" patronage). I had my own emerging disciplinary identity, just like the field, and I took up the majoritarian values informing the research, its approaches, and its power within the university.

Jane taught her graduate courses with a true mentoring model, what Theresa Enos (1997) described at the time as "mentoring discussion groups" in which "research is seen as invention" (142) and students are encouraged to imagine pathways to publication, rather than just the semester's seminar paper. Throughout it all, Jane's guiding hand helped us through the overwhelming range of material and encouraged us to develop our own methodological stances—to approach whatever work called to us. I got the sense that she was being the mentor that she herself never had, and she basically encouraged us to pursue our own research dreams, not hers. Despite her status as a pre-tenure assistant professor, I asked Jane to direct my dissertation because I trusted her judgment, respected her respect of different perspectives, and knew that she'd always push me to consider questions for myself rather than simply take up her answers. After all, she was brilliant in her mentoring dialogues, always pushing us to consider possibilities and context. Whatever question we might bring to her, she'd often start her reply with an about-to-dialogue smile and say, "It depends...."

II. MENTOR, ADVISOR, OFFICEMATE

During my third year, our department was temporarily relocated, and workspace was compromised, so Jane took me in as an officemate for the duration. Relieved to get out of the graduate "bullpen" cubicles, I was honored by the trust it signaled and the investment she had in mentoring me. She embraced an unconventional role that treated me as a peer and colleague. As Penny Gold writes, "there is an unavoidable dynamic of power in advisee-advisor relationships. . . . Your career is quite literally in the hands of your advisor. . . . The best advisors will treat you like a junior colleague—which you are, indeed, in the process of becoming" (Goldsmith, Komlos, and Gold 2001, 47). By sharing her office space, Jane lowered the threshold of the power dynamic between us and made concrete her long-term investment in my success.

For many graduate students, access to advisors is an obstacle, whether through email delays or chapter drafts that take weeks (or months) for review. Our office arrangement was a gift given in terms of time, presence, and access. Advocating for mentoring students of color, Gail Okawa (2002) observes, "When the mentors make themselves highly accessible and available to their mentees, this accessibility translates, from the mentees' view, into presence—in person or on the phone or on email: contact time" (527). Indeed, in practice the mentoring I received was "shared, reflective, and democratic" on an almost daily basis (528), but it would be years before I would better understand that the nature of this mentoring—and varying perspectives on time—could provide a form of anticolonial resistance to the dominant legacies of academic culture. Okawa notes that the European notion of time is quantifiable and commodified: either a transactional weapon or an egalitarian means "toward the goal of emancipating their mentees from the constraints of the dominant academic culture" (528). Jane's office sharing was a push against that culture, just like her critiques of heteronormative assumptions in the field's scholarship or her support of collaboratively written and other nonnormative dissertation approaches.

As the months went on, I faced a deadline to form a dissertation project, and Jane did not push me in any one direction. I was torn between three projects that I had started in coursework, each one suggesting a different career path, and I wanted to include them all. Jane encouraged me to try, to find a way, to write my way through it. I started drafting an introduction on the field's diverse research history, which ballooned into one hundred manuscript pages, and Jane grounded me to focus on what I had discovered in the process, at the end. She congratulated me on writing my way *to* a thesis: I had written a "zero draft," what Joan Bolker (1998) describes as "a point where it becomes possible to imagine, or discern, a shape to your material, to see the method in your madness. . . . Nothing is even necessarily usable, but you've got something" (1998, 50). I had drafted a document the length of my MA thesis, but it was just a working-through of my thinking to discover my project. A radical revision was some harsh medicine that I wouldn't have otherwise been ready to take. By that point, however, I had come to trust and respect Jane's advice on multiple levels, so I started drafting all-new chapters.

I had found my real project: not just a history, but what I foolishly considered "The" history of research methodologies in rhetoric and composition. It was audacious in scope, especially for a novice researcher, but I had taken a lead from Robert J. Connors (1997), who wrote that his *Composition-Rhetoric* history was intended just as a starting point: "It means to construct coherent explanations for historical facts and causality, taking archival research as a starting place and consistent control. . . . I want mostly to tell a story, to identify and pin down as much basic textual evidence as possible, so that further discussion from a theoretical base can then proceed from shareable data" (19–22). I admired Connors, and now I know the privilege that *he looked like me*: a burly white man who held the stories of the field. He was a version of the "me" I could become.

I saw Connors's approach as a way to draft a history while negotiating the critiques of "master narratives" proliferating in critical theory and cultural studies, yet I hoped that I could do more for the voices excluded from the field's history, to "read our research histories through a theoretical approach that not only accounts for the turbulence of historiography but also allows for dominant and marginalized historical narratives to co-exist" (Lucas 2002, 57). My aims did not go nearly far enough, though, because "the margins" in my project were still delimited by the field's dominant whiteness. Despite my intentions, I now see that I was still complicit in majoritarian storytelling. Indeed, my dissertation drew from, and contributed to, the narratives (Mikhail Bakhtin, Pierre Bourdieu, and Aristotle) that uphold patriarchal white supremacy and its legacies in the academy.

III. META, HODOS, LOGOS AND HISTORIES: SITUATED, TEMPORAL, AND DYNAMIC

Despite the majoritarian thinking that shaped my project, Jane's mentoring allowed me to pursue my research inspirations, and their legacies, positioning myself as a methodology specialist—and eventually securing a tenure-line position to do so. I understood research methodologies as a complex set of practices that included fundamental assumptions, philosophic frameworks, orientations that drive methods, and systematic approaches to research problems. I wanted to fight against the mundane view that methodology was just the logic or theory behind a method, and a deep dive into etymology revealed depth, complexity, and dynamics. I highlight the linguistic roots of the term "methodology" here not to center its Western origins but to foreground the range of signification emanating from the term, too often constrained to those legacy structures or the mere "application of method."

I learned that "method" is a compound noun derived from the Greek *méthodos* (μεθοδοσ), a combination of the root prefix *meta-* (μετα) and the root *hodos* (όδόσ), which taken together loosely translate to "a going after, pursuit" of "a way, path." The prefix **meta-** signals an observant or transcendent quality of a term, but it also signals location (before, after, between, beside), temporality (following, occurring later), and dynamism (involving change, intensified action). In addition, **hodos** also signals location and dynamism in its very definition—of place (a road, way, or path) or as an action or manner (traveling, journeying, ways of doing)—and has a temporal dimension, too, as in the derivative words "episode," "period," and "exodus." Taking the Greek word **lógos**, too, beyond my sophomore-level definitions revealed that while lógos obtained meanings of speech, discourse, and word—and someone who treats of or deals with a particular topic or subject—I was more drawn to the larger philosophical concept of "reason thought of as constituting the controlling principle of the universe and as being manifested by speech" (Danner and Noël 1992, 393). As such, lógos imports literally the workings of the universe in its significations of computation and reckoning; relation, correspondence, and proportion; explanation; debate of the soul; and verbal expression (see Ayto 1990; Barnhart 1995; Danner and Noël 1992; Klein 1967; Liddell and Scott 1996; and Onions 1966). While it is not surprising to find time and place integral to dynamic action, often the notion of "method" conjures images and definitions of universal, static, and rigid systems or formulae when in fact the full import of method should be *an always situated, temporal, and dynamic practice*. Methodology, then, is an understanding of how those practices are tied up in webs and networks of meanings, relationships, and articulations that extend from local community contexts to the larger cosmos.

Teaching my first graduate seminar in research methodologies, I was eager to include this sense of complexity while drawing from Jane's syllabus as the "mentor text" for my own. While still informally called "the methods course," my colleagues and I named the new seminar Research Practices in Composition and Rhetoric in 2006 to emphasize its broader and more complex range. We expected that methodologies would be discussed in all of our seminars, but we wanted one that would account for the available methods, showcase the knowledge production in the discipline, and, ideally, serve as a staging area for dissertations. I saw "mentoring as a 'pay it forward' activity" (Eble and Gaillet 2019, 283), and I wanted Research Practices to be a launching pad for graduate students' careers—or at least create conditions for writing their way toward them. Jane framed the course that way for me and my classmates, and I wanted to replicate it.

Our disciplinary research story had been cast largely in terms of dominant Western methodologies, wherein the widely accepted methods shaped our understanding by inscribing a sense of "movements" and "periods." Research eras were shaped into and shaped by a dominant history, one that usually dramatized the origins, development, and acceptance of rhetoric and composition as a discipline. The early 2000s marked a proliferation of these perspectives, with efforts to periodize a progress narrative using various approaches (see table 2.1): a "growing garden" metaphor (Goggin 2000), institutional vitality (North 2000), a familial generational model (Zebroski 1999; Connors 1999), and simple decade divisions (Bizzell, Herzberg, and Reynolds 2000). As Debra Journet, Beth Boehm, and Mary Rosner (1999) chose the years 1963–1983 as the "Birth of Composition," they acknowledged the arbitrary and selective framing of the two decades, which "almost inevitably produces a story that privileges growth, change, and success" (xxii). In a department where literature colleagues still dismissed the field's legitimacy or intellectual parity, such stories were essential to tell; *time to be commodified, with amelioration.*

Earlier versions of Research Practices devoted weeks to historiography, with the "history of research" unfolding throughout the semester, usually beginning with the 1963 Braddock Report which forecasted future research interests while presenting a compendium of research based on "scientific methods" on writing (Braddock, Jones, and Schoer 1963). North called the report the "charter of modern Composition"; it argued for practice based on research, thereby setting the stage for what North (1987) called a "methodological land rush" (7), tacitly framing its role in white settler colonialism. From there, the course turned to the "research community" of the 1970s, when "coherent research programs emerged marrying empirical methods to theoretical conceptions" (Nystrand, Greene, and Wiemelt 1993, 271). With these, and other, origin stories in place, the course would take up methods: from discourse / textual analysis to quantitative / experimental approaches

Table 2.1. Early 2000s views of historical periods in rhetoric and composition

Bizzell, Herzberg, and Reynolds (2000)	1930s–1950s: Beginnings of Modern Composition Studies: New Criticism	The 1960s: Classical Rhetoric, Writing Processes, and Authentic Voice	The 1970s: Cognitive Processes, Basic Writing, and Writing Across the Curriculum	The 1980s: Social and Historical Approaches to Rhetoric	The 1990s: The Challenge of Diversity
Goggin's (2000) Garden	Preparing the Ground 1950–1965	Sowing the Seeds 1965–1980		Fruits of the Garden 1980–1990	A Pot-Bound Garden 1990–2000
Zebroski's (1999) Four Zones of Identity Formation	Proto-Community 1950s–1960s		Mythic First Generation 1970s–1980s	Revolt of the Second Generation 1990s	Third Generation Consolidation and Thereafter
Connor's (1999) Generations of Scholars	First Generation late 1940s–early 1960s	Second Generation early 1960s–1970s	Third Generation 1970s–1987	Fourth Generation 1987–	
North (2000)	The Great Expansion 1945–late 1960s		The Great Contraction early 1970s–late 1980s	The (Surp)Rise of Heterogeneity late 1980s–2000	

and then to qualitative / ethnographic research, followed by historiography, archival research, institutional critique, and "digital futures."

Thanks to Rickly's survey work in 2005, we learned about common denominators in such methods seminars—often the only space for explicit mentoring around methodology—with typical and frequently used texts: Kirsch and Sullivan (1992), Lauer and Asher (1988), and MacNealy (1999). Rickly (2007) advocates for such courses to emphasize the application of methods "in a heuristic, contextual manner" and give students the opportunity "to conduct actual research studies," rather than focus too much on critical reading of research reports (395). Importantly, too, she calls for that research to take place within the " 'safe' context of a class" and argues that "support for conducting research should be offered frequently, throughout a graduate student's career" (395). Over the next decade, I took heed of Rickly's sage advice and added a research-design assignment, scaled back the reading of research reports, and included two edited collections in 2012 that marked a renewed interest in research practices (Nickoson and Sheridan 2012; Powell and Takayoshi 2012).

Along the way, I cut more content to make room for newer conversations, newer considerations, and a decolonial stance that could displace the central figure of Western empirical research and its capitalist narrative of (disciplinary) progress—and eliminate the periods and eras that had previously driven the course. Initially, "mapping" was a central metaphor in the syllabus, based on North's (1987) four methodological communities and prominent locations of knowledge-making (2–6). But by 2016, I downgraded North's work from a central point of reference to just a historical example of one classification scheme, and by 2020 I removed it altogether. In its place were Bagele Chilisa's (2012) *Indigenous Research Methodologies*, and then Linda Tuhiwai Smith's (2012) *Decolonizing Methodologies: Research and Indigenous Peoples* and Leigh Patel's (2016) *Decolonizing Educational Research: From Ownership to Answerability*.

Initially assigned as a corrective to dominant Western ideologies, such readings challenged my own assumptions about the very course in which I assigned them. As Smith (2012) writes, "from an indigenous perspective Western research is more than just research that is located in a positivist tradition. It is research which brings to bear, on any study of indigenous peoples, a cultural orientation, a set of values, a different conceptualization of such things as time, space and subjectivity, different and competing theories of knowledge, highly specialized forms of language, and structures of power" (44). Smith critiques Western history for its totalizing and universalizing aims, singular and coherent chronology, and patriarchal motives linked to self-actualization and development (31–32), all traits that had defined my initial Research Practices course. From its origin stories in structures dominated by white men to its period-based "eras" of disciplinary conquest, the course—and my whole scholarly upbringing and orientation—landed squarely in the center of such critiques. My dissertation had, after all, been an attempt to document and synthesize the "cultural archive" of research in the discipline: "systems of research classification, representation, and evaluation . . . rules of classification, rules of framing and rules of practice" (45). Just as my early forays into research methodologies allowed me to unlock the mysteries of scholarly publication, I had initially hoped to illuminate those systems and rules to enable my graduate students to do the same. However, these epistemological critiques clarified for me that the premise behind a singular methodology course was anchored in the "positional superiority" of Western, imperial knowledge systems (via Edward Said): "The ways in which knowledge and culture were as much part of imperialism as raw materials and military strength. Knowledge was also there to be discovered, extracted, appropriated and distributed. Processes for enabling these things to occur became organized and systematic" (Smith 2012, 68). Such critiques raised awareness of positional superiority, but the course still upheld Western research values and remained predicated on the cultural archive of a discipline, because it was anchored to a survey model, a subject to study rather than practices for engagement.

Complementing these Indigenous perspectives was *Re/Orienting Writing Studies: Queer Methods, Queer Projects*, whose editors ask us "to challenge the heteronormative orientations that have guided inquiry in writing studies since its inception" (Banks, Cox, and Dadas 2019, 5). They foreground the importance of "orientation" in research in terms of "how (and why and even to what extent) the researcher turns toward the objects, participants, or contexts of study" (3), yet they recognize how traditional methods and methodologies are not objective or free from ideology and how normative frameworks obscure knowledge-making possibilities:

> Where these practices—surveys, focus groups, observations, rhetorical analyses, and so forth—become commonplace, where they represent normative/unquestioned activities or epistemologies, they demonstrate not only the ways that each has become an active method for orienting a researcher (and thus also preventing other orientations, other views from taking the foreground) but also how each has become a normative orientation for the field, a well-trodden path whose existence actively replicates itself from researcher to researcher, from discipline to discipline. (4)

The problem of replication as a normative practice echoes not only from the perception of available methods (and the courses that introduce them) but to the larger systems of replication engrained in graduate education—and the mentoring practices therein.

Ultimately, my changes to the course led me to conclude that the all-in-one methodologies survey had "run its course" as a useful instrument for doctoral education. We removed it as a requirement, and I will not teach it again. Just as Okawa (2002) highlights "the reciprocal nature of the mentoring process" (528), I was mentored by the mentor texts I assigned to my students. Likewise, my own graduate mentees have been mentors for my own pedagogy, like James Chase Sanchez who—with his coauthors—critiques survey texts like *The Rhetorical Tradition*, which serve as the centerpiece for many survey courses, because they "omit non-White, non-male authors and sufficient attention to structural racism. . . . Normalizing representations of disciplinary history that inhibit criticism about the influence of racism and coloniality on canon formation and research traditions makes it difficult to study these issues" (Lockett et al. 2021; 18–19; see also Dixson et al. in this volume). Our research course needed restructuring not only to dismantle imperial Western knowledge practices and raise awareness about the normative orientations of methodologies but also to include a diverse representation of voices and perspectives within the legacies of racism and colonialism.

As my colleague Carmen Kynard (2013) reflects on such histories and disciplinary structures, she writes, "Very little that I had been shown as the canon, as the key moments, as the critical issues, as the seminal edited collections, as 'the' history, as the landmarks and signposts, as the categories, or as the inventive engines seemed to include me" (12). Efforts to redress such representational erasures and omissions, however, cannot be token additions or simple expansions of existing frameworks. We cannot leave the underlying structures and assumptions intact and just "add" more to inherently flawed legacy frameworks when our graduate students need research practice, support, and mentoring to establish themselves—and contribute to the redefinition of—the discipline so that it does include them. Similar to Charlotte Bunch's famous quip about feminism in 1979, we cannot just "add women and stir" (qtd. in Messer-Davidow 1985, 8) to correct the deficiencies of traditional white patriarchal education.

IV. OPPORTUNITIES IN TIME

In place of the methods survey, the way forward—for now—suggests graduate seminars that take up the very critiques that replace them. Research methodologies must be taught within a mentoring model that highlights invention rather than replication, promotes creative research orientations over static methods, enables low-stakes work on actual research design and implementation, and not only sets the stage for dissertation work and the research that follows but also demystifies peer review and publication. I will no longer teach "the methods course" survey, because I feel it unethical to do so; it perpetuates the problem behind a normalized mask of a coverage model.

I will continue to mentor graduate students as they find their own methodological paths, as I did in my recent graduate seminar on autoethnography and counterstory, drawing from some of the same thinking that I brought to this essay and to my teaching (see Flahive, in this volume, for similar aims through *testimonio*). After all, for its challenges to canonical Western research practices and subject representation, autoethnography embraces—rather than obscures—scholarship that's undeniably subjective, political, and socially just. Emerging from critical race theory, counterstorytelling draws on the knowledge of racially and socially marginalized people from their own perspectives and experiences while calling attention to their stories of resistance and struggles for justice. As Aja Y. Martinez (2020) writes, "Counterstory is methodology that functions through methods that empower the minoritized through the formation of stories that disrupt the erasures embedded in standardized majoritarian methodologies" (3). And as Yosso (2006) concludes, counterstories can "(1) cultivate community among socially and racially marginalized groups, (2) challenge the perceived wisdom of majoritarian stories, (3) nurture community memory and resistance, and (4) encourage readers to continue working toward social and racial justice with determined urgency" (165). Counterstory draws from (auto)biographical and composite-character approaches, and like autoethnography, it certainly does have academic ends—but it doesn't necessarily end with the academic, often having much broader aims and wider audiences. We might say that counterstory and autoethnography travel well together in their challenges to the academy.

Just as Jane encouraged me to write my way through it, I hope to pay forward the gift in the future, encouraging young scholars not only to pursue their research dreams but question the norms that shape the possible paths getting there. As we mentor graduate students into and through the discipline, we must encourage critique of the disciplinary and programmatic structures—from coursework through exams and the dissertation—and protect the students who challenge those structures (see Dixon et al., in this volume, for detailed suggestions and guidelines). While I felt some sense of loss in giving up the methods survey that had defined so much of my journey, the lessons learned as I reconstructed a new perspective are invaluable, particularly as we reimagine and revise what meaningful graduate education should be. Just as Jane taught me to look through feminist and LGBTQ lenses when I was a doctoral student, my graduate students continue to teach me how to envision the potentialities of a new university, where antiracist and translingual practices can be pervasive and embedded in the very fabric of our programs—and our mentoring. As Elise Dixon, Trixie Smith, and Malea Powell (this volume) conclude, "We have more to learn than we have to teach, that we do our best creating when we begin with listening, when our mentors start from a place of listening too." I have tried to see my privilege as a surplus that I am obliged to redistribute, not just through efforts to reform and transform but through giving whatever time I can spare in the same ways it was so generously given to me. A lifetime of thanks to Jane—as well as my graduate students who have mentored me to continue questioning and challenging my paths, both past and present.

REFERENCES

Ayto, John. 1990. *Dictionary of Word Origins*. New York: Arcade Publishing.
Banks, William P., Matthew B. Cox, and Caroline Dadas, eds. 2019. *Re/Orienting Writing Studies: Queer Methods, Queer Projects*. Logan: Utah State University Press.
Barnhart, Robert K., ed. 1995. *The Barnhart Concise Dictionary of Etymology*. Vol 2. New York: HarperCollins.
Bizzell, Patricia, Bruce Herzberg, and Nedra Reynolds. 2000. *The Bedford Bibliography for Teachers of Writing*. 5th ed. Boston: Bedford/St. Martin's.
Bolker, Joan. 1998. *Writing Your Dissertation in Fifteen Minutes a Day*. New York: Henry Holt.
Braddock, Richard, Richard Lloyd Jones, and Lowell Schoer. 1963. *Research in Written Composition*. Urbana, IL: NCTE.
Chilisa, Bagele. 2012. *Indigenous Research Methodologies*. Thousand Oaks, CA: Sage.
Chomsky, Noam. 2000. "Propaganda and Indoctrination." ZNet Daily Commentary. December 10, 2000. https://chomsky.info/20001210/.
Condon, Frankie. 2012. *I Hope I Join the Band: Narrative, Affiliation, and Antiracist Rhetoric*. Logan: Utah State University Press.
Connors, Robert J. 1997. *Composition-Rhetoric: Backgrounds, Theory, and Pedagogy*. Pittsburgh, PA: University of Pittsburgh Press.
Connors, Robert J. 1999. "Composition History and Disciplinarity." In *History, Reflection, and Narrative: The Professionalization of Composition, 1963–1983*, edited by Mary Rosner, Beth Boehm, and Debra Journet, 3–21. New York: Ablex.
Danner, Horace G., and Roger Noël. 1992. *A Thesaurus of Word Roots of the English Language*. Lanham, MD: University Press of America.
Eble, Michelle, and Lynée Lewis Gaillet. 2019. "Re-inscribing Mentoring." In *Retellings: Opportunities for Feminist Research in Rhetoric and Composition Studies*, edited by Jessica Enoch and Jordynn Jack, 283–303. Anderson, SC: Parlor Press.
Enos, Theresa. 1997. "Mentoring—and (Wo)mentoring—in Composition Studies." In *Academic Advancement in Composition Studies: Scholarship, Publication, Promotion, Tenure*, edited by Richard C. Gebhardt and Barbara Genelle Smith Gebhardt, 137–145. Mahwah, NJ: Lawrence Erlbaum Associates.
Fleckenstein, Kristie S., Clay Spinuzzi, Rebecca J. Rickly, and Carole Clark Papper. 2008. "The Importance of Harmony: An Ecological Metaphor for Writing Research." *College Composition and Communication* 60 (2): 388–419.
Goggin, Maureen Daly. 2000. *Authoring a Discipline: Scholarly Journals and the Post–World War II Emergence of Rhetoric and Composition*. Mahwah, NJ: Lawrence Erlbaum Associates.
Goldsmith, John A., John Komlos, and Penny Schine Gold. 2001. *The Chicago Guide to Your Academic Career*. Chicago: University of Chicago Press.
Journet, Debra, Beth Boehm, and Mary Rosner. 1999. "Introduction." In *History, Reflection, and Narrative: The Professionalization of Composition, 1963–1983*, edited by Mary Rosner, Beth Boehm, and Debra Journet, xiii–xxiii. New York: Ablex.
Kirsch, Gesa, and Patricia A. Sullivan, eds. 1992. *Methods and Methodology in Composition Research*. Carbondale: Southern Illinois University Press.
Klein, Ernest. 1967. *A Comprehensive Etymological Dictionary of the English Language*. Amsterdam: Elsevier.
Kynard, Carmen. 2013. *Vernacular Insurrections: Race, Black Protest, and the New Century in Composition-Literacies Studies*. Albany: State University of New York Press.
Lauer, Janice M. 1997. "Graduate Students as Active Members of the Profession: Some Questions for Mentoring." In *Publishing in Rhetoric and Composition*, edited by Gary A. Olson and Todd W. Taylor, 229–235. Albany: State University of New York Press.
Lauer, Janice M, and J. William Asher. 1988. *Composition Research: Empirical Designs*. Oxford: Oxford University Press.
Liddell, Henry G., and Robert Scott. 1996. *A Greek-English Lexicon*. Oxford: Clarendon.

Lockett, Alexandria L., Iris D. Ruiz, James Chase Sanchez, and Christopher Carter. 2021. *Race, Rhetoric, and Research Methods.* WAC Clearinghouse / University Press of Colorado. https://doi.org/10.37514/PER-B.2021.1206.

Lucas, Brad E. 2002. "Histories of Research in Composition and Rhetoric: Temporal Species and the Perils of Pedagogy." PhD diss., University of Nevada.

MacNealy, Mary Sue. 1999. *Strategies for Empirical Research in Writing.* Boston: Allyn and Bacon.

Martinez, Aja Y. 2020. *Counterstory: The Rhetoric and Writing of Critical Race Theory.* Urbana, IL: CCCC/NCTE.

Messer-Davidow, Ellen. 1985. "Knowers, Knowing, Knowledge: Feminist Theory and Education." *Journal of Thought* 20 (3): 8–24.

Miller, Susan. 1991. *Textual Carnivals: The Politics of Composition.* Carbondale: Southern Illinois University Press.

Nickoson, Lee, and Mary P. Sheridan, eds. 2012. *Writing Studies Research in Practice: Methods and Methodologies.* Carbondale: Southern Illinois University Press.

North, Stephen M. 1987. *The Making of Knowledge in Composition: Portrait of an Emerging Field.* Portsmouth, NH: Boynton/Cook.

North, Stephen M. 2000. *Refiguring the PhD in English Studies: Writing, Doctoral Education, and the Fusion-Based Curriculum.* Urbana, IL: NCTE.

Nystrand, Martin, Stuart Greene, and Jeffrey Wiemelt. 1993. "Where Did Composition Studies Come From?: An Intellectual History." *Written Communication* 10 (3): 267–333.

Okawa, Gail Y. 2002. "Diving for Pearls: Mentoring as Cultural and Activist Practice among Academics of Color." *College Composition and Communication* 53 (3): 507–532.

Onions, C. T., ed. 1966. *The Oxford Dictionary of English Etymology.* Oxford: Clarendon Press.

Patel, Leigh. 2016. *Decolonizing Educational Research: From Ownership to Answerability.* New York: Routledge.

Powell, Katrina M., and Pamela Takayoshi, eds. 2012. *Practicing Research in Writing Studies: Reflexive and Ethically Responsible Research.* New York: Hampton Press.

Rickly, Rebecca. 2007. "Messy Contexts: Research as a Rhetorical Situation." In *Digital Writing Research: Technologies, Methodologies, and Ethical Issues,* edited by Heidi McKee and Danielle Nicole DeVoss, 377–397. New York: Hampton Press.

Rickly, Rebecca, and Kelli Cargile Cook. 2017. "Failing Forward: Training Graduate Students for Research—An Introduction to the Special Issue." *Journal of Technical Writing and Communication* 47 (2): 119–129.

Smith, Linda Tuhiwai. 2012. *Decolonizing Methodologies: Research and Indigenous Peoples.* 2nd ed. London: Zed Books.

Wilson, Shawn. 2008. *Research Is Ceremony: Indigenous Research Methods.* Winnipeg: Fernwood.

Yosso, Tara J. 2006. *Critical Race Counterstories along the Chicana/Chicano Educational Pipeline.* New York: Routledge.

Zebroski, James Thomas. 1999. "The Expressivist Menace." In *History, Reflection, and Narrative: The Professionalization of Composition, 1963–1983,* edited by Mary Rosner, Beth Boehm, and Debra Journet, 99–113. New York: Ablex.

Zuberi, Tukufu, and Eduardo Bonilla-Silva, eds. 2008. *White Logic, White Methods: Racism and Methodology.* Lanham, MD: Rowman and Littlefield.

3
GENTEFYING OR GENTRIFYING?
Mentoring Up to Code on the Methodological Block

Eric A. House, Kelly Medina-López, and Kellie Sharp-Hoskins

"Mija, don't find a seat. Build one. You have all the tools."
—Kelly's Dad

This collaboration emerged in the context of converging commitments—to students, to mentoring, to methodology, to tearing down white supremacy—and diverging experiences. Embodied quite differently, we all grew up in the southwest United States: San Diego, California; Tucson, Arizona; Las Cruces, New Mexico. Talking about being kids (and teenagers) in the 1990s, sharing pictures of our sweet retro styles and haircuts, and brainstorming a name for the collab (E2K—for Eric, Kelly, and Kellie—sounded like the name for a 1990s music group, and we have used it in our emails to each other when writing this chapter) helped us to even out the unevenness in the group: who has known each other longer, who shares cultural literacies, who has worked with whom and in what ways. Despite differences in our embodiments and lived experiences, in the process of sharing with each other the stories and sentences below, we created a homeplace for E2K: an intellectual space where the three of us *fit*. But smoothing out the seams of our collaboration is not our goal. That is, while we argue for scholarly practices attuned to methodological fit, we're more interested in the ways we create and mentor (methodological) places in the field and less interested in making anyone fit in existing spaces. As we explain below, we're interested in gentefying, not gentrifying; making community places for meetups and hangouts, book clubs and BBQs, places *para la gente*.

In the sections that follow we begin by engaging with the theoretical forebears of this project—feminisms by Black, Indigenous, and women of the global majority (BIWGM)[1]—to articulate how we understand methodological homeplaces as they emerge *in relation* to the bodies and lives that build and use them. Building on their legacies, we propose a methodology for mentoring that accounts for how bodies *fit* (in) spaces (or not). Guided by a commitment to spatial practices that do not dispossess, bypass, or whitewash students' (home) languages, literacies, and embodied expertise, we include some of our own stories to discuss mentoring para la gente; that is, gentefying, not gentrifying, the spaces and places of rhetoric and writing studies. We invite readers to accompany us as we build such methodologies and as we use this space to reflect on the places each of us create and occupy in our field. We ask readers to be critical of the places they create and inhabit, acknowledging the roles our mentoring practices play in disciplining others according to the codes of rhetoric and writing studies.

BUILDING METHODOLOGICAL HOMEPLACES

BIWGM feminisms—within and beyond rhetoric and writing studies proper—teach us that there is no such thing as one-size-fits-all methodology; such a formulation radically discounts relationships between epistemology, embodiment, and research. Indeed, "fit" is an appropriate spatial rendering of the inadequacy of methodologies that elide embodied knowledge because they offer no space for experiences, perspectives, or bodies that fall outside pre-set norms. Across the academy, BIWGM recount experiences of mis-fit and discomfit / discomfort as they enter academic spaces ill-designed for their languages, their bodies, and their lives. Narrating her first experiences in a university, Bernadette Calafell (2010) writes, "I was initially uncritical about my place in the space, completely blaming myself for what I was feeling. All I knew was that I felt extremely awkward and out of place" (109). While institutional discourses pathologize these feelings of mis-fit or awkwardness, Calafell (2010) identifies their cause as a defining feature of institutions designed to fit some bodies and not others: "I would come to understand that I was overwhelmed by the whiteness of the place. The whiteness was not just marked by bodies and personas that seemed vastly different and in many ways 'free' . . . but also by the feeling and the affect of the place" (109). The overwhelming whiteness of the university wasn't (isn't) confined to the phenotypes of peers or professors but emerged (emerges) in the ways of knowing, being, belonging, and fitting—the methodologies—of the university.

In the face of institutions and disciplines characterized by methodologies anathema to questions of differential embodiments, privileges, and power, BIWGM feminists thus articulate the "need for many women of color scholars in rhetoric to find and create our own homeplaces" (Calafell 2010, 105). It is, as Calafell invokes Cherríe Moraga and Gloria Anzaldúa (1981) to explain, "theory in the flesh . . . where the physical realities of our lives—our skin color, the land or concrete we grew up on, our sexual longings—all fuse to create a politic born of necessity" (Anzaldúa and Moraga 1981, 19). With what she later calls a "methodological pastiche," Calafell creates her homeplace in relationship to theories and methodologies that *do* fit, that anticipate and welcome her body and knowledges and make her comfortable. She describes feeling *at home* for the first time in the academy when reading Lisa Flores's (1996) "Creating Discursive Space through a Rhetoric of Difference: Chicana Feminists Craft a Homeland," which itself invokes the necessity of crafting a homeland in the face of hostile theory and methodology. For her part, Flores cites Sandra Cisneros's main character in *The House on Mango Street*, Esperanza, who "longs for a house . . . of which she can be proud and in which she can feel comfortable" (qtd. in Flores 1996, 142).

The comfort of home sought by Esperanza, Flores, and Calafell is not superficial but, as Moraga and Anzaldúa propose, a "refusal of the *easy* explanation to the conditions we live in. There is nothing *easy*," they continue, "about a collective cultural history of what Mitsuye Yamada (1981) calls 'unnatural disasters'; the forced encampment of Indigenous people on government reservations, the forced encampment of Japanese American people during WWII, the forced encampment of our mothers as laborers in factories / in fields / in our own and other people's homes as paid or unpaid slaves" (19). Instead of ease, the comfort of a methodological homeplace indicates achieved fit between theory and body, between methodology and experience, where the place is shaped by who is there as much as the inhabitants are shaped by the place (see also Ahmed 2012). It is, in the words of bell hooks ([1990] 2014) specifically characterizing the necessity of constructing homeplaces for Black people, "a safe place where black people could affirm one another and by so doing heal many wounds inflicted by racist domination" (42). This happens in part through what Leslie R. Anglesey and Melissa Nicholas (this collection) call the "connective tissue" that flows across bodies and binds us together. Like the space we crafted as E2K for this collaboration, a methodological homeplace offers comfort and fit because it emerges *in relation* to bodies and lives; it is built both *by* and *for* those who use it.

Kelly helps us conceptualize methodology in this way in "Rasquache Rhetorics: A Cultural Rhetorics Sensibility," which offers "a robust approach to meaning making by allowing users to pull from the compendium of theories, ideas, experiences, tangible tools, and intangible epistemologies they can access" (Medina-López 2018, 2). Creating a homeplace is not about "simply approach[ing] the disciplinary table but build[ing] a new one out of the bits and pieces we have at hand" (2018, 3). And the table must *fit* the sensibility of those who use it, not be honed and polished to the specifications of the field as it exists but crafted for the use and taste of those who build it. Affirming the need to build this table anew (rather than merely bring more chairs to it, for example), Jaqueline Jones Royster (2000) recalls her own methodological invention practices, for which she was not "privileged to have a guide" (2000, 52). Without a guide, Royster invented "a range of techniques" "adequate to the complexity" of her embodiment, identifications, and research (52). These techniques did not pre-exist her work.

GENTEFYING THE NEIGHBORHOOD

Writing over the span of twenty years, Medina-López (2018), Calafell (2010), Royster (2000), and Flores (1996) each confront a discipline ill-equipped to offer them a homeplace. But none seek a methodological home built by others. Indeed, Kelly "hear[s] her dad whisper, 'Mija, don't find a seat. Build one. You have all the tools'" (Medina-López 2018, 12). Considering the relationships between methodology and mentoring posited by this collection, then, we ask: What does—or can—mentoring look like when those *without* an existing methodological homeplace nonetheless have the knowledge, materials, and tools to build one? How can mentors help them build successful, sound, and *fitting* homeplaces without taking over? How can they check in and check up on the process without invoking the authority of the realtors association (governed by unspoken racial redlining), the homeowners association (eager for tended lawns and approved paint colors, regulated by codes both tacit and explicit), the neighborhood watch (looking out for bodies that do and don't belong), or law enforcement (trained to violently enforce racialized norms of community belonging)? How can they, invoking the experience of Victor Villanueva (1993), "slip through the cracks in the hegemonic bloc" (xvi)?

Answering these questions, we propose, requires spatially building out our sense of methodological (home)places so that they are situated in communities wherein mentoring practices include not only welcoming others into our homes and working to help them feel at home but simultaneously helping them build and inhabit their own—in the neighborhoods and on the blocks they choose, with the tools and the materials they carry (and whatever they may want to borrow), and with their own architectural and design styles. This work hinges on both differentiating and acknowledging the deep entanglements of space (which we draw on Nedra Reynolds [2004] to define as "the more conceptual notion—a realm of practices") and place ("defined by people and events" [181]). Following Reynolds, we understand that whereas "space . . . structures our habitats but cannot be inhabited . . . places touch people's lives and evoke memories and emotions" (2004, 181). As we illustrate below with our own stories, this work is metaphorical *and* material. It includes imagining rhetoric and writing studies in spatialized terms and acknowledging the physical, embodied spaces and places of the field (its copyrooms, offices, and conferences); it includes acknowledging that bodies are tangible and require a spectrum of physical accommodations (see also Anglesey and Nicolas, this collection). Mentoring attuned to spatial relations—which have emerged over long and short histories—means we consider how our own methodological homeplaces invite or preclude visitors / newcomers. Metaphorically, we can ask if they feel safe in the neighborhood or out of place: Do they feel relaxed in our living rooms or nervous that they will break something? Do they want to stay and share stories or quickly leave after a (formal) visit? It also means that we consider how, as mentors, we move and act in the community (of rhetoric and writing studies): which neighborhoods do we visit and which do we avoid? Which do we imagine as "good" neighborhoods and what makes us understand them as such? Who do we consider neighbors or strangers and how do we interact with them? But these metaphoric questions simultaneously structure and resonate across our material, lived spaces: students *feel* fit (or not) in our classrooms and offices. They see the books on our shelves and the looks on our faces and understand whether and when they can make themselves *at home*.

In this chapter, we build on articulations of methodological homeplaces in order to build out a theory of mentoring on the methodological block, but our building metaphors are not without ideological baggage. In the land(scape) of late capitalism, haunted by historic and ongoing colonial occupation and enslaved and exploited labor, where eminent domain replaces land sovereignty, "building" is never a neutral activity. Working in these spatial terms allows us to consider the land we occupy and how we take up space and call for *gentefying*, not gentrifying, our methodological neighborhoods. Marieke Ahrens (2015) explains in "'Gentrify? No! Gentefy? Sí!" that gentefication "allud[es] to the Spanish word la gente (the people), middle-class Latinos aim to improve the neighborhood from within the community in order to maintain the area's Latino character and to avoid the displacement, exclusion, and sociospatial polarization typical of gentrification" (9). Invoking this terminology to conceptualize methodology and mentoring allows us to address their relational complexities: methodologies are built in part from, and in context of, mentoring relationships that foreclose, forestall, or foment possibilities (see also Dixon, Smith, and Powell in this collection). While those developing methodologies can (and often do) use creativity, resilience, and embodied knowledges to build their own homeplaces in the absence of positive mentoring relationships, we see our work as contributing to more sustainable and equitable disciplinary communities.

Creating strong, affirmative communities, we argue, means acknowledging and rejecting white flight (where those with resources abscond to insular, sometimes gated communities) and gentrification (where those with wealth claim existing neighborhoods, displacing residents, erasing histories, and expunging character) and foregrounding our commitments to respecting land sovereignty, to sharing architectural plans and construction materials and tools without demanding uniformity, and to making spaces habitable. Emphasizing building relationships—between land and bodies, land and capital, land and access—gives us a framework to conceptualize how building, decorating, and surveilling happen in the tangible work of signaling methodological commitments (in how we build space and inhabit homeplace) and in the epistemological work of supporting, resourcing, and welcoming students to build and inhabit (methodologies) themselves. In committing to gentefication, then, we explore both how we (visibly, tangibly) signal what kind of homeplaces we have built and the epistemological tools we've used to build them.

In the sections that follow, we use this framework to critically assess a range of experiences we have had, both mentoring and being mentored. Positioned and embodied differently, we show the impact that mentoring practices can have on contributing to conditions of possibility for building methodological communities marked by equity, hospitality, and reciprocity, where those making choices about what they build (and how) have the support they need to make places that fit and feel safe. We begin this work by turning to specific spaces where this building and signaling happens (itself linked to real estate, homespaces, and racial capital)—institutional spaces—and how we are granted and governed by these spaces and come to find fit there.

BUILDING ON THE BLOCK

As an undergraduate student intimidated by her professors, Kelly used to walk past faculty offices and make mental notes about the professors who inhabited those places: this door has a questionable comic about grammar (not safe), this one has a United Farm Workers flag (safe), this door is wide open (welcoming), this door is blank and there are papers shoved under it (unwelcoming). As she moved through university hallways, she thought about the predominantly Brown, low-income southern New Mexico barrio she grew up in; this house has a neighborhood watch sticker (not safe); this house has a shrine to La Virgen and tons of plants in all kinds of planters, coffee cans, old tires (safe); those neighbors are sitting on their porch (welcoming); this house has bars on the windows and a big mean dog (unwelcoming). Even as a young child, Kelly connected the homes in her neighborhood to the epistemologies of their inhabitants. Neighborhood Watch and Bars-on-the-Window shared similar ideologies about the neighborhood and the people who lived there: that they posed a threat and merited surveillance. They did not fit. Tons-of-Plants and Sitting-on-the-Porch felt like part of the community and were comfortable with their neighbors. They fit. This barrio epistemology, of which houses held friends and which houses to avoid, transferred to Kelly's experience as an undergraduate navigating the unfamiliar neighborhood of faculty offices. It was a methodology for identifying mentors: a way to find fit.

As a professor with her own office, Kelly knew that the majority Latinx, first-generation students at her university might use their barrio epistemologies in similar ways. She was careful about the signs she picked and what they might signal to the nervous students who passed by. One (literal) sign she put up was small, hand painted, and quoted Ejército Zapatista de Liberación Nacional (EZLN) leader Subcomandante Marcos reading "Disculpe las molestias, esto es una revolución" (pardon the inconvenience, this is a revolution) (see figure 3.1). The quote is one of Kelly's favorites—in particular, the absolute irony of it, and its applicability to being BIPGM in academia. The story, at least, is this: on January 1, 1994, Subcomandante Marcos is leading tourists out of San Cristóbal, Chiapas, as the EZLN initiate armed conflict in hopes of gaining land back and basic human rights for the Indigenous populations of México. As he escorts the tourists out of town, he tells them, "Disculpen las molestias, esto es una revolución" ("Disculpen" 2014). An Indigenous man fighting for basic needs apologizing to tourists who were grumpy because they couldn't sleep off their hangovers: sorry, but this is a revolution. It's the apology that's ironic, but it's the fact that the EZLN mobilizes the conflict either way—inconvenient or not—that makes the quote worth embodying; sorry you're being inconvenienced, I've been inconvenienced all along.

Figure 3.1. Hand-painted sign, "Disculpe Las Molestias, esto es una Revolución."

The sign is the first thing a first-generation Latinx (potential) mentee notices when she sits down to negotiate her mentoring relationship with Kelly: What does that mean? Where is it from? And, just a remark: it's in Spanish! After discussing the quote and its language politics in the context of an English department, Kelly and her mentee get to work on their mentor agreement, a formal, collaborative charter required of their undergraduate research program. Halfway through their conversation, the mentee starts to express serious doubts about her fit as a researcher in the program: the other student researchers are already in a lab! They're doing *actual* research! I'm so far behind! Kelly's thoughts immediately turn to Royster, Calafell, Flores, and even *The House on Mango Street*'s Esperanza herself. "What did you do yesterday?" Kelly asks, "I went to the library. I got this!" the student rustles through her backpack and pulls out Anzaldua's *Borderlands/La Frontera*. "You mean, you did *actual* research?" The student turns her head to the side, confused. "How will you learn more about the family stories you want to include in your project?" Kelly asks. "I need to talk to my *abuelita*, she's the one that knows them all. I'll probably go to her house and help her cook dinner for my *tíos* this weekend so I can ask her to tell me then." "You mean, you're going to do *actual* research?" This time, it clicks. The mentee's eyes get wide, "this is the lab, isn't it?!" Kelly points to her own Brown body, "this is my lab," and then to her mentee's, "and that's yours. Everywhere our bodies go, and everything they experience, is our research. You've been researching your whole life. You're actually so far *ahead*."

Two weeks pass and the mentee comes back to Kelly's office for another check-in. There is a noticeable change in how she occupies the space. She's comfortable, as if she feels like she *fits* there. "They asked about my lab, and my research," she says. "What did you tell them?" "Well, I tried to explain it but they didn't really get it, so I just said 'Disculpen las molestias, esto es una revolución.' "

"Next time, don't apologize," Kelly says. Just like Kelly as an undergraduate used her barrio epistemology to identify and distinguish safe, welcoming faculty from unsafe, unwelcoming faculty, her mentee did similar work, identifying a tangible sign Kelly used to decorate her space as indicating something about Kelly's intangible scholarly commitments and sorting out whether or not she felt safe and welcomed in both the tangible space of Kelly's office and in Kelly's intangible ways of being and knowing signaled by the sign. A few weeks later, an email went around to all faculty saying that office windows could not be obstructed. This meant the sign would have to be moved somewhere less visible. As Kelly removed the sign and the other markers she had put up—Undocu-Allies and Safe Zone stickers, a small Zia symbol, a California Faculty Association flyer—she wondered about the institutional codes governing how and by whom she was surveilled while occupying her university space. What would happen if she didn't comply with the email? Put up curtains? Blacked her window out? Would the homeowners association send her menacing emails? Would the neighborhood watch mark her as a threat? Would law enforcement be called?

Kelly recalled how, in the 1990s, Sandra Cisneros caused controversy in her historic San Antonio neighborhood when she gentefied her house by painting it bright purple, a color choice not approved by the Historic Design and Review Committee. When asked by the committee to prove purple was a historically accurate color choice linked to the Tejano population of the area, she found, instead, the intentional erasure of Tejano identity from the city, including the "redevelopment" of the "historically valuable" neighborhood of Laredito "into a jail, parking lot and downtown police station" (Cisneros 1997, 1). Indeed, one of most historically significant Tejano neighborhoods in San Antonio was gentrified by the carceral legacy of slavery and the tangible violence of police brutality and mass incarceration of Black and Brown bodies on the very real estate that had been systematically robbed from those same bodies. Kelly made sure the sign was still visible through her office window and thought about stopping by the hardware store for a bucket of bright purple paint.

Like the upper-middle-class, predominantly white suburbs of the broader United States, where curb appeal is tightly regulated to produce the fiction of safety, universities are mythologized as safe, crime-free spaces, where each homeowner has passed through peer-review background checks and ascribes to the vision and values of the neighborhood. If owning a home in the 'burbs is considered "making it" in the American dream, a dream that redlining, covenants, and other structuralized racisms have prevented BIPGM from attaining, then "owning" a faculty office is the academic equivalent, and the same codes apply. They are the codes of white supremacy codified as building codes of the academy: the ordinances that check us, that require inspection, and subject us to approval or denial through administrative processes. Kelly's student was both bumping up against these codes and learning to build despite them, in spite of them. Rather than signal to the student how she might "pass inspection," Kelly encouraged her to build her own space and make her own fit.

The point of sharing this moment is not to indict specific people; while individuals write and live by the (white supremacist) codes, they aren't the (whole) problem. Moreover, the problem can't be solved only by individuals trying to make sense of their positionalities. White supremacist and colonial codes of the academy are upheld every time it is narrated to newcomers as a place where only particular building materials are used, only specific paint colors *fit* the neighborhood aesthetics, and no yard signs are allowed (see also Dixon, Smith, and Powell in this collection). Our hope is that this discussion shifts where we place our attention if, as a field, we take the lived experiences of BIPGM scholars and students seriously. Kelly's experience illustrates that mentees already have (many, most of, sometimes all) the tools they need to build their own places as well as a sense of what fits and feels comfortable, suggesting that the role of the mentor is to support and affirm, welcoming them to the neighborhood or validating their choice to build elsewhere. Eric's experience (detailed below) expands our sense of mentoring possibilities by highlighting the creative potential within the mentor/mentee relationship. Through practices rooted in Black resistance and Black creation, his experience suggests that mentoring in context of the field's methodologies can find purpose in direct opposition to the structures of white supremacy, whether that be through creation of new homeplaces or disruption of the old.

Eric's situation invites us to consider the role of mentoring in further creating and disrupting methodologies. To return to the neighborhood metaphor, it asks us to consider the impact of throwing a barbeque without asking the neighbor's permission to park family and friends' cars on their curbs, or of creating murals and graffiti on pristine walls and picket fences. Eric's experience corroborates the idea that mentoring should invite students to build their own methodological places, but it also invites construction through destruction; it reminds us that the methodological block our field sits on didn't appear in a vacuum. It was intentional and material, built and maintained to look and feel a certain way. But if we're serious about addressing systemic inequities, we might need to deface a wall or two, maybe rack up a couple noise complaints to remind residents that only *some* people feel safe in suburbia.

SPEAKING OF HOME

Eric's experience as a mentee navigating graduate school mirrors Calafell's warning that feelings of isolation often lead to self-doubt and mis-fit, specifically since it's the codes legitimized by white supremacy that promise success and visibility. As one of the few Black people associated with his department, Eric was encouraged to theorize and think through Blackness within the field but struggled when the ways of communicating Blackness and its intricacies were filtered through non-Black methods and performances. In other words, he was encouraged to understand his role as decorating a prefab home instead of building his own. Moreover, his existence in the field (on the block) was always that of a guest; he often felt welcomed, and there were those who built their own disciplinary homeplaces in which he could feel comfortable visiting with and learning from them. But making oneself at home in another's space isn't quite the same as having your own place.

The type of homeplace Eric required needed to be political in order to effectively address the effects of white supremacy. bell hooks (1990) explains that such homeplaces have often been constructed by Black people in order to address the humanity of Black bodies living within white supremacy. As she states:

> Historically, African-American people believed that the construction of a homeplace, however fragile and tenuous (the slave hut, the wooden shack), had a radical political dimension. Despite the brutal reality of racial apartheid, of domination, one's homeplace was the one site where one could freely confront the issue of humanization, where one could resist.... This task of making homeplace was not simply a matter of black

women providing service; it was about the construction of a safe place where black people could affirm one another and by so doing heal many wounds inflicted by racist domination. (42)

For Eric, these homeplaces were first realized through connecting with Black scholars in the field at regional and national academic conferences who modeled—within their work and their conversations—the type of scholarly existence he longed for. It was important that Eric see their research methodologies affirm Blackness and call out white supremacy, but it was even more important that each meeting, formal or informal, establish the sort of neighborhood feel where his existence in the field was also affirmed. As bell hooks (1990) states, that sort of affirmation, which is cognizant of the effects of white supremacy, is critical for homeplaces to be spaces "where we return for renewal and self-recovery, where we can heal our wounds and become whole" (49).

On Resistance

Like Kelly's with her mentee, Eric's experience suggests that mentors should help establish politicized homeplaces where mentees can work through the white supremacist codes that underwrite disciplinary structures. But mentorship inspired by Black feminist methodologies also recognizes that the impacts of white supremacy must be addressed outside of the home, and Eric's experiences suggest that our disciplinary homeplaces cannot become so insular that we forget they exist within community spaces. His story pushes against practices that individualize or isolate a homeplace, demonstrating that the spaces we navigate—and how we do so—always impact those around us. It is the reason why building and neighborhood codes and homeowners associations exist. It is how residents and visitors, returning to Kelly's words, develop neighborhood/barrio epistemologies and literacies, understanding where and how their bodies fit *in relation* to others' spaces. Certain codes exist to give homeowners the perception of individualism (they can pick paint colors or whether to install shutters), but in reality, the codes, often embedded in legacies of white supremacy, suggest that any structure built and maintained through difference will always be seen as an aberration (homeowners can only pick paint colors from a limited set of options). It will always be the burden of those living in difference to justify their practice and existence. They will always be surveilled, their choices measured against predefined neighborhood standards that create its *feel*. And, of course, the feeling of the neighborhood has consequences. "Good" neighborhoods, "safe" neighborhoods,

neighborhoods with "good schools" are not accidental: they reflect generational wealth and historic redlining.

So, what would it look like to support a student building a methodology that flouts the neighborhood codes while ignoring neighbors' suspicious looks? If discipline or displacement are always realities—gentrification is more popular than ever, neighborhood watch is fundamentally dangerous for Black and Brown bodies—how do we support student choices without denying their differential effects? How can they understand practices of resistance that push just enough to make the neighbors uncomfortable? We propose that mentoring methodology must center critical resistance and advocating for communal spaces receptive to difference. In other words, gentefying the methodological neighborhood is about not just including a variety of homeplaces but including spaces for neighbors to meet, talk about community concerns, review and revise the HOA. As Eric's experience attests, it is the shared or communal spaces on the block where methodology founded in difference can be realized and affirmed.

Although Eric's first requirement was establishing a homeplace, that was only one step in realizing a community across difference. The next step was to outwardly challenge and resist racist codes through performances, and Eric was able to do so through the relationship with his mentor, Dr. Stephanie Troutman Robbins. It was important to build and connect with Black scholars across the field in order to establish a homeplace in it, but it was even more important that he learn how to live and thrive in spite of the codes that made his existence in academia an anomaly. His mentor illustrated the need to continually call out the issues with current codes based in white supremacy, gentefying the space so that it might be sensitive to and inviting of difference.

While there was much that Dr. Troutman Robbins did to help Eric work through his graduate studies, three main practices of her mentoring specifically illustrate the potentials of gentefying as an approach to mentoring: checking in, modeling resistance, and encouraging resistance. Her first strategy centered the overall humanity of a mentee, separate from any of the disciplinary work they did. These check-ins would go longer than many obligatory greetings that folks do before getting down to business. Dr. Troutman Robbins's attention to Eric's overall well-being recognizes that much of the work that BIPGM in our field do is deeply historical and always embodied. It takes a lot of energy to constantly work through scholarship, both contemporary and ancient, that refuses to acknowledge the intellect and humanity of BIPGM. It also takes a lot of energy to stare at books and computer screens, sifting through information in order to make it all make sense. Dr. Troutman Robbins's approach, to attend to the humanity of it all, first and foremost affirmed Eric's existence in the space and gave him permission to feel all the things before settling in and working through all the things.

Another approach that Dr. Troutman Robbins took in her mentoring practices was to model resistance in all spaces in her life, from the page, to classrooms, to publications, to communities. Her work not only continually demanded calling out social injustices, it was also smart and critical; guided by Black feminisms and transposed from a different (more equitable) neighborhood. Her practices pushed against expectations in academia (the codes of the HOA) by demanding that the work not only be intellectually sound but also have impact on the neighborhood—affirming the humanity and lived experiences of those traditionally left out of or silenced by the institution. Modeling this approach to scholarly work had a major impact, illustrating to Eric that community-building in mentoring practices means affirming lived experiences and not displacing others for the sake of homogeneity.

Lastly, Dr. Troutman Robbins encouraged Eric to resist, through a variety of performances ranging from the type of scholarship he pursued to the way he dressed in "academic" spaces. It is important that this step came after the previous emphasis on mentoring as modeling, since Eric was comfortable performing various resistances only after witnessing Dr. Troutman Robbins be unapologetic in her own performances of resistance. Once again, to return to the metaphor, Dr. Troutman Robbins's performance invited Eric to step out of the individual homeplace in order to become a member of the larger community—on campus, in the field, in academia itself—and to do so on his own terms. The act of stepping out didn't ignore the codes that give structure to the block; as previously mentioned, Dr. Troutman Robbins's approach to the work was smart and critical, aware of the power dynamics that shape the neighborhood (discipline). But the act of stepping out of the house and into the community allowed Eric to recognize that there was nothing inherently natural about the neighborhood codes. The codes are socially constructed, and sometimes those constructions need to be called out for what they are and what they allow. The process of gentefying the block requires performances of resistance, of claiming space and sovereignty in the face of cleaning up the neighborhood; mentors modeling such resistances invite mentees to further transform the block into a place that welcomes difference rather than one that seeks to white it out.

NEW CODES

Much like Gloria Ladson-Billings's (1995) early equation of culturally relevant approaches to teaching with plain old "good teaching" (159), the mentoring practices of Dr. Troutman Robbins could easily be summed up as "good mentoring." This parallel invites another question inspired by Ladson-Billings (1995): If such practices are considered good mentoring, why does so little of it occur for BIPGM graduate students in our discipline (159)? Why do so many BIPGM graduate students in our discipline have mentoring horror stories? As we have argued in this piece, our discipline's history of mentoring has favored practices of gentrification and homogenization, practices that make methodological neighborhoods hostile to BIPGM students—and eventually faculty.

In addition to outright displacement (moving in on intellectual territory through a logic of imminent domain), mentoring often takes the form of gentrification, investing in a neighborhood only when it looks like it will offer a good return on investment. A mentor who sees students as rehab projects, only interested in buildings that can be remade to look good as new, or one who visits different (scholarly, intellectual) neighborhoods only to find materials or sites they can salvage or claim, is signaling the type of neighbor they will be: a nightmare. Mentors who only authorize building projects in the image of their own are building academic 'burbs: exclusive, homogenous, and often dangerous for BIPGM. While the 'burbs feel safe to some—a place to settle in and build a life—they are alienating for others: a constant reminder of how they do not fit.

As we imagine and recreate the future of the discipline as more dynamic, inclusive, and equitable, we must consider how the codes we tacitly accept and live by (no loud music, no block parties, no bright purple paint, no signs in the yard) signal to students how they fit in (or not) on the methodological block. The extant codes of the academy, like the racial covenants and neighborhood watch of neighborhoods, enforce norms to preclude difference or change. As mentors, however, we can participate in changing the neighborhood: throw barbeques, hang out in the park, welcome new architecture and homebuilders. We can make and share space while students are making their way and making their place. We can put up signs—literally and metaphorically—to signal our commitments. We can check in on our mentees without checking up on them: affirmation not surveillance. We can show them how we know the rules, break the rules, and rewrite the rules of belonging. We can learn to recognize new-to-us (methodological) tools, (epistemological) know-how, and (embodied) expertise, ready to share our own without taking over.

NOTE

1. As the purpose of this essay is to disrupt institutionalized and academic whiteness (in particular, as it's attached to mentoring), we also choose to do so through our terms. Rather than "of color," "people of color" (POC), or "Black, Indigenous, and people of color" (BIPOC), we replace "of color" with "of the global majority" (e.g., Black, Indigenous, and women of the global majority, BIWGM) or "Black, Indigenous, and people of the Global Majority" (BIPGM). "Of the global majority" is an inclusive term that marks the identity of non-white people without reifying whiteness (inaccurately) as the default and disrupts US-centric racial politics from which POC/BIPOC emerge as categories (see also Portelli and Campbell-Stephens 2009).

REFERENCES

Ahmed, Sara. 2012. *The Cultural Politics of Emotion*. New York: Routledge.

Ahrens, Marieke. 2015. "'Gentrify? No! Gentefy? Sí!': Urban Redevelopment and Ethnic Gentrification in Boyle Heights, Los Angeles." *aspeers* 8: 9–26.

Calafell, Bernadette M. 2010. "Rhetorics of Possibility: Challenging Textual Bias through Theories of the Flesh." In *Rhetorica in Motion: Feminist Rhetorical Methods and Methodologies*, edited by Eileen E. Schell and K. J. Rawson, 104–117. Pittsburgh, PA: University of Pittsburg Press.

Cisneros, Sandra. 1997. "My Purple House—Color Is a Language and a History." Latino Link, August 31, 1997. http://genconnection.com/English/house.html.

"Disculpen las molestias. Esto es una revolución." 2014. *La última en llegar*, January 2, 2014. https://llegalaultima.com/2014/01/02/disculpen-las-molestias-esto-es-una-revolucion/.

Flores, Lisa A. 1996. "Creating Discursive Space through a Rhetoric of Difference: Chicana Feminists Craft a Homeland." *Quarterly Journal of Speech* 82: 142–156.

hooks, bell. (1990) 2014. *Yearning: Race, Gender, and Cultural Politics*. 2nd ed. New York: Routledge.

Ladson-Billings, Gloria. 1995. "But That's Just Good Teaching! The Case for Culturally Relevant Pedagogy." *Theory into Practice* 34 (3): 159–65.

Medina-López, Kelly. 2018. "Rasquache Rhetorics: A Cultural Rhetorics Sensibility." *Constellations: A Cultural Rhetorics Publishing Space* 1 (1): 2–23.

Moraga, Cherríe L., and Gloria Anzaldúa. 1981. "Entering the Lives of Others." In *This Bridge Called My Back: Writings by Radical Women of Color*, edited by Gloria Anzaldúa and Cherríe L. Moraga, 19. Waterton, MA: Persephone Press.

Portelli, John P., and R. Campbell-Stephens. 2009. *Leading for Equity*. Toronto: Edphil Books.

Reynolds, Nedra. 2004. *Geographies of Writing: Inhabiting Places and Encountering Difference*. Carbondale: Southern Illinois University Press.

Royster, Jacqueline Jones. 2000. *Traces of a Stream: Literacy and Social Change among African American Women*. Pittsburgh, PA: University of Pittsburgh Press.

Villanueva, Victor Jr. 1993. *Bootstraps: From an American Academic of Color*. Urbana, IL: National Council of Teachers of English.

4
THE LEGACY OF CARE
Origins and Expectations of Mentoring in Writing Center Methodologies

Devon Fitzgerald Ralston

Before I became a writing center administrator, my understanding of mentoring as a practice was limited and often intellectually focused: serving as a thesis director or advisor, writing letters of recommendation, or acting as a reference for students in my classes. While I likely would have said that mentoring was a part of my work, including my pedagogy, my perspective shifted significantly once I stepped into the role of writing center director at Winthrop University. Not only was mentoring more central to my work, I also began to recognize that the spaces I might have turned to for advice regarding this work—scholarly texts, my own mentors, and colleagues—could not fulfill my need to more fully embrace these expectations. In fact, one of my college friends, who is a corporate regional manager responsible for many diverse groups and teams, provided the most guidance as I struggled in the first few months in the position. This chapter emerged, like a lot of writing center scholarship, out of my own experiences, but more particularly my questions, conflicts, and frustrations.

There are a few goals at its center. The first is to trace the legacy of writing center methodologies in the move from the classroom lab to the stand-alone space. The history laid out in writing center scholarship is crucial to understanding how the identities of writing center administrators become enmeshed in writing center work. An aim of this chapter is to uncover and draw attention to mentoring as central to writing center administration.

The second goal is to argue for a deliberate and visible methodology of mentoring, one that values administrator identities, roles, and contexts within local institutions as well as the field at large. Conversations within a field are important to gauge what is privileged. Since a guiding principle of writing center methodology is that writing is collaborative and social, scholarly conversations embrace this notion on listservs, informally and formally in conference spaces, in our primary journals (*Writing Lab Newsletter, Writing Center Journal, Praxis, Southern Discourse in the Center*), in training materials like textbooks, and in scholarly publications (books and edited collections). In the *Oxford Guide for Writing Tutors*, Lauren Fitzgerald and Melissa Ianetta (2016) identify types of writing center scholarship: lore, historical research, theoretical research, empirical research, and rhetorical research, which they define as arguments from a "community's shared values in an attempt to motivate a change in attitude or action from the reader" (9). I thread lore, historical research, and rhetorical research together throughout this piece, beginning with history.

This chapter argues that when writing centers moved from methods of tutoring (part of instructional labs, remedial, hands-on practice) to stand-alone spaces outside classrooms, the methodologies of the work became entangled with the atmosphere of the physical space, and with the ethos of the writing center director, whose decisions from decor to recruitment become the way students know what a writing center is, the purpose it serves within the university and how they should work within it. Most students who become writing center tutors have little to no experience with writing center studies as a field and typically take either a preparation course or are consistently trained in professional development events throughout the year. As such, writing center administrators' responsibility to provide a foundation for tutor knowledge and practices through direct instruction and mentoring is a significant one. Yet little scholarship within writing center research focuses on mentoring, and even less provides a methodology for mentoring. What does this say about the value of mentoring to the field? To our students and tutors? To tenure and promotion committees?

Dave Healy (1995) explains that "outside the academy, we expect professionals to have some sort of 'calling' to their profession and to have devoted themselves with considerable intentionality and focus to their chosen specialty—whether in medicine or law or whatever" (38). Within the university, however, faculty are often nominated for or appointed to administrative roles without such intentionality or explicit training. A 2017 survey of writing center directors, in fact, shows that 20 percent of directors were appointed to their positions (Valles, Babcock, and Jackson 2017). What this means, ultimately, is that there is often little guidance of how to manage a new administrative role. As Elizabeth Chavin and Beth Towle discuss elsewhere in this collection, research methods in writing center work are also often left up to individual administrators not necessarily trained in writing center administration.

In this piece, I share an autoethnography of how I came to this work. Not only does this approach enact a common research methodology of writing center administration, the narrative itself also emphasizes a common path to writing center administration—in particular, where faculty or staff "end up" in such positions. But first, it is useful to briefly examine the history of writing center methodologies as reflected in writing center studies scholarship. To understand the complexities of writing center methodologies requires some patience. The history of writing center scholarship in particular is messy and not always linear.

THE LEGACY OF CARE

Most writing center scholarship emerged in the 1970s, when writing centers were professionalizing but, according to Peter Carino (1995), writing center work was happening before writing centers as places were formalized. Early writing centers, often called labs, were designed to enhance writing instruction, acting as an extension of the classroom. Elizabeth Boquet (1999) explains that labs were not considered sites but rather methods, focusing particularly on the grammatical elements of writing. Eventually the methods evolved into sites as writing center work moved outside of the classroom and became additional assistance rather than an extension of coursework. In doing so, Boquet explains that the physical spaces of writing centers worked in opposition to their "auto-tutorial counterparts" and were characterized with "creature comforts—couches, plants, coffee pots, posters" (473). In separating themselves from the structured classroom, the atmosphere and comfort of writing centers becomes an important aspect of the collaborative work occurring within.

Early writing center scholarship focuses on how to establish writing centers, defining their purpose and setting expectations for how to conceptualize a writing center and its staff. Two foundational articles, Stephen North's (1984) "The Idea of a Writing Center" and Muriel Harris's (1995) "Talking in the Middle: Why Students Need Writing Tutors," emphasize the interactivity between tutors and writers, and the importance of talking about writing. North's piece is particularly influential to writing center methodologies; "creating better writers not better writing" is a guiding foundation to the field as a whole. North (1984) also stresses the importance of autonomy for writing center directors. He writes, "The first rule in our Writing Center is that we are professionals at what we do" (441). Harris's (1995) article describes the place of the writing center, acknowledging the importance of how the physical space orients tutors and clients. She uses the term "haven" and stresses the priority of creating a space outside of the classroom. So, almost from their inception, methods of tutoring and the spaces in which tutoring occurs become imbued with care. In fact, Harris's "What's Up and What's In: Trends and Traditions in Writing Centers" discusses a writing center conference where a book of recipes sat among handouts and brochures. Harris writes that rather than questioning this inclusion, most writing center directors seemed excited to share it with their tutors. "Providing nourishment is a constant activity in writing centers," Harris (1990) explains. She writes of writing center scholarship that "there is a very noticeable tradition of perceiving writing centers as nurturing, helping places which provide assistance to other writing centers and sustenance to students to help them grow, mature, and become independent" (17).

Kinkead and Harris's (1993) *Writing Centers in Context,* one of the first book-length publications on writing centers, profiles twelve writing centers throughout the country at various universities. In the book's introduction, Harris describes the Purdue Writing Center as

> a mix of comfortable, old donated couches, tables, plants, posters, coffeepots, a recycling bin for soda cans and paper, and even a popcorn machine, all of which signal (we hope) that this mess is also a friendly, nonthreatening, nonclassroom environment where conversation and questions can fly from one table to another. (6)

These early profiles of writing centers set expectations of the physical space of a writing center, but also its atmosphere or mood. Jackie Grutsch McKinney (2005) explains the consequences of the legacy of these early profiles. She writes,

> An unintended result, however, might be that these objects become prescriptions for these spaces; to be legible—to be read—as a "writing center," a space needs to have a particular array of objects. And because many writing center professionals seem to be operating under the tacitly accepted notion that writing centers should be welcoming, cozy, comfortable, friendly spots where talk about writing can happen, one prescription wins out: writing centers should be like home. (7)

Grutsch McKinney argues that fortifying such a narrative using the metaphor of home is problematic, not only because it is significantly gendered but also because students' home lives may be markedly different than those of the people who create, direct, or decorate writing centers. I would add to Grutsch McKinney's critique by suggesting that the cozy environment not only sets expectations of the physical writing center but also sets expectations for those who direct them. A recent survey of writing center directors showed that since 1995, writing center directors have been predominantly female, which makes the gendered nature of care particularly fraught. (Valles, Babcock, and Jackson 2017). Mary Trachsel (1995) notes that "writing centers are often socially constructed as feminine sites where something like the domestic, care-giving service of the academy is carried out, and this may be true regardless of whether the work is undertaken by women or by men" (26). Beyond early scholarship, metaphors often used to describe the center's work include "care-giving," "midwifery," and "nurturing," extending this gendered identity not only of the physical space but also of the work itself. Grutsch McKinney (2013) argues that "looking *at* our spaces instead of *through* them" limits what can be valued as labor.

For many directors, decisions about everything from decor to software becomes their responsibility. While writing centers vary from university to university, the legacy of writing center work since its early days of taking care, of setting up cozy spaces, of being a place for help with writing, which is recognized as a vulnerable act, influences writing center directors and, thus, the tutors they train.

On the surface, the daily labor of writing center directorship looks very similar today to the way Valerie Balester and James McDonald (2001) described it over twenty years ago:

> Directors are called upon to write budgets and reports, recruit and train staff, prepare educational materials, design and fill out countless forms, make appointments, communicate with writing instructors and staff, train faculty from various disciplines in writing instruction, write grants, organize workshops and mini-courses, teach classes for tutors, placate irate students and faculty—and so on (68).

However, often implicit in this work is that it be undertaken with care, that directors act as guides, mentoring students through the messy work of tutoring writing, of "making better writers." This relational and emotional labor has only recently become a focus of writing center scholarship, but it is certainly a part of almost all director responsibilities. Chavin and Towle argue in this collection, for example, that the future of mentorship in writing centers should be theorized from a feminist and decolonized perspective emerging from writing center administrators' daily practices.

While this is not an exhaustive review of early writing center scholarship, nor work focused on the physical space of writing centers, it is clear that an expectation of care has been firmly established. I felt the pressure of this legacy acutely when I became writing center director, first in an interim position and then later taking on the role more permanently.

EXPECTATIONS

I began my career, as most writing center directors seem to, as a writing center tutor. I loved helping students find a topic or a way to say something meaningful. I also struggled as a go-between. Sometimes, I was just as frustrated as the students with a complicated prompt or with very few details for an assignment. After a semester and a summer in the writing center, I became a teaching assistant, and by my PhD program, I was exclusively in the classroom. As I moved through my career, I remained connected to universities' writing and learning centers. I provided resources, encouraged students in all my classes to make use of the center, and participated in workshops, but my roles were always from outside of the center looking in.

When I accepted my current position in rhetoric, professional writing, and composition at Winthrop University, I did not anticipate a return to writing center work. Then there was a medical emergency, and I was asked to step in to direct the center and teach the tutor training course.

Once I decided to serve as interim director in the fall of 2016, the director who was on medical leave shared many of her materials with me in the form of a stack of large black binders. It was, honestly, a bit daunting. Because my research focus was elsewhere, I was unfamiliar with the scholarship of contemporary writing center studies, and yet I could see, from the policies to the textbooks for the course, that I approached writing and tutoring from different pedagogical and philosophical places in the composition landscape. Since my assignment as director was temporary, I did not feel it was my role, then, to make sweeping changes, so I tried to follow the syllabus and the guidance in the binders. Even though I had a great deal of support in the department from my chair and colleagues, and despite my previous tutoring work and administrative experience in other programs when that director retired in 2017 and I stepped fully into the directorship, I kept wondering, "How do *I* do this job?"

I understood the daily tasks. I had a job description, yet I knew from previous years' experience that much about writing center work is not present in these documents. Further, there were many emotions wrapped into this question for me. When the position was temporary, I was focused on managing the day-to-day concerns. I was not focused on establishing a vision or mission, because I was merely a substitute. So, when the responsibilities came to me and I was the director, I had to quickly adjust my thinking about the role and how I could make an impact. Suddenly, tutors were looking to me to guide them, and to help them succeed both in- and outside of the writing center. And while I'd been preparing as I shadowed the previous director and acted as an associate director, I felt the weight of expectations about how *I* would do the job. How would a white, forty-something, queer, feminist digital rhetoric scholar who drinks too much coffee and frequently forgets to charge her phone direct a writing center, direct *this* specific writing center that had been influenced by the same director for over twenty years?

In *Facing the Center*, Harry Denny (2010) explains that "these very pressures of identity—and their attendant politics—are ever-present" and that "students, tutors, administrators and faculty must confront who they are, whether the identity in question is one from the margins or whether the context forces awareness of one's privilege or position at the center" (16). I am a white, cis-gender female. I am queer. I am recently tenured faculty. I teach professional writing and composition. I research pop culture, digital rhetoric, and intellectual property, and I direct the writing center. All of these personal and professional identities contribute to what I bring to writing center directing. Dave Healy (1995) argues that "if we are to understand the issue of professional status among the people who run writing centers, we need to know more about who they are and how they conceive of their own roles" (27). Nikki Caswell, Rebecca Jackson, and Jackie Grutsch McKinney's (2016) *Working Lives of New Writing Center Directors* has started such conversations, and Travis Webster's (2021) *Queerly Centered* continues to research the emotional labor of queer writing center directors. I believe much more research with an explicit focus on mentorship is essential not only for a more robust understanding of our work but also for a legacy that includes diverse voices and the pressures BIPOC directors face.

From the beginning of my role as director, the tension between the expectations of my role and my comfort within it felt significant. Because my ethos was drastically different from that of the previous director, it was challenging to find common ground in our approaches to writing center administration. It also meant that any changes I wanted to implement would likely feel extreme for the tutors who had been used to one way of doing things. Thus, the question of how *I* do this work was one born not only of concern for meeting localized expectations but also an implicit and unspoken question: How do I do this work differently? What is *my* vision for Winthrop's writing center?

What both Denny's and Webster's research shows is that writing center administrators frequently grapple with the tension evident in questions about how to direct a writing center in their particular set of circumstances. For me, questions ranged from the practical (when do I hold the first staff meeting) to the personal (do I come out to the tutoring staff?) and the strategic (what kinds of professional development can I provide as institutional and student needs evolve)? The kinds of questions that were front-of-mind provide insight into the ethos I wanted to build as Winthrop's new writing center director. From policies to hiring and training, writing center directors carry out writing center methodologies and practices. As such, the ethos of a writing center director circulates through and intersects the center's ethos. Ethos, I argue, is also where the roots of mentoring as a methodology begin. My understanding of ethos and its function in writing center administration, and more particularly to mentoring, builds on feminist rhetorical scholars and remains a potential space for feminist praxis. See Bartlett et al. on slow mentoring in this collection for a feminist-centered mentoring model that foregrounds knowledge-making in the context of personal and professional lives rather than productivity and success. Such a model allows for the kinds of collaboration privileged in writing center methodologies and acknowledges feminist ethos (the importance of which I address below) in significant ways.

While I have what feels like a well-articulated pedagogical philosophy for my classroom, I have only recently begun to develop a philosophy specific to mentoring, particularly in my role as director. As such, when I was asked to make decisions or provide guidance, I was without a deliberate methodology for the work of mentoring, which likely would have assuaged at least some of the internal conflict and tension I initially felt.

ADMINISTRATOR ETHOS

Michel Foucault (1997) talks about ethos as the subject's mode of being and a certain manner of acting visible to others. One's ethos was seen by his dress, by his bearing, by his gait, by the poise with which he reacts to events, and so on. Ethos, in this sense, displays cultural "markers," such that the speaker's task is "to open a space" through language that allows the self to be heard and, saliently, to be seen (117).

Rhetorical scholar Kate Ronald's (1990) claim that "ethos is the appeal residing in the tension between the speaker's private and public self" (39) presents a postmodern view of ethos that links credibility and identity. Similarly, Susan Jarratt and Nedra Reynolds (1992) echo this view of ethos as a fluid and dynamic set of identifications, arguing that "these split selves are guises, but they are not distortions or lies in the philosopher's sense. Rather they are 'deceptions' in the sophistic sense: recognition of the ways one is positioned multiply differently" (56). As I consider the identities that I bring to writing center administration, this recognition provides some comfort to the previous tensions with which I began my work.

Michael Halloran (1982) argues, "To have ethos is to manifest the virtues most valued by the culture to and for which one speaks" (60). In the context of writing center studies, then, culture exists within both the localized writing center and the culture of the field through its scholarship and lore.

Feminist scholars argue that ethos is formed through the negotiation between private experience and the public, rhetorical act of self-expression. According to Nedra Reynolds (1993), "ethos, like postmodern subjectivity, shifts and changes over time, across texts, and around competing spaces" (336). However, Reynolds additionally discusses how one might clarify the meaning of ethos within rhetoric as expressing inherently communal roots. Karlyn Kohrs Campbell (1982) echoes this emphasis when she writes, "Ethos does not refer to your peculiarities as an individual but to the ways in which you reflect the characteristics and qualities that are valued by your culture or group. In fact, the Greek meaning for 'ethos' as 'a habitual gathering place' calls forth an image of people coming together." (qtd. in LeFevre 1987, 45–46). We can think of ethos as intersecting culture, community, and socially created spaces. In a sense, then, ethos belongs not to the speaker but to the community. What this means is that we must "open spaces" to make ethos visible and deliberate. Since the writing center director's ethos drives a center's policies, philosophies, and methods, centering mentoring as a methodology works to open a space for ethos.

There is an intimacy in writing center work, not just for the tutors in sessions as they read and talk about writers' ideas and beliefs but also in the relationship between tutors and the writing center director who recruits, hires, and mentors them. And because writing center tutors navigate the emotional labor of working with student writing and it is a director's responsibility to help tutors manage that labor, the boundaries often made clear in the classroom seem to blur within the writing center ecology. As Caswell, Grutsch McKinney, and Jackson (2016) argue, "The tasks the writing center directors are responsible for are labor intensive, ongoing, often unplannable, and highly relational" (173). Because mentoring is personal and ethos-driven, and because it often feels intangible and unrecognized in annual reports or tenure cases, I believe that, as a field, we haven't been deliberate about mentoring, despite the both implicit and explicit presence of mentoring as a writing center methodology. Articulating a mentoring methodology (Bartlett et al.'s "Slow Mentoring," for example) would provide writing center directors with an individualized dynamic guide for establishing centering practices as well as a space for reflection.

I want to say here that I recognize the contested nature of "mentoring" as a term. Janice Lauer (1997) and Theresa Enos (1996) critique the hierarchical structure of many mentoring relationships as well as the exclusionary practices: who gets to speak or act as a mentor and why? Because the practice of mentoring grows out of a patriarchal ideal, then, the power structures of most mentoring relationships carry the baggage of such stratified power. Michelle Eble and Lynée Lewis Gaillet (2008) write, "The predominant theory of mentoring—master-apprenticeship model—was problematic and based on exclusion and tokenism. Only the lucky were mentored, and the predominant mentoring model was difficult to institute and promote" (308). Foucault (1997) believed that introspection into the self, the careful attention to the self, a turn to ethos was in itself a resistance to dominant power structures, and the feminist turn of ethos is to create a collaborative space. I try to mentor with such resistance in mind.

At Winthrop, students must take a course before they apply to be a tutor. Revising this course was perhaps the most deliberate way to make my own ethos more visible once I stepped into the directorship. We spend a good deal of time talking about our beliefs about writing. I talk openly and draw connections to how I see my beliefs taking up space in the operations manual and in our marketing materials, but also in the students I hire as they become more aware and invested in writing center work. The course may be the first time many of them are exposed to writing center studies as a field of scholars and practitioners made up of directors, staff, and students who write and publish about their own experiences. Mentoring via texts and text selection is an important part of training tutors, not only as an introduction to the field but also as a way to open spaces for better understanding its legacy. Course texts help to inform the practices of the writing center. The assignments ask students to consider their own beliefs about writing and the ways they have been mentored in writing, and at the end of the semester, students articulate their own tutoring philosophies.

Because my own mentoring derives from a distinctly queer and feminist background, which means valuing my students' / tutors' / tutees' / clients' experiences, including but not limited to their writing and learning experiences that involve past writing instruction, attitudes toward their language, handwriting, and grammar. Further, it means paying attention to my students' lived realities. For some that means working multiple jobs to contribute to their household. For others, it means struggling with mental health. All too frequently, it means my students are processing traumas. They may face physical or emotional violence or the death of a parent or loved one. The lived realities of students on campus are vastly different from my own. I want to open a space where those realities are honored.

Once part of the writing center ecology, tutors are invited into my life in much different ways than students I teach. I bring food to meetings and often buy pizza for the tutors on busy days during finals week. I come out to my tutors but don't often mention details of my life with the students in the tutor preparation course, though once they begin tutoring full-time, I talk more openly about life. And because I teach the preparation course every fall, I come out to a new slate of students each year, anxious about how students will respond. Though we have campus LGBTQA organizations and are noted for being queer-friendly, particularly for the area, I am still aware that many of my students have deeply religious beliefs that may create tension when I disclose my queerness.

I also understand the importance for my LGBTQA students to see a queer person being successful. Additionally, because the work I ask students to do in the center requires them to be vulnerable and open-minded as they meet vulnerable writers, I feel a certain responsibility to be transparent about who *I* am, which in itself requires quite a bit of vulnerability. Once I do so, I end up opening a space for students to share their experiences outside of class, outside of the center, outside of my job responsibilities.

In *Cruel Optimism,* Lauren Berlant (2012) is concerned with the ways politically conceived fantasies of the good life (in this case, writing center lore) can clash with the material conditions of everyday existence. Berlant writes, "Fantasy is the means by which people hoard idealizing theories and tableaux about how they and the world 'add up to something'" (2). What happens when those fantasies start to fray— "depression, dissociation, pragmatism, cynicism, optimism, activism, or an incoherent mash?" What Berlant is describing is, I think, part of why I often feel conflicted as I mentor.

I came to writing center work as a student tutor, never imagining that I would be a director. I have a deep commitment to our core writing courses, especially composition, and more so to the students in those courses. This is all part of the way I, specifically, *show up* to this work. How can I draw distinct connections to my history, my identities as part of a mentoring practice? It is necessary for me to be deliberate about this, especially upon reflection after my first semester as director, where it felt like many of the changes that I enacted were a direct response to the established practices that stood in place for so long and that did not reflect my ethos. I wanted to articulate not only for myself but also to my students why I was doing things differently and why their understanding of such practices mattered.

I started with policies. I revised language and eliminated many of the policies that did not align with empowering the students who work there. I eliminated the dress code. I added pronoun preferences to our registration forms. I rewrote punitive policies such as "If you are running late, your pay may be impacted" to now read: "Please let a receptionist or tutor know immediately if you are running late so we can adjust the schedule as needed and reassign your appointment." I divided the manual into sections, asking current tutors for suggestions on what needed revising. In 2018, the graduate students and I modified the tutoring job descriptions. We use Slack for communication, which allows tutors to post and answer one another's questions. This equalizes information and creates a way for us to build knowledge together. I aim to model interactions where power is shared, where I listen to tutors, where I acknowledge our collective vulnerabilities. While collaboration is at the core of writing center work, and thus such policies and approaches may be the norm across writing centers throughout the country, the changes I proposed were a distinct response to local and institutional contexts where such practices were not in play. Furthermore, I wanted to make an immediate impact in order to establish my ethos as director.

TOWARD DELIBERATE MENTORING

Because the work of budget requests and reporting, where the focus is on justifying our work to administrative bodies, places attention on the students we serve, the initiatives we undertake and how the challenges of evolving to meet student needs leave little room to emphasize mentoring practices, there are often gaps between what our institution values, what the field values, and where we, as administrators, want to spend our energy. In recognizing the legacy of care, in acknowledging that the roots of writing center directorship are intertwined with expectations of comfort, of nurturing, we can better understand how writing center work is framed (and gendered) in terms that may no longer suit the individual directors undertaking the job.

As writing center scholarship evolves, it challenges practitioners to reimagine our roles and complicates the legacy of such roles. Since 2018, there has been a significant turn toward wellness and self-care, to emotional labor and concerns over burnout (Johnson, Kervin and Barrett, Featherstone). Most significantly, *WLN: A Journal of Writing Center Scholarship*, one of the prominent writing center journals, published a special issue on wellness in early 2020. Most of the articles address how to help tutors carry the emotional labor of their work in tutorials, how mindfulness can benefit tutorials, or how to handle particularly emotional sessions. Neisha-Anne Green's (2018) "Moving beyond Alright: And the Emotional Toll of This, My Life Matters Too, in the Writing Center Work" explores the emotional labor that comes with being one of the few people of color in the field. She also emphasizes the vulnerability and danger that tutors and administrators of color experience in doing their work. Green argues the importance of professional development, research, and praxis that includes connections between race and wellness care. Many of the essays in *Counterstories from the Writing Center* (Faison and Condon 2022) emphasize narratives that challenge much of the current lore and engage in moments where advocacy has failed or been performative.

In *The Everyday Writing Center*, Geller et al. (2007) emphasize writing centers as communities of practice. They write, "One of the necessary conditions both for individual and organizational learning is a shared conviction that one's presence, one's engagement, and one's contributions matter" (125). The lived experience of administrators and tutors is essential to our praxis, our methodologies, and our ways of knowing and understanding writing center work. However, race, class, sexuality, gender, linguistic background, and disability must be seen as part of what matters in mentoring.

I propose we work together as administrators to unearth mentoring, to center it as a methodology, one that is deliberate and focused and one that can be flexible and evolving as we open spaces for previously underrepresented voices. As such, I have developed a brief heuristic toward more deliberate mentoring practices.

In *Facing the Center*, Harry Denny (2010) calls on those of us who work in writing centers to "infuse our everyday practices with the currency of academic life: intellectual questioning and theorizing of what's possible" (146). Mentoring is a practice where we can enact Denny's call. Not only do I believe we need research focused on mentoring as a methodology, I also believe applying the heuristic could be a starting point.

Beyond simply applying the heuristic to a mentoring philosophy, there are ways to make mentoring more visible beyond the writing center itself. When determining ways to be more deliberate, consider ways to include mentoring as a component of yearly departmental and college-level assessment. In defining yearly outcomes, I look for opportunities to align to institutional goals. For example, our university's quality enhancement plan (QEP) includes a component focused on professionalization and

Table 4.1. Toward more deliberate mentoring practices

Praxis	Legacy
Describe a specific mentor/mentee experience.	It's important to trace one's own mentoring experiences, since we often carry lived experiences into our own practices (positive or negative).
In what ways could you be more deliberate in considering ethos as part of mentoring? Can you draw specific connections from your beliefs to your policies, training, etc.? Do you vocalize these connections?	Writing center directors' ethos influences policies, philosophies, methodologies, practically all parts of writing center administration. If there are places where your ethos isn't represented, perhaps change is in order.
How frequently do you talk to your tutors about their writing beliefs, tutoring philosophies, practices?	Inviting student voices into your own practices models mentoring and may provide an opportunity for mentor texts.
In what ways do you want mentoring to be more visible? What are your mentoring goals? How do you plan to achieve them?	It may be necessary for some mentoring to be informal or implicit. To be more deliberate in mentoring, specify where and how you want to show up and, perhaps more importantly, for whom you want to show up.

employable skills. In laying out my goals for the year, I explicitly discuss mentoring students toward professionalization not only by encouraging them to develop and present research projects at regional writing center conferences and providing training opportunities for online tutoring but also by including how tutors will produce and publish our podcast, as well as reestablishing a tutor excellence award. In the past I might not have been explicit about these goals as mentoring goals, but in aligning mentoring to institutional initiatives, I'm able to create a more tangible value for mentoring and create an opportunity to assess such goals. Other parts of the heuristic can be applied to daily practices like talking openly about beliefs about writing, and how tutoring philosophies are defined, and drawing attention to mentoring as it happens.

In the five years that I have directed the writing center, I have, admittedly, stumbled my way through many situations, from HVAC leaks to interpersonal conflicts. What I have learned most is that the more deliberate I am with the decisions I make when I connect actions to my identities, beliefs, and values, the more comfortable I feel navigating the complexities of what it means to direct the writing center at Winthrop University. I hope that, as writing center directors, as writing studies mentors, we can reach a more nuanced understanding of the expectations writing center directors face, expectations complicated by various identities and local contexts, as well as our own field's legacy. I see this chapter as an opening, an invitation for more conversations about administrative work, mentoring methodologies, and how it all matters.

REFERENCES

Balester, Valerie M., and James McDonald. 2001. "A View of Status and Working Conditions: Relations between Writing Program and Writing Center Directors." *WPA: Writing Program Administration* 24 (3): 59–82.

Berlant, Lauren. 2012. *Cruel Optimism*. Durham, NC: Duke University Press.

Boquet, Elizabeth H. 1999. " 'Our Little Secret': A History of Writing Centers, Pre- to Post-Open." *College Composition and Communication* 50 (3): 463–482.

Campbell, Karlyn Kohrs. 1982. *The Rhetorical Act*. Belmont, CA: Wadsworth.

Carino, Peter. 1995. "Early Writing Centers: Toward a History." *Writing Center Journal* 5 (2): 103–115.

Caswell, Nicole, Jackie Grutsch McKinney, and Rebecca Jackson. 2016. *The Working Lives of New Writing Center Directors*. Logan: Utah State University Press.

Denny, Harry C. 2010. *Facing the Center: Toward an Identity Politics of One-to-One Mentoring*. Logan: Utah State University Press.

Eble, Michelle F., and Lynée Lewis Gaillet. 2008. *Stories of Mentoring: Theory and Praxis*. Parlor. West Lafayette, IN: Parlor Press.

Enos, Theresa. 1996. *Gender Roles and Faculty Lives in Rhetoric and Composition*. Carbondale: Southern Illinois University Press.

Faison, Wonderful, and Frankie Condon. 2022. *Counterstories from the Writing Center*. Logan: Utah State University Press.

Fitzgerald, Lauren, and Melissa Ianetta. 2016. *Oxford Guide to Tutoring: Practice and Research*. Oxford: Oxford University Press.

Foucault, Michel. 1997. "The Ethics of Concern for Self as a Practice of Freedom." In *Ethics, Subjectivity and Truth*. New York: The New Press.

Geller, Anne, Michele Eodice, Frankie Condon, Meg Carroll, and Elizabeth H. Boquet. 2007. *The Everyday Writing Center: A Community of Practice*. Logan: Utah State University Press.

Green, Neisha-Anne. 2018. "Moving beyond Alright: And the Emotional Toll of This, My Life Matters Too, in the Writing Center Work." *Writing Center Journal* 37 (1): 15–34.

Grutsch McKinney, Jackie. 2005. "Leaving Home Sweet Home: Toward a Critical Reading of Writing Center Spaces." *Writing Center Journal* 25 (2): 6–20.

Grutsch McKinney, Jackie. 2013. *Peripheral Visions for Writing Centers*. Logan: Utah State University Press.

Halloran, Michael S. 1982. "Aristotle's Concept of Ethos, or If Not His, Somebody Else's." *Rhetoric Review* 1: 58–63.

Harris, Muriel. 1990. "What's Up and What's In: Trends and Traditions in Writing Centers." *Writing Center Journal* 11 (1): 15–25.

Harris, Muriel. 1995. "Talking in the Middle: Why Writers Need Writing Tutors.' " *College English* 57: 27–42.

Healy, Dave. 1995. "Writing Center Directors: An Emerging Portrait of the Profession." *WPA* 18 (3): 26–43.

Jarratt, Susan C., and Nedra Reynolds. 1992. "The Splitting Image: Postmodern Feminism and the Ethics of Ethos." In *Ethos: New Essays in Rhetorical and Critical Theory*. Dallas, TX: Southern Methodist University Press.

Kinkead, Joyce, and Jeanette Harris, eds. 1993. "Writing Centers in Context: 12 Case Studies." Urbana, IL: NCTE.

Lauer, Janice. 1997. "Graduate Students as Active Members of the Profession: Some Questions for Mentoring." In *Publishing in Rhetoric and Composition*, edited by Gary A. Olson and Todd W. Taylor, 229–236. Albany: State University of New York Press.

LeFevre, Karen Burke. 1987. *Invention as a Social Act*. Carbondale: Southern Illinois University Press.

North, Stephen M. 1984. "The Idea of a Writing Center." *College English* 46 (5): 433–446.

Reynolds, Nedra. 1993. "Ethos as Location: New Sites for Understanding Discursive Authority." *Rhetoric Review* 11 (2): 325–338.
Ronald, Kate. 1990. "A Reexamination of Personal and Public Discourse in Classical Rhetoric." *Rhetoric Review* 9 (1): 36–48.
Trachsel, Mary. 1995. "Nurturant Ethics and Academic Ideals: Convergence in the Writing Center." *Writing Center Journal* 16 (1): 22–45.
Valles, Sarah Banschbach, Rebecca Day Babcock, and Karen Keaton Jackson. 2017. "Administrators and Diversity: A Survey." *Peer Review* 1, no. 1 (Spring). https://thepeerreview-iwca.org/issues/issue-1/writing-center-administrators-and-diversity-a-survey/.
Webster, Travis. 2021. *Queerly Centered: LGBTQA Writing Center Directors Navigate the Workplace.* Logan: Utah State University Press.

PART 2

Sustainability at the Slash

5
BUILDING RESEARCH TRAJECTORIES THROUGH MUTUAL MULTIGENERATIONAL MENTORING IN WRITING PROGRAM ASSESSMENT

Gregory J. Palermo, Qianqian Zhang-Wu, Devon Skyler Regan, and Mya Poe

Successful writing program administrators are attuned to current research on writing, sustained professional development for teachers in their programs, and financial and policy implications of running a writing program (Malenczyk 2016); they are also keen to cultivate rich learning experiences for diverse members in the community (García de Müeller and Ruiz 2017; Pytlik and Liggett 2001). As a result, many WPAs take an active role in mentoring graduate students on program operations, curriculum development, and even program assessment. Moreover, organizations such as Writing Program Administrators–Graduate Organization (WPA-GO) and Writing Across the Curriculum–Graduate Organization (WAC-GO) have been developed to help foster a sense of community for graduate students interested in writing program administration and Writing Across the Curriculum as well as foster multigenerational mentoring that extends knowledge transfer across generations (Presswood and Schwarz 2020; Russell et al. 2020). Together, such efforts can provide graduate students entry points into the complexities of running writing programs. But such mentoring is not without its challenges. For example, in writing program assessment, the technical nature of the methods can limit opportunities for sustained participation; graduate students often do not have coursework on assessment or quantitative analysis. And undergraduate students are constrained to semester-long study through the credit-bearing model of higher education, making sustained, compensated research opportunities limited.

The implications of such challenges are not insignificant. For graduate students, their limited role in program assessment often precludes the opportunity to engage in meaning-making, including the renegotiation

https://doi.org/10.7330/9781646425822.c005

of legitimate practices that defines disciplinary boundary work (Klein 1996, 1–2), and the chance to reflect on the generative methodological "friction" they experience when learning new methods (Horner and Lu 2013). Undergraduate research is often imagined as a site for weaving together the discourses students encounter in disciplinary contexts and synthesizing the learning that happens in isolated classroom spaces (Graff 2009); however, the labor students do in programmatic research often stops at exposing students to practices already in use rather than emphasizing their innovation. Finally, for new generations of faculty WPAs, there is a missed opportunity to go beyond handing down "best practices" in assessment research to shape cutting-edge approaches that are attuned to justice, data ethics, and multilingualism. In other words, we see new WPAs grasp onto a few key ideas or best practices of writing assessment rather than drawing on the epistemological potential of assessment as research.

To address these issues, the Northeastern University Writing Program undertook a multigenerational program-assessment project with two core goals. The methodological goal of the project was to develop a method for outcomes assessment that was more "linguistically responsive" to the needs of our university's significant international student population (Benda et al. 2018; Poe and Zhang-Wu 2020). Our mentoring goal, more significant to this chapter, was to affirm the collaborative renegotiation of terms and methods that comprise disciplinary boundary work and that also extend through multigenerational mentoring. Our chapter reflects on the various dimensions of our grant-funded, multigenerational model of program assessment and how we attempted to reflexively meet the learning needs of project collaborators during the COVID-19 pandemic.

This approach has yielded an innovative program assessment design more attuned to the shifting demographics of our writing program students today and that validates the very human aspects of research. We recognize that not all readers, especially since early 2020, have had reliable access to the supports that made our project possible in our institutional context. That said, resource precarity, shifting labor models, and disciplinary fragmentation require writing program administrators and researchers to think in innovative ways about how to research productively and accountably while mentoring students. Born out of a need for program assessment support and sustained through the COVID-19 pandemic, our project survived because of our multigenerational team. We hope that our reflections may provide the motive, if not the model, for projects that prioritize cross-generational collaboration, justice-oriented assessment methods, and mutual care.

MULTIGENERATIONAL MENTORING

Multigenerational mentoring, also known as cross-generational mentoring, engages faculty and students from multiple levels. In the private sector today, multigenerational mentoring is a normalized organizational process (Knight 2014). In contrast, higher education still often relies on a hierarchical model of mentorship: tenure-track faculty secure grant monies that employ graduate and undergraduate students while tenured faculty mentor pre-tenure faculty through the tenure process. Hierarchical models of mentoring can be useful to navigate institutional processes, especially to provide access to resources otherwise unavailable to students. Cross-generational mentoring, however, is critical throughout higher education to help fill curricular gaps in disciplinary knowledge-making, as well as to foster the interdisciplinary skills and habits that benefit future faculty in the academic "pipeline" (DeZure 2017, 566). In an ideal situation, multigenerational mentoring allows for cross-generation learning, such that different members of the team can bring their own skills and expertise to the project.

Writing program assessment may not seem like an obvious choice for multigenerational mentoring. Much program assessment relies on the routinized practice of articulating learning outcomes, gathering student writing samples and surveys, scoring the writing samples, and reporting the findings to institutional stakeholders and accrediting bodies. But more recent calls for justice-oriented assessment, translingual orientations to assessment, along with the increasing need for analysis of analytics data, suggests that WPAs need collaborative expertise in conducting ethical program assessment.

Program-review projects have been heralded as sites for graduate students' "situated learning"—Michelle LaFrance and Alisa Russell's (2018) term for "first-hand" exposure to different disciplines' languages for talking about writing as well as what goes into maintaining a sustained research project (224). In some cases, like in LaFrance and Russell's (2018) case study of a writing program at George Mason University, "authentic" experiences with program assessment are paired with graduate courses in research methods (209–211). In other cases, graduate students are mentored in program-assessment methods exclusively in research-based or administrative roles beyond coursework, like in Zelenik et al.'s (2002) reflection on a PhD student–led team assessing a cross-disciplinary, integrated teaching initiative at Iowa State University. Multigenerational mentoring that is cross-disciplinary, especially, provides for the application of mixed qualitative and quantitative methods to answer common research questions, including, for example, surveys, interviews, and statistical analysis (Zelenik et al. 2002, 232). Moreover, program assessment provides graduate students the opportunity to learn about institutional processes, including "the most challenging aspects of university life, in all its political, structural, and interpersonal complexity" (Anson and Rutz 1998, 119).

Graduate students, however, are not the only beneficiaries of multigenerational projects in writing assessment. Multigenerational collaboration can be a formal and informal site of socialization for pretenure faculty within the discipline (Mullen and Forbes 2000) and a site for early career scholars to foreground their disciplinary expertise when working with faculty across the curriculum (Hughes 2020). Intraprogram collaborations may be complemented by organization-level programs that pair early-career scholars with mid-to-late-career mentors, across institutions, for the reciprocal exchange of methodologies as well as for networking (see also Russell and Polk in this collection). While multigenerational mentoring in program assessment is a time-intensive commitment for mid-to-late-career faculty, it offers potential to draw on knowledge of new methods (e.g., computational) for the analysis of assessment data. It also offers a way to bring new faculty into the assessment process early, so the learning curve is not as steep later. And most importantly, the inclusion of undergraduate students in program assessment provides a true student voice to questions of student learning.

When they are consciously multigenerational, assessment projects can be sites for bringing the collaborative ethos, collective identity formation, and inclusive practices that we as a field are committed to in our writing classrooms to writing program administration (Anson and Rutz 1998, 119). According to Mary Alm (1998), process-oriented "intimate collaboration" works not only to divide labor but to create "intellectual friendships" among feminist-oriented scholars through writing and thinking together dialogically (126). This kind of work, Anson and Rutz (1998) argue, "define[s] compositionists and place[s us] in cultural opposition to [our] institutions" (119). The emphasis of multigenerational mentorship that includes "developing professionals" in equitable governance and decision-making is in stark contrast to projects that may place students in a hierarchical dynamic of mentorship (Holberg and Taylor 1996). Resisting a hierarchical team research model is part of what our English department colleague Julia Flanders (2010) has called "a tradeoff between autonomy and synergy" in collaboration—not only between the individual expectations of collaborators, but with the institutionalized research norms with which we are in dialogue as we pursue the commonalities that bring us together while respecting our differences (67). We also must contend with the "ghost advising" labor that this negotiation involves, and that disproportionately falls on individual scholars who are women and people of color to make up for structural deficiencies (Parham 2018, 679–680).

One structural deficiency in writing studies to be addressed with multigenerational mentoring, especially, is the rarity of opportunities for undergraduate researchers to be intimately involved in program assessment. There is sparse literature published about undergraduate work on assessment projects, and not because undergraduate contributions are not valued in writing studies. Following Grobman and Kinkead's (2010) call to involve undergraduate students in every aspect of English studies, a recent CFP for *College English* dedicates its July 2022 special issue for research papers from undergraduate students, highlights the value to acknowledge and share these apprentice researchers' diverse "funds of knowledge" (González, Moll, and Amanti 2005). Our field has established spaces for undergraduate authors in publications like *Queen City Writers* and *XChanges*. Still, there is a lack of sustained funding that would match, for example, initiatives in the scientific fields such as the National Science Foundation's (NSF) Research Experiences for Undergraduates (REUs), leaving truly multigenerational initiatives in writing studies to arise mostly within local programs' needs and funding structures.

MULTILINGUAL WRITING OUTCOMES STUDY

Thanks to internationalization of higher education and global mobility, US college campuses have become "fundamentally multilingual spaces, in which students and faculty bring to the acts of writing and communication a rich array of linguistic and cultural resources" (Conference on College Composition and Communication 2020). Attracting over 14,000 international students from 140 countries, Northeastern University has been one of the leading international student host institutions in the country for the last ten years, according to the Institute of International Education's annual "Open Doors" report (2022). In response to the increasingly culturally and linguistically diverse campus environment, the NU Writing Program has initiated a series of efforts to better support multilingual students since 2009. Among them, the Multilingual Writers Research Project (MWRP) has been one of our endeavors to improve the quality of the NU Writing Program curriculum and instruction to address linguistic diversity at our local setting.

In the latest iteration of the MWRP led by Mya (director of the writing program) and Qianqian (director of multilingual writing), we designed an assessment study of outcomes for the program's Advanced Writing in the Disciplines courses. Rather than simply tick off whether students had met the outcomes, we wanted to understand how outcomes were shaped by the complexity of multilingual students' identities, writing performances across contexts, and their within-group variabilities. The assessment study, which spanned from fall 2019–summer 2021, included a survey of students' linguistic identities, holistic- and trait-scoring data from three different text types (descriptive, research, reflective) in advanced writing courses, student interviews, and corpus analysis of student writing (for more details, see Poe and Zhang-Wu 2020).

Our assessment project was supported by a 2019 grant from the Northeastern University College of Social Sciences and Humanities (CSSH) Multi-Generational Research Teams Program. These competitive grants

> support the development of multi-generational research teams that engage faculty, graduate, and undergraduate students to advance faculty research. The development of such teams furthers [the] college's mission to support faculty-initiated research as well as expand research opportunities for students at all levels. In addition, this team-based approach allows for the engagement of progressive mentoring models. Such models provide opportunities for mutual learning between faculty and students with diverse levels of research experience.[1]

The multigenerational research grant is one of several types of college-level grants available to faculty. As part of the larger Northeastern institutional context that prides itself on experiential learning, CSSH is especially interested in promoting interdisciplinary, community-based, and undergraduate research opportunities (Northeastern University n.d.).

Additional support for the project was also provided by the Northeastern University Project-Based Exploration for the Advancement of Knowledge (PEAK) Awards, which lend undergraduate researchers experience with applying for funding and financially support their projects.

In our case, the Multi-Generational Research Teams and PEAK grants provided funding to bring in one graduate (Greg) and one undergraduate (Devon) research assistant to facilitate the design, implementation, and analysis of the study. Thanks to the multigenerational collaboration, we were able to have weekly meetings, form reading groups, brainstorm ideas, and work together throughout the project. Although the project started off in a traditional face-to-face program-assessment format with in-person scoring of student writing and in-person team meetings, we quickly shifted to Zoom in March 2020. Since spring 2020, our team has worked completely remotely due to the pandemic and has even given multiple presentations on this project through online venues. Through video-conferencing technology, screen sharing, and the Google suite of tools, the Multilingual Assessment Outcomes Project progressed and is now in its final stages of dissemination of data.

MULTIVOCAL PERSPECTIVES ON THE MULTILINGUAL ASSESSMENT OUTCOMES PROJECT

We have been able to meet three stated goals of the Multi-Generational Research Teams grant: to advance faculty research, expand undergraduate research opportunities, and provide opportunities for mutual mentoring. As we detail in the narratives below, the mutual mentoring aspects of the Multilingual Assessment Outcomes Project have been especially rich. Through these narratives, our goal is to provide a multivocal perspective on mutual mentoring (Akkerman et al. 2006). Since mutual learning is a key focus of the multigenerational grant, we treat all members on the research team as collaborators with unique identities and expertise, instead of traditional subordinate/supervisor relationships. Therefore, we chose to adopt a multivocal approach to structure this part of the chapter to make sure all members of the team could discuss what the project meant to them.

Although we start with Mya's narrative because she was the writing program director, we could have easily started this section with Devon's, Qianqian's, or Greg's narrative, and readers would be able to see the same thread arise. For example, we each found ourselves reflecting on the effects of the pandemic on our collaboration, how this project is complicating our understanding of multilingualism, and what we have learned about where and how research education happens.

Mya Poe, Associate Professor of English and Writing Program Director

As someone who has worked in writing assessment for more than twenty years, I have tried to use collaboration to work against the field's lack of infrastructure for mentoring new researchers while also including perspectives from historically marginalized researchers in writing assessment research. In this way, assessment research moves from normative practice to a site of learning and social action. Much of my mentoring work has been—for better and worse—through editorial collections and special journal issues. This multigenerational project gave me the opportunity to think about how I would frame assessment methodologies and make writing assessment a site of political action at Northeastern. Three things became immediately obvious in the design of the study—the need for interdisciplinary collaboration, the need for methods negotiations, and the need to attend to generational differences. What would only become obvious later is how mutual mentoring would change the way I think about my own linguistic identity and how I work as a researcher.

For me, the value of this team was rooted in complementary expertise. For example, because the project was pitched as a study of multilingual writing assessment, it was obvious that I needed expert advice on second-language writing research. Qianqian, the director of multilingual writing, was just the expert we needed for the project. I knew that I could learn much from Qianqian. Yet, I also wanted to be careful of her time as an untenured faculty member. This project needed to serve Qianqian as a source of publishing opportunities. Qianqian helped us transform the MLWRP survey instrument from an instrument that used older terms about L1 and L2 to an instrument that centered students' multilingual identities, locations of use, and educational backgrounds. In addition to expertise in second-language writing research, I knew the project needed someone with data expertise. I knew Greg from graduate courses, so I knew his expertise in digital humanities and his "chops" with computational methods. Although I had dabbled in corpus linguistics research methods, I was not proficient enough in such methods to realize their full potential, and I had no experience with Python. I suspected that Greg would bring new ideas to the project regarding data management and visualization. Greg helped make data management more efficient, and he became a source of leadership when it came to data ethics. Finally, Devon brought computational experience to the project through her digital humanities courses in literature. She also brought the undergraduate perspective to the project and helped me see things in the scoring of student writing that I could not see from my position as a faculty member. Devon's understanding of the undergraduate experience at Northeastern helped us understand how students would read the data. Furthermore, while the Writing Program Assessment Committee (WPAC) helped us with scoring of student writing, it was Greg and Devon that de-identified the writing samples, tracked the scoring, and coded in R so we could more easily analyze the data. The ease with which they could process data allowed Qianqian and I to ask additional questions about the data later, such as tracking connections between survey responses, scoring data, and corpus linguistics analysis.

Just as the project was entering the third phase of scoring in March 2020, the university went online. We could no longer meet in person, and we even debated canceling the final scoring session. Yet, with the support of our mutual mentoring team, the assistant director of the writing program, and the WPAC, we were encouraged to continue. The scoring got finished, but what happened in the transition to virtual work also brought about a different kind of dynamic to our multigenerational work. Mutual mentoring became about care—the need to stay connected in a world of upheaval. Mentoring extended beyond data or methods to the commitments for people about whom we care.

Finally, the Multilingual Writing Outcomes Study has made me rethink my own linguistic identity. For someone who grew up with parents committed to the eradication of their own linguistic difference, this project has made me reflect on linguistic loss and how such perspectives have long fueled program assessment. In reading such rubrics, one finds that "knowledge of conventions" is not merely about some kind of product or process knowledge, but it is often hitched to notions of cognition (Dryer 2013). If we were to value students' linguistic repertoires instead, we would not be scoring so-called correctness but rather flexibility and resourcefulness. We would be valuing the creative work of language use in action. As a WPA and an assessment researcher committed to justice-oriented assessment, I believe it is imperative that we establish writing outcomes for critical language awareness (Gere et al. 2021).

Qianqian, Assistant Professor of English and Director of Multilingual Writing

I am an applied linguist with a background in Teaching English to Speakers of Other Languages (TESOL) and bilingual education research. As an early career scholar with a newly minted PhD degree, I am currently working as an assistant professor wrapping up my first year on the tenure track. To me, this collaborative project has been extremely beneficial professionally and personally. Its interdisciplinarity and collaborative nature facilitated ongoing professional development among members on the research team. The lens of investigation of this project has complicated my understanding of multilingualism, which consequently informs my future research and teaching.

First, this interdisciplinary initiative has offered me an exciting professional development opportunity, thanks to which everyone on the team was able to contribute and learn in different ways. In traditional faculty-led research initiatives, faculty members were very likely to be the only experts or bosses, and students often worked passively as assistants who were in charge of various assigned tasks. In contrast, in this project all members work as co-constructors of knowledge who adopt their agency and draw upon their unique area of expertise to contribute to this interdisciplinary research initiative. Specifically, Mya (primary investigator) is a scholar in writing assessment, Greg (graduate student) is a PhD student in digital humanities, Devon is an undergraduate student researcher on writing analytics, and I am an expert on multilingual research (Co-PI). Our different strengths and expertise have naturally established a mutual-learning community where everybody jigsaws, learns from each other, and contributes to the design, implementation, and analysis of the project throughout every step along the way. This is extremely important during the COVID-19 global pandemic, when such togetherness and mutual support could benefit all of us academically and psychologically.

Second, this project has complicated my understanding of multilingualism. An applied linguist, I used to see multilingualism from the angle of language performance. From this perspective, multilingual students could be defined as those from culturally and linguistically diverse (and often minoritized) backgrounds who possess rich linguistic repertoires and are able to function linguistically based on the situational contexts. Yet, the dynamic institutional context of this program assessment project has pushed me to expand this working definition through the lens of super-diversity (Vertovec 2007). This has allowed me to understand multilingual students' experiences beyond the rigid L1/L2 divide and pay attention to complex linguistic identities among our learners. At Northeastern University, because learning a second language has been a requirement for college admission, the phenomenon of linguistic diversity is not a specialized concept relevant to a small group of students (e.g., international students, students of color) but instead a common characteristic among all students (Poe and Zhang-Wu 2020). In fact, with the internationalization of higher education and global mobility, almost all students in our local context are raised in multilingual families or exposed to linguistic diversity as they grow up. In the era of super-diversity, students' countries of citizenship and ethnicities are often messily aligned with their linguistic identities. For example, it is almost impossible to determine the L1, L2, or L3 of a Chinese American student (ethnicity) born in the United States (citizenship) to parents speaking Mandarin and English at home who grew up in South Korea before returning to the United States for college education. Working on the multilingual program-assessment project has made me realize that linguistic labels like L1/L2, native/nonnative speakers, domestic/

international students are overly simplified to capture the linguistically super-diverse nature of our students. I have adopted super-diversity as an important theory to frame my methodology and analysis for my projects ever since, which is extremely helpful to think beyond fixed linguistic categories and understand multilingual students as whole persons with dynamic experiences and identities.

Finally, participating in this social justice–oriented program-assessment project and exploring the experiences and needs of multilingual students using asset-based approaches has prompted me to rethink my own linguistic identity as a first-generation immigrant of color, a nonnative English-speaking professor of English, and a young mother of a multilingual and multicultural child. These reflections have consequently informed my pedagogical practices, in which I invite students to explore the linguistically super-diverse reality in global contexts by thinking critically about the intersectionality of super-diversity, language, race, identity, and power. Such instructional practices provide students with valuable opportunities to contextualize their linguistic experiences and identities in the greater sociopolitical context, helping them move away from deficit perceptions of English-only and begin embracing cultural and linguistic super-diversity.

Greg, PhD Candidate in English

Since joining the PhD program in Northeastern's English department in 2015, my primary goal has been to bridge the digital humanities (DH) and writing studies communities and the methodological commitments they share, providing space for transfer when there are different approaches (Friend 2018; Palermo 2017). I can trace this emphasis on transdisciplinary methodology to my time as an undergraduate student in the Edgar Fellow Program at SUNY Geneseo. Mentors at SUNY Geneseo encouraged me to write on the knowledge-making practices common to English and physics. I've since accrued most of my humanities-oriented graduate training with data in mentorship contexts, possible largely because Northeastern has two established digital humanities (DH) centers: one on the faculty side (the NULab for Texts, Maps, and Networks in CSSH) and one on the library side (the Digital Scholarship Group in Snell Library). These contexts have included digital project and editorial work, formal workshops associated with projects on methods, and an informal "open office hours" sharing and presentation space. NULab faculty have been able to consistently offer courses like The Shape of Data in the Humanities and Humanities Data

Analysis as part of a graduate certificate program—these courses are concerned with methodological debates that digital humanists take up within and across disciplinary contexts. For example, such courses drew my attention to issues of power in how knowledge is curated and used (Gebru et al. 2021; Olson 2001), the role of the analyst's choices about scale and data diversity preservation in data-driven research (Rawson and Muñoz 2016), and the necessity of counter-data practices and collaborative building in justice-oriented work with data (D'Ignazio and Klein 2020; Flanders 2019). These methodologies are not widely embraced in writing studies, even given an increasing emphasis in the field on corpus analysis and data-driven research.

When Mya secured the multigenerational grant from the college, I applied for the opportunity to build on my coursework with her in Writing Assessment and Rhetorical Genre Studies—that is, methods-based courses that also addressed data transformation in gathering and analyzing data. At the same time, working with Qianqian and Devon gave me the opportunity to work with new colleagues. My disciplining in program assessment and mentorship happened alongside an interdisciplining of the "transversal intersections" of Mya's, Qianqian's, Devon's, and my backgrounds and job roles (Klein 2015, 26–35). For example, Qianqian's scholarship on super-diversity shaped how I treated the categories I used to "split-apply-combine" our initial scoring data in my exploratory analysis (Wickham 2011), as well as the language of the questions we wrote together for the survey we would use to further facet the data. Devon's needs as a student and pragmatic differences between our student institutional roles (for example, who had access to what kind of software through our ITS) shaped how we shared the labor necessary to de-identify student samples of writing in preparation for scoring. While these tasks were what Di Pressi et al. (2015) might call "mechanical" contributions, rather than the more "substantive contributions" for which they recommend students be credited as collaborators (cf. Mann 2019), even these parts of the project involved moments when Devon and I discussed our methodological and ethical research decisions. Due to the pandemic, we were often not in the same room for these discussions but rather witnessing, supporting, and regrounding each other at a distance.

Devon, Senior Undergraduate in English

I joined this project in early 2020 as an English student seeking to broaden my knowledge of and experience in more technical aspects of the discipline. After three years, I had only a vague idea of what "English research" looked like. I had also taken a handful of computer science classes and was eager to keep in practice with coding while exploring how programming and other digital tools can be used to complement real-world humanities research with expansive and justice-oriented goals.

Language was never a barrier in school—I am a native English speaker with the privilege of education, which grounded me in college writing conventions and predisposed me to success. But this privilege also left me disillusioned. Like Mya's, my family subscribed to an eradicationist perspective on cultural and linguistic difference: assimilate and prosper under the American dream, guided by education that seeks to push its own narrative of excellence. Since middle school, I was pressured to apply to private school in spite of the financial burden it would put on my single mother and of my own reluctance; I didn't want to be a wonky cookie-cut in a room of rich kids where I'd never fit in. This pressure peaked after ninth grade, when the special needs program I was in recommended trade school in its evaluation of my individualized education plan (IEP). For my grandparents, higher education was everything in transcending the poverty my grandfather was born into, but it perpetuated the narrative that one must struggle to achieve, and the erasure of anyone failed by or left out of this pipeline. If *they* did it, anyone can. This view prevailed at the private Episcopalian high school I attended from tenth through twelfth grade; a conviction in itself blinded by the bubble of extreme wealth and privilege that permitted it to exist (est. 1965 in southern Florida). I was always skeptical of this dynamic, but in a vague and anecdotal sense—only later did I piece together my unease as indicative of the systemic forces perpetuating this championed elitism and other forms of colonial gatekeeping. Over the course of my concurrent learning and unlearning, it's become particularly important to me to uplift marginalized perspectives and open linguistic resources to all, especially those left out of hegemonic ideas about who can be successful. In its critical examination of how writing practices aid student success across backgrounds, using data-driven research and analysis, this project offered for me a material continuation of these goals.

Activists and scholars alike have critiqued academia's disinterest in critically examining its own practices (e.g., Ayres 2021). Assata Shakur famously stated, "Nobody will give you the education you need to overthrow them." Yet this is not to say there aren't educators committed to changing the limiting frameworks of academia from within. I'm lucky enough to have found them in my mentors and collaborators as well as a handful of inspirational professors. A pivotal moment in my experience of the undergraduate curriculum was Ryan Cordell's course Technologies of Text (ToT), which served as a nexus of thought in bridging literary and writing studies. ToT raised critical inquiry about the creation of texts and the contexts they circulate in, from the dawn of the codex to the contemporary. The empirical research methods introduced—that is, how text can be turned into data and analyzed with programs like R—offered support for me as an emergent researcher, introducing multiple points of entry and understanding.

Upon joining the Writing Program Assessment Project, I was immediately enmeshed in my mentors' research interests. Mya's and Qianqian's work elucidates the justice-oriented dimensions of my field so often obscured by the powers that be and nonetheless undertaken by those dedicated to change and reaching new understanding. Greg has strong working knowledge of the digital humanities in pursuit of this aim. Here was a team of folks working to critically analyze academic conventions while making sure I was supported in my research and paid for my time. This praxis was evident at every step in my involvement—as well as readily sharing resources, they actively sought out and incorporated my input. Even when I felt unsure or inadequate, my collaborators uplifted me with refreshing transparency about their own struggles and doubts.

As the pandemic hit just a month or so into my time on the project, it shook up everything. Yet I think in some way the spotlight it put on existing disparities intensified the need for justice and the feeling that our work was a meaningful contribution to that end. Having this pocket of community and consistency was a grounding experience during the wild unease of the pandemic, and ultimately left me with a stronger understanding of institutional politics and reflective awareness of my own positionality and ability to enact change.

CONCLUSION

Traditionally, the concept of mentorship in writing studies has mainly focused on graduate students and early-career faculty members. Such mentoring relationships are critical to the professional success of new members of the writing community. Yet, following Grobman and Kinkead's (2010) call to involve undergraduate students in every aspect of English studies, the field has started to pay attention to the important role of mentoring undergraduate researchers. Echoing this trend, our multigenerational project has adopted an inclusive, bottom-up approach to include the voices of undergraduate (Devon) and graduate (Greg) researchers and early-career (Qianqian) and more established

(Mya) scholars. Throughout the project (from grant-funding, to design, to pilot, to implementation, to analysis, to dissemination), we built off each other's complementary expertise, including assessment, multilingualism, data analysis, and feminist approaches to team-building, to foster a mutual mentoring relationship.

The methodological and theoretical benefits of a multigenerational, interdisciplinary mentoring approach for our project were multiple. Locally, we now have an approach to program assessment that forwards the Northeastern Writing Program's commitments to linguistic diversity. The timing of this project could not be more important; Northeastern is moving to a program assessment model in which general education outcomes assessment will be owned by the faculty senate. Our data on the outcomes of multilingual students, the significance of educational backgrounds, and the role of genre are evidence that will help us retain some control over program assessment values.

The project has also complicated our understanding of terms like multilingualism and super-diversity, and our own linguistic identities. At the beginning of the project, we found ourselves debating terms like "home language," "heritage language," and "first language." Through this project, we see how a concept like super-diversity that situates language practices at specific sites can be a useful framework to understand shifting linguistic identities in context.

Finally, we would be remiss if we did not discuss the impact of the pandemic on this project. Given the many ways our lives were upended with additional caregiving responsibilities and the impact of COVID-19, our project became as much about mutual care as it did about multigenerational research. As our project moves into the dissemination phase and the grant funding is completed, we are left reflecting on the lasting effects of multigenerational mentoring. One noticeable effect has been on our composing process. We now write together. We schedule Zoom meetings to discuss ideas, then write together on a shared document for twenty to thirty minutes. In the shared document, we see the false starts, revisions, and gaps. We comment and compose together. Thus, shared textual production has been one lasting practice of mutual mentoring during a pandemic. Our team members continue to grow: Devon is in her final year of college, Greg has completed his dissertation and is a full-time teaching-track faculty member at another institution, Qianqian is well on her way to tenure, and Mya is transitioning to a new administrative role post-sabbatical.

In conclusion, what began as a pre-pandemic, multigenerational, grant-funded project to develop a method for outcomes assessment that was more linguistically responsive to the needs of our university's significant international student population became a way for the four of us to affirm disciplinary boundary work and draw on each other's humanity during what Devon rightly calls the "wild unease of the pandemic."

NOTE

1. Thomas Vicino, Multi-generational research team pilot program, Email, October 24, 2019, emphasis added.

REFERENCES

Akkerman, Sanne, Wilfried Admiraal, Robert Jan Simons, and Theo Niessen. 2006. "Considering Diversity: Multivoicedness in International Academic Collaboration." *Culture and Psychology* 12 (4): 461–485. https://doi.org/10.1177/1354067X06069947.

Alm, Mary. 1998. "The Role of Talk in the Writing Process of Intimate Collaboration." In *Common Ground: Feminist Collaboration in the Academy*, edited by Elizabeth G. Peck and JoAnna Stephens Mink. Albany: State University of New York Press.

Anson, Chris M., and Carol Rutz. 1998. "Graduate Students, Writing Programs, and Consensus-Based Management: Collaboration in the Face of Disciplinary Ideology." *WPA: Writing Program Administration* 21 (2–3): 106–120.

Ayres, Zoë (@ZJAyres). 2021. "Academia: we teach you critical thinking / Also academia: don't critically think about improving academia though." Twitter, May 5, 2021. https://twitter.com/ZJAyres/status/1389835049860833281.

Benda, Jonathan, Michael Dedek, Chris Gallagher, Kristi Girdharry, Neal Lerner, and Matt Noonan. 2018. "Confronting Superdiversity in US Writing Programs." In *The Internationalization of US Writing Programs*, edited by Shirley K. Rose and Irwin Weiser, 79–96. Logan: Utah State University Press. https://doi.org/10.2307/j.ctt22h6qmq.7.

Conference on College Composition and Communication. 2020. "CCCC Statement on Second Language Writing and Multilingual Writers." Conference on College Composition and Communication, May 2020. https://cccc.ncte.org/cccc/resources/positions/secondlangwriting/.

DeZure, Debora. 2017. "Interdisciplinary Pedagogies in Higher Education." In *The Oxford Handbook of Interdisciplinarity*, edited by Robert Frodeman, 2nd ed., 558–572. Oxford: Oxford University Press. https://doi.org/10.1093/oxfordhb/9780198733522.013.45.

D'Ignazio, Catherine, and Lauren F. Klein. 2020. *Data Feminism*. Cambridge, MA: MIT Press.

Di Pressi, Haley, Stephanie Gorman, Miriam Posner, Raphael Sasayama, and Tori Schmitt. 2015. "A Student Collaborators' Bill of Rights." *HumTech—UCLA* (blog). June 8, 2015. https://humtech.ucla.edu/news/a-student-collaborators-bill-of-rights/.

Dryer, Dylan B. 2013. "Scaling Writing Ability: A Corpus-Driven Inquiry." *Written Communication* 30 (1): 3–35.

Flanders, Julia. 2010. "Collaboration and Dissent: Challenges of Collaborative Standards for Digital Humanities." In *Collaborative Research in the Humanities: A Volume in Honour of Harold Short*, 67–80. Brookfield, VT: Ashgate Publishing Company.

Flanders, Julia. 2019. "Building Otherwise." In *Bodies of Information: Intersectional Feminism and the Digital Humanities*, edited by Elizabeth Losh and Jacqueline Wernimont, 289–304. Minneapolis: University of Minnesota Press. https://doi.org/10.5749/j.ctvghjgr9.

Friend, Christopher R. 2018. "Outsiders, All: Connecting the Pasts and Futures of Digital Humanities and Composition." In *Disrupting the Digital Humanities*, edited by Dorothy Kim and Jesse Stommel, 1st ed., 401–417. Santa Barbara, CA: Punctum Books.

García de Müeller, Genevieve, and Iris Ruiz. 2017. "Race, Silence, and Writing Program Administration: A Qualitative Study of US College Writing Programs." *WPA: Writing Program Administration*. 40 (2): 19–39.

Gebru, Timnit, Jamie Morgenstern, Briana Vecchione, Jennifer Wortman Vaughan, Hanna Wallach, Hal Daumé III, and Kate Crawford. 2021. "Datasheets for Datasets." arXiv, December 1, 2021. http://arxiv.org/abs/1803.09010.

Gere, Anne Ruggles, Anne Curzan, J. W. Hammond, Sarah Hughes, Ruth Li, Andrew Moos, Kendon Smith, Kathryn Van Zanen, Kelly L. Wheeler, and J. Crystal Zanders. 2021. "Communal Justicing: Writing Assessment, Disciplinary Infrastructure, and the Case for Critical Language Awareness." *College Composition and Communication* 72 (3): 384–412.

Gonzalez, Norma, Luis C. Moll, and Cathy Amanti, eds. 2005. *Funds of Knowledge: Theorizing Practices in Households, Communities, and Classrooms*. 1st ed. New York: Routledge.

Graff, Gerald. 2009. "Presidential Address 2008: Courseocentrism." *PMLA* 124 (3): 727–743.

Grobman, Laurie, and Joyce Kinkead, eds. 2010. *Undergraduate Research in English Studies*. Champaign, IL: National Council of Teachers of English.

Holberg, Jennifer L., and Marcy M. Taylor. 1996. "Apprenticeship versus Partnership: Graduate Students as Administrators." *Composition Chronicle: A Newsletter for Writing Teachers* 8 (9): 6–8.

Horner, Bruce, and Min-Zhan Lu. 2013. "Toward a Labor Economy of Literacy." In *Literacy, Economy, and Power: Writing and Research after "Literacy in American Lives,"* edited by John Duffy, Julie Nelson Christoph, Eli Goldblatt, Nelson Graff, Rebecca S. Nowacek, and Bryan Trabold. Carbondale: Southern Illinois University Press.

Hughes, Bradley. 2020. "Galvanizing Goals: What Early-Career Disciplinary Faculty Want to Learn about WAC Pedagogy." *WAC Journal* 31 (1): 23–65. https://doi.org/10.37514/WAC-J.2020.31.1.02.

Institute of International Education. 2022. "Leading Institutions." Opendoors. November 14, 2022. https://opendoorsdata.org/data/international-students/leading-institutions/.

Klein, Julie Thompson. 1996. *Crossing Boundaries: Knowledge, Disciplinarities, and Interdisciplinarities*. Charlottesville: University of Virginia Press.

Klein, Julie Thompson. 2015. *Interdisciplining Digital Humanities: Boundary Work in an Emerging Field*. Ann Arbor: University of Michigan Press.

Knight, Rebecca. 2014. "Managing People from 5 Generations." *Harvard Business Review*, September 25, 2014. https://hbr.org/2014/09/managing-people-from-5-generations.

LaFrance, Michelle, and Alisa Russell. 2018. "Preparing Writing Studies Graduate Students within Authentic WAC-Contexts: A Research Methods Course and WAC Program Review Crossover Project as a Critical Site of Situated Learning." *WAC Journal* 29: 207–229.

Malenczyk, Rita, ed. 2016. *A Rhetoric for Writing Program Administrators*. 2nd ed. Anderson, SC: Parlor Press.

Mann, Rachel. 2019. "Paid to Do but Not to Think: Reevaluating the Role of Graduate Student Collaborators." In *Debates in the Digital Humanities 2019*, edited by Matthew K. Gold and Lauren F. Klein, 268–278. Minneapolis: University of Minnesota Press.

Mullen, Carol A., and Sean A. Forbes. 2000. "Untenured Faculty: Issues of Transition, Adjustment and Mentorship." *Mentoring and Tutoring: Partnership in Learning* 8 (1): 31–46. https://doi.org/10.1080/713685508.

Northeastern University. n.d. "Northeastern 2025." https://www.northeastern.edu/2025/.

Olson, Hope A. 2001. "The Power to Name: Representation in Library Catalogs." *Signs* 26 (3): 639–668.

Palermo, Gregory. 2017. "Transforming Text: Four Valences of a Digital Humanities Informed Writing Analytics." *Journal of Writing Analytics* 1 (1). https://wac.colostate.edu/docs/jwa/vol1/palermo.pdf.

Parham, Marisa. 2018. "Ninety-Nine Problems: Assessment, Inclusion, and Other Old-New Problems." *American Quarterly* 70 (3): 677–684. https://doi.org/10.1353/aq.2018.0052.

Poe, Mya, and Qianqian Zhang-Wu. 2020. "Super-Diversity as a Framework to Promote Justice: Designing Program Assessment for Multilingual Writing Outcomes." *Composition Forum* 44 (Summer). http://compositionforum.com/issue/44/northeastern.php.

Presswood, Amanda, and Virginia M. Schwarz. 2020. "Mentorship, Affordability, and Equity: Ways Forward in Writing Program Administration." *XChanges: An Interdisciplinary Journal of Technical Communication, Rhetoric, and Writing Across the Curriculum* 15 (1).

Pytlik, Betty P., and Sarah Liggett, eds. 2001. *Preparing College Teachers of Writing: Histories, Theories, Programs, Practices.* 1st ed. Oxford: Oxford University Press.

Rawson, Katie, and Trevor Muñoz. 2016. "Against Cleaning." *Curating Menus* (blog). July 6, 2016. http://curatingmenus.org/articles/against-cleaning/.

Russell, Alisa, Jake Chase, Justin Nicholes, and Allie Sockwell Johnston. 2020. "The Writing Across the Curriculum Graduate Organization: Where We've Been, Where We Are, and Where We're Going." In *Diverse Approaches to Teaching, Learning, and Writing Across the Curriculum: IWAC at 25,* edited by Lesley Erin Bartlett, Sandra L. Tarabochia, Andrea R. Olinger, and Margaret J. Marshall, 45–53. Fort Collins, CO: WAC Clearinghouse. https://doi.org/10.37514/PER-B.2020.0360.2.03.

Vertovec, Steven. 2007. "Super-Diversity and Its Implications." *Ethnic and Racial Studies* 30 (6): 1024–1054. https://doi.org/10.1080/01419870701599465.

Wickham, Hadley. 2011. "The Split-Apply-Combine Strategy for Data Analysis." *Journal of Statistical Software* 40 (1). https://www.jstatsoft.org/article/view/v059i10.

Zeleznik, Julie M., Rebecca Burnett, Thomas Polito, David Roberts, and John Schafer. 2002. "Ranks, Roles, and Responsibilities: Crossing the Fine Lines in Cross-Disciplinary Mentorship." In *The WAC Casebook: Scenes for Faculty Reflection and Program Development,* edited by Chris M. Anson. Oxford: Oxford University Press.

6
EXPANDING THE WAC NETWORK
The Cross-Institutional Mentoring Project

Alisa Russell and Thomas Polk

This chapter describes the experiences of graduate students and faculty mentors who participated in the Cross-Institutional Mentoring Program (CIMP) during the 2020–2021 academic year. The CIMP is a voluntary, formal mentorship program that pairs graduate students (and some early career faculty) with WAC scholar-practitioners at different institutions for a full academic year. As early officers in the WAC Graduate Organization (WAC-GO), one of our first endeavors was to launch the CIMP to broaden access to mentoring within WAC. We had both been the recipients of good mentoring in WAC that had helped us learn about the field and develop a passion for the work, and we began to realize that many of our peers who were interested in WAC work (even if they didn't yet know WAC was a thing) weren't so fortunate; they didn't have the same access to mentoring that we had and weren't always sure how to find it (Russell et al. 2020).

So, in 2017, WAC-GO launched the CIMP as a formal mentoring program with the specific aim of increasing access to WAC mentoring and familiarizing more writing studies practitioners (specifically graduate students but including early career scholars) with WAC's methodologies. As a *formal mentoring program*, the WAC-GO leadership team operates as a third party, coordinating the mentoring relationships but remaining outside of them (Chao, Walz, and Gardner 1992, 620). In some ways, this resembles other formal mentoring programs in the field, such as the WPA-GO Breakfast Buddies at CCCC, but the CIMP distinguishes itself by supporting a sustained, year-long relationship as opposed to a one-time event. Every August, we distribute a call for mentors and mentees over email lists, social media, and major listservs across writing studies. This call asks interested participants to complete a pairing survey (appendix 6.A), and we create pairs based on their responses. Once we've organized pairs, we introduce them to one another over email, distribute a best practices document, send occasional check-in emails to all participants throughout the academic year to encourage mentoring practices and invite any questions and concerns, and distribute an end-of-program survey in May. Otherwise, the mentoring relationship and activities are in the hands of the mentors and mentees.

In the remainder of this chapter, we present a study of the CIMP that we conducted during the 2020–21 academic year in order to explore the role of a formal, cross-institutional mentoring program in the development of WAC methodologies for both newcomers and established scholar-practitioners. We prompted participants to think of WAC methodologies with our own loose characterization—approaches to researching in WAC studies, teaching based in WAC pedagogies, and administering WAC-related programs; however, our participants' interpretation and responses to those prompts provide a felt sense of how these methodologies live and breathe, defying strict definitions. After reviewing the rationales behind a formal, cross-institutional mentoring program, we describe the mentoring pairs as reported across five surveys, and we explore which characteristics might foster sustained, meaningful cross-institutional mentoring relationships. We especially draw out intersections between identity and influence before revisiting the program rationales in light of these findings.

WHY A FORMAL, CROSS-INSTITUTIONAL MENTORING PROGRAM?

Mentoring literature across higher education (i.e., Jacobi 1991), business (i.e., Kram 1985), and psychology (Levinson et al. 1978) suggests that a formal, cross-institutional mentoring program like the CIMP can play an important role in developing methodologies, because they (1) increase access to mentorships, (2) promote diversity and inclusion, and (3) contribute to the sustainability of a field of study.

First, a formal faculty/graduate student mentorship program can provide more equal access to mentoring opportunities that the "organic" development of informal relationships just can't guarantee. Since faculty are usually drawn to students who share their interests or show a strong sense of belonging from the start, we fear that "what makes students attractive as a [mentee] is what makes them successful with or without a mentor" (Johnson 2007, 202), whereas those students with differing interests or those who are uncertain of their place in the field may be left without a mentor. John Weidman, Darla Twale, and Elizabeth Leahy Stein (2001) sum up this dilemma of access and the promise of formal programs beautifully:

Once admitted to a graduate program, *certain incumbents* become privileged entrants into the private world of the scholar. The select few who penetrate the private domain are permitted to share that life with increasing opportunity and support for participating in research, publication, and presentations at professional meetings. Entry into this guarded enclave comes more easily through teaching and research assistantships, fellowships, internships, externships, and preceptorships than coursework. (76–77; our emphasis)

As Weidman et al. argue, a structure outside of regular coursework often facilitates stronger connections to the field, and we believe a cross-institutional mentoring program presents a more equal and available means for doing so. As we mentioned before, many of our peers were uncertain about finding and establishing a mentoring relationship, and we believe a formal program like the CIMP makes these opportunities more visible.

Furthermore, Wendy Sharer, Jessica Enoch, and Cheryl Glenn (2008) emphasize that mentorship is "most powerful when it involves scholars at diverse institutions" (142). These mentorships expand one's network, present opportunities for collaboration, provide different institutional perspectives, and operate outside of one's own institutional expectations/politics. We believe the opportunity to expand one's network across institutions is particularly important for students who are interested in WAC but attend a school without a WAC program or scholar. It's further important for students who are interested in WAC to gain perspective on how WAC might play out in various institutional and local contexts. This dimension of the CIMP also resonates directly with the very title of Lu Liu et al.'s (2008) piece "It Takes a Community of Scholars to Raise One: Multiple Mentors as Key to My Growth," in which she argues that a network of both formal and informal mentors across institutions critically contributed to her development as a graduate student. We take pause at her conclusion, though, in which she puts the onus of seeking out mentors on graduate students—that they must "take the initiative" and work to keep the mentorships alive. We agree that there is some initiative and investment that must be taken by graduate students (like completing the pairing survey for the CIMP), but we also hope that a formal program makes finding mentors (especially those outside of one's home institution) more possible, manageable, and equitable.

Because of this increased accessibility, we further posit that a formal mentoring program like the CIMP can promote diversity and inclusion. In fact, most formal mentoring programs in higher education were formed in order to ensure marginalized student populations benefit from rich mentorship (Crisp and Cruz 2009, 530; Mullen 2008, 300). This is made possible when invitations to mentoring relationships are advertised widely with concrete paths to inclusion—an opposition to the shoulder-tapping or discrete selection that can happen in "organic" mentorships. We see increasing the diversity and inclusion of a field as directly related to its sustainability: diversity brings innovation of thought and enriches the field's methodologies. For WAC in particular, many of the founders and key figures are moving (or have moved) into retirement, and the field broadly is concerned about its vitality moving forward (see Palmquist et al. 2020; Polk 2020). Thankfully, Jerel Slaughter and Michael Zickar (2006) found that faculty/graduate student mentorships result in a strong commitment to the profession at large (282), a finding which certainly resonates with both of our experiences in coming to (and staying in) WAC primarily through mentorships (see Palmero et al., this collection, for a model of multigenerational mentoring with similar effects). As Johnson (2007) puts it, "By facilitating a culture conducive to mentorship, universities and entire professional fields may help ensure inertia in the cycle of active career development" (199). We see a formal, cross-institutional mentoring program like the CIMP as one that may be integral to the rich culture of mentorship sustaining a field.

With these three proposed benefits in mind—access, inclusion, and sustainability—we wanted to observe how a program like the CIMP might impact the development of WAC methodologies for those cast in the roles of both mentors and mentees[1] in one of these formal, cross-institutional relationships. What kind of influences on WAC research, teaching, and administrative practices would participants report based on their activities and evolving relationship over an academic year? And how might those reported influences enrich our understanding of how a formal, cross-institutional mentoring program might best be implemented to reach these benefits of access, inclusion, and sustainability?

EXPERIENCING THE CIMP

In the rest of this chapter, we explore the above questions by presenting data from eight mentoring pairs enrolled in the CIMP's 2020–21 academic year (Wake Forest University IRB0002393). After the initial pairing survey, we distributed four surveys (appendix 6.B) throughout the year intended to gather what kind of activities happened in the cross-institutional mentorships and how those activities influenced the development of WAC methodologies. Each survey included three prompts:

1. Describe how these activities have or have not influenced your approach to research in WAC studies.

2. Describe how these activities have or have not influenced your approach to teaching based in WAC methodologies.

3. Describe how these activities have or have not influenced your approach to administering WAC-related programs.

The end-of-spring survey asked five additional questions about participants' experiences in the CIMP as a whole.

Although we collected data from eight mentorships, this chapter highlights five pairings to demonstrate the range of methodological influence. The three pairings not narrativized here fall into what might be described as a "failure to launch" category—pairings that did not engage beyond initial communications. While two of these pairs fell off in responding to the surveys, one pair filled out the surveys until the end (even though they were not connected) to describe the mitigating factors; we briefly describe some of this pair's experiences in a later section. In the next section, we introduce the main pairings (all names are pseudonyms) and describe their activities.

Exploring Administration

Penny (director of a writing-intensive curriculum program at an R1 university) and Anna (a rhet-comp master's student at an R1 university without a formal WAC program) kept to a ninety-minute video call every other week through the academic year, with emails and even occasional texts in between. Penny and Anna covered a large range of topics in their regular video calls: they discussed PhD programs, especially ones that might allow Anna to specialize in WAC; the "history and labor surrounding writing studies as a whole"; how various programs conduct professional development; major scholars and literature in WAC studies; and the regular facilitation and management of WAC programs across institutional contexts. It seems a lot of Penny and Anna's conversations consisted of Anna asking Penny questions about the ins and outs of how WAC programs happen across institutions, or the "day-to-day work of running a WAC program," as Penny calls it. By the final survey, Anna writes, "I rely on my WAC-Mentor more than anyone else I know." She and Penny plan on continuing their mentorship past the CIMP program.

Expanding Scholarly Influences

Eric (director of a first-year writing program at an R1 university) and Beth (pre-tenure faculty and director of writing at a regional campus) are a bit of an anomaly in this study for two reasons: Eric is the only participant who was also a participant in an original pilot study of the CIMP (Russell and Nicholes 2019), and Beth is the only non–graduate student that served in a mentee role. Their relationship revolved around sharing updates on their ongoing projects: Eric especially learned about disability studies, an area of scholarship he was previously less familiar with but one in which Beth specialized. Beth was able to recommend research that Eric incorporated into his current book manuscript, and Eric also reports that Beth provided "advice about accessibility that [he] applied in [his] own teaching and in mentoring of FYC teachers." In turn, Eric shared relevant scholarship for Beth to review for her ongoing research projects in assessment, he read parts of her dissertation to discuss what ways forward the project might have, and he gave feedback and advice on Beth's writing curriculum proposal that finally passed at the end of the year. Beth sums up her final survey with: "I certainly hope to stay connected to my mentor."

Linda (director of a new WAC program at a liberal arts college), who described herself as "fairly green" and not "heavily steeped in the [WAC] literature as a graduate student," and her mentee (a graduate student who was a nonparticipant in the study) chose a book about reading's place across the curriculum, along with some other literature, to read and discuss together over regular video meetings and emails. Through this activity, Linda reports that she benefited from the "shared conversations" as they "tackled WAC literature together." She further describes her mentee's influence: "My mentee's outside perspective has helped me to understand the value of particular ideas, approaches, and programming innovations I'm considering for my WAC faculty." Linda also supported her mentee by discussing job market options, reviewing materials for "limited regional searches that include[d] both academic and non-academic positions," and by "connecting her mentee with networking contacts."

Navigating Disparate Contexts

In the mid-fall survey, Tim (professor emeritus and past director of multiple WAC programs) and Lisa (EdD candidate at a national R1 university and writing instructor at an international university) had discussed their shared research interests in transnational WAC, and Tim had shared multiple resources that Lisa describes as giving her "a more complete picture of how WAC works in different countries." But then Tim and Lisa did not connect again through the rest of the academic year. Lisa explains in the final survey, "I would have continued to contact my mentor and work on WAC but the recent changes in my university's EdD program and the current geopolitical situation have caused me to change my thesis topic to one that is unrelated to WAC." She was also on a leave of absence the second half of the year.

Likewise, Olivia (director of a WAC program at a large state university), a public health scholar, and Liam (a graduate student halfway through a rhet-comp MA-to-PhD degree at an R1 university and coordinator of his university's WAC program) write about the influence of learning each other's institutional contexts and disparate WAC models, and they even brainstormed a collaborative research project early. By the end-of-fall survey, though, Liam writes, "To be honest, we have not checked in very much at all in the past month or so. I feel like my mentor does not really have the time." By the mid-spring survey, the mentorship had sputtered out entirely. Liam had also decided by this time that he was not going to stay in WAC—not because of this mentoring program or Olivia's influence, he noted, but "as a result of [his] own research trajectory."

MENTORING: RECIPROCITY, REGULARITY, AND IDENTITY

Looking across these mentorships allows us to reflect on what a formal, cross-institutional mentorship makes possible and how those possibilities might best be reached. As with most things in life (and in mentorship), the answer is somewhere between "it's complicated" and "well, it depends." In analyzing this data, we believe more than ever that mentorship is more art than science. However, two main features came up across almost all of the respondents' survey answers for making or breaking their cross-institutional mentoring experience: (1) reciprocity and (2) regularity.

Those with meaningful, sustained mentorships all mention how important it was that both parties were able to mutually support one another, collaborate, and work as more like "colleagues" than teacher/student. In other words, expertise and influence needs to flow both ways. Some of the less successful mentorships seemed to lack this reciprocity, with the mentors noting little to no influence on their professional practices. Agreeing with some of our respondents, we believe this reciprocity becomes more possible to establish in a cross-institutional mentorship that isn't marred by one's institutional structures, expectations, or politics. Anna explains this as collaborating "without it feeling like it has to be presented in a certain way," while her mentor Penny reflects,

> I loved the chance to support and interact with someone with no expectations of what they were meant to do in or for my own program. I have a graduate assistant and interns in my program, and although I enjoy mentoring them, I have to balance their needs and interests with the needs of the program itself. With my CIMP mentee, I could center her interest and needs completely, and it was great to have that simple, supportive role.

Similarly, Beth was able to discuss tenure and credit changes with a mentor who did not have a stake in her institutional context. Both Eric and Beth go on to note that being able to share and support one another out of their areas of expertise was especially generative. Beth reflects, "I really appreciated how mutually supportive our mentoring relationship is. I like to be able to give something back, and Eric actively sought out my advice too."

As a complication, though, reciprocity seems to only be possible if the mentor and mentee have aligned their goals, interests, and expectations. For example, Liam was hoping his mentor, Olivia, would be able to "cue [him] into scholarly conversations that [he] was not encountering on [his] own," but Olivia's discipline was public health and not writing studies, so he "did not get that exposure." Olivia also cites Zoom (and general pandemic) fatigue, as well as realizing that Liam was losing interest in WAC program administration, as reasons their mentorship was interrupted. Because of all these factors, Liam saw the "outside-ness" of the relationship in opposition to the way those in the more successful mentorships saw it: "The relationships that I have with my faculty on-campus seem much more important to me, not just because these people are the ones who sign my paperwork and stuff." We find Liam and Olivia's experience to be an interesting counterexample to Eric and Beth's relationship. Where Eric and Beth were able to benefit from each other's diverse disciplinary expertise and experiences, Liam—who might have been able to import some new ways of seeing WAC given Olivia's background—struggled to find the relevance of her experience.

The other essential feature of cross-institutional mentorships seems to be setting up regular structures and times. The more successful pairs did this in a number of ways: Penny and Anna scheduled biweekly Zoom calls to talk about any manner of topics; Eric and Beth set up phone calls and reached out based on ongoing projects; and Linda and her mentee chose a book to read and discuss together at regular intervals. Across these approaches, there was a reliable touchstone for the relationship, and these pairs decided on these structures at the beginning of the academic year. On the flip side, the less successful pairs all cite time as a constraint, often saying that they hadn't connected since the last survey.

We suspect the lack of connection happens if times to connect are not decided on near the beginning of the academic year. Without the expected regularity, every outreach can feel like reinventing the wheel or even like bothering the other.

Of course, context matters—most of the mentorships that faltered did so because of contextual or logistical factors beyond the participants' control. Participants cite factors as varied as program changes, COVID-19 stress, Zoom fatigue, changed research interests, and even tumultuous geopolitical situations. For example, Tim and Lisa both describe their pairing as ideal, but between the changes to Lisa's EdD program and her city's geopolitical situation, even a great pairing couldn't sustain the mentorship. One of our "failure-to-launch" mentees, Ellie, sums up this conundrum when she writes, "Because of real world stress, I was not able to connect with my mentor." As researchers, we are so grateful for these types of responses because they reveal an essential piece of mentoring: the very issues mentorship is meant to address can be the issues that keep it from being successful. We say this because in reading Ellie's responses, we couldn't help but lament that her mentor, Fiona, probably would have been able to offer advice, validation, and comfort to Ellie's concerns. But we also know that being a graduate student often means being "on" all the time—that there's pressure to be a good mentee. We think it's relevant that Ellie also notes in her final survey that she had "never really had any mentoring relationships." If she had never experienced that process of trust-building, reciprocity, and support, it's no wonder it felt so overwhelming and like another academic obligation to do so. Throw a pandemic on top of all of that, and here we are. Of course, Ellie's mentor, Fiona, perhaps has the best response we could think of: "We have to work with folx where they are, not where we think they should be." Both reciprocity and regularity, then, directly relate to whether participants describe this mentorship as one of the best in their lives or a failed experiment.

However, a successful mentorship isn't as easy as merely planning for reciprocity and regularity: these practices are encompassed by and enmeshed in participants' emergent identities. While we set out to collect some data that would help us contextualize those social-material notions of identity (i.e., professional status) that we as a field recognize as consequential to research, the two of us grew to appreciate the significance of intrapersonal characteristics of identity (e.g., dispositions, prior experiences, and motivations) as our study unfolded. That is, the social-material conditions of our professional lives might enable us to dedicate more or less time to a mentoring relationship, but intrapersonal factors, such as our motivation for participating in that relationship, also shape our commitment to it. In other words, while someone might *have* the time, they might not *make* the time. Eric especially has insight on this dynamic since he was able to compare his experience in the CIMP this year with the pilot year. He writes,

> This experience has been so different than my first mentoring experience with WAC-GO that it really emphasizes to me how complex these relationships are. I think with my first experience my mentee was very busy, was getting some good mentoring already at her institution, and was also just not clicking with me on a personal level. It's made me realize that for a successful mentoring experience a lot of factors need to be in place.

We believe part of what Eric is referring to is an intermingling of social-material and intrapersonal notions of identity as they are enacted within the many contexts that impact any mentorship. But identities are not easily captured, and they are thus very difficult to take into account when pairing mentors and mentees. In the pairing survey over the years, we've had some participants make special requests, like to be paired with a woman of color, or another academic parent, or someone also interested in feminist methods. We always try to honor these requests, but honoring them doesn't automatically equal a successful mentorship. We wish it were as easy as drawing clearer lines of cause and effect between identifying factors and a successful mentoring relationship. Institutional positions, backgrounds, disciplines, personality types, race and ethnicity, gender, sexual orientation, disability, socioeconomic levels, and so on—we haven't found clear ways of predicting how these complex identities will play out in a mentoring relationship. We only know after the fact if they have been successful, and always on a case-by-case basis.

While the two of us remain committed to identifying pairings with strong potential for success (and certainly encourage other organizers of formal mentoring programs to also do this), we also believe that matched mentors and mentees might individually and collaboratively reflect on how their identities are shaping the relationship. We quote here from a follow-up email that Penny sent us after her final survey, because it demonstrates this reflexive practice so thoughtfully:

> I mentioned in my survey that both my mentee and I are the first in our family to attend graduate school. (We are also nearly first in our family to attend college—that is, while we are each not the first, we both come from families without strong academic traditions, which means families that have not been able to help us navigate academia.) I have been able to share what I have learned about how academia works, and this seems to have helped her understand things that were puzzling to

her. I'm talking here not just about things like how to evaluate potential PhD programs—though we talked about things like that too—but about academic politics and the kinds of performative actions one sees (e.g., in the Q&A part of a conference session, or in departmental meetings). My mentee also is a person of color, and we have talked regularly about race and racism in academia in general, and in our field. Although I am a white scholar—albeit one committed to self-education and anti-racist work—my mentee has said that my listening, support, and perspectives have been helpful to her.

One part of this pairing is luck—that Penny and Anna were able to bond and support one another over their first-gen identities. But another part is a reflexive attention from both the mentor and mentee to the role of identity in the development of WAC methodologies and in academia; they talked openly about race and recognized how those identities shaped their relationship, their work, and their development. Similarly, Eric also mentioned being "aware that implicit sexism can hinder a mentoring relationship involving an older man and a younger woman," and that he "tried [his] best to be conscious of the potential for negative gender/age dynamics" in his discussions with Beth. When we listen to Eric's response, we know his reflexive attention to power and gender contributes to this successful mentorship, but we also recognize that Eric is motivated to attend to these aspects of identity. We thus believe that conscious attention to identity, and evolving identity formation over time, is a key aspect of any "successful" mentorship.

METHODOLOGY: THE QUESTION OF INFLUENCE

When the two of us designed our survey, we talked a lot about the term "influence" in our prompt formulation: for example, "Describe how these activities have or have not *influenced* your approach to research in WAC Studies." We played with a variety of words there—"affected," "improved," "developed." We kept asking ourselves: If we are looking to uncover the relationship between mentorship and WAC methodologies in this program, then what is it that happens between those two things? We landed on *influence*. My, that was a big assumption baked into our survey instrument! Or at least our survey data quickly showed that people clearly define *influence* and its association with WAC methodologies differently than we do. Thus, beyond whether these mentorships seemed successful or not, the way each characterized *influence* encourages us to reflect on the very heart of mentorship—what it is, what it does, and what it means—in the development of methodologies (in this case, WAC methodologies).

Some respondents took *influence* to mean *a specific change*. For example, Linda writes early on, "I'm not sure I have a concrete change to share, but I'll say that I've learned from my mentee." We would have thought learning from your mentee would be considered influence or change, but Linda and others in this study saw influence as a specific adjustment or shift from current thinking or acting. Relatedly, many respondents seemed to only report influence if they could put things into action. For example, Liam consistently writes, "I do not teach a WAC course," as a reason his mentorship did not influence his WAC pedagogies. A similar sentiment is shared when, even though Anna spent a majority of her mentorship time discussing program administration, she still answers, "I'm not a WPA, so I can't administer any programs sadly." Based on her other responses, it seems clear to us that her approach to administering WAC-related programs was being influenced, but we also appreciate that it wasn't recognized as influence without action.

In yet another characterization, others saw influence as a culmination of learning across time. For example, Penny does not report any influence until the very last survey. In her previous surveys, she simply describes talking to her mentee as "a delight" and that she comes out of their conversation "re-energized for all [her] WAC work." Only in the final survey does Penny describe these same effects as influence; she writes, "The excitement about this work affects everything." In this case, it seems that either the idea of influence changed for Penny over the course of the mentorship, or the ongoing effects of the mentorship finally culminated in some kind of influence.

These interpretations of influence also intersect with how participants interpreted WAC methodologies, which our survey names in terms of "your approach to research in WAC Studies"; "your approach to teaching based in WAC pedagogies"; and "your approach to administering WAC-related programs." Even the more sustained mentorships have gaps where they did not report any influence in one area right beside great influence in another area, and this is usually because they see these WAC methodologies as specific activities. As we noted above, several participants answered that they don't teach a WAC course or administer a WAC program, and thus they reported there was no influence. Another interesting trend is how interconnected the respondents saw these three areas of research, teaching, and administration. Some would write a long answer about what they were getting out of their work with their mentor or mentee in the first prompt box about research, and then write something like "See above" for the other two questions. Others separated out answers for the three separate prompts (although it's difficult to say whether respondents see the three areas as distinct or were merely responding to the survey design as best they could).

Of course, some influences that our participants note do not fit into the prompts on our survey, which is focused on the development of WAC methodologies, but are no doubt some of the most valuable parts of the mentoring experience. We're grateful as researchers that the participants found ways of noting these aspects of their mentorship in the interstitial spaces of the surveys, because, ultimately, we believe these parts *did* end up influencing the development of WAC methodologies. For example, some participants write at length about enjoyment they got out of their mentorship. Similarly, almost all participants regularly mark that they "engaged in personal (i.e., non-WAC or academic) conversations" with their mentor or mentee. And what about the pairs that spent their discussion time demystifying academia, reviewing program/job options, or pumping up confidence in each other's projects? We see these all as influences, including influences on WAC methodologies, because we are whole people. And we believe mentorships are one space in academia where we can be seen as whole people—WAC methodologies being just one part of the whole, but inextricable from it. And so, we are once again back at identity as an all-encompassing but nebulous feature of these mentoring relationships and the development of WAC methodologies. If *influence* is what happens between mentorship and methodology, then we must account for its wide range of characterizations and intersections with identities.

CONCLUDING THOUGHTS

We'd like to end by simply exploring some questions around the three proposed benefits of a formal, cross-institutional mentoring program that we listed earlier: (1) increased access to mentorships, (2) promoting diversity and inclusion, and (3) contributing to the sustainability of a field of study. In terms of access, mentors described how wonderful it was to have mentees that they either don't have access to at their universities or that they can't have an equal relationship with because of institutional expectations, while mentees described either not having any WAC mentors at their institutions or desiring an expanded perspective beyond their institution. We are left wondering, though, about the relationship between mentoring and *action*. What if cross-institutional mentoring offers access to mentors/mentees but their influence can't be realized because of the lack of opportunity to put the learning into action (e.g., no WAC program, not teaching WAC courses, not working on WAC projects, etc.). Is access an *ongoing* condition (meaning it can't be granted or achieved just once but must be continually made visible)? If so, how can we support and foster access to mentors and to the development of WAC methodologies beyond the CIMP? Can access in the past lead to access in the future? If so, can we consider what happens in the CIMP as a kind of *potential* influence that is critical for later fruition? And how does that shape what we do in the CIMP?

We see these possibilities around access as directly related to increasing the diversity and inclusion of our field. There are still some skeptics who believe mentoring relationships can only be successful if they happen "organically," because those mentorships are believed to be rooted in an altruistic "ethics of care" (Downs and Goldstein 2008, 150). But do these "organic" mentorships happen equitably? Sustainably? Intentionally? Mentor Penny provides a searing articulation of these questions:

> This has gotten me thinking about the importance of direct support of graduate students from minoritized groups, not just for those individuals, but for the field. If we truly want the diversity of our scholarly community to reflect the diversity of our communities and our schools, as I believe most of us really do, I think we need more of the kind of direct, sustained, personal mentoring the Cross-Institutional Mentoring Project is creating. This work does not show up in publication records, or in major named initiatives, but I believe it makes a difference, one scholar at a time, that will change our field as much as the big picture work of big name scholars will.

In other words, a commitment to inclusion requires intentionality to create identifiable and equitable access points. And those who volunteer for the CIMP are clearly brimming with ethics of care! To Penny's point, do publications about increasing the diversity and inclusion of our field hold weight without one-on-one mentoring acts behind them?

Finally, we are left pondering the sustainability of a discipline or field, in our case WAC studies, especially in terms of reciprocity between mentors and mentees. It's easy to think of mentorship as a way of bringing new scholars into a field to literally continue the work, but what about the effect new scholars have on established scholars? If influence toward sustainability is seen largely as unidirectional, that might lead to the stifling of innovation or might indicate a field oriented toward its re-creation but not its *reimagining*. For example, we see this reimagining made possible in Gregory Palmero et al.'s (this collection) exploration of a multigenerational assessment project that prompted all involved—from tenured faculty to early-career faculty, to graduate student, to undergraduate student—to critically question and collaboratively develop their beliefs about linguistic identities. Is sustained reciprocity a possible answer to not only socialize newcomers but (re-)socialize the established? Should we focus less on bringing newcomers in and more on creating some fresh amalgam between the two? And can cross-institutionality provide a particularly rich space for the invigoration or innovation of methodologies?

APPENDIX 6.A: PAIRING SURVEY

1. Name
2. Email
3. Interested in becoming a mentor or mentee?
4. How did you originally become interested in WAC/WID work?
5. In what ways are you currently involved in WAC/WID work?
6. Why are you interested in becoming a mentor or mentee for the Cross-Institutional Mentoring Project?
7. What kind of mentorship would you be most interested in offering or receiving in this program? (Very interested, interested, somewhat interested, not interested)
    a. Developing Scholarship, that is, writing for WAC/WID audiences, designing WAC/WID studies and methods, etc.
    b. Learning Administration, that is, understanding daily WAC operations, troubleshooting problems, cultivating stakeholders across the university, etc.
    c. Understanding Career Paths, that is, learning about jobs in WAC, preparing for the job market, etc.
8. What would you most hope to accomplish in a WAC/WID–focused mentoring relationship?
9. What activities would you be interested in doing with your cross-institutional partner? (Check all that apply)
    - Video-chat semi-regularly
    - Share/read thesis and dissertation chapters
    - Share/read articles or works-in-progress
    - Email regularly
    - Meet/socialize at conferences
    - Collaborate on projects / co-author papers or presentations
    - Other
10. Any other info that would help us pair you with a mentor or mentee?

APPENDIX 6.B: MID-FALL SURVEY (OCTOBER 2020); END-OF-FALL SURVEY (DECEMBER 2020); MID-SPRING SURVEY (MARCH 2021); END-OF-SPRING SURVEY (MAY 2021)

1. Which mediums did you use to connect with your mentee/mentor since the last survey? (Check all that apply.)
    a. Video
    b. Email
    c. Phone
    d. Text or social media messaging
    e. Document sharing platforms
    f. In-person
    g. Other
2. What activities have you engaged with your mentor/mentee since the last survey? (Check all that apply)
    a. Set (or revisited) goals for the mentorship
    b. Conversed about a variety of WAC topics/issues
    c. Read and discussed WAC literature
    d. Shared regular updates/questions about current WAC work
    e. Shared/read thesis and dissertation chapters
    f. Shared/read articles or other works-in-progress
    g. Collaborated on co-authored projects
    h. Discussed and/or reviewed job market options and materials
    i. Engaged in personal (i.e., non-WAC or academic) conversations
    j. Other
3. Describe how these activities have or have not influenced your approach to research in WAC Studies.
4. Describe how these activities have or have not influenced your approach to teaching based in WAC pedagogies.
5. Describe how these activities have or have not influenced your approach to administering WAC-related programs?

    [Note: Questions 6–10 were only on the end-of-spring survey]

6. Looking back over the whole of your involvement in the CIMP, did your mentor/mentee seem to be a good pairing for you considering your goals, experiences, interests, etc.? Why or why not?
7. What seemed to facilitate this mentoring relationship?
8. What seemed to constrain this mentoring relationship?
9. How would you describe your cross-institutional mentoring relationship in the context of your other mentoring relationships?
10. Any other comments on your experience in the CIMP?

NOTE

1. We originally used the terms "mentor" and "mentee" in the pairing survey and general pitch of this program, and that's why our chapter and our participant responses mirror those terms. Since the conception of these "mentor" and "mentee" roles no doubt shaped the mentoring relationships in this study, we will continue using them in this chapter. However, in future iterations of the CIMP, we will most likely drop these hierarchal terms altogether and opt for terms that emphasize the reciprocal nature of these relationships, that is, mentoring partners.

REFERENCES

Chao, Georgia T., Pat M. Walz, and Philip D. Gardner. 1992. "Formal and Informal Mentorships: A Comparison on Mentoring Functions and Contrast with Nonmentored Counterparts." *Personnel Psychology* 45, 619–636.

Crisp, Gloria, and Irene Cruz. 2009. "Mentoring College Students: A Critical Review of the Literature between 1990 and 2007." *Research in Higher Education* 50: 525–545.

Downs, Doug, and Dayna Goldstein. 2008. "Chancing into Altruistic Mentoring." In *Stories of Mentoring: Theory and Praxis*, edited by Michelle F. Eble and Lynée Lewis Gaillet, 149–152. West Lafayette, IN: Parlor Press.

Jacobi, Maryann. 1991. "Mentoring and Undergraduate Academic Success: A Literature Review." *Review of Educational Research* 61 (4): 505–532.

Johnson, W. Brad. 2007. "Student-Faculty Mentorship Outcomes." In *The Blackwell Handbook of Mentoring: A Multiple Perspectives Approach*, edited by Tammy D. Allen and Lillian T. Eby, 189–210. Oxford: Blackwell.

Kram, Kathy E. 1985. *Mentoring at Work: Developmental Relationships on Organization Life*. Lanham, MD: University Press of America.

Levinson, Daniel J., Charlotte N. Darrow, Edward B. Klein, Maria H. Levinson, and Braxton McKee. 1978. *The Seasons of a Man's Life*. New York: Ballentine.

Liu, Lu, with Irwin Weiser, Tony Silva, Janet Alsup, Cindy Selfe, and Gail Hawisher. 2008. "It Takes a Community of Scholars to Raise One: Multiple Mentors as Key to My Growth." In *Learning the Literacy Practices of Graduate School: Insiders' Reflections on Academic Enculturation*, edited by Chrstine Pearson Casnave and Xiaoming Li, 166–185. Ann Arbor: University of Michigan Press.

Mullen, Carol A. 2008. "Conclusion: Mentoring, Change, and Diversity; Findings and Lessons." In *The Handbook of Formal Mentoring in Higher Education*, edited by Carol A. Mullen, 297–319. Norwood, MA: Christopher-Gordon Publishers.

Palmquist, Mike, Pam Childers, Elaine Maimon, Joan Mullin, Rich Rice, Alisa Russell, and David Russell. 2020. "Fifty Years of WAC: Where Have We Been? Where Are We Going?" *Across the Disciplines* 17 (3). https://wac.colostate.edu/atd/archives/volume-17-2020/wac50/.

Polk, Thomas. 2020. "Something Larger Than Imagined: Developing a Theory, Building an Organization, Sustaining a Movement." *WAC Journal*, 31. https://wac.colostate.edu/docs/journal/vol31/polk.pdf.

Russell, Alisa, Jake Chase, Justin Nicholes, and Allie Sockwell. 2020. "The Writing Across the Curriculum Graduate Organization: Where We've Been, Where We Are, and Where We're Going." In *Diverse Approaches to Teaching, Learning, and Writing Across the Curriculum: IWAC at 25*, edited by Leslie Erin Bartlett, Sandra L. Tarabochia, Andrea R. Olinger, and Margaret J. Marshall, 45–53. Fort Collins, CO: WAC Clearinghouse. https://wac.colostate.edu/docs/books/iwac2018/chapter3.pdf.

Russell, Alisa, and Justin Nicholes. 2019. "The Role of Faculty-Graduate Student Mentorship in WAC Studies: Evaluating the Cross-Institutional Mentoring Project." White Paper Series, Writing Across the Curriculum Graduate Organization.

Sharer, Wendy, Jessica Enoch, and Cheryl Glenn. 2008. "Performing Professionalism: On Mentoring and Being Mentored." In *Stories of Mentoring: Theory and Praxis*, edited by Michelle F. Eble and Lynée Lewis Gaillet, 129–144. West Lafayette, IN: Parlor Press.

Slaughter, Jerel, and Michael J. Zickar. 2006. "A New Look at the Role of Insiders in the Newcomer Socialization Process." *Group and Organization Management* 31 (2): 264–290.

Weidman, John C., Darla J. Twale, and Elizabeth Leahy Stein. 2001. "Socialization of Graduate and Professional Students in Higher Education: A Perilous Passage?" *ASHE-ERIC Higher Education Report* 28 (3): 2–135.

7
PROFESSIONALIZING MENTORSHIP
The New Ethos of Academic Publishing

Jessica Clements and John Pell

Publishing journal articles is a traditional measure of academic success in many disciplines—writing studies is no exception. And the methodology of publishing journal articles looks something like this: spend several years in graduate school learning to write and talk in the language of your area; research journals to determine impact factor and ranking as well as fit; write your manuscript, ask colleagues to review your manuscript, re-write your manuscript (iteratively, until "ready" to submit); check and double-check submission instructions, then submit; wait and wait some more for double-blind peer review; celebrate your "revise and resubmit" (buckling up for more back-and-forth) or place rejected manuscript out of sight and mind until you can stomach starting the process over again (both results typically involve tearfully navigating the overly critical anonymous suggestions of the infamous "reviewer 2").

We draw out this narrative not to undermine the importance of peer review but to highlight the problematic "how"; innumerable failures are amplified in the traditional academic publishing process with only a privileged few who seem to have an easier time jumping largely invisible hurdles, hurdles rendered more or less visible through systemic inequities in traditional academic publishing methodology.

> Dr. Jennifer Ortiz (she/her)
>   @Ortiz_PhD
>
> If you believe that PhD students and junior faculty should suffer through grueling academic rituals and life circumstances simply because you had to endure them, you are toxic. If you're not reaching back to ease the struggle of others, you're what's wrong with academia.
>
> 2:35 PM September 30, 2021 Twitter for Android
>
> Shit Academics Say
>   October 1, 2021 at 9:00 AM

https://doi.org/10.7330/9781646425822.c007

As freshly minted co-managing editors of an independent writing studies journal and practicing writing program administrators, we believe we can craft a productive counternarrative to Godbee's (2017) "epistemic injustice" by inherently intertwining the methodology of academic publishing with explicit (tactical, cross-institutional) mentorship. Adapting contemporary scholarship on mentorship and co-authoring (Day and Eodice 2001; Duffy 2020; Geller and Eodice 2013), we suggest that an ethic of mentorship challenges the meritocratic impulses of academic publishing that obfuscate the nuances of the publishing process for new scholars with little, if any, formal mentorship on how to navigate the peer-review process. Professionalizing mentorship as a tactical methodology for both author and reviewers affords a more inclusive disciplinary identity, one that is accessible to the disparate and vulnerable voices deserving of an audience in our field. Integrating mentorship into the editorial process foregrounds the notion that supporting an author's continued development might be a viable alternative for understanding the work of editors beyond their perceived gatekeeping function.

This change in editorial focus can be disorienting. Therefore, we want to emphasize that productive mentor/mentee relationships take time and explicit education. We are no strangers to what WAC scholar Bradley Hughes (2020) calls "the long game."

A qualitative study comprising the analysis of micro narratives capturing the lived experiences of young scholars and their dialogical engagement in the academic publishing review process would lend exigence to our claims. We might have engaged in the not unproblematic process of obtaining institutional review board approval for such a methodological intervention, but in *Present Tense*'s spirit of challenging exclusionary paths to publication, we begin by offering the phenomenological evidence that is already all over social media: Twitter, the discourse of our everyday lives, with specific attention to the epically harsh statements of #reviewer2.

RHETORICAL EXIGENCE: THE NOTORIOUS R2

Denny Pencheva
@dr_denny_penny

Replying to @NickAnguelov and @DimitarBechev

I'll see you and raise you: A journal asked me to review an article in my capacity as an expert in the field, after desk-rejecting my article as unfit for the thematic scope of said journal. This is how #reviewer2 is born, just saying.

10:09 AM March 1, 2021 Twitter Web App

Double-blind peer review by field experts is at the heart of the gauntlet that is contemporary academic publishing. The admirable goals behind this anonymous review process are to ensure fit with the journal's focus, soundness of methods, meaningful contribution, and general adherence to genre conventions. Unfortunately, not all reviewers are created equal, and lack of training in editorial response (coupled with the general dangers of anonymous online communication) can (and do) result in a toxic cycle of shaming and otherwise excluding the contributions of early-career scholars and others who don't fit the ivory tower (read: white, self-sufficient male) mold.

Anecdotally, Reviewer 2 is considered to be grumpy and aggressive, vague and unhelpful, hyperfocused on their own favorite methods, and otherwise unlikely to treat the anonymous author as a peer worthy of their scholarly time and attention. The following tweets offer direct quotations from such exhausting academic "colleagues" in the enigmatic enterprise of contemporary academic publication.

- @Megan_ EL_Brown offers evidence of one of the more egregious transgressions: "How * * *not* * * to phrase your peer review: 'I gave up reading your paper' . . . #MedEd #PhD #Reviewer2" (May 26, 2021).
- @SzydlowskaBM demonstrates grit in their response to the following commentary regarding "fit": "'Such speculations make interesting talk at cocktail, but it is not the sort of thing that ought to be published under serious scientific aegis.' . . . The #reviewer2 comment on Lawrence Morley paper on 'continental drift'! #AcademicChatter—Never get discouraged!" (June 1, 2021).
- And, @nocode_dc brings up the significant context of surface-level language issues: "Why is it so difficult for #reviewer2 to understand that stating 'I don't mean to be offensive . . .' means exactly the opposite? Not because you are a native English speaker you are allowed to be offensive. My English can be improved, not so sure about people . . . #anonymous" (May 26, 2021).

These are micro examples of a macro problem. Peer review is intended to uphold shared standards of rigor and ethics, to ensure that collective intelligence moves a field forward in robust conversation. It is intended to assist journal editors in establishing a manuscript's potential place in the journal's epistemic domain. And it is intended to help burgeoning scholars find their voice in meaningful advancement of disciplinary knowledge. As a rhetorical endeavor, then, peer review encapsulates multiple purposes for multiple audiences. It is a challenging service. A service, by nature, is voluntary—unpaid. And academics too often find that this service is unrecognized and otherwise unrewarded

(Watling, Ginsburg, and Lingard 2021). Given both lack of reward and lack of training for engaging in this complicated and time-consuming process, it is no wonder we end up with a plethora of Reviewer 2s, who "give up" on reading manuscripts, unabashedly declare the ill fit of potential authors' proposals for *any* serious knowledge-producing contexts, and hedge their offensive comments before they continue being, well, offensive.

Beginning to parse the structure of peer review as it currently exists gives us some important insight into how such problems might arise, but it is the delineation of the outcomes that sound the alarm bell:

> Reviewer 2 can push the imposter syndrome button for both novice and more experienced writers, causing them to doubt their . . . abilities. They can consign papers with good potential to a desk drawer for eternity. They can cost journals future submissions and the field future knowledge. And perhaps most disturbingly, they can disproportionately harm underrepresented groups. A 2019 study found that intersectional groups such as women of colour and non-binary people of colour were most likely to report direct negative impacts on . . . aptitude, productivity, and career advancement after receiving an unprofessional peer review. (Watling, Ginsburg, and Lingard 2021)

The costs—individual imposter syndrome to future communal field knowledge—are great. We must also recognize that the costs are greatest, as Watling, Ginsburg, and Lingard (2021) note, for those operating outside the model of the white, self-sufficient male.

> Dr. John Bahadur Lamb
> @SecuritySheep
> #AcademicTwitter #acwri I have serious hangs ups about #writing caused by #Reviewer2 experiences. This is so bad I actively avoid #writing
> Recently I was told work the problem so This is a commitment to post a picture of what I have written each week. #KeepMeOnTrack
> 5:48 AM June 6, 2021 Twitter for iPhone

Facebook groups like "I Should Be Thriving: Advancing Gender/Ethnic/Class Minorities in Academia" exist because of the general lack of scaffolded writing support in the academy, to offer support to writers largely rendered invisible by traditional publishing practices. More often than not, such social media discourse showcases the cycles of blame and shame that circulate around academic publishing talk, including and especially the transgressions of Reviewer 2. They also stand as evidence that underrepresented minority writers in particular are at a disadvantage because of current practices.

While it is beyond the scope of this chapter to analyze this social media discourse, we offer this glimpse as evidence of the larger problem in which we seek to intervene: traditional academic publishing processes privilege a select few, whereas sponsoring formal mentorship on how to navigate the peer-review process would afford a more inclusive disciplinary identity.

This begs the question: How did academic publishing get to this point *and* where do we go from here?

SCHOLARLY CONTEXT: WRITERLY DEVELOPMENT

In *After Whiteness*, Willie James Jennings (2020) outlines what he sees as the quintessential problem of contemporary theological education and, by extension, of higher education writ large: "Western education . . . as it now exists works against a pedagogy of belonging" (10). We suggest the same of academic publishing. Academic publishing has been a performance of "white, self-sufficient masculinity," defined, in Jennings's words, as "a way of being in the world that aspires to exhibit possession, mastery, and control of knowledge first, and of one's self second, and if possible of one's world" (29). White, self-sufficient masculinity is a paradigm that defines what counts as scholarship—and who counts as a "serious scholar"—an exclusionary enterprise, a "notorious intellectual hierarchy" (50) scarred by a "relentless Eurocentrism" (52). If one desires to "publish" rather than "perish," they must don the voice of the objectively clear, white male persona and rigorously pursue subjects that have already been deemed of import to a Eurocentric canon, usually with as much explicit guidance as "Your tenure clock is ticking." Belonging, on the other hand, including listening to and learning from those traditionally locked out of the game of academic publishing due to varying degrees of difference from the white, self-sufficient masculine model *can* begin with attention (49). But "our paying attention also requires a commitment to be *patient* in weaving *deep lines of connection* between what we teach, whom we teach, and the world we inhabit together with them" (59; emphasis added)—to the emotionally laborious (but ultimately valuable, we argue) service of mentoring.

While "mentoring" writers is often commented upon in the writing studies discipline, the primary loci of inquiry tend to be first-year writers and graduate students completing dissertations. We find ourselves asking, how can seasoned professional scholars provide support for developing writers in contexts more akin to low-stakes affairs like writing groups or writing retreats than the hardscrabble world of academic publishing? As Eric Hayot (2014) notes in *The Elements of Academic Style*, such models of professionalization rely too heavily upon the good will of individual faculty members or colleagues. In order to enrich our conversations about writing instruction in the context of professional development, we must integrate the "*institutional* patterns" (9; emphasis in original) of instruction and mentorship and how well it helps writers develop acumen with the "professionally normative forms," namely conference papers, journal articles and book chapters, grant proposals, and full-length book projects.

For Hayot (2014), writers need mentors to help them develop their craft in the confines of *non-professional* and *low-stakes* environments, a place where writers are able to craft their voice under the supervision of experienced writers and trusted allies. Through a myriad of practices (conferences, peer-review, and copious feedback), emerging writers develop skills necessary for success in publishing. While Hayot's manuscript does not directly address Jennings's (2020) critique of what counts as a "serious" scholarly voice, Hayot (2014) does remind writers that they "owe every act of narration and description to the panoply of norms into which, like newborns into language, we all emerge" (218). Taking a clear social constructionist route, Hayot concludes that "recognizing the social world of your work; understanding the difference between how you work and how you must, given professional norms, present the process to the world" is the central task of the developing authors. In this model of professional development, "publish or perish" can be understood as an assessment of an author's preparedness. During their apprenticeships as a student, did they develop the requisite skills necessary for success as a scholar? Does the author employ practices that allow them to produce the requisite number of pages per week necessary to maintain their publishing goals?

Even though Hayot's (2014) take on writerly development nods to the complexities of the larger scholarly communities from which professional academic prose emerges, he nonetheless assumes that the role of emerging scholars is to adopt the "voice" of their discipline through focused encounters with discrete scholarly forms most often composed by members of those disciplinary communities. Hayot argues that professional development of this kind can and should occur during graduate preparation, but such an approach would require institutions to provide greater sustained support for graduate students and their faculty mentors. Hayot is dubious about the notion that such sweeping change will occur, so, like many scholars writing about how to create successful writing lives, Hayot turns his attention to individual authors' writing practices.

William Banks and Kerri Flinchbaugh (2013) make a similar observation concerning the scholarship on professional writing development.

"In many of the texts," they write, "used to encourage writers, we have seen a marked focus on observable dispositions (physical activities)" (229). The emphasis on physical practices obfuscates the underlying assumption informing a focus on writerly practices: faculty already see themselves as writers. But, as Banks and Flinchbaugh argue from their experiences as mentors to both faculty and graduate students, such assumptions may be unwarranted: "Faculty do not see themselves primarily as *writers* but as teachers/professors and researchers" (228). For those interested in helping faculty develop confidence as *writers*, Banks and Flinchbaugh argue that perhaps the initial stages of such support structures begin with encouraging faculty to change their self-perceptions.

Drawing upon the notion of *ethos*, so central to rhetorical scholarship, Banks and Flinchbaugh (2013) seek to augment traditional professional-development strategies (workshops, seminars, writing groups, etc.) with a "different sort of intervention, one based not so much in dispositions as one based on a rhetorical refiguration of writerly identity" (231). Instead of simply providing faculty with strategies and exercises that will produce more prose, Banks and Flinchbaugh encourage faculty to engage in reflective practices that provide space to consider their writerly ethos. "Ethos" as a critical term, Banks and Flinchbaugh argue, "provides a language and a theory for disrupting simple identity categories," which often have a categorical fixity based on binary relations, that is, writer/teacher or writer/researcher (232). From a rhetorical perspective, to be a writer is not a categorical imperative; rather, "to be a writer" is a disposition we embody in particular moments: "ethos is a rhetorical self, a self we choose based on current exigencies" (232). When confronted with writing exigencies, then, Banks and Flinchbaugh encourage faculty to "experience themselves as writers"; that is, understand that "writer" is one of the many personal and professional *ethoi* they can choose to adopt.

Following Banks and Flinchbaugh (2013; and the WAC scholarship of which they are a part more broadly), we might ask the following question: How can the editorial process contribute to people "experiencing themselves as writers?" To be clear, we (editors of a professional journal) understand that our engagements with writers are limited, and we are cautious to make any grand claims about the impact the editors have on writers' self-perceptions. Moreover, while mentorship and collaboration are concepts often discussed and critiqued within WAC scholarship, there is little written about how mentorship might function in professional spaces that do not have the luxury of face-to-face connection or serendipity often found in the classroom or conference room of a particular institution. However, we are invested in imagining small ways that mentorship can occur in less contextualized professional settings, particularly settings like the editorial process, where authors sojourn into territories and encounter new exigencies bound up in the discourse of that particular publication.

Helping potential authors change self-perceptions as well as helping those currently in editorial power to be more inclusive involves creating a culture of transparency in mentorship: "It is only by understanding the way that people behave . . . behind the veil of peer-review anonymity that we can hope properly to modify reviewing conventions for the better" (Eve et al. 2021). Pulling back the veil and critiquing existing academic publishing practices allows us to intervene in a positive way, and it's not necessarily about sweeping changes. As we hope our review of current scholarship on writing mentorship makes clear, there seem to be gaping holes in writing studies and mentorship of academic publishing (i.e., it happens in the undergraduate composition classroom or graduate rhetoric and composition program—or it doesn't happen at all); we believe there is room to talk about smaller, more manageable interventions. We can do small things and not overwhelm the service agenda of the already burdened mid-career scholar, for example, to make a big difference. Investing in such micro interventions *to eventually build systemic change* can create positive feelings for the writer, feelings about self as professional, and an ethos of viewing oneself as an "author." Comments from Reviewer 2, then, seem more manageable, more helpful, part of a larger, positive process. We can also intervene *with* Reviewer 2 to avoid discourse in reviews that attack the scholar's ethos as a writer. We can be a journal that shapes authors' ethos productively in mentoring initial responses and in how we encourage our reviewers to respond, as we illustrate below. We can participate in changing the writing studies publishing narrative from "you must *prove* that you're an author" to "as a valued writer in our field, we encourage the following . . ." That is, we can provide editorial guidance that acknowledges a scholar's writerly ethos as belonging to the larger disciplinary community.

PRESENT TENSE AND MENTORING

> *"Comments to the Editors:*
> *I don't believe this paper should have been sent out for review. It reads like undergraduate student work."*

Earlier in this chapter, we talked about the notorious R2, and how R2s' stinging comments can crush the drive of burgeoning scholars trying to make it in the field of writing studies. The above comment, however, illustrates that such stinging comments can come from your own editorial board and wound your own sense of authority as you try out the new position of managing editor. Though such comments might have value in creating empathy around the imposter syndrome many of us feel as we navigate the yet obtuse academic publishing process, we want to flip the script and let such comments serve as a reminder that we can do a better job of molding our review board into more effective mentors.

In addition to serving as managing editors of a writing studies journal, we serve as writing program directors at a small liberal arts school in the Pacific Northwest. We bring up this unique intersectional identity because, *as* writing program administrators, we are no strangers to the utility and unique value of peer mentorship in evolving more effective writers. Even more plainly, you cannot separate writing center scholarship, for example, from peer mentorship. The foundational premise of writing tutoring is that consulting with a slightly more advanced (and productively educated) peer will result in producing more effective writers (not just more successful writing products). What writing center scholarship also tells us is that crafting effective writing mentors does not happen overnight; it involves continually engaging in ongoing education to create confidence through explicit mentoring strategies both in the peer mentor and the peer mentee (see, for example, Clements 2019). We believe this methodology can be levied at multiple levels of the publishing process to afford hands-on multi-institutional collaboration, an ethos that eliminates the visage of traditional academic publishing as a zero-sum game and replaces it with a metaphor of dynamic mentoring relationships. But, again, productive mentor/mentee relationships take time and explicit education.

Drawing upon our expertise as writing program administrators, we find value in the big-picture methodologies that drive, for example, contemporary WAC programs (programs charged with unifying inquiry and stimulating engagement with writing across a variety of disparate stakeholders): sustainable development theories, systems thinking, resilience theories, and so on (Polk 2020). We see potential in operationalizing an ethos of tactical, cross-institutional mentoring arrangements—ongoing arrangements that speak to an intentionality in the structuring of editorial leadership systems, in how we mentor new and existing editors, and, specifically, in looping in graduate and undergraduate interns. Phelan and Weber (2021) describe how writing centers, for example, have long operated on methodologies that incorporate the voices of such early-career contributors: "True to the collaborative ideology on which writing centers are built, student voices are still included [in *The Writing Lab Newsletter*] alongside those of directors and accomplished scholars" (1). The introduction to our most recent issue of *Present Tense* further outlines our methodological goal:

> From our initial communication with authors to the comments authors receive from reviewers, we want the editorial processes of *Present Tense* to reflect the generous and collaborative spirit we believe is one of the hallmarks of our field.
>
> We want every author that submits to *Present Tense*, regardless of whether their work is published in the journal, to walk away from the process encouraged and energized because of the meaningful interactions with reviewers and editors whom provided careful and thoughtful responses to their work. For years, *Present Tense*—given its focus on contemporary discussions of culture and theory—has served as a weathervane, providing insight into the direction of research in our field. We believe *Present Tense* will continue to serve this function; however, we also want *Present Tense* to serve as a model for academic publishing where collaboration and generosity usurp competition as the primary editorial ethos. (Clements et al. 2021).

"Collaboration and generosity" can only "usurp competition as the primary editorial ethos" of academic publishing, however, if we renovate systems of peer review to sponsor and continually support resilience rather than engender ill will by enforcing solitary working conditions that breed emotionally charged feedback, entrenching the cycle of diverse voices self-isolating from contributing to field knowledge. Both the hands-on and multi-institutional nature of this mentoring work are necessary to create sustainably supportive epistemological circles, to provide "meaningful interactions with reviewers and editors whom provided careful and thoughtful responses to their work."

Part of this work involves borrowing from feminist methodologies that afford the creation of diverse networks of teacher-scholars, nurturing communities that preclude the birth of Reviewer 2. To do this, we look inward at the structure of our editorial board and make sure we are best serving our field in our current positions as well as opening up positions to those traditionally underrepresented in academic publishing. There is immediate room, for example, to welcome new voices into the team of style editors, a low-stakes position within the larger editorial enterprise. We will also launch a comprehensive editorial board mentoring program, in which we engage in ongoing efforts to educate our editors and review board in the process of response that engenders *belonging*. We do this by walking alongside our editors and review board—seasoned and brand-new—through resources such as

Cagle et al.'s (2021) *Anti-Racist Scholarly Reviewing Practices: A Heuristic for Editors, Reviewers, and Authors*, in order to read with a more inclusive eye and write with a more inclusive heart. Writing with a more inclusive heart, for example, starts with our managing editors' response to submissions that are not ready to circulate to the review board. Rather than a boilerplate "we are not going to publish you at this time" message, we offer the following artifact as evidence of such efforts:

> Thank you for your submission to *Present Tense: A Journal of Rhetoric in Society*.
> We, the Managing Editors, have read your manuscript. We find the topic to be important and the piece generally well written; however, in its current version, the manuscript's central argument needs further development before it is sent out for external review.
> *Present Tense* strives to be a venue where authors receive constructive feedback and professional mentorship. We also want every issue published to include rigorously peer-reviewed scholarship that represents the best thinking in our field. We believe this process begins by providing our disciplinary colleagues with thoughtful criticism that fosters their professional development.
> Our journal's commitment to professional development and mentorship means that we will, on occasion, invite authors to revise and resubmit work not yet ready for external review. We believe your piece falls into this category. Having engaged with your manuscript, we offer the following detailed comments as guides to your revisions, should you choose to continue publication with *Present Tense*.
> [200+ words that speak to suggestions for improving the submitted manuscript]
> We hope you find our comments helpful in your writing process even if you choose to submit your work to another venue. Please feel free to reach out to us with further questions regarding potential publication with *Present Tense*.

A gesture easily overlooked, we start by *thanking* the author for offering the experience of perusing their work. We validate the importance of the subject matter, which is integral given the often-Eurocentric dominance in topics of import to the field. We help the author know our goal is constructive criticism because we believe direct feedback will lead to publication of their voice among the "best thinking in our field." We offer *detailed guidance* alongside the invitation to resubmit to *Present Tense* or publish elsewhere, because this author's voice has inherent value even if *Present Tense* is not the right venue at the present time.

To complement feminist growth methodologies, we return to writing program administration and its "collaborative ideologies" alongside the agency of things in social actor network theory; the *Writing Lab Newsletter*, for example, is anthropomorphized by Phelan and Weber (2021), who describe its mentoring role as follows: "It is a valuable resource not only because of the information it shares, but also because it provides a supportive, inquisitive network of peers and colleagues to which one can turn" (9). When forwarding authors' works to the *Present Tense* review board, we invite them to become part of a similar pay-it-forward mentorship model. That is, once an author has been published in *Present Tense*, we encourage that author to "pay it forward" by serving as a mentor for those authors whose works have received a revise-and-resubmit status from the review board. Authors who have previously published with *Present Tense* have valuable insider knowledge regarding the publication process, and a position of power from which they can guide authors who are newer to the publishing process. As with the education process of the review board, the mentorship process involves explicit education for authors in what it means to be a good mentor, including how to offer holistic support of mental, emotional, and professional needs.

WRITING STUDIES JOURNALS AND MENTORING

Writing studies as a field, then, has started to heed the call of intertwining scholarly publishing, mentorship, and *belonging*. *WLN: A Journal of Writing Center Scholarship*, for example, embraces the mentoring ethos through its "Digital Resources." In addition to its open-access digital edited collections and archived #WCChat discussions on Twitter, which bring together the voices of writing center scholars and the community concerning writing center issues, *WLN* provides archived videos of online webinars in which "*WLN* editors meet in real-time with prospective authors to discuss and workshop issues related to publishing in the academic journal" (IWCA 2021b). Past webinars have included "Introduction to Publishing in *WLN*," "WCA as Hero: A Scholar's Journey to Publication," "Finding Ideas for Scholarship in Everyday Writing Center Work," and "Writing the Tutors' Column: From Submitting to Revising," extending explicit scholarly publishing mentorship to undergraduate scholars (IWCA 2021b). *WLN* also performs inclusive mentorship through its low-stakes publishing environment blog, *Connecting Writing Centers Across Borders*, "a space for writing center people across the globe, especially for those who don't have other writing center specialists nearby, to interact" (IWCA 2021a). In that regard, *WLN* offers not only a space where global writing studies scholars can exercise preparedness to enter the existing publishing system but also a space where seasoned scholars can listen and learn from their early-career and diversely geographically oriented colleagues. Such dialogic attention is but one important step in creating the *methodology of mentorship* we seek to espouse through *Present Tense*, an *ethos* of belonging through mentoring in the academic publishing world.

WLN's efforts in creating access to previously occluded academic publishing process information are duly noted. *constellations*, "an online double-blind peer review publishing space focused on cultural rhetorics scholarship, teaching, and practice," is another example of a team of writing studies scholars explicitly invested in demystifying the peer-review process through mentorship (Constellations 2021a). On their FAQ webpage, they outline seven steps in answer to the question "What does the review process look like once I submit?" Most relevant to this chapter is step 5: "Once your piece reaches either Accept with Major Revisions or Accept with Minor Revisions status, you will be assigned a mentor if you choose to have one. The mentor will help you work through the revision process (see below for an explanation of how that is done)" (Constellations 2021b). Further down the page, *constellations* defines the role of publishing mentor as supporter, helper, interpreter, and revision strategist: "[Because] we believe in transforming the editorial and publication processes to be more supportive, we offer the opportunity to work with a mentor" (Constellations 2021b). While we applaud this transparency and move toward sustained support, we also note the onus is on the author to request and submit to the mentorship process, a notoriously difficult task for those in the position of *needing* help. In a break from *constellations* but in alignment with our identities as writing program administrators, we invest *Present Tense* in mentoring methodologies that situate the seasoned writer as more actively responsible for shaping young writers' confidence and flexibility in scholarly writing processes; while seasoned writers may "opt out" of our one-to-one mentoring paradigm, the default is to be "opted in."

The Coalition of Feminist Scholars in the History of Rhetoric & Composition, sponsor of the *Peitho* journal, similarly commits to mentoring in the publishing process: "The journal's editors will match writers with mentors when a manuscript shows promise but it is either not ready to go out for review or comes back with suggestions for significant revision. Mentors work one on one with writers to help them evolve their manuscripts from draft to re-submission" (CFSHRC 2021b). A newer, more prescriptive initiative of the coalition comprises an online mentoring program in which "mentor-mentee pairs . . . collaboratively establish a schedule whereby the mentee can make good progress on an agreed-upon project (i.e., job market/prepping application materials; planning research projects/fieldwork; writing/revising materials for publication; developing a syllabus; applying for grants; etc.) within six months or less" (CFSHRC 2021b). Such efforts nod toward the deep lines of connection needed for successfully evolving academic publishing ethos through mentorship—but put a six-month cap on the mentoring relationships. This is why the coalition's most recent efforts deserve attention: "The Fellowship Pods Program [is] a non-hierarchical fellowship program to foster community-building among its membership. The program is designed to respond to members' calls for a re-imagining and restructuring of coalition networks that have fostered a culture of elitism and bias" (Pettus 2021). Fellowship Pods are established as yearlong collaborative endeavors meant to produce dialogue and collective action for the explicit purpose, as the coalition notes, of combating elitism and bias in publishing. There is much to be excited about in the coalition's commitment to "disrupt[ing] charismatic models of leadership in the Coalition," or, in other words, taking a long, hard look at oneself and how power is constructed and enacted through existing academic publishing loci, which we feel has great potential to serve as a model for systematic and comprehensive change (Pettus 2021). At *Present Tense*, we seek to emulate the coalition's investment in such feminist methodologies as we operationalize our methodological mentorship on our platform of fast-paced digital publication: "We welcome and *sustain* all who do feminist work, inclusive of all genders, sexualities, races, classes, nationalities, religions, abilities, and other identities, in their research and/or classrooms" (CFSHRC 2021a; emphasis added).

Kairos, "a refereed open-access online journal exploring the intersections of rhetoric, technology, and pedagogy," offers a comprehensive approach to mentoring in academic publishing, one we seek to, in some ways, also emulate at *Present Tense* (Kairos 2021). In their spring 2021 issue, *Kairos* co-editor, Cheryl Ball, outlined several public-facing "Outreach and Mentoring Goals," including open houses (quarterly video drop-in sessions where potential authors can chat with *Kairos* editors about submission ideas), Lunch with an Editor (monthly video chats with writing studies journals editors), Chat with an Editor (monthly or quarterly one-to-one chats with humanities editors), Friday #AskanEditor @kairosrtp (weekly Twitter streams monitored by seasoned editorial staff), KairosCamp ("throughout the year" two-week online institutes to help authors build webtexts suitable for journals like *Kairos*), Ask the Authors (in tandem with each published issue, "10-minute, process-based interviews with authors who have recently published in the journal"), Kairos Research Network (ongoing discussion among *Kairos* staff, discussing works in progress with one another), and webinars (monthly videos relating to *Kairos*, digital publishing, and field professionalization: "creating a video-based class-like experience") (Ball 2021).

Kairos's goals were birthed when "*Kairos* participated in the Technical and Professional Communication editors' Listening Sessions on inclusivity in TPC publishing" (Ball 2021) and speak quite clearly to Cagle et al.'s (2021) "Anti-Racist Scholarly Reviewing Practices: A Heuristic for Editors, Reviewers, and Authors" 2021 call: "We ask: How might we dismantle the existing exclusionary and oppressive philosophies and practices of reviewing in the field of technical and professional communication and replace them with philosophies and practices that are explicitly anti-racist and inclusive?" The authors of this chapter encourage deep perusal of Cagle et al.'s (2021) work as well as participation in *Kairos*'s many open-access mentoring opportunities.

Kairos, like *Present Tense*, operates on an academic publication methodology that weds innovation and open access, which also "recognizes that scholarly publishing traditionally functions within white supremacy. . . . [*Kairos*] works to actively reject those systems of oppression by creating anti-racist publishing practices that are inclusive and equitable for authors, staff, and peer reviewers" (Ball 2021). *Present Tense* seeks to extend publication mentorship methodology to systematically include not only early-career scholars, potential authors, and authors whose work is already on the publication docket but also, and most specifically, those authors who have submitted but will not, at this time, be published in our journal; our methodology places special attention on the molding of effective mentors for sustainable, systemic mentoring as a (the) key component of academic publishing.

CONCLUSION

Mentorship within the professional contexts of academic publishing can help counter some of the invisible hurdles that map, as we note, onto larger systems of inequity in the discipline. As a reminder, when we look at the hallmarks of white supremacy culture, we see its scarring lineage in the current state of publishing even within writing studies: a sense of perfectionism in which it is "more common . . . to point out either how the person or work is inadequate" and in which "mistakes are seen as personal"; a sense of urgency in our limited time to publish and to serve as reviewers for those who seek to publish "that makes it difficult to take time to be inclusive, encourage democratic and/or thoughtful decision-making, to think long-term, to consider consequences"; paternalism, and a lack of transparency in the publishing process (rejection, acceptance, or somewhere in between) in which "decision-making is clear to those with power and unclear to those without it"; power hoarding by the same types and kinds of individuals in editorial leadership positions; individualism and, more specifically, a lingering insistence on individual publication in tenure and review processes (i.e., creating a "desire for individual recognition and credit"); and an overreliance to the Enlightenment goals of objectivity or "impatience with any thinking that does not appear 'logical' " or otherwise falls outside the purview of Western rhetorical tradition (Okun 2021).

While none of these problems can be erased overnight, writing studies journals can make a commitment to more extensive and expansive (systematic!) mentorship that drives toward an ethos of transparency and *belonging*. Open-access, multimodal-friendly online journals have led the charge in public-facing mentorship opportunities for more transparent and inclusive academic publication practices. It is worth noting, in fact, that a product of the pandemic and shift to online learning has made connecting disciplinary peers at different career stages a more popular option through things such as professionalization webinars or social media discussions in writing studies writ large. We hope readers of this chapter will consider the virtues of such access and not only continue these practices but also further imbibe such mentoring opportunities throughout the entirety of the editorial process. That is what *Present Tense* seeks to offer: a model for generative, collaborative publication even and especially in the non-public-facing arenas of publication; supporting authors even and especially if their work is not quite ready to be sent into the circulation of a review board. We want to welcome such authors into the dynamic network that academic publishing could be: not closed circles of editors and review boards but dynamically inclusive circles that are continually evolving through the input of dialogic mentoring relationships.

REFERENCES

Ball, Cheryl. 2021. "Outreach and Mentoring Goals." *Kairos: A Journal of Rhetoric, Technology, and Pedagogy* 25 (2). https://kairos.technorhetoric.net/25.2/loggingon/mentoing-outreach.html.

Banks, William P., and Kerri B. Flinchbaugh. 2013. "Experiencing Ourselves as Writers: An Exploration of How Faculty Writers Move from Dispositions to Identities." In *Working with Faculty Writers*, edited by Anne Ellen Geller and Michelle Eodice, 228–245. Logan: Utah State University Press.

Cagle, Lauren E., Michelle F. Eble, Laura Gonzales, Meredith A. Johnson, Nathan R. Johnson, Natasha N. Jones, Liz Lane, et al. 2021. "Anti-Racist Scholarly Reviewing Practices: A Heuristic for Editors, Reviewers, and Authors." https://ihr.asu.edu/node/3518.

Clements, Jessica. 2019. "The Role of New Media Expertise in Shaping Writing Consultations." In *How We Teach Writing Tutors*, edited by Karen Gabrielle Johnson and Ted Roggenbuck. https://wlnjournal.org/digitaleditedcollection1/Clements.html.
Clements, Jessica, John Pell, Shreelina Ghosh, Matt Cox, Don Unger, Ryan Skinnell, Megan Schoen, et al. 2021. "Volume 9.1: Introspection." *Present Tense: A Journal of Rhetoric in Society* 9 (1). www.presenttensejournal.org/editorial/volume-9-1-introspection/.
Coalition of Feminist Scholars in the History of Rhetoric and Composition (CFSHRC). 2021a. https://cfshrc.org.
Coalition of Feminist Scholars in the History of Rhetoric and Composition (CFSHRC). 2021b. "Mentoring." https://cfshrc.org/mentoring/.
Constellations. 2021a. "About." *Constellations: A Cultural Rhetorics Publishing Space*. https://constell8cr.com/about/.
Constellations. 2021b. "FAQ." *Constellations: A Cultural Rhetorics Publishing Space*. https://constell8cr.com/faq/.
Day, Kami, and Michele Eodice. 2001. *(First Person)2: A Study in Co-Authoring in the Academy*. Logan: Utah State University Press.
Duffy, William. 2020. *Beyond Conversation: Collaboration and the Production of Writing*. Logan: Utah State University Press.
Eodice, Michele, and Anne Ellen Geller, eds. 2013. *Working with Faculty Writers*. Logan: Utah State University Press.
Eve, Martin Paul, Daniel Paul O'Donnell, Cameron Neylon, Samuel Moore, Robert Gadie, Victoria Odeniyi, and Shahina Parvin. 2021. "Reading Peer Review—What a Dataset of Peer Review Reports Can Teach Us about Changing Research Culture." The London School of Economics and Political Science, March 31, 2021. https://blogs.lse.ac.uk/impactofsocialsciences/2021/03/31/reading-peer-review-what-a-dataset-of-peer-review-reports-can-teach-us-about-changing-research-culture/.
Godbee, Beth. 2017. "Writing Up: How Assertions of Epistemic Rights Counter Epistemic Injustice." *College English* 79: 593–618.
Hayot, Eric. 2014. *The Elements of Academic Style: Writing for the Humanities*. New York: Columbia University Press.
Hughes, Bradley. 2020. "Galvanizing Goals: What Early-Career Disciplinary Faculty Want to Learn about WAC Pedagogy." *WAC Journal*, 31. https://wac.colostate.edu/docs/journal/vol31/hughes.pdf.
International Writing Centers Association (IWCA). 2021a. "About Us." Connecting Writing Centers Across Borders. www.wlnjournal.org/about-us/ (site discontinued).
International Writing Centers Association (IWCA). 2021b. "Digital Resources." *WLN: A Journal of Writing Center Scholarship*. www.wlnjournal.org/#resources.
Jennings, Willie James. 2020. *After Whiteness*. Grand Rapids, MI: William B. Eerdmans Publishing Co.
Kairos. 2021. "About Kairos." *Kairos: A Journal of Rhetoric, Technology, and Pedagogy*. kairos.technorhetoric.net/about.html.
Okun, Tema. 2021. "White Supremacy Culture." Dismantling Racism. www.whitesupremacyculture.info/uploads/4/3/5/7/43579015/okun_-_white_sup_culture.pdf.
Pettus, Mudiwa. 2021 "Announcing the Fellowship Pods Program." Coalition of Feminist Scholars in the History of Rhetoric and Composition. https://cfshrc.org/announcing-the-fellowship-pods-program/?fbclid=IwAR1r1-gTCWwif-JNYdEXN0L3s0YLjm6kpEi042e4DdWUETtn57iTUlrLtfc.
Phelan, Molly, and Jessica Weber. 2021. "Our Documented Growth as a Field and Community: An Analysis of the Writing Lab Newsletter." *WLN: A Journal of Writing Center Scholarship* 45. https://wlnjournal.org/studies_phelan.pdf.
Polk, Thomas. 2020. "Something Larger Than Imagined: Developing a Theory, Building an Organization, Sustaining a Movement." *WAC Journal* 31. https://wac.colostate.edu/docs/journal/vol31/polk.pdf.

Watling, Chris, Shiphra Ginsburg, and Lorelei Lingard. 2021. "Don't Be Reviewer 2! Reflections on Writing Effective Peer Review Comments." *Perspectives on Medical Education* 10: 299–303. https://link.springer.com/article/10.1007/s40037-021-00670-z.

8

SLOW MENTORSHIP
A Feminist Methodology for Un/Becoming

Lesley Erin Bartlett, Jessica Rivera-Mueller, and Sandra L. Tarabochia

This chapter is an invitation to engage in a methodology for mentorship that prioritizes the *people* involved in the mentoring relationship. While common approaches to mentorship are often seen as a means to an end, the approach we describe is primarily concerned with the means—process, relationships, and, we daresay, feelings—while keeping ends in mind. Currently, specific ends we are working toward include publication, tenure, and promotion; however, we believe our approach to mentoring is capacious enough for a range of goals and contexts. And we believe that working toward goals can be affirming and humane, particularly when we work together.

Our aim in this chapter is to offer slow mentorship as a holistic, countercultural alternative to neoliberal approaches to mentoring that values "excess," identity work, and agency. Contrary to hierarchical, often assigned, mentoring relationships, the site of our approach to slow mentoring is a voluntary peer writing group. The three of us, Lesley, Jessica, and Sandy, were in the graduate program in Composition and Rhetoric at the University of Nebraska–Lincoln. Although we did not enter or leave the program together, our time at UNL overlapped and we were friends. We all worked with the same dissertation chair, Professor Shari Stenberg, whose feminist influence on our work is strong. After graduate school we went separate ways, but we found our way back to one another and have been meeting online more or less monthly to share writing and discuss our research for almost a decade.

We've lived ourselves into slow mentorship. In many ways, this chapter is about how we've come to understand and theorize what we have been living, consider what might have shaped its evolution, and re-discover what we are learning already exists—so that we may offer it to others. Over time our group has become a space for what Godbee and Novotny (2013) call "feminist co-mentoring," or "(reciprocal and mutual) teaching, learning, and laboring together" (178). We are in different stages of our careers (Sandy is tenured and Lesley and Jessica are on the tenure track), yet none of us holds power over the others. We honor the unique experience and expertise each of us brings in non-hierarchical ways, creating a context for what VanHaitsma and Ceraso (2017) call "horizontal mentoring."

Ribero, Milena, and Arellano's (2019) "comradismo as a culturally specific mentoring approach for Latinas in Rhetoric and Composition" (334) resonates with our experience of horizontal mentorship. Although we do not all identify as Latinas, we agree that what the authors propose is certainly "useful to people of different positionalities" (336). In particular, we are grateful for their notion of a kinship relationship. Kinship, or "chosen family," refers to deliberate social relationships that grow out of shared values and involve deep intimacy and involvement that acknowledges participants as whole people (344).

Horizontal co-mentoring relationships we cultivate in our writing group are ripe for slow mentorship and will be the focus of our chapter. We understand that not every reader will be drawn to slow mentorship, an approach that values relationships, practices, processes, and habits of mind and body that are not always "productive," "efficient," or "appropriate" uses of time according to the values of the (neoliberal) university. But we believe that many readers will feel enlivened and seen as they read, and we hope our chapter helps those readers find each other. In what follows, we start by identifying our key terms as they relate to mentorship: slowness, unbecoming, and methodology. Next, we describe what we call the tenets of slow mentorship, using examples from our own experiences and prompting readers with questions for their own reflection. Finally, we explore implications of slow mentorship by reflecting on how our experience in this group shapes how we approach mentoring in more traditional, often hierarchical contexts and relationships.

SLOWNESS

In our current educational climate, mentoring practices are too often infused with neoliberal mindsets; the current "common sense" of mentoring focuses on productivity and efficiency—publish as much scholarship as you can in as little time as you can, take every opportunity to "professionalize," produce evidence of "success" in teaching and research, build the CV, smooth over the cracks, hide the mess. Although we understand the allure of mentoring models designed to support success according to traditional academic reward structures, we are troubled by neoliberal approaches to mentoring that privilege speed over intentionality, generalizability over individuality, adaptability over transformation, lack of friction over meaningful conflict made invisible and thus devalued. We think here of the teachers and scholars featured in Amy Goodburn, Donna LeCourt, and Carrie Leverenz's (2012) collection *Rewriting Success in Rhetoric and Composition Careers* and in Kristin Bivens et al.'s (2013) *Harlot* piece "Sisyphus Rolls On," for example, which challenge the "narrow representation of success" and "hierarchical constructions of academic mentoring" (Rose 2020) promoted in *Women's Ways of Making It in Rhetoric and Composition* (Ballif, Davis, and Mountford 2008), once considered a "comprehensive guide for achieving success in the 'feminized' field of rhetoric and composition" (Leone 2010, 402).

We hope to contribute to the ongoing conversation about the need to forge mentoring models that disrupt limited definitions of academic success and look to the Slow Movement for inspiration. Maggie Berg and Barbara K. Seeber's 2016 book *The Slow Professor: Challenging the Culture of Speed in the Academy* is just one example of many academic texts that draw on the Slow Movement, which "challenges the frantic pace and standardization of contemporary culture" (x) and pushes back on "the corporatization of higher education" (vii) and the neoliberal mindsets that come along with it (see, e.g., Micciche 2011; Mountz et al. 2015; Tremmel 2017). Slow scholars value "deliberation over acceleration," time for deep reflection, open-ended inquiry, and dialogue (Berg and Seeber 2016, xviii). Slow scholars resist the "language of crisis" that compels hasty action and visible outcomes, and privilege instead mindful behavior and persistent incremental progress (xviii). Slow scholars hold time and space for emotion, including pleasure, and relationship-building. While several scholars bring the principles of the Slow Movement to educational contexts, none that we're aware of have put them in conversation with approaches to mentoring. We see promise in sharing how the notion of "slowness" as feminist practice has defined our experience of academic mentorship.

UNBECOMING

In the title of this chapter, we frame slow mentorship as a feminist methodology for "un/becoming" because for us the process of knowledge-making in the context of our lives often means "becoming and performing identities" other than those we are taught to covet. In fact, sometimes it means actively "unbecoming" the scholars we are *supposed to* want to be. Invoking Jessica Restaino (2019), we acknowledge unbecoming as methodologically essential for slow mentorship in order to honor and celebrate "failure [as] an inseparable, inherent part of complex forms of knowledge making" (53). In that spirit, we reject the finality and the linear, progressive trajectory lurking behind the incessant charge to become successful academics. With Restaino, we embrace Jack Halberstam's (2011) insistence "on the meaning-making, activist inspired slant of failure, loss, and 'unbecoming'" (53). That is, we see slow mentorship as a means of resisting dominant "tendencies toward universalizing method, genre, text, and process in how we do our work," and investing in the reality that so often "failing, losing, forgetting, unmaking, undoing, unbecoming, not knowing may in fact offer more creative, more cooperative, more surprising ways of being in the world" (quoted in Restaino 2019, 53).

Traditional forms of mentoring rooted in neoliberal ideology assume a mentor who has *become* a successful scholar residing in the center, helping a mentee who has not yet *become* successful move from the margins inward (Glenn 2018). In the spirit of Matzke and Tassoni's "mentorship-that's-not-a-mentorship" (this volume), our use of un/becoming blurs easy boundaries between margins and center, troubles the dichotomous mentor-who-is versus mentee-who-is-not-yet relationship, rejects assumptions that the center is always the ultimate goal, and challenges the linear, one-directional trajectory toward that objective. We offer slow mentorship as a possible methodology toward that end.

SLOW MENTORSHIP AS METHODOLOGY

We believe a foundational connection exists between the mentorship one offers and receives and the research, writing, and teaching one can imagine doing. Our engagement with a range of scholarship, including the intellectual, emotional, and physical labor exerted by minds, hearts, and bodies of Black (Faison and Treviño 2020; Green and Condon 2020; hooks 1994; Mckoy 2021), Indigenous (Riley-Mukavetz 2020; Wilson 2008), Latinx (Faison and Treviño 2020; Martinez 2016, 2020; Ribero, Milena, and Arellano 2019; Treviño and Ozias 2022), and queer (Dadas 2016, 60–72; Patterson 2019; Waite 2017) scholars, teaches us again and again that our relationships and ways of coming to know never exist outside racist, sexist, homophobic, classist, ableist, and colonial histories and systems of oppression. Scholars who have and continue to publish and model robust approaches to mentorship and methodology help us recognize the necessity of paying attention to *how* we know as we work within and against these systems. Slow mentorship as a methodology is a process for coming to know that foregrounds critical questions about how we come to know, from whom we come to know, and what that knowing, which is always provisional, makes possible and for whom—questions that might otherwise be ignored or dismissed.

Informed by our commitments as feminist scholars who "embrace as a resource that which is habitually exiled" (Stenberg 2015, 32) and refuse rigid boundaries (between mind/body, intellect/emotion, personal/rigorous, objective/subjective, public/private, etc.), the slow mentorship model values knowledge and knowledge-making practices often rejected in traditional models. Honoring theories of the flesh (Moraga and Anzaldúa 2015), for example, we value knowing that originates in the body; challenging neoliberal discourses of emotional management, we "view emotion as a rich (and rational) resource for knowledge" (Stenberg 2015, 40). Acknowledging different sites of meaning-making broadens what we can know as individuals and as a field. Taking a feminist rhetorical approach to mentoring as methodology, like rhetorical approaches to feminist pedagogy, means performing based on "context, exigency, power dynamics and subjects involved," making "room for multiplicity, inclusion, and agency" (Stenberg 2015, 39–40). In the face of neoliberal purposes, this approach "offer[s] ways to hold multiple, even contradictory, purposes together," so as to take into consideration mentors, and mentees' material needs given existing conditions "as well as to highlight and enact the feminist ideas that may otherwise be obscured in the neoliberal university" (Stenberg 2015, 40).

In our writing group meetings, we come alongside each other in pursuit of the questions that we take up in our writing. Bringing our shared and divergent knowledge and experience, we offer questions and participate in conversation to support each writer in reaching the next step in their project. In this process, we do not school each other into performing already-established methodologies. Slow mentorship is not a process for helping each other enact already-established methodologies; instead, it is its own process, one for synthesizing the questions, passions, and commitments that matter to us. In this way, our writing group meetings provide a context for bringing our whole selves into a space and allowing for those dimensions to interact in new, perhaps creative, ways. Through questioning and conversation, we are able to listen to ourselves rhetorically, better seeing how and why we are making knowledge (Ratcliffe 1999).

Slow mentorship as a methodology focuses more on the process of coming to know than the achievement of knowing. In this way, it is a purposeful way of learning and unlearning, which distinguishes it from simply an approach to mentoring. We recognize scholars need to come to know in ways that are recognizable by their fields through the use of established methodologies. We help each other do this work. However, we also recognize that we are never just gaining and sharing knowledge; we are un/becoming and performing identities. Therefore, slow mentorship as a methodology values our humanity first. It is not focused primarily on productivity. It is focused on knowledge-making in the context of our lives.

In what follows, we offer several tenets of slow mentorship, the principles that drive this methodology we've been living and cultivating with and for one another for years. Our hope is not so much that readers apply or execute the tenets but that they live and feel into them. In that vein, we invite readers to do the following: notice when the tenets of slow mentorship are present or could be present in your current mentoring relationships. Notice when you want them to be and when your instinct is to resist them. Consider which conditions, structures, behaviors, and relationships make them im/possible. How do they resonate with your own processes of un/becoming the person and scholar you want to be? How might awareness of the tenets of slow mentorship help you find others with shared values and commitments? How might the tenets themselves offer a scaffold for cultivating mutual vulnerability and trust that in turn activate and reinforce the tenets?

TENETS OF SLOW MENTORSHIP

Slow Mentorship Attends to Excess over Efficiency

Drawing on pop culture analyst John Fiske, Orner, Miller, and Ellsworth (1996) describe excess as that which "exceeds the norms proposed as proper and natural by those with social control" (72), what Cheryl Glenn (2018) calls "everything else" (159). Many structures of the academy are designed to control excess (Orner, Miller, and Ellsworth 1996, 72). Naming what we are taught to consider excessive (to the writing process, to institutionally defined productivity, to living a successful scholarly life) and the mechanisms by which excess is controlled (typical career trajectories, "research protocols, proper forms of academic writing, and curricular norms and standards") allows us to reposition what we are disciplined to call excess as valid and valuable stories, realities, desires, commitments, emotions, responsibilities, and so on that have been historically and discursively repressed.

Surfacing, naming, and repositioning excess are feminist acts. As Karen Kopelson (2006) points out, "the notion of 'excess' has for some years now served as a productively disruptive trope for a variety of postmodern feminist theories working to counter and subvert dominant, masculinist logics" (para. 1). Slow mentorship, for us, has meant troubling the dominant logics of academia, questioning what constitutes excess, and lifting up that which is considered excessive in our institutional contexts. For another example of attention to excess in mentoring relationships, see Anglesey and Nicolas (this volume). As a methodology, slow mentorship supports a process of coming to know what matters to us as scholars, as women, as humans even when what matters is presumed excessive and must often be embraced at the expense of efficiency—a goal rooted in dominant, masculinist logics that demand trimming the excess. Slow mentorship makes room for "ways [our] bodies, subjectivities, pleasures, fears, histories, and power relations overflow the protocols, norms, and forms that are intended to 'contain' them" (Orner, Miller, and Ellsworth 1996, 73).

For example, we've all had the experience of repeatedly sharing the same draft or messy set of notes with the group for feedback. We frame and reframe our projects, trying on different approaches and insights. We've all been part of other writing groups where this recursive process was implicitly (or not so implicitly!) discouraged in favor of a linear progression of writing development: brainstorm (on your own), draft, receive feedback, revise, and submit. In that trajectory, the mess we share with each other is considered wheel-spinning, getting stuck, wasting time—the writers' and the group members' time. On the contrary, in the space of slow mentorship, we see this as the very process of coming to discern what matters. We stand with each other through the messy processes of writing, bringing the lonely, hair-pulling labor that happens behind the scenes to the center of our work together. "Stuck" is not efficient, but it is real, essential, and it belongs here.

Tending to excess as part of slow mentorship is a radical act. According to Mountz et al. (2015), "Caring happens in private spaces under neoliberalism" (1247). The move to pay "explicit attention to excessive moments, identities, acts" bids caring to "come out of hiding in private times and spaces" (1247). To bring caring to the fore is risky because it counters dominant neoliberal cultural logics. Many university structures, some made more blatant by institutionalized responses to the pandemic, privilege surveillance and management. Tedious processes for justifying remote teaching accommodations demand divulgence of personal medical history, for example, while rigid bureaucratic policies stipulate syllabus statements and limit instructor control over classroom practices around masking and social distancing. Assuming a standard, easily managed neoliberal subject, such procedures thwart care (for self and others) by framing vulnerability as weakness, and the complexity and mess of human lives as excessive and unruly, wrenches in the machine. They discourage generosity, mutual trust, and shared priorities rooted in holistic health and well-being.

In this context, we need opportunities to creatively and collaboratively strategize about how to navigate the risk of bringing an ethic of care "out of hiding." Attending to who we are as humans and welcoming all that weighs on our minds and hearts as we live full lives as mothers, daughters, sisters, life partners, citizens in a suffering democracy, and so on in mortal bodies in the midst of a pandemic, sometimes means we start talking about writing forty minutes into an hour-and-a-half meeting. When we welcome "the unacceptable excess being exiled from the dominant logic," we are establishing new "codes for conducting ourselves in the world" (Ratcliffe 1999, 203). We resist "being" the scholars we are institutionally disciplined to be, and commit to un/becoming, to accepting and celebrating our failures—failure to write and meet efficiently, for example. We "choose to listen for the exiled excess and contemplate its relation to our culture and ourselves" (203). In doing so, we decide who and how we want to be in our lives and in our work and support one another in (re)making and manifesting those decisions over and over again.

For me, Lesley, sharing life-things that seem excessive to the work at hand is a hallmark of slow mentorship. As we draft this chapter, I am working toward tenure, teaching remotely, parenting a toddler while pregnant with twins, selling a house, buying a house, and trying to meet all the other obligations that accompany my current version of adult life . . . in a global pandemic. While there is an overwhelming amount of privilege in that list, there is also an overwhelming amount of, well, overwhelm. In our group, these facts of life are welcome and valued. Jessica, Sandy, and I know about each other's lives outside the university, and the trust we have built as a result of welcoming "excess" makes our scholarly work possible. Each of us pursues scholarship that takes up topics or uses approaches that don't always fit traditional academic molds. Often, the work that is most meaningful to us feels risky. For example, Sandy and Jessica recently supported me as I authored a book chapter that included critiques of assessment processes at my institution. I didn't realize how anguished I would feel as I tried to articulate what felt like an important argument for teachers' and students' agency while also striving to treat the work of my colleagues fairly and with respect. My worries about how the writing would be received by colleagues at my institution could have been considered excessive to the argument I was making, but Sandy and Jessica understood how intertwined my concerns were. Making space for "excess" creates a context where we trust each other enough to stumble toward the risky scholarship we all care about doing.

Our examples of how we've attended to excess in our group are not meant to be models. Rather, we invite you to consider how this tenet functions methodologically; (how) does it surface your assumptions, and the assumptions of those around you, about the place of excess in knowledge-making and un/becoming in your context? What aspects of your life have you bracketed from your work (writing, research, teaching) and mentoring relationships? Why have you bracketed them? Were you given explicit advice to do so? Were you responding to more subtle signals about which dimensions of self are appropriate and which are considered excessive? What have you lost or what do you stand to lose by continuing to exile excess? Who benefits? What have you gained or what do you stand to gain by attending to excess?

Slow Mentorship Creates a Context for Holistic Identity Work

Because slow mentorship attends to excess, it creates a context for holistic identity work. For us, holistic identity work means exploring how all aspects of our identities shape our processes for un/becoming academics. In this way, slow mentorship, like Ribero, Milena, and Arellano's (2019) conception of comadrismo, "injects a much-needed feminist ethos into academic life" (353). Slow mentorship acknowledges the integral connection between our personal and professional lives and provides a context for grappling with the ways these connections shape our understandings of who we want to un/become. This context supports and sustains our un/becoming, because it helps us articulate connections across our identities *and* values the labor involved in that identity work. As Ribero, Milena, and Arellano (2019) point out in their argument for comadrismo, "It's important to receive feedback from other comadres who understand not only where you are coming from and the premises upon which you build your arguments, but also from comadres who value the type of knowledge production you are engaging in" (350). Slow mentorship is enacted through our shared commitment to un/becoming and valuing the messy, recursive nature of that process.

The horizontal nature of our relationship has been an important part of creating a context for slow mentorship to flourish. In our group, we do not fear consequences for sharing negative emotions or challenging experiences; therefore, we don't feel pressure to deny or suppress aspects of our identities that we might want to suppress in more hierarchical mentoring contexts. Because we are not responsible for each other's progress toward particular goals, we can be more responsive to each other; we can practice empathy. In fact, we understand empathy as another important part of creating a context for slow mentorship. With Lisa Blankenship (2019), we believe that empathy is a way of constructing meaning that is "informed by deep listening and its resulting emotions" (5). Empathy is "coming alongside or feeling with the experiences of an Other rather than feeling for or displacing an Other, which is usually associated with pity or sympathy" (Blankenship 2019, 6). Empathy helps us attend to how our lived experiences are situated and "stresses the idea that we are not all simply individuals devoid of context" (Mirra 2018, 8). Therefore, empathy "comes with the urgency to persevere, not through assimilation but through strategies that sustain the soul" (Ribero, Milena, and Arellano 2019, 348). The context created by slow mentorship is a place for discovering, sharing, and modeling these strategies with one another, thereby normalizing these strategies and "asserting [our] right to belong" in our respective fields (Godbee and Novotny 2013, 190). As we walk alongside each other intellectually, emotionally, spiritually, we gain a deeper sense of ourselves and our work. As we've learned about each other's work over time—the origins, the evolution, the rootedness in other aspects of life—we have been able to reference our long-term knowing and help members recall and make connections that might otherwise remain underdeveloped.

I, Jessica, have never wanted to fit in to academia. In making this claim, I draw from Brené Brown's scholarship. Brown explains that "fitting in is about accessing a situation and becoming who you need to be to be accepted. Belonging, on the other hand, doesn't require us to change who we are; it requires us to be who we are" (2010, 25; emphasis in original). My ongoing struggle has been to belong in an institution that would rather have me—someone with a multiracial and working-class background—fit in. This tension has emerged in a variety of ways through my educational journey from undergraduate student to tenure-track professor. And now, the truth is that my ways of knowing have been shaped by my time in academia. For this reason, the identity work that I engage in through this group is so important for my process. Because Lesley and Sandy know me, our conversations provide a context for me to imagine my role in and relationship to academia. Our conversations, for example, have helped me craft language to negotiate my professional responsibilities with my supervisors, an action that has made room for the professional activities that are central to my reasons for being a teacher educator. Through discussing big and small decisions, Lesley and Sandy help me navigate my desire to be a teacher-scholar who is wholly herself and my quest to make room for others to belong, too.

Once again, we invite you to engage in methodological reflection inspired by this tenet of slow mentorship. When have you been expected to "fit in"? When have you enjoyed a sense of belonging? What structures, conditions, behaviors, or relationships contributed to those feelings? When have you felt supported in the identity work to un/become different versions of yourself? When have you been thwarted in discovering or pursuing your own ends in view? What is the relationship between the methodologies, the ways of coming to know (in research, teaching, writing), you feel compelled to embrace and who you are un/becoming as a scholar and person? (How) do your mentoring relationships cultivate (or not) ways of coming to know that align with who you are un/becoming?

Slow Mentorship Cultivates "Located Agency" as a Form of Resistance

Slow mentorship makes space for the cultivation of what Shari Stenberg (2015) calls "located agency." For Stenberg, and for us, located agency is distinctly feminist. Stenberg writes, "Rather than assuming that agency stems from acclimation to dominant structures, a feminist agency interrogates the dominant modes and practices that constitute belonging (Rowe 2005) in the first place so as to illuminate possibilities for alternative ways of moving in and among our locations" (Stenberg 2015, 100). The slow mentorship methodology we practice in our writing group resists the full embrace of neoliberal approaches to mentorship that single-mindedly focus on efficiency and productivity above all else, as the tenets attest. Neoliberal approaches to mentorship rarely make time or space for questioning and critiquing established norms and standards. The focus of neoliberal agency is to fashion oneself to fit existing norms in order to fit in—to ignore, deny, or cut away what doesn't align with the dominant structure (to the extent that such cutting away is even possible). For us, the energy associated with neoliberal agency is misdirected. We see better ways to use our energy—ways that invite a holistic approach to our work and lives and that encourage connection with others.

Don't get us wrong; we want to progress in our academic careers. However, we want something more and different than strictly meeting established standards. We want to pursue work that aligns with our deepest-held values and is true to how we understand ourselves and what we have to contribute rather than pursuing work because it seems trendy or marketable; we want to do our work in connection with others rather than in competition; we want to do and enable work that pushes institutions to be more equitable—work that, by its nature, disrupts the status quo—rather than ignoring inequitable institutional conditions in service of meeting established standards and keeping powerful stakeholders comfortable. Pursuing these aims requires the kind of located agency that slow mentorship fosters. With Stenberg, we argue that "there is . . . a possibility for agency in questioning the conditions of belonging, and this allows us to become participants in our own making and reflexive about the process—and in so doing, we foster alliances with others" (2015, 103).

The holistic identity work described in the second tenet enables the *enactment* of located agency. The slow, holistic identity work that happens in our writing group makes us better equipped to take intentional action informed by our values. Often, we take these intentional actions in contexts that embrace neoliberal values without question. Stenberg (2015) writes, "In the neoliberal model, self-commodification and acclimation—belonging in and to the dominant structure—serve as the pathway to agency. . . . Feminist scholars, alternatively, have long promoted a different means to agency—one that involves embracing a marginal position as a source of knowledge and authority" (2015, 99). Disrupting the "common sense" of neoliberal values in institutional contexts that operate from those values takes energy, courage, and preparation. Slow mentorship prepares us to act in such moments, and our group provides a haven to process whatever happens (good or ill) as a result of enacting located agency.

The slow mentorship methodology we practice in our writing group positions us, as Stenberg puts it, as *participants in our own making*. We aren't only participants in our own making, though. We *help each other* participate in our making. We encourage each other to see what could be possible and to be brave in pursuit of those possibilities. We participate in *each other's* making. As Laura Micciche (2011) writes, "Agency is relational. It entails a conglomeration of resources and activities that exceed a single agent but engulf her in a field of energy and activity" (78). Because slow mentorship makes space for people's locations—and values those locations as relevant to the "real work"—new possibilities for not only belonging but reflection and action emerge.

In a recent writing group meeting, I, Sandy, initiated a discussion about where to submit an article I'd been working on. Several years post-tenure, I was experimenting with poetic inquiry to represent the lived experience of faculty writers, and I was both thrilled and hesitant to submit my work for review. I deeply appreciated Lesley and Jessica's engagement with my drafty writing and thinking over several months and their vigorous encouragement of the direction my work was taking, which felt incredibly risky, if also vital and personally compelling. When I asked for advice about where to submit my manuscript, Lesley adamantly urged me to submit to College Composition and Communication. *I was honored by Lesley's excitement and her resoluteness that my piece deserved the wide audience a publication in CCC would garner. At the time, I was asking myself questions about who I wanted to be as a scholar, a thinker, a researcher, a feminist, a writer. Without the shackles of the tenure clock, I felt freer to participate in my own making, to think more deliberately about the audience I wanted to reach and the scholarly communities and conversations I wanted to call home, about where I belonged. I decided not to take Lesley's advice. In feeling welcome to express her strong recommendations and through her faith in my autonomy, Lesley fostered located agency. She made space for my complex and shifting location as I set my own (new) terms for belonging and took courageous action to live out evolving values and principles.*

Where and when do you claim agency? From where does that agency stem? When has agency been acknowledged and bolstered? When has agency been contained or dismissed? For you, what is the relationship between ongoing identity work and where and how you exercise agency? How do you recognize agency? On whose terms? To what ends do you exercise agency? At what expense? Are the ends worthwhile? For whom? (When) is the energy it takes to garner and exercise agency sustaining? Depleting? Which of your relationships cultivate agency? Which narrowly define or constrain it?

CONCLUSION

Slow mentorship changes how we *feel* as we labor within and against institutional structures driven by neoliberal logics. We all still strive for tenure and promotion in our institutions, fret about how we are building our CVs, worry about annual evaluations, and participate in the high-stakes system of peer review for publication. At the same time, regularly practicing the tenets of slow mentorship—attending to excess, creating a context for identity work, and cultivating located agency—sustains a sense of holistic belonging that feels, well, good. In making space for all aspects of our lives and identities we strengthen those dimensions in ways that fuel our work and generate the energy it takes to resist the systems and structures that would have things—our work, our lives, our identities—and our experience of those things be otherwise.

Although our experience of slow mentorship is rooted in horizontal co-mentoring, we believe the tenets can inform approaches to mentoring in more traditional, hierarchical relationships as well. We've each reflected on how our experience with slow mentorship in this group has informed how we orient to situations where we have more institutional power than mentees—when we mentor new faculty colleagues, direct graduate student theses and dissertations, teach graduate seminars in pedagogy and research methods, and support student writers in graduate and undergraduate classrooms. Slow mentorship in these contexts, we've found, means acknowledging unequal power dynamics and being honest about how power inequities affect the tenets we've described. As teachers and traditional mentors, we certainly look for opportunities to make room for excess, support meaningful identity work, and recognize located agency. However, we must also admit when power dynamics complicate that work, and find ways to leverage our institutional positions to encourage and protect the work of slow mentorship in other spaces. For example, we might encourage the graduate students whose committees we are chairing to form a cohort, and talk explicitly with the group about the tenets of slow mentorship and how those practices might support horizontal relationships. As mentors aware of the value of slow mentorship, we can check in with our mentees to see if they are finding spaces outside our relationship to attend to the tenets, and support them in seeking out or creating those spaces. We know from experience how vital and powerful it can be to have those in positions of power validate practices not typically recognized or valued in the spaces we seek to belong. We can imagine making similar moves as course instructors, helping undergraduate and graduate students in our classes reflect on the tenets of slow mentorship and support each other in finding or creating opportunities to put them into practice.

As we conclude, we are painfully aware of the possibility that slow mentorship may seem just another way to force individuals to take responsibility for untenable working conditions that demand systemic change. Transformation is necessary, and we hope that our articulation of how slow mentorship looks within and beyond our writing group inspires new ways to push for change on a broader scale. At the same time, we hope readers find slow mentorship valuable for working within and against current structures, for participating in their own making. As a methodology, slow mentorship focuses primarily on who we are un/becoming as we make knowledge, rather than exclusively on what we do to make knowledge. At its heart, through valuing excess, creating a context for holistic identity work, and cultivating located agency, slow mentorship is about changing ways of *being* and coming to know.

REFERENCES

Ballif, Michelle, Diane D. Davis, and Roxanne Mountford. 2008. *Women's Ways of Making It in Rhetoric and Composition.* New York: Routledge.

Berg, Maggie, and Barbara Karolina Seeber. 2016. *The Slow Professor: Challenging the Culture of Speed in the Academy.* Toronto: University of Toronto Press.

Bivens, Kristin Marie, Martha McKay Canter, Kirsti Cole, Violet A. Dutcher, Morgan Gresham, Luisa Rodriguez-Connal, and Eileen E. Schell. 2013. "Sisyphus Rolls On: Reframing Women's Ways of 'Making It' in Rhetoric and Composition." *Harlot: A Revealing Look at the Art of Persuasion,* no. 10. https://cornerstone.lib.mnsu.edu/eng-fac-pubs/24/.

Blankenship, Lisa. 2019. *Changing the Subject: A Theory of Rhetorical Empathy.* Logan: Utah State University Press.

Brown, C. Brené. 2010. *The Gifts of Imperfection: Let Go of Who You Think You're Supposed to Be and Embrace Who You Are.* Center City, MN: Hazelden.

Dadas, Caroline. 2016. "Messy Methods: Queer Methodological Approaches to Researching Social Media." *Computers and Composition* 40 (June): 60–72. https://doi.org/10.1016/j.compcom.2016.03.007.

Faison, Wonderful, and Anna K. (Willow) Treviño. 2020. "Race, Retention, Language, and Literacy: The Hidden Curriculum of the Writing Center." In *Learning from the Lived Experiences of Graduate Student Writers,* edited by Shannon Madden, Michele Eodice, Kirsten T. Edwards, and Alexandria Lockett, 92–107. Logan: Utah State University Press. https://doi.org/10.7330/9781607329589.c004.

Glenn, Cheryl. 2018. *Rhetorical Feminism and This Thing Called Hope.* Carbondale: Southern Illinois University Press.

Godbee, Beth, and Julia C. Novotny. 2013. "Asserting the Right to Belong: Feminist Co-Mentoring among Graduate Student Women." *Feminist Teacher* 23 (3): 177–195. https://doi.org/10.5406/femteacher.23.3.0177.

Goodburn, Amy M., Donna LeCourt, and Carrie Leverenz, eds. 2012. *Rewriting Success in Rhetoric and Composition Careers.* Anderson, SC: Parlor Press.

Green, Neisha-Anne, and Frankie Condon. 2020. "Letters on Moving from Ally to Accomplice: Anti-Racism and the Teaching of Writing." *Diverse Approaches to Teaching, Learning, and Writing Across the Curriculum: IWAC at 25,* edited by Lesley Erin Bartlett, Sandra L. Tarabochia, Andrea R. Olinger, and Margaret J. Marshall, 277–292. Fort Collins, CO: WAC Clearinghouse; University Press of Colorado. https://wac.colostate.edu/docs/books/iwac2018/approaches.pdf#page=293.

Halberstam, Jack. 2011. *The Queer Art of Failure.* Durham, NC: Duke University Press.

hooks, bell. 1994. *Teaching to Transgress.* New York: Routledge.

Kopelson, Karen L. 2006. "Radical Indulgence: Excess, Addiction, and Female Desire." *Postmodern Culture* 17 (1). https://doi.org/10.1353/pmc.2007.0006.

Leone, Eden. 2010. "A Review of: *Women's Ways of Making It in Rhetoric and Composition,* by Michelle Ballif, Diane Davis, and Roxanne Mountford," *Rhetoric Society Quarterly* 40 (4): 402–404. https://doi.org/10.1080/02773941003800089.

Martinez, Aja. 2016. "Alejandra Writes a Book: A Critical Race Counterstory about Writing, Identity, and Being Chicanx in the Academy." *Praxis: A Writing Center Journal* 14 (1). http://www.praxisuwc.com/martinez-141.

Martinez, Aja. 2020. *Counterstory: The Rhetoric and Writing of Critical Race Theory.* Champaign, IL: Conference on College Composition and Communication; National Council of Teachers of English.

Mckoy, Temptaous. 2021. "'. . . Had Y'all Simply Listened to Black Women': A Call for Intentional Listening and Impactful Anti-Racist Action." Keynote address presented at Thomas R. Watson Conference, virtual, April 22, 2021.

Micciche, Laura R. 2011. "For Slow Agency." *Writing Program Administration* 35, no. 1 (Fall–Winter 2011): 73–90. https://link.gale.com/apps/doc/A279262792/AONE?u=iastu_main&sid=bookmark-AONE&xid=274aabd5.

Mirra, Nicole. 2018. *Educating for Empathy: Literacy Learning and Civic Engagement*. New York: Teachers College Press.

Moraga, Cherríe, and Gloria Anzaldúa, eds. 2015. *This Bridge Called My Back: Writings By Radical Women of Color*. Albany: State University of New York Press.

Mountz, Alison, Anne Bonds, Becky Mansfield, Jenna Loyd, Jennifer Hyndman, Margaret Walton-Roberts, Ranu Basu, et al. 2015. "For Slow Scholarship: A Feminist Politics of Resistance through Collective Action in the Neoliberal University." *ACME: An International Journal for Critical Geographies* 14 (4): 1235–1259. https://acme-journal.org/index.php/acme/article/view/1058.

Orner, Mimi, Janet L. Miller, and Elizabeth Ellsworth. 1996. "Excessive Moments and Educational Discourses That Try to Contain Them." *Educational Theory* 46 (1): 71–91. https://doi.org/10.1111/j.1741-5446.1996.00071.x.

Patterson, G. 2019. "Queering and Transing Quantitative Research." *Re/Orienting Writing Studies: Queer Methods, Queer Projects*, edited by William P. Banks, Matthew B. Cox, and Caroline Dadas, 54–74. Logan: Utah State University Press.

Ratcliffe, Krista. 1999. "Rhetorical Listening: A Trope for Interpretive Invention and a 'Code of Cross-Cultural Conduct.'" *College Composition and Communication* 51 (2): 195–224. https://doi.org/10.2307/359039.

Restaino, Jessica. 2019. *Surrender: Feminist Rhetoric and Ethics in Love and Illness*. Carbondale: Southern Illinois University Press.

Ribero, Ana Milena, and Sonia C. Arrellano. 2019. "Advocating Comadrismo: A Feminist Mentoring Approach for Latinas in Rhetoric and Composition." *Peitho* 21 (2), 334–356.

Riley-Mukavetz, Andrea. 2020. "Developing a Relational Scholarly Practice: Snakes, Dreams, and Grandmothers." *College Composition and Communication* 71 (4): 545–565. https://search.ebscohost.com/login.aspx?direct=true&AuthType=ip,shib&db=mlf&AN=202018744855&site=ehost-live.

Rose, Jeanne Marie. 2020. "Mother-Scholars Doing Their Homework: The Limits of Domestic Enargeia." *Peitho* 22 (2). https://cfshrc.org/article/mother-scholars-doing-their-homework-the-limits-of-domestic-enargeia/.

Stenberg, Shari J. 2015. *Repurposing Composition: Feminist Interventions for a Neoliberal Age*. Logan: Utah State University Press.

Tremmel, Michelle. 2017. "Forget Formulas: Teaching Form through Function in Slow Writing and Reading as a Writer." *Composition Studies* 45 (2): 113–129. https://search.ebscohost.com/login.aspx?direct=true&AuthType=ip,shib&db=asn&AN=125991882&site=ehost-live&custid=s8875136.

Treviño, Anna K. (Willow), and Moira Ozias. 2022. "A Need for Writing Coalitions: A Chicana's Fotos y Recuerdos—Anticipating (Dis)Identification." In *White Benevolence: Deconstructing White Womanhood in the Writing Center*, edited by Wonderful Faison and Frankie Condon, 44–56. Logan: Utah State University Press.

VanHaitsma, Pamela, and Steph Ceraso. 2017. "'Making It' in the Academy through Horizontal Mentoring." *Peitho* 19, no. 2 (Spring/Summer): 210–233.

Waite, Stacey. 2017. *Teaching Queer: Radical Possibilities for Writing and Knowing*. Pittsburgh, PA: University of Pittsburgh Press.

Wilson, Shawn. 2008. *Research Is Ceremony: Indigenous Research Methods*. Black Point, NS: Fernwood Publishing.

PART 3

Methodological Innovations

Bridging the Slash

9
WHO MENTORS THE MENTORS?
How Writing Center Pedagogy, Labor, and Administrator Status Impact Methodologies

Elizabeth Geib Chavin and Beth A. Towle

Writing center (WC) studies has long been positioned as the kicked dog of writing studies—unsupported, underserved, and ill-treated by the larger discipline and its professional organizations and graduate programs (Geller and Denny 2013). This marginalization narrative, according to Jackie Grutsch McKinney (2013), has largely hindered WCs that take it as the only narrative, not opening themselves to the possibilities inherent in finding alternate stories of how WCs and their administrators operate within and beyond institutions (54–55). Nowhere can we see these dual narratives—marginalization versus a reclaiming of what's possible—more than in the history of WC scholarship. While early WC research began in the oft-criticized tradition of "lore"—telling stories based on the lived experiences of WC administrator-scholars (Grutsch McKinney 2013, 45–47)—current research is diverse, rigorous, and deeply collaborative. WC studies has come a long way since the nationwide writing center boom of the 1970s and the founding of the subfield's most prestigious journal, the *Writing Center Journal*, in 1980. Those early years of WC scholarship were based largely in personal experiences, eschewing empirical research methodologies (Driscoll and Perdue 2012, 13) and done by people who often just "stop over" in WC work as part of a longer trajectory in writing studies (Lerner 2014, 75). However, as both formal and informal research networks have developed, an increased call for empirical research, a growing interest in cross-institutional or collaborative research studies, and renewed focus on the labor and status inequities for writing center administrators (WCAs) have allowed the subfield of WC studies to produce better, stronger, and replicable research in the last decade. These changes have allowed for more methodologies in WC research, and for WC scholars to actually develop their own

https://doi.org/10.7330/9781646425822.c009

methodological approaches. And this work would simply not exist without the mentorship at the heart of WC practices.

When mentorship is discussed in WC work, it is often applied to the collaborative relationship between consultants and writers. The subject of WCA mentorship is present in WC scholarship but is often situated as an activity that focuses on mindfulness (Clary-Lemon and Roen 2008; Concannon et al. 2020; Mack and Hupp 2017) or professional development through a focus on administration (McBride and Rentscher 2020). Rarely is mentorship explored as a methodological framework in which WCAs, WC scholars, and consultants support one another in research through formal and informal networks. We see a need for more work on how mentorship operates between WCAs, WC scholars, and WCAs-in-training. What we do is based in mentorship, so not only do we see mentorship as important within WC studies but also as developing networks outside our WCs and professional WC organizations.

In our definition of mentorship, collaboration and positionality are central tenets, with WC administrator-scholars working together to build new knowledge or change our WC praxis to be more equitable and just. Mentorship is methodological, meaning it is built into how we understand our research and knowledge-making practices. For example, an experienced WCA working with a graduate student on a dissertation can impart knowledge based in experience but also have their perspective changed by graduate students' emerged understanding of the subdiscipline and their position within it. Collaboration, through reciprocal conversation where agency is prioritized, is the foundation for mentorship practices. Mentorship also requires careful consideration of positionality—through mentorship, collaborators acknowledge their relation to a larger objective, demonstrating the student-colleague's respective expertise and discourses. Therefore, we argue, mentorship should lead to knowledge and disrupt power differentials.

In this chapter, we discuss the last couple of decades of WC research and the influence of mentorship networks. We first share our own positionalities as a new WCA and faculty member (Beth) and a graduate student writing a WC dissertation (Elizabeth). We believe these narratives demonstrate our own complicated relationships with WC studies and our own evolution as WCAs and scholars, because positionality is absolutely ingrained in both the history and the contemporary values of WC research and is a central component of our definition of mentorship. Once we establish our own positions, we discuss the unique status, labor, and educational backgrounds of WCAs and how these material issues impact WC research, followed by a conversation about how we see these complications playing out in the methodological history of WCs. Finally, we reflect on where WC studies is now and how it might continue to evolve over the next decade, particularly as we decolonize our research practices and turn toward intersectional approaches in methodology and mentorship.

OUR POSITIONAL NARRATIVES
Beth and Elizabeth

As we present our own narratives, we note that mentorship—especially the receiving of it—has been notably more available for both of us as cis white women in a subdiscipline primarily composed of cis white women. WC studies is reckoning with the whiteness of our professional spaces, and we acknowledge our roles in perpetuating notions of WCs as white spaces. While both of our conceptions of mentorship are rooted in feminism, we also understand that white feminism perpetuates violence, too. We realize that our positionalities, even when we face difficulties, are significantly easier to navigate than those of WCAs and scholars who face racism, homophobia, and ableism every single day. It is our job, then, as both mentors and mentees to listen to others in our subfield with very different experiences than ours, which is why we find it so important to share our own positions here. We cannot fully know the daily lived experience of other WCAs or scholars. Our hope here is that we bring attention to how WC methodology has historically failed to take all perspectives into consideration, but also recognize that WC studies is making an effort (and *needs* to make the effort) to be more diverse in both its material and knowledge-making practices.

Beth

When Elizabeth and I were discussing our own experiences with WC administration and research for this chapter, I said, "It feels like everything I do is mentorship." And it is true that most of my work involves mentoring others or providing opportunities for mentoring, especially now that I am a tenure-track (TT) faculty-administrator. I mentor writers, consultants, and students, and, as the leader of our workshop and outreach program, I mentor faculty and staff all across campus. But this mentorship extends far beyond my own campus. As someone who has worked in WCs for fourteen years and did a WC dissertation, I also mentor new scholars or graduate students in the subfield of WC studies. I see this mentorship work as a way to pay it forward. Mentorship has benefited me through the entirety of my education and my development as a teacher and WCA. Through WC networks—both homegrown networks my dissertation director helped me develop as well as membership in groups such as the International Writing Centers Association (IWCA)—I have had the chance to share and improve my scholarship and thinking about WCs, as well as get help preparing for the job market and my new role as TT faculty. This mentorship is especially important to me as a first-generation student from a working-class background. I see this mentorship as being connected to the tenets of collaborative learning. One of the very first pieces of WC scholarship I read when I began working as a peer tutor was Kenneth Bruffee's (1984) "Collaborative Learning and the 'Conversation of Mankind,'" which had a profound impact on me as a student and eventual scholar. Bruffee's call for collaboration as a form of community-building directly influences how I teach students, direct my WC, and work with colleagues. More recent work on collaboration, such as Georganne Nordstrom's (2021) *A Writing Center Practitioner's Inquiry into Collaboration*, which examines the ethics of collaboration, and William Duffy's (2020) *Beyond Conversation*, about co-authoring, continues to shape my view that collaboration and mentorship often happen together, that to be a mentor is also to be a collaborator in learning and knowledge-making. It is this view that impacts the definition of mentorship as it relates to methodology that we present in our introduction.

However, I also recognize that I come from a relatively unique position: I am a TT associate director with an independently funded WC and a disciplinary home as an assistant professor in the English department at my regional comprehensive university (we will see how uncommon this is later in the chapter when we discuss the status of WCAs). Even more rare is that I co-direct the center with a fellow TT faculty director who also has a doctorate in writing studies with a focus in WCs. It is nearly unheard of to have two TT writing studies faculty co-directing a mid-size WC (fifteen to twenty peer, graduate, and professional tutors) with significant financial support. Because my co-director and I both have backgrounds in WCs, we developed a collaborative relationship where we work together on projects that serve all of our campus stakeholders—students, faculty, staff, and administrators. We both also share a strong partnership with the campus writing program administrator (WPA). Because we are all pre-tenure faculty, all women, and all relatively young, we have built support for each other that we find difficult to receive through the larger institution.

Outside of these campus relationships, I've maintained many of the mentorship networks I built during the job market process, and my former doctoral advisor still mentors me on research and publication. Now that I am several years beyond graduate school, I in turn mentor others with dissertation projects and job materials. I regularly work with Elizabeth and her cohort on fellowship and grant applications, questions about IRB, and idea-sharing sessions for their research. These types of mentorship networks are important because they give us new ways of looking at our work while also carving space for true collaboration built in active listening and mutual labor. As faculty, I advise or read theses on WC research as well as teach research methods at both the graduate- and undergraduate-consultant levels. The models of mentorship provided to me over the years in WC studies have absolutely made me a better, more giving, and more collaborative mentor now that I have the ability to take on more of the position of expertise.

Elizabeth

As in Beth's case, mentorship is an implied and integrated aspect of my work, but it's often unnamed and sometimes unrecognized. As a graduate student and instructor, my positionality in the classroom is much different than that of neighboring faculty and staff. I don't hold the stature of an associate or assistant professor. My older-but-not-too-much-older positionality seems to be approachable for students, particularly young women. As the assistant director of Writing Across the Curriculum and Workshops, I often spend more time justifying my expertise to faculty and instructors across campus than my WC's director and associate directors do. I am currently the only woman graduate student in my department focused in WC studies. At the same time, I still see people in close and relatable positions who look like me. Our administrative staff is predominantly white, as is our campus population. The students and consultants we work with in the WC, however, come from a vast variety of backgrounds—varying in race, gender, sexual orientation, class, and religion. As much as I see mentorship as a positive, foundational component to my success as a graduate student, our university circles are always in danger of fostering non-equitable spaces.

While I do see strong mentorship relationships within my identifiable circles—my initial incoming grad cohort, cohort of graduate women, rhet/comp faculty support system, and community of graduate writers I meet across campus—I see a noticeable difference in WCs. The undergraduate students I used to mentor in our tutor training practicum now mentor me as small group discussion leaders as we check in, share success stories, and work through our struggles and hesitations of tutoring.

I learned from Beth as she mentored undergraduate consultants, which heavily influenced my role in the classroom; I supported her through dissertation drafting, as she does with me now, and as I approach the job market, she coaches me on the lessons she learned. My WC director and faculty advisor referred to me as "a colleague" as we co-taught and pedagogically reenvisioned our undergraduate practicum. Directors, assistant directors, and consultants regularly collaborate on publications and conference presentations. My current three-person graduate cohort of aspiring WC directors share weekly conversations about emotional labor as students and professionals in our connected and unique positionalities. Through writing tutorials with graduate students across campus, we've learned together through conversation and unintentional mentorship that science and engineering methodologies have connections to rhetorical decision-making, concepts of space, and philosophies of human interaction, all of which are important to writing and WC studies. The people who enter WC spaces all take part in a mentorship-based methodology that we build, foster, and rework.

At the start of graduate school, I had a large support system during my first few years of teaching introductory composition—an assigned faculty mentor, a cohort of new instructors, and over one hundred colleagues. As I pulled away from composition to teach undergraduate tutor training at the WC, I quickly learned how different mentorship looks. My departmental colleagues were not as familiar and interested in WC pedagogy. As I focused on my career in WCs, I learned that subject-specific mentorship is tied to relatable knowledge, and relatable knowledge in WC theory and pedagogy seems more isolated than it should be. I fed into the "kicked dog" narrative when I noticed connections between theory and pedagogy of composition and WC studies that many composition scholars didn't see—missed collaboration opportunities between rhetorical lessons that composition instructors teach and the rhetorical scaffolding techniques that consultants use with writers. Agency, voice, reflection, accountability, and synthesis all surround the work of consultants and instructors, but the how, what, where, when, and why of that work always seemed so segregated to me.

As my graduate school journey comes to a close, I reflect on my time as both a mentor and a mentee, realizing there is a common thread that seeps into my research, activism, pedagogy, and everyday informal interactions—mentorship has become a methodological framework that helps to push against colonized "grand narratives" (Grutsch McKinney 2013, 86–87). When I first found WCs, I was an undergraduate struggling with grief, misplaced anger, and unfocused drive. I struggled in some of my English literature classes, but it wasn't because I was a bad writer or unmotivated. I needed support and people to challenge me. I needed to find agency in my writerly voice and a space where I could give that support back to others. WCs quickly became a space where being a student–consultant mentee and mentor naturally meshed.

WRITING CENTER ADMINISTRATOR-SCHOLARS: EDUCATION, LABOR, AND STATUS

In the 1920s, WCs became a remedial supplement for writers who struggled in their writing classrooms, which shifted in the 1940s as "tension emerge[d] between the institutional space of the WC and the individual pedagogies enacted in that space" (Boquet 1999, 467). As open enrollment and minority populations increased in the 1970s, instructors dealt with overcrowded classrooms and increased standardization, and students struggled with a one-size-fits-all writing curriculum. Writing courses began to rely on the help of WCs, which transpired into complicated relationships with the larger field of writing studies, as WCAs and scholars fought for their disciplinary worth with hopes of no longer being a response to institutional crises. Over time, writing support reached disciplines campus-wide, complicating that worth and institutional positionality. WCs were and still are in a unique position in higher education institutions. Consultants do not hold the same hierarchical relationships as professors; consultants don't have power over grades, and their sole objective is to support the students who seek help; and consultants see cross-disciplinary writing through a vantage point unlike any other space on campus. Tutor training became a higher priority, focusing on the diversity of students, their disciplinary contexts, and how identity is interconnected with what, how, and why students write. Consultants became writing mentors. Administrators became writing consultant mentors. Consultants and administrators became cross-disciplinary mentors for all-things-writing. The very existence of WCs is built on a need for support. In this historical arc of WC history, mentorship becomes a methodological approach for learning tutor pedagogy, enacting that pedagogy, and sustaining writerly communities across administration, teaching, and tutoring.

Unfortunately, this complicated history means that there are issues of labor and staffing in WCs that have directly impacted its emergence as a distinct subfield in writing studies. WC administrators enter the subdiscipline from many different educational and disciplinary backgrounds. Only 61 percent of WC directors and 45 percent of associate or assistant directors hold doctorates, according to the 2018–2019 Writing Centers Research Project (WCRP) survey. Some of those doctorate graduates hold PhDs in writing and rhetoric studies, but only a sliver of those wrote WC-focused dissertations. WCAs also come from doctorate programs in English, second-language studies, or education. The rest of the WCAs in the WCRP survey have MAs or MFAs from a wide range of disciplines, and 9 percent of associate or assistant directors have only a bachelor's degree (Writing Centers Research Project 2020). There are WCAs who never stepped foot in a WC before they began directing one themselves, and there are others who lived, breathed, and sweated WCs for years before, like Beth, getting their "dream job" in a university WC.

Part of the reason WCAs come from such diverse disciplinary backgrounds is because the position of writing center administrator is not the same at every institution. According to the National Census on Writing's most recent data, gathered in 2017, only about 28 percent of WCAs have TT positions, compared with 31 percent in nonfaculty staff positions. The rest are non-tenure-track (NTT) faculty or hybrid faculty/staff positions. WCs are located in a myriad of places across campus, too, which means their administrators may or may not be part of an actual department. Only about 31 percent of WCs in the WCRP survey were located within English or writing/rhetoric departments, with the rest located in learning commons, libraries, or other student success centers (National Census on Writing 2021). Beth's WC, while directed by two English faculty members, is technically independent, with its own funding line and reporting chain located in the provost's office. Elizabeth's WC, meanwhile, is closely connected to the English Department and funded primarily by the liberal arts college. This diversity of WC locations, each with their own attendant complexities of funding structures, bureaucratic oversight, and staffing, plays a role in both how WCAs are positioned on their campus and the actual job descriptions of those administrators. And, of course, the inequity of positions directly impacts the ways in which WCAs are able to develop and publish research.

The variety of education and training in WCs, coupled with the issue of insecure positionality within institutions, has historically had a depressing impact on the quality of research in WC studies. Dana Lynn Driscoll and Sherry Wynn Perdue's 2014 study, which looked at the definitions of and beliefs about research among 133 WCAs across the country, found that a quarter of participants said they had "never heard" of RAD (replicable, aggregable, and data-driven, as defined by Richard Haswell [2005]) research and another quarter "dismissed [it] as impossible or not useful for writing centers" (Driscoll and Perdue 2014, 114).

These high numbers are due to the lack of training in writing research methods, unclear definitions of what research is, and the assumption that the primary goal of WC research is assessment that serves upper-level administration. Several years later, in a 2017 study about how institutional status impacts research, Perdue and Driscoll found that WCAs in NTT faculty or staff positions struggled to find the time, financial resources, or institutional support to do research (2017, 195). While this is not necessarily true of all staff or NTT faculty (some of the most prominent scholars in WC studies come from these positions), it is still a problem that WC studies must reckon with, because so much of the subdiscipline is made up of these positions. Professional organizations like IWCA or regional WC associations fill the gap somewhat by offering research grants, but that is simply a Band-Aid on a larger problem. Additionally, because so many people in WCs are not specifically trained in WC scholarship as part of their graduate experience, WCAs are pressured to educate themselves on research methods.

THE ROLE OF MENTORSHIP IN WRITING CENTER RESEARCH

This gap in methodological training, then, is where mentorship comes in. Experienced WC scholars from across position types mentor newer scholars through a variety of ways: through IWCA's mentor pairing program and through social media like the Directors of Writing Centers Facebook group. These options are add-ons or alternatives to the more traditional mentorship that happens through doctoral advising, scholarly conversations through peer-reviewed publications and conference proposals, and networking through conferences. IWCA, as the major professional organization for WCAs, is a primary conductor for mentorship opportunities. Each summer they host a weeklong Writing Center Institute for new administrators who need support in the everyday management of a WC, tutor education pedagogies, and research. IWCA also hosts more informal gatherings, such as a summer writing group. (For an example of a formal, intentional mentorship program, we recommend Alisa Russell and Thomas Polk's chapter in this collection.)

These mentorship models specifically geared toward helping WCAs with research have a direct impact on our methodologies. WC studies has historically been stigmatized by the notion that our research is purely lore, storytelling about one's own center as a way to engage with larger conversations about WC practice. And that's not a wholly inaccurate depiction of WCs for much of their existence in the twentieth century (Boquet and Lerner 2008, 184–186). However, starting in the late 1990s and building particularly in the last ten years, WCs have shifted toward empirical research. The prestigious *Writing Center Journal (WCJ)*, as well as the oldest journal in the field, the *Writing Lab Newsletter*, both include language in their calls for submissions about particular interest in publishing empirical research. It is increasingly rare to see theoretical work published in these journals now, as the focus has especially shifted to being empirical after the publication of Driscoll and Perdue's 2012 study, which found that only 16 percent of all *WCJ* articles published between 1980 and 2009 used RAD methods (Driscoll and Perdue, 2012, 28). These distressing findings were echoed in Neal Lerner's 2014 study of pre-2010 *WCJ* publications and citations, in which he found that "knowledge making is marked by the prevalence of single-authored publications, one-time authors, and cited sources that either rely on the obscure, or non-repeatable, or on a small set of self-referential work" (93–94). Lerner's findings demonstrate that, for the majority of the time WC studies was considered its own subdiscipline, the amount of robust research being published was relatively paltry. Lerner was especially concerned by the number of single-authored articles, because they seemed in direct opposition with WCs' "ethos of collaborative work" (68).

That number has greatly changed in the near-decade since Driscoll and Perdue and Lerner published their articles; it's rare now to find articles published in *WCJ* that aren't empirical or co-authored. There are a variety of reasons for this change in scholarship over the last decade, including increased formal and informal mentorship in WC organizations and networks. Established WC scholars often spend significant time working with newer scholars on how to best recruit participants, develop data collection methods, and analyze data using new programs, such as Lori Salem showing other scholars how to use Chi-squared Automatic Interaction Detection (CHAID) analysis trees for large amounts of institutional data, or experts in specific types of research publishing in Jo Mackiewicz and Rebecca Day Babcock's (2019) recent comprehensive collection about WC theories and methodologies. Without the kind of formal training most writing studies scholars receive as part of their doctoral education, WCAs rely on these models of mentorship to build their understanding of research. Mentorship becomes a way of collaborating with WCAs and tutors on larger-scale, data-driven projects that might not otherwise exist. Because empirical research requires time, space, and resources, several collaborators are often the only way such projects happen. In this sense, mentorship is a platform allowing new methodologies to prosper among collaborators.

MENTORSHIP'S IMPACT ON WRITING CENTER METHODOLOGIES

These networked ways of learning methodologies have a significant impact on the methodologies themselves. WC scholarship is often deeply collaborative; co-authorship is now very common in WC publications. It goes beyond writing and publication, though. Because the very core of WC practice is collaborative, research is as well. It often involves the insight of tutors, student writers, and other WCAs. We are one of the few writing studies subdisciplines that routinely publishes with student researchers, particularly undergraduates, in our major journals or presents with them at conferences. We work across our campuses and across institutions, too. Beth's research, which examines issues of class and marginalization in WCs, would not exist without the collaboration of the other WCAs she interviews, the feedback from other people at her institution working in assessment or first-generation support programs, and mentorship networks that encourage this work or offer feedback. Elizabeth's work with local community organizations and her strong relationships with other doctoral students studying WCs in her graduate program continuously inform her dissertation research. WC methodology is now, first and foremost, based in the collaborative.

Because our research is collaborative, our methodologies outside of assessment tend to come out of qualitative approaches. Our assessment practices are still largely rooted in the quantitative—"bean counting," as Neal Lerner (1997, 1) has called it—in order to justify our existence through the use of data about usage, GPA outcomes, and demographic information. However, our scholarship outside of local assessment is often qualitative in nature. That doesn't mean we only do qualitative work—there is some great cross-institutional work being done around large-scale data analysis right now—but it does mean that we tend to look at the world through a constructivist or transformative lens. We look for the stories our work tells us, and because our work requires empathy and understanding, we want to tell the stories that are true to the complex human experience we find in our institutional networks. There are certain qualitative approaches that are especially common to WC work, such as discourse analysis, case studies, and grounded theory, all of which account for the networked nature of tutoring and administrative work. Additionally, methodologies specifically accounting for networks, such as institutional ethnography, are used to study issues of labor, positionality, and institutional histories, as seen in Michelle LaFrance's (2019) *Institutional Ethnography* and Michelle Miley's (2017) "Mapping Writing Center Work through Institutional Ethnography." These methodologies are used in WCs because of the collaborative, mentorship-focused work that informs the most basic practices of the discipline. The ways in which existing methodologies have been taken up and transformed by WC scholars is incredibly important, despite being largely ignored by the broader writing studies discipline.

Unfortunately, while WC studies has made significant strides over the last decade in making research more accessible to WCAs from diverse institutional contexts, we have not worked hard enough as a subfield to decolonize our research methods. The importance of opening up methodologies beyond traditionally white, male, and capitalistic understandings of writing and collaboration is vital to WCs' increased focus on social justice. There is significant work still needed in decolonizing our research to prevent hegemonic understandings of education and students (Patel 2016; Smith 2012), in opening up cross-cultural ways of knowing (Powell, et al. 2014), and in honoring the many identities held by writers, tutors, and WCAs (Denny 2010). (In her chapter in this collection, Devon Fitzgerald Ralston discusses the impact identity has on how we enact mentorship within our centers.) Some of this work must come from a change in mentorship networks, with less focus on passing down methods or skills and more focus on justice, questioning power dynamics, and diversifying networks through both official avenues like the IWCA Mentorship Program, conferences, and professional organization memberships and through our everyday collaborative practices.

THE NECESSARY FUTURE OF WRITING CENTERS: A FOCUS ON SOCIAL JUSTICE

Decolonization

While WC research has benefited from an increased focus on empirical research and RAD methodologies, we are aware as a subdiscipline that WC research cannot solely rely on these typically white, westernized knowledge-making systems. Rebecca Hallman, Ezekiel Choffele, and Trixie Smith (2015) argue that WC studies has much to learn from cultural rhetorics and should "seek to constellate the qualitative methods of oral history, narrative inquiry, and storytelling to demonstrate how stories can be used in WC research" (Hallman, Choffele, and Smith 2015). The rise of cultural rhetorics has had a profound influence on how writing scholars think about the cultural context and histories of how we make and record knowledge. This focus in writing scholarship coincides with calls for decolonizing our WCs and therefore our methods and models of mentorship in WC studies. While Anis Bawarshi and Stephanie Pelkowski's 1999 article advocating for a postcolonial WC model is often cited within the field, it has taken time for us to apply this thinking to our methodologies (Bawarshi and Pelkowski 1999). The work of newer scholars like Romeo Garcia, Wonderful Faison, and Neisha-Anne Green have asked us to consider how our pedagogies, spaces, methods, and mentorship models have perpetuated racism and colonization in WCs, and we are beginning to finally respond as a subdiscipline. Regional organizations and new journals in particular have been at the front of this movement toward inclusion and diversity of knowledge-making practices. The Mid-Atlantic Writing Centers Association (MAWCA), for example, has established a research grant for WCAs of color or WCAs who serve traditionally underserved populations, such as at HBCUs. *The Peer Review*, an IWCA-supported journal established in 2015, focuses on issues of social justice, decolonization, and methodological inquiry beyond what is being published in established mainstream WC journals. We see this work of decolonization as having a profound impact on how we will theorize, conduct, and write about research in the next decade and beyond in WC studies. Additionally, we hope that this work forces us to reckon with how mentorship has been exclusionary to people of color, making us a white field that has done harm to the often marginalized students we seek to serve. Along with intersectional feminism and a renewed focus on community collaboration, we hope to see a completely revolutionized subdiscipline within the next decade through the transformation of how we position mentorship in WCs. This transformation requires journals and organizations to include more diverse voices in their leadership and in the knowledge they value (particularly, moving beyond a Eurocentric empiricism), as well as more inclusive mentorship models based not in expert-novice relationships but rather horizontal, collaborative relationships. Of course, more work is needed to truly change WC studies, but it can begin a shift in the subdisciplinary narrative.

Feminist Mentoring

As mentioned in our narratives, we see WCs as feminist spaces. Many WCAs and consultants learn that language is gendered, racial, and classed, and that respect is tied to the body, not the language, lessons learned from the biographic and ethnographic accounts of Keith Gilyard (1991), Geneva Smitherman (1977), and Victor Villanueva (1993). Sometimes intersections of identity are the reason a writer is timid, confused, at a loss, or overstressed. Through awareness of "intersectionality," a term coined by Kimberlé Crenshaw (1989), and through enactment of mentorship-based responses, feminism and mentorship work together as a methodology for supporting one another in less hierarchical ways. Feminist methodology, as Verta Taylor and Leila Rupp remind us, is self-reflexive, epistemological, and focused on how knowledge is carried across formal and informal mediums (Taylor and Rupp 2005, 2116). Mentorship, too, carries epistemology through everyday conversations with students and peers in a self-reflexive state. As mentors and mentees, our positionality affects how we interact with others who hold their own unique positionality. As we reflect on the impact of mentorship through our personal experiences and of the historical underpinnings of WCs, we think of our peers who never have the choice to "pass" or "blend in" with whatever sociocultural majority is dominating a space at a moment; we think about the unrecognized and emotional labor involved. We think about Geller et al.'s "Everyday Racism" (2007), where Krista, an African American WC consultant, was regularly asked by colleagues "if she needed to make an appointment" when showing up for her shifts (87–88). And we echo Frankie Condon's (2012) sentiment that "those of us who are white may need to admit we have not yet begun, really, to craft epistemological and rhetorical practices or a performative antiracist narrative tradition," which painfully limits our contributions with "multiracial, antiracist coalitions in doing the work of antiracism" (33). WC theory and pedagogy should be grounded in equity—writing consultants are trained to see language as a vehicle for accessing others and as a symbol of oppression. Enacting intersectional feminist methodology in WC research means approaching public(s) with an awareness of unequal power and institutionalized hierarchies across social, economic, and political spheres. Feminist mentoring as we described here, is one framework or way of thinking about mentorship as a methodology. We see these intersectional models of feminism continuing to take shape in WC work, especially as it relates to mentorship.

Community Engagement

Because WCs often pride themselves on being less authoritative and more collaborative, they are spaces focused on meeting writers where they are in the moment. From a pedagogical standpoint, WCs are "particularly well suited for ethical and sustainable community work" (Nichols and Williams 2019, 88) and, we argue (cautiously), well-suited due to our mentorship-based methodologies and feminist frameworks. WCAs have the privilege and capability of asking tough questions about writing support: How might a parent who's applying for an industry job receive help on their resume? What support might a nontraditional prospective student receive on composing their college applications? How might a non-academic-affiliated community member receive help on a legal appeal letter? However, sustainability, reciprocity, and agency need priority. WCs may be "well suited" for community engagement work, but only with accessible approaches that serve both academic and non-academic parties. Sustainability is hindered as consultants are only in a WC for a few years, as grad students who take on administrative positions move on to other institutions, and as WCAs have institutional boundaries to work within. We think of Nicole I. Caswell, Rebecca Jackson, and Jackie Grutsch McKinney's (2016) book, *The Working Lives of New Writing Center Directors*, here; we see various forms of labor and institutional expectations that are expected of WCAs, and when we add collaboration with local spaces into that mix, that labor becomes even more complex. Even if all institutional logistics fall into place, there is a larger ethical factor at play that overrides well-thought-out pedagogy; if faculty, students, or consultants are involved, there is always risk of disseminating westernized systems of education back into communities. As WC community engagement continues to find its way, we wonder what space mentorship-based methodologies have. We hope mentorship becomes an extended practice, a way of thinking and problem solving, and a foundation for equitable spaces.

CONCLUSION

Mentorship is embedded within the pedagogical and philosophical ideologies of everyday WC praxis and in our scholarship. Despite the often frequent lack of access to resources, time, and TT positions, WCAs have produced a rich body of research that has largely emerged out of collaborative methodologies that are the result of ingrained mentorship and mentoring practices. Mentorship is perhaps the single most important factor in how WCAs learn to do research, develop research projects, and use or transform existing methodologies to learn more about how people write, work, and operate within complex institutional networks.

Looking forward, we see a new wave of WC professionals as more graduate students are intentionally seeking WCA positions. The influx of graduate students wanting to specialize in WCs, combined with increased calls for fairer labor practices in the subdiscipline, also provides us an opportunity. Elizabeth's work in meta-analysis methodologies and community WCs; Beth's work on first-generation and working-class student support in WCs; and the work of our colleagues in studying the connection between WCs and empathy, language, social justice, and institutionality demonstrate the wide range of topics, but also the emerging methodological perspectives, in contemporary WC work. Looking back at the history of WCs can feel bleak, especially as we see how long it took for WC researchers to produce scholarship on par with other subdisciplines in writing studies. But the future looks bright. New methods, paradigms, and models of mentorship are emerging from WCAs, who themselves often had to go outside the traditional mentoring of graduate programs to learn and make change in WCs. We expect to see traditional mentoring have a larger role in how graduate students, for example, are trained in research, but we also see a continued need and desire for the type of collaborative mentoring across expertise, age, and position type that has helped WCs become a mainstay of American higher education institutions.

REFERENCES

Bawarshi, Anis, and Stephanie Pelkowski. 1999. "Postcolonialism and the Idea of a Writing Center." *Writing Center Journal* 19, no. 2 (Spring/Summer): 41–58. https://www.jstor.org/stable/43442836.

Boquet, Elizabeth. 1999. "'Our Little Secret': A History of Writing Centers, Pre- to Post-Open Admissions." *College Composition and Communication* 50, no. 3 (February): 463–482. https://doi.org/10.2307/358861.

Boquet, Elizabeth, and Neal Lerner. 2008. "Reconsiderations: After 'The Idea of a Writing Center.'" *College English* 71, no. 2 (November): 170–189. https://www.jstor.org/stable/25472314.

Bruffee, Kenneth A. 1984. "Collaborative Learning and the 'Conversation of Mankind.'" *College English* 46, no. 7 (November): 635–652. https://doi.org/10.2307/376924.

Caswell, Nicole I., Rebecca Jackson, and Jackie Grutsch McKinney. 2016. *The Working Lives of New Writing Center Directors*. Logan: Utah State University Press.

Clary-Lemon, Jennifer, and Duane Roen. 2008. "Webs of Mentoring in Graduate School." *Stories of Mentoring: Theory and Praxis*, edited by Michelle F. Eble and Lynee Lewis Gaillet, 178–192. Anderson, SC: Parlor Press.

Concannon, Kelly, Janine Morris, Nicole Chavannes, and Veronica Diaz. 2020. "Cultivating Emotional Wellness and Self-Care through Mindful Mentorship in the Writing Center." *Writing Lab Newsletter* 44, no. 5–6 (Summer): 10–17. https://wlnjournal.org/archives/v44/44.5-6.pdf.

Condon, Frankie. 2012. *I Hope I Join the Band: Narrative, Affiliation, and Antiracist Rhetoric*. Logan: Utah State University Press.

Crenshaw, Kimberlé. 1989. "Demarginalizing the Intersection of Race and Sex: A Black Feminist Critique of Antidiscrimination Doctrine, Feminist Theory, and Antiracist Politics." *University of Chicago Legal Forum* 44 (1): 138–167. http://chicagounbound.uchicago.edu/uclf/vol1989/iss1/8.

Denny, Harry C. 2010. *Facing the Center: Toward an Identity Politics of One-to-One Mentoring*. Logan: Utah State University Press.

Driscoll, Dana Lynn, and Sherry Wynn Perdue. 2012. "Theory, Lore, and More: An Analysis of RAD Research in *The Writing Center Journal*, 1980–2009." *Writing Center Journal* 32 (2): 1–39. https://doi.org/10.7771/2832-9414.1744.

Driscoll, Dana Lynn, and Sherry Wynn Perdue. 2014. "RAD Research as a Framework for Writing Center Inquiry: Survey and Interview Data on Writing Center Administrators' Beliefs about Research and Research Practices." *Writing Center Journal* 34, no. 1 (Fall/Winter): 105–133. https://doi.org/10.7771/2832-9414.1787.

Duffy, William. 2020. *Beyond Conversation: Collaboration and the Production of Writing*. Logan: Utah State University Press.

Geller, Anne Ellen, and Harry Denny. 2013. "Of Ladybugs, Low Status, and Loving the Job: Writing Center Professionals Navigating Their Careers." *Writing Center Journal* 33 (1): 96–129. https://doi.org/10.7771/2832-9414.1758.

Geller, Anne Ellen, Michele Eodice, Frankie Condon, Meg Carroll, and Elizabeth H. Boquet. 2007. "Everyday Racism: Anti-Racism Work and Writing Center Practice." *The Everyday Writing Center: A Community of Practice*, edited by Anne Ellen Geller, Michele Eodice, Frankie Condon, Meg Carroll, and Elizabeth H. Boquet, 87–109. Logan: Utah State University Press.

Gilyard, Keith. 1991. *Voices of the Self: A Study of Language Competence*. Detroit, MI: Wayne State University Press.

Grutsch McKinney, Jackie. 2013. *Peripheral Visions for Writing Centers*. Logan: Utah State University Press.

Hallman, Rebecca, Ezekiel Choffele, and Trixie Smith. 2015. "Re(Focusing) Qualitative Methods for Writing Center Research." *The Peer Review* 0 (Fall). https://thepeerreview-iwca.org/issues/issue-0/refocusing-qualitative-methods-for-writing-center-research/.

Haswell, Richard. 2005. "NCTE/CCCC's Recent War on Scholarship." *Written Communication* 22, no. 2 (April): 198–223. https://doi.org/10.1177/0741088305275367.

LaFrance, Michelle. 2019. *Institutional Ethnography: A Theory of Practice for Writing Studies Researchers*. Logan: Utah State University Press.

Lerner, Neal. 1997. "Counting Beans and Making Beans Count." *Writing Lab Newsletter* 22, no. 1 (September): 1–3. https://wlnjournal.org/archives/v22/221.pdf.

Lerner, Neal. 2014. "The Unpromising Present of Writing Center Studies: Author and Citation Patterns in 'The Writing Center Journal,' 1980–2009." *Writing Center Journal* 34, no. 1 (Fall/Winter): 67–102. https://www.jstor.org/stable/43444148.

Mack, Elizabeth, and Katie Hupp. 2017. "Mindfulness in the Writing Center: A Total Encounter." *Praxis: A Writing Center Journal* 14 (2). www.praxisuwc.com/mack-and-hupp-142.

Mackiewicz, Jo, and Rebecca Day Babcock. 2019. *Theories and Methods of Writing Center Studies: A Practical Guide*. New York: Routledge.

McBride, Maureen, and Molly Rentscher. 2020. "The Importance of Intention: A Review of Mentoring for Writing Center Professionals." *Praxis: A Writing Center Journal* 17 (3). http://www.praxisuwc.com/173-mcbride-and-rant.

Miley, Michelle. 2017. "Looking Up: Mapping Writing Center Work through Institutional Ethnography." *Writing Center Journal* 36 (1): 103–129. https://www.jstor.org/stable/44252639.

National Census on Writing. 2021. "2017 Four-Year Institution Survey." University of California San Diego, March 22, 2021. https://writingcensus.ucsd.edu/survey/4/year/2017 question_name=s4y2017admin57&op=Submit#results.

Nichols, Amy McCleese, and Bronwyn T. Williams. 2019. "Centering Partnerships: A Case for Writing Centers as Sites of Community Engagement." *Community Literacy Journal* 13, no. 2 (Spring): 88–106. https://doi.org/10.25148/clj.13.2.009071.

Nordstrom, Georganne. 2021. *A Writing Center Practitioner's Inquiry into Collaboration: Pedagogy, Practice, and Research*. New York: Routledge.

Patel, Leigh. 2016. *Decolonizing Educational Research: From Ownership to Answerability*. New York: Routledge.

Perdue, Sherry Wynn, and Dana Lynn Driscoll. 2017. "Context Matters: Centering Writing Center Administrators' Institutional Status and Scholarly Identity." *Writing Center Journal* 36 (1): 185–214. https://www.jstor.org/stable/44252642.

Powell, Malea, Daisy Levy, Andrea Riley-Mukavetz, Marilee Brooks-Gillies, Maria Novotny, and Jennifer Fisch-Ferguson. 2014. "Our Story Begins Here: Constellating Cultural Rhetorics." *Enculturation* 18, no. 25 (October). http://enculturation.net/our-story-begins-here.

Smith, Linda Tuhiwai. 2012. *Decolonizing Methodologies: Research and Indigenous Peoples.* Ireland: Zed Books.

Smitherman, Geneva. 1977. *Talkin and Testifyin: The Language of Black America.* Detroit, MI: Wayne State University Press.

Taylor, Verta, and Leila J. Rupp. 2005. "When the Girls Are Men: Negotiating Gender and Sexual Dynamics in a Study of Drag Queens." *Signs: Journal of Women in Culture and Society* 30, no. 4 (June): 2115–2139.

Villanueva, Victor. 1993. *Bootstraps: From an American Academic of Color.* Pullman: Washington State University Press.

Writing Centers Research Project. 2020. "Writing Centers Research Project 2018–2019 Survey Results." Purdue University, February 18, 2021. https://owl.purdue.edu/research/writing_centers_research_project_survey.html.

10
RETHINKING MENTORSHIP THROUGH INSTITUTIONAL ETHNOGRAPHY AND WRITING CENTER PEDAGOGY
Mapping Up to Engage in Transformative Work

Anna Sicari

As a writing center scholar and director, my work has always centered around mentorship, as writing center pedagogy focuses on key concepts and values Amy McCleese Nichols and Bronwyn T. Williams (2019) detail: "Institutional interaction, ongoing critiques of power structures, and collaborative goal-setting and decision-making" (89). While writing center work goes beyond the one-on-one tutoring sessions, the philosophy of working with writers individually and holistically in a space that values reciprocity of learning is key to my own philosophy of mentorship. Michelle Miley (2018), a writing center scholar, discusses this idea of reciprocity of learning in her article "Mapping Boundedness and Articulating Interdependence between Writing Centers and Writing Programs." The writing center is a place that encourages learning to occur and happen in all different places—the consultants / peer tutors, the director, the students that we work with. Writing center work is—at its heart—relational work; we are aware that the work that we do in the institution is grounded in our work with one another. Like writing center work, mentorship is relational—it is dynamic and should be a space of reciprocal learning. I am also a strong advocate of the writing center being a space that encourages institutional change, and it has the potential to be a leading unit in working and learning from and with difference as higher education attempts to take on antiracist, and social justice, initiatives. If the goal is to create institutional change as we mentor and collaborate with others, particularly and especially with colleagues and academics of a new generation, values and practices of writing center pedagogy are crucial to engage.

This essay will show how institutional ethnography (IE) as a methodology can better inform our mentorship practices, and how our work in mentorship, particularly when grounded in writing center pedagogy, can help us understand how IE works; that is, mentorship is a practice that can shed light on how IE can better help us understand how practices get normalized and reenacted. As Marie Campbell and Frances Gregor write in their primer for IE researchers, *Mapping Social Relations: A Primer in Doing Institutional Ethnography* (2004), "People participate in social relations, often unknowingly, as they act competently and knowledgably to concert and coordinate their own actions within professional standards" (31). While scholarship has been done on mentorship, very often people mentor based on what they have experienced themselves and witnessed others experiencing in their local departments; mentorship can show how IE is useful for educators, particularly those in the field, to do better, particularly if the field is recognizing and understanding its limitations and privileging of white practices and standards. In this chapter, I will examine three different case studies on mentorship that I experienced and, utilizing IE, map the knowledge from these experiences to better understand the complicated power dynamics, differing positionalities, and institutional policies and practices that informed these experiences, as well as the traditional academic cultures and philosophies that served as models for me. These case studies are representative of the different relationships we form in our everyday work lives: a conversation with an undergrad tutor, a meeting with a graduate student working on their doctoral dissertation, and collaboration with a colleague I am co-authoring with. Using IE to better understand discourses that dominate understandings of mentorship, and to tease out the ruling relations in these institutional relationships, I will examine ways in which the values of writing center pedagogy (collaborative decision-making, institutional interaction, and ongoing critiques of power) created a space of mystery for responsive mentorship (Hinsdale 2015) through the interpersonal relationships to enact institutional change, albeit through the one-on-one. These case studies will serve as models on how both IE and WC pedagogy can help rethink mentorship if we, as mentors and writing studies scholars, are to do the *work* in transforming the institutional structures that continue to harm and exclude.

WRITING CENTER PEDAGOGY, INSTITUTIONAL ETHNOGRAPHY, AND RESPONSIVE MENTORSHIP

For the sake of this chapter, and my own specific use of WC pedagogy to inform mentorship, I am focusing on the writing center values of institutional interaction, ongoing critiques of power structures, and collaborative goal-setting and decision-making, as these values have been crucial. These values would not occur without a focus on communal listening and radical relationality; two pedagogical values the WC offers. These values allow for the WC to be radical, if we use them to intentionally learn from difference and question norms and practices the institution perpetuates. Laura Greenfield (2020) writes, "These norms stand to be interrogated and engaged differently, not merely by students presumed falsely to be 'outside' the system but equally so by students who feel very much at home within it. A radical politics reminds us we are all responsible for resisting these systems, and therefore the standardized methods stand to be resisted as well" (123). To better interrogate standard practices and policies regulated by institutional power, I believe it is extremely necessary for writing center directors and scholars to utilize IE, and here I am acknowledging Michelle Miley's (2018) particular call for IE in the WC, if we are to better illuminate how bad practices become normalized; IE as a methodology and as a practice (to cite work being done by scholars Melissa Nicolas and Michelle LaFrance) can help us better understand the positioning of the WC and institutional interactions, and how this will help us become better mentors.

While there are many different stakeholders and individuals in academic institutions who still view the writing center as a "fix-it" shop (Boquet 1999; Boquet and Lerner 2008; Grutsch McKinney 2013; Lerner 2014), and there are valid criticisms of the writing center existing as a space of regulation (Burrows 2016; Denny 2010; Condon and Young 2016; Garcia 2017; Grimm 1999; Greenfield 2020; Lockett 2019; Sicari and Garcia 2022), the potential of the writing center and the dynamic learning that can occur in that space is necessary to examine and better understand. Writing center pedagogy places a premium on listening to learn, and here I will explicitly emphasize the importance of listening to learn with and empower individuals who walk in our doors, and validate their experiences and writing. The focus on the interaction and exchange in learning is important, as the WC values reciprocal knowledge and mutual trust and respect; with a de-emphasis on traditional academic hierarchies, all who enter the space ideally recognize that we can learn from one another when we listen to our stories and perspectives. As I have argued elsewhere, "through one-with-one writing sessions, writers and tutors have the opportunity to have a meaningful dialogue, openly discussing the feelings and emotions associated with writing and surviving the academy" (Sicari

2018, 201). While "surviving" might seem to some as a bleak approach to academic work, particularly when discussing transformational practices and institutional change, I draw from the theoretical work on Black feminist scholars such as Audre Lorde and, most recently, Alexis Pauline Gumbs (2012), when she writes in "The Shape of My Impact," "Survival has never meant bare minimum, mere straggling breath, the small space next to the line of death. . . . Survival is a promise. It is not a promise that any university or non-profit organization can make to me." While I certainly do not want to appropriate the lives and experiences of Black women that Gumbs is directly referring to in this essay, I do want to apply her theory on survival, particularly in relation to academic institutions, as a white woman WC director and scholar who aims to be a better accomplice in antiracist, social justice work. Gumbs discusses the need for those who the institution does *not* love—that is, those who are not white, not male, not able-bodied—to survive through community, through the relational. The writing center can be that space—if the field recognizes that the people who walk through the doors are people we need to learn from to create a community for change. For more work on how the writing center is a space for mentorship, please see Devon Fitzgerald Ralston's chapter in this collection.

Institutional ethnography is grounded in standpoint theory; that is, IE begins in people's lived experiences. Dorothy Smith (2005), the developer of IE, discusses how important her own lived experience was and is to institutional ethnography, as she explored her experiences in the workplace as a woman. Her involvement with the feminist movement and participation in consciousness raising is especially important, as IE is a methodology designed for women and marginalized bodies to speak from their perspectives and lived experience as a starting place to research. Mentorship, as we know, is personal, and research on mentorship needs to better address the lived realities of mentoring relations. IE allows for us to better understand institutional interactions as we better understand the people involved in such interactions through an examination of texts, ruling relations, and institutional discourses. As Michelle LaFrance and Melissa Nicolas (2012) write in their article "Institutional Ethnography as Materialist Framework for Writing Program Administrators," "As a form of critical ethnography, IE does not seek to generalize about or to understand the 'structures' commonly found at similar institutional locations. Rather, IE asks ethnographers to focus on individuals and to understand their personal experiences as uniquely responsive to the social organizations of institutions" (134).

This idea is key to needed research on mentorship and my argument, as this essay focuses on and starts with individuals and personal experiences, namely, my research narrative through IE and my observations and reflections on notes I took during these mentoring experiences and conversations I had during and afterward with the participants. I will note here that I received consent from the participants in these narratives to include them in this book chapter, and they helped me with my analysis. This essay focuses on local institutional discourses and national discourses of the field and teases out how individuals experience and are shaped by (and shape) discourses.

Gruwell and Lesh (2021) ask an important question in their CFP, "How might our performances of mentorship shape our methodologies?" I believe it is important to dwell on the performative and embodied aspects of mentorship, and how these acts shape how and what we come to know. In Shannon Madden et al.'s (2021) text, *Learning from the Lived Experiences of Graduate Student Writers,* they write, "Perhaps it is time to reconsider our mentoring practices. The traditional model of apprenticeship through which graduate students learn to perform research by carrying out faculty designs . . . is a colonized model. . . . As becomes clear, knowledge innovations will require new research methods and patterns of communication (Hendry 2009; Tardy 2016); as such, they will also require new mentoring models" (16). This chapter argues that mentoring models can and should shape our research methodologies (and vice versa), if we choose to learn from difference and shape our performances based on responsiveness and relationality. Much scholarship on feminist mentorship (Godbee and Novotny 2013; Melonçon et al. 2015) discusses the need to flatten hierarchies within existing mentorship relationships; E. Shelley Reid (2008) discusses the importance of peer mentorship and ways to better develop and support peer mentoring relations, and Gail Y. Okawa (2002) writes on mentoring as a "cultural and activist project" in which multiethnic mentoring networks should be formed so people can learn from each other's cultural perspectives to change the mentoring paradigm. These are models of mentorship that, as a field, we need to learn from, and I believe IE allows us to map the differing relationships and models and, through use of texts and interviews, helps us create new knowledge from the data.

Responsive mentorship is important to my own work as a mentor, particularly as a cis-gender white woman, and it serves a model of mentorship that can be created and developed by institutional ethnography and simultaneously better help us understand and rethink IE as a methodology for institutional change. Mary Jo Hinsdale (2015) writes on the importance of mystery in mentorship: "Differences of ethnicity, sexuality, ability, and first-generation status contribute to mystery. . . . Transformative, decolonizing mentorship across difference strives to hold students' otherness and mystery in the foreground so that we might recognize the imperative to respond to them" (103). Hinsdale advocates to enter mentoring relationships through mystery, so that we allow for differences to shape the relationship, with an understanding that there will be trust relationally and in the process. Hinsdale urges mentors to disrupt traditional academic norms and discourses, to fight against the "rational community" of the academy to better respond to protégés of difference, those who have been excluded from academic structures, and learn from them through listening, mutual trust, acknowledgment of privilege, and even vulnerability. IE, like Hinsdale's use of mystery, is, to cite Dorothy Smith (2006), a "process of discovery" and always starts with the individual and their embodied experiences in the workplace; IE allows us to examine how these individual experiences and relationships are often coordinated beyond their local settings; that is, they are shaped and influenced by academic discourses and structures, the rational community. IE can allow us to discover when mystery happens in mentorship through looking at coordinated influences, dominating texts, and how mystery can occur because of working within such confines; mystery can allow us to complicate IE further, as we look at ways difference might impact ruling relations and standpoint.

Responsive mentorship, WC pedagogy, and institutional ethnography inform and intersect to provide new knowledge in how we form relations with others to make new knowledge. IE encourages us to learn from the relational, and WC pedagogy and responsive mentorship provide paths to better create relationships of reciprocal learning and trust for institutional change; in turn, mentorship allows us to better inform our methodologies, as we draw from the local to "map up" and think about the role difference plays in research methodologies, specifically IE, as we learn about "how things happen"; in workplace settings, learning from difference can help us better learn "how we can make things happen," particularly in white-dominant institutions. The next section takes us to case studies in which I will analyze and unpack lived mentoring experiences through IE, WC pedagogy, and responsive mentorship; these cases will involve failures of mine and how such issues were resolved through mentoring methodologies.

MENTORING RELATIONSHIPS ACROSS THE ACADEMY: THREE STORIES

Learning from Lived Experience: A Conversation with an Undergrad Tutor

Days in the writing center are almost always busy, and while this certainly helps create a dynamic space in which "learning happens everywhere," it can also hinder my ability to be self-reflexive and to "listen for silence and mystery." One busy day, an undergraduate tutor, a young Black woman pursuing a degree in English, came in to tell me about a difficult session she had with a writer. This was an individual she knew already—they were in several English classes with her throughout her college career and she told me, up front, "I don't like him." Busy and prepping for class, I asked her to tell me what happened in the session. She gave me the background of their relationship, he would talk over her, never valued her input in peer review, often was a class favorite among professors. She said that he told her immediately he knew he didn't have to come to the writing center, but it was a required assignment in one of his advanced writing courses he was taking, and that all sessions were booked except for her. Despite this blatant outward sign of disrespect, she went ahead with the session, in which she said he either contested her suggestions and thoughts or nodded as to dismiss. She told me she didn't know how to deal with such racist bullshit, and before coming to me, she looked to our handbook's section on tutors' "rights and responsibilities." In the WC handbook, there is a list of tutors' rights, one being "the right to a safe and respectful working environment." She felt that right, particularly the respectful component to that right, was violated, and yet she was not sure; she felt this was certainly a microaggression, but did the writing center have policy against microaggressions? And what exactly was her right? Did we have the right to refuse services to someone acting disrespectful in a session? Did we have, she pressed, antiracist policy that tutors, particularly tutors of color, could use in situations like this? We started scanning the handbook together (a handbook inherited to me that I have made changes to here and there but have not fully revised, as we have been focusing on the mission statement and website). We did not have an antiracist policy anywhere in our handbook. While I turned my attention to other ruling texts—our mission statement and the website, which describes our pedagogy and practices—I had ignored an important document due to the constant, everyday business and perhaps my own disregard for handbooks that focus too much on policies and procedures and professionalism. However, a handbook is certainly a boss text; to quote Smith (2006), it is a text that is "foundational media of co-ordinating people's work activities, including talk . . . in institutional complexes" (65).

As relationality is important, I want to establish that this young woman and I have a close relationship; I am an advisor on her undergraduate thesis and have worked with her the past two years in the WC. I believe that is why she was able to come to me to ask about policies, or lack thereof, in the writing center and ways in which she can be protected from racism. I also want to acknowledge, however, that I am a white woman—my understanding of racism is severely limited, and while I can think about my experiences with gender and sexism and how they intersect—and they do—my privilege cannot be denied. Carmen Kynard (2015) writes about the importance of Black mentors centering Black lives in the academy; one way, as a white woman, that I can center Black lives is to keep listening to those with lived experience and to adopt an ethics of love (hooks 1994). Hinsdale (2015) writes, "To choose love . . . is to remember to drop our defenses, to stop our inner dialogue so that we can listen fully and deeply—to truly hear what a student is saying. . . . In choosing love, we accept the need for an 'ethical hesitation,' in which we are . . . unsure of our abilities to relate across difference" (133). Love and working with the whole person are important in my understanding of ruling relations, especially if we are to think about the institutional hierarchies and how they impact mentoring relationships. Ruling relations is a core concept to IE, and they are, as Smith (2006) details, "that extraordinary yet ordinary complex set of relations . . . that organize us across space and time" (10). Ruling relations draw on complexes of power that organize our daily practices. The ruling relation in this situation is that of an advisor/advisee relationship and a boss/employee relationship—extremely hierarchical and influenced by power and authority. In this situation, we were examining a boss text—the handbook—to see if there was antiracist policy in place and how the lack of this policy allows for racist incidents to happen on an everyday level. The layers of institutional power in this conversation between me and the WC consultant are important to document and reflect on, as it draws on how mentoring relationships across difference can help us rethink our lack of antiracist policies in institutional texts.

In this situation, there were several factors involved that taught me about mentorship as a methodology and how methodology can better inform mentorship; WC pedagogy and responsive pedagogy allowed me to be open and collaborative-goal-oriented with the consultant (see Ralston's chapter on mentoring in the writing center for more); it asked me to listen deeply, with an "ethical hesitation" that allows me to be unsure of difference, to rethink institutional interactions and hierarchies, and to learn from the WC consultant's lived experience and what policies mean to different people without the privilege I have. IE as a methodology helped guide our conversation as we untangled together the ruling relations (what policies mean to me as a director versus what policies mean to her as a tutor) in the situation and examined the boss texts that dominate institutional conversations—that is, racism is not allowed in the writing center—and helped us shed light on policy and antiracist work. I believe this example asks IE to examine more the power dynamics that occur within marginalized positions and ways in which starting from those positions can shed light on racism in the academy and racist behavior in our mentoring practices.

Unsettling Knowledge for Institutional Change: Working with a Graduate Student under Normative Practices and Policies

My first year on the tenure track, I was asked to direct a dissertation by a graduate student whom I already formed a close relationship with. Both of us white women, we were invested in antiracist work in the writing center and program and worked together to "check our privileges" and to recognize the work that is needed to do antiracist work. I will also admit that this doctoral student often helped me prioritize antiracist work, as during my first year I was tempted to appease all those who came to the WC to collaborate on projects. I learned from this student—as she learned from me—and I was excited to help her on her journey with a qualitative study, a study that focuses on her work with antiracist workshops to local institutional communities, churches, schools, higher education, and so on. While this grad student herself was not an outsider to the academic community, her project certainly "disrupted the rational community" (Hinsdale 2015) and did not come without costs (Ahmed 2017). My commitment to collaborative work and ongoing critique of power structures made our working situation enjoyable; together we formed goals and timelines, both regarding her project and how the work can inform the writing center. To me, it was the type of mentoring relationship I always believed in.

I knew at the time that one of her advisors had serious issues with this student's project, but I was a first-year junior faculty member, still convinced that good work—even if unconventional—will shine through any potential obstacle. As the student was preparing for a qualifying defense, in which she was defending a chapter from her dissertation, I discussed with her the high risk / high reward model and the potential costs that could come from her work. This chapter was a critical autoethnography, drawing from citation sources used by scholars such as Sara Ahmed and

Leigh Patel, in which she was investigating her own whiteness and complicity in racism with Black colleagues doing antiracist work. Her work was grounded in research justice and a commitment to ethical love. I knew that the advisor who I was concerned about would have questions regarding her methodology, and she had a certain way of looking at these papers and what made for "publishable papers." The ruling text dominating this conversation was the qualifying paper guidelines document, with one line being key and central to this advisor's own understanding of the defense: "Note that the qualifying paper is expected to demonstrate breadth and depth of knowledge in the field and to be as close to publishable as possible."

Prior to the student's defense, we again discussed explicitly institutional interaction and power dynamics involved in the advisory committee (I as junior faculty member to a senior faculty member[1] on the committee). While this student's methodology foregrounds this experience as research, I was concerned about the advisor's thoughts on "demonstrating depth of knowledge" and what a "publishable" paper looks like. In this student's presentation, she cited the long list of antiracist scholars, both within writing studies and beyond, that informed her work; how critical autoethnography is an important methodology in such work; how her paper is adding to the discussion. I still believed her work was very strong and that despite any particular mindset centered on notions of traditional academic discourse and boss texts that dominate the department, she would have passed successfully. It was clear to both of us, twenty minutes in, that this was not going to be the case. The experience itself was painful—to both of us—and stemmed deeply in how, to quote Michelle LaFrance and Melissa Nicolas (2012) in their article "Institutional Ethnography as Materialist Framework for Writing Program Research and the Faculty-Staff Work Standpoints Project," "social mechanisms grant practices of legitimacy. The social order comes to sanction doing, knowing, and being" (130). The senior colleague in the room, confronted with a methodology unfamiliar to them, and disturbed by any disruptions, was the one who sanctioned what was legitimate scholarship and what was not. This piece was not legitimate scholarship. This senior colleague was informed by their understanding of the boss text and the qualifying paper guidelines, and traditional academic conventions and norms with publishing.

As a mentor, I failed the student in not being able to push back as I normally would—not fully understanding the dominant texts and discourses that informed the conversation. Had I been more familiar with IE, I would have perhaps had a better response in my defense of the work. I would have also been more cautious with my advisement to the student and this paper if I better understood how things happened at my institution and was more aware of the power of workplace norms LaFrance (2020) discusses, that "assumed norms of practice speak to, for, and over individuals" (23). While I did explicitly discuss institutional interactions and the high risk/high reward model, I was still quite naïve in how powerful dominant norms of practice were, particularly for graduate students, as there is an indoctrination of "I made it—you have to make it too" (citing Cheryl Glenn in a conversation). While we were able to have this paper pass through "significant revisions," and an understanding that the advisor must first look at the revised paper to sign off on it—another practice within my institution that I was unaware of—we both felt like failures. As the student revised the paper to fit a more traditional, academic model with a heavy lit review and less focus on the personal, I began to question my own understanding of responsive mentorship; perhaps as a junior faculty I cannot allow those I am advising to "disrupt the rational community" and must better help navigate them through academic norms.

Reflecting back on this experience and discussing it in-depth with the student, I do believe IE would have helped guide me to be a better mentor in the situation, with a better understanding of how important the local discourse is in defenses and policies; much of the behavior from that day stemmed from a way to establish academic rigor and dominance, as our field was not respected by other programs, such as literature. The paper needing to be "as close to publishable as possible" stems from graduate students in the past trying to take "an easy way out," in the program, as rhetoric/composition was once considered a softer, less rigorous discipline in the department. This history, which has changed considerably, does not excuse behavior—but it does better situate the mentor and grad student trying to learn from difference to be prepared. Together, the student and I discussed a ruling text in the field, that is, the *CCCC Statement on Professional Guidance for Mentoring Graduate Students* and ways in which this text would help us rethink our conversation with this one particular advisor. I also regret that this experience challenged the values I had as a mentor, values I learned from scholarship and pedagogy, so that the student revised the paper to fit more academic norms—making it perhaps "more publishable" in the eyes of the one advisor but less impactful in what it was trying to do through critical autoethnography. This experience helps illuminate how IE can better help us radically defend graduate students and others trying to push back on conventional norms through research about the local; it also helps illuminate how responsive mentorship, grounded in writing center pedagogy, requires both parties to take significant risks and to be fully aware of such risks. Hinsdale (2015) writes, "Even as I ask them to complete certain tasks, I explicitly tell them I do it to disrupt the bonds of power that grow from history. Mentors are caught in similar webs—disciplinary norms, departmental and university protocols all exert pressure on their relationships with students" (137–138). Mapping out these webs with students through IE is a powerful exercise for responsive mentorship, and one that needs to happen if we are to disrupt power. Using ruling texts such as the *CCCC Statement on Mentoring* as texts to use horizontally in our everyday practices is helpful in working within such webs, and more documentation on how such statements are being used and listened to is needed.

The Issues with Peer Review: Mentoring Relationships in Academic Publishing

The final case study focuses on a recent collaborative project with a co-author and their response to feedback from a Reviewer 2. This case study reflects on the need to better mentor peer reviewers, many (if not most) of whom are mentors of junior writers, to change the academic pipeline and how ruling texts can help aid in the mentoring process. My co-author and I are early-career faculty and scholars, I am a white woman, and my colleague is a person of color. As we wrote, we often negotiated tasks and prioritized competing concerns. Our work in writing centers made us good collaborators, and the process was truly enjoyable; we learned from our work together and through our commitment to critiquing institutional interactions and collaborative goal-making. We sent the piece, which was very much focused on lived experience, out for review with a journal. We got back the reviewer reports, with a good response from Reviewer 1, and a response from Reviewer 2 that required a whole restructuring of the paper.

In this situation, Reviewer 2's report was the ruling text, as it shaped the conversation I had with my co-author about next steps; like the situation with the graduate student, this reviewer did not appreciate the "lack of cohesion" (the paper connected a series of vignettes to different arguments) of the paper and disagreed with implications made. While I saw Reviewer 2 as frustrating but manageable, thinking about ways to include better transition phrases and reorganize some of the vignettes, my co-author was upset with the feedback, did not want to change the piece, and found the review to be problematic. In talking with my colleague, and hearing her concerns, it was clear she was right;

this reviewer was attempting to change an important element of the piece (trauma writing) and used their partial knowledge on a subject to dominate the report. However, I was preoccupied with wanting to get this piece published, as tenure loomed over me—an important institutional practice that shapes how and why we do what we do. Through our own responsive relationship and our commitment to WC pedagogies, we came to a compromise with each other and with Reviewer 2, pushing back on certain suggestions that changed the meaning of our paper and revising to make more explicit certain connections. We made this clear through the reader report, as well as documented our conversation to the journal.

In their article, "Editing as Inclusion Activism," Blewett et al. (2019) discuss the need for journals and editors to radically rethink their policies, practices, and norms if we are to change racist, sexist, and ableist structures within the academy. They write, "Journal editing is a site where inclusion activism is needed in our field, particularly given the importance of journal publishing to emerging and junior scholars and the tendency for journals to operate as echo chambers in which, for example, citation practices reproduce established hierarchies of power" (275). My experience with my co-author reminded me of how I, as a white woman of privilege, might be more inclined to reproduce hierarchies of power in order to get tenure, yet my co-author has more at stake with changing her words and writing; it also makes me aware that one can use certain institutional processes during publication, such as the letter to the editors, to push back against a reviewer with a problematic report (and I am aware that comes with high risks). In this experience, my co-author embodied inclusion activism and I learned from my co-author how to utilize ruling texts from IE and WC pedagogy to push back on problematic journal editing.

In this experience, both my co-author and I were let down by Reviewer 2, and their lack of intentionality and mentorship, and instead used the peer review process as a way for us to mentor each other. With the patience of my colleague, I allowed ethical hesitation to take over before rushing to revise and listen with difference on the need to push back. In this narrative, we mapped our compromises using the reader report to not only defend our position but to use the report as a text for Reviewer 2 to learn from for future reviews. IE can help journal editors revise their mentoring practices through an analytic examination of ruling texts, such as journal mission statements, guidelines, and expectations of peer reviewers (and I must reference here the excellent document from Cagel et al., "Anti-Racist Scholarly Reviewing Practices:

A Heuristic for Editors, Reviewers, and Authors," as a hopeful ruling text for journal editors). IE will better help journal editors tease out ruling relations and power dynamics involved in the review process, possibly rethinking who they ask to be reviewers or revising how these reviews are being written, through mapping up. Creating such maps will better help journals within the field to learn from one another and be in better communication. Mentoring practices, such as responsive mentorship, should be taught alongside the use of IE to reviewers and editors as they rethink their work from being academic gatekeepers to mentors of and with difference, and reader reports can help create a better dialogue between authors and reviewers as we in the field rethink the power dynamics in the editorial process.

A CONCLUSION

In all three case studies, I believe a focus on marginalized positionalities was key in these mentoring relationships, and IE can be used as a methodology for those in such positions within institutions if there is more of a focus of difference within standpoint and ruling relations. Mentoring relationships can grow from IE as it maps out our relations with one another and shows how ideology and history inform our conversations and work. Putting IE in our mentoring practices is important in grounding the relational in WC pedagogy and responsive mentorship, making sure authority does not reside in one person or in one entity. IE helps practitioners be more reflective in their process, and reflexivity is crucial in bettering our mentoring practices. Mentoring, particularly when grounded in WC pedagogy and responsiveness, can help the field and our research methodologies rethink power dynamics and difference as well as how knowledge is created, shared, and understood by different networks and groups of people.

In the vignettes detailed in this essay, there were feelings of unfamiliarity and discomfort, and I had to reflect on my own privilege as a white woman and come to terms with my own failures in how these experiences happened, and I used IE, responsive mentorship, and WC pedagogy to learn from these situations. These insights from the case studies can better help us create and rethink our policies for marginalized positions, navigate institutional discourses and norms for "unconventional projects," and revise journal expectations and standards for inclusion work. Mentoring is about networks, as is IE, and ways in which networks can be coordinated; very often, such coordination creates power dynamics that exclude, but who is to say that this must be? Laura Greenfield's

(2020) definition of radicalism is important to me when thinking about the institution: "Radicalism refers to the belief that (1) truth is a human construction; (2) power is not possessed but exercised, and therefore power is neither inherently good nor bad; and (3) authority resides not in people or entities but in ethically engaged praxis (reflective action)" (59). We can allow for IE and mentoring to coordinate radicalism within our networks, allowing for a more ethically engaged praxis and institutional change. IE is particularly helpful in that it allows us to be rooted in the relational, in the one-on-one interaction, and to map these experiences to build bigger webs as we start from the local to examine patterns of power that occur nationally. As mentoring is relational, and very much focused on the one-on-one, we can learn from these experiences to bring new knowledge to our research and teaching practices if those of us committed to the field of writing studies are to start from a place of learning from and with difference and to not place authority in a person or entity but rather in the collaborative reflective action, the process of mentoring, itself.

NOTE

1. I'd like to point out that I am using the term "senior faculty," as that is the language used both officially and informally at the institution where I work; as IE asks us to start with the local context, I believe it is important to use the identifying terms / labels faculty use locally to shed light on how even our everyday language can unconsciously create and perpetuate hierarchies and power dynamics. I am using the term "junior faculty" similarly in this section-story.

REFERENCES

Ahmed, Sara. 2017. *Living A Feminist Life*. Durham, NC: Duke University Press.
Blewett, Kelly, Christina M. LaVecchia, Laura R. Micciche, and Janine Morris. 2019. "Editing as Inclusion Activism." *College English* 81 (4): 173–196.
Boquet, Elizabeth. 1999. "Our Little Secret: A History of Writing Centers, Pre- to Post-Open Admissions." *College Composition and Communication* 50 (3): 463–482.
Boquet, Elizabeth, and Neil Lerner. 2008. "Reconsiderations: After the Idea of a Writing Center." *College English* 71 (2): 170–189.
Burrows, Cedric. 2016. "Writing While Black: The Black Tax on African American Graduate Writers." *Praxis: A Writing Center Journal* 14 (1).
Campbell, Marie, and Frances Gregor. 2004. *Mapping Social Relations: A Primer in Doing Institutional Ethnography*. Lanham, MD: AltaMira Press.
Condon, Frankie, and Vershawn Young. 2016. *Performing Antiracist Pedagogy in Rhetoric, Writing, and Communication*. Fort Collins, CO: WAC Clearinghouse.
Denny, Harry. 2010. *Facing the Center: Toward an Identity Politics of One-to-One Mentoring*. Logan: Utah State University Press.
Garcia, Romeo. 2017. "Unmaking Gringo Centers." *Writing Center Journal* 36 (1): 29–60.

Godbee, Beth, and Julia Novotny. 2013. "Asserting the Right to Belong: Feminist Co-Mentoring among Graduate Student Women." *Feminist Teacher: A Journal of Practices, Theories, and Scholarship of Feminist Teaching* 23 (3): 177–195.

Greenfield, Laura. 2020. *Radical Writing Center Praxis: A Paradigm for Ethical Political Engagement.* Logan: Utah State University Press.

Grimm, Nancy. 1999. *Writing Center Work for Postmodern Times.* Portsmouth, NH: Heinemann.

Grutsch McKinney, Jackie. 2013. *Peripheral Visions for Writing Centers.* Logan: Utah State University Press.

Gruwell, Leigh, and Charles Lesh. 2021. *Mentorship and Methodologies: Reflections, Praxis, and Futures.* CFP for Edited Collection.

Gumbs, Alexis Pauline. 2012. "The Shape of My Impact." *The Feminist Wire.* https://thefeministwire.com/2012/10/the-shape-of-my-impact/.

Hinsdale, Mary Jo. 2015. *Mutuality, Mystery, and Mentorship in Higher Education.* Rotterdam, Zuid-Holland: Sense Publishers.

hooks, bell. 1994. *Outlaw Culture: Resisting Representation.* New York: Routledge.

Kynard, Carmen. 2015. "Teaching While Black: Witnessing Disciplinary Whiteness, Racial Violence, and Race Management." *Literacy in Composition Studies* 3 (1): 1–20.

LaFrance, Michelle. 2020. *Institutional Ethnography: A Theory of Practice for Writing Studies Researchers.* Logan: Utah State University Press.

LaFrance, Michelle, and Melissa Nicolas. 2012. "Institutional Ethnography as Materialist Framework for Writing Program Research and the Faculty-Staff Work Standpoints Projects." *College Composition and Communication* 64 (1): 130–150.

Lerner, Neil. 2014. "Writing Center Pedagogy." In *A Guide to Composition Pedagogies,* edited by Gary Tate, Amy Rupiper Taggart, Kurt Schick, and H. Brook Hesler, 301–316. Oxford: Oxford University Press.

Lockett, Alex. 2019. "Why I Call It the Academic Ghetto: A Critical Examination of Race, Place, and Writing Centers." *Praxis: A Writing Center Journal* 16 (2).

Madden, Shannon, Michele Eodice, Kirsten T. Edwards, and Alexandria Lockett. 2021. *Learning from the Lived Experiences of Graduate Student Writers.* Logan: Utah State University Press.

Melonçon, Lisa, Patricia Sullivan, Michele Simmons, Kristen Moore, and Liza Potts. 2015. "Intentionally Recursive: A Participatory Model for Mentoring." *Technical Communication* 67 (2): 54–67.

Miley, Michelle. 2018. "Mapping Boundedness and Articulating Interdependence between Writing Centers and Writing Programs." *Praxis: A Writing Center Journal* 16 (1).

Nichols, Amy McCleese, and Bronwyn T. Williams. 2019. "Centering Partnerships: A Case for Writing Centers as Sites of Community Engagement." *Community Literacy Journal* 13 (2): 88–106.

Okawa, Gail Y. 2002. "Diving for Pearls: Mentoring as Cultural and Activist Practice among Academics of Color." *College Composition and Communication* 53 (3): 507–532.

Reid, E. Shelley. 2008. "Mentoring Peer Mentors: Mentor Education and Support in the Composition Program." *Composition Studies* 36 (2): 51–79.

Sicari, Anna. 2018. "Centering the Conversation: Patriarchy, Academic Culture, and #MeToo." *Composition Studies* 46 (2): 200–202.

Sicari, Anna, and Romeo Garcia. 2022. "Have We Arrived Yet? Revisiting and Rethinking Responsibility in Writing Center Work: The Need for Transformative Listening and Mindfulness of Difference," *Praxis: A Writing Center Journal* 19 (1).

Smith, Dorothy. 2005. *Institutional Ethnography: A Sociology for the People.* Lanham, MD: AltaMira Press.

Smith, Dorothy. 2006. *Institutional Ethnography as Practice.* Washington, DC: Rowman & Littlefield.

11
CONNECTING ROLES AND PURPOSES IN UNDERGRADUATE EMBEDDED MENTORING

Keaton Kirkpatrick

Acknowledging that mentoring has different definitions across contexts, this chapter follows an empirical study researching what embedded student mentors do in classrooms, how mentoring programs benefit students, and how mentoring is understood by faculty, mentors, and students in one co-taught course at a rural northern California university. Since embedded models of undergraduate mentoring are not widely discussed in writing studies, this study explores how defined purposes of mentoring are understood in classrooms and how those purposes affect mentors' roles in a class space. By describing how mentors are perceived by faculty, mentors, *and* students in the same class, this study complements research attending to either mentors *or* students. Specifically, this research seeks to understand how mentors act in a classroom and how their actions are interpreted.

Applying to a variety of contexts, mentoring evades a single definition. However, there are patterns of practice distinguishing mentors from other support roles at the university. Differentiating mentoring from other developmental relationships, Sambunjak and Marušić (2009) argue that successful mentors balance educational, personal, and professional aspects in their practice. These are broadly aligned with Nora and Crisp's (2007) four major domains of mentoring: psychological or emotional support (personal), support for goal-setting and career paths (professional), academic subject knowledge support (educational), and the existence of a role model. The role model domain offers mentees the opportunity to "learn from the mentor's current and past actions, as well as achievements and failures" (Crisp 2009, 179). Role models may embody all of the developmental aspects, since they are what learners aspire to become (Speizer 1981), though they encourage imitation rather than metacognitive development. Role modeling naturally happens in mentoring—especially when mentees value the approaches and expertise of the mentor—but it should not be seen as an integral part of mentoring.

Complicating ideas of mentors and classrooms, course-embedded mentoring models place trained student mentors directly into classrooms to support students. For first-year undergraduate students, this approach is especially promising because of its focus on educational, personal, and professional development. However, the purposes and effects of this model should be considered in different contexts; as Crisp (2009, 191) argues, mentoring programs need to be as "individualized as possible to meet the needs of a diverse student population." By focusing on one model at one university, this study acts as an example of an individualized program designed to support students in large-enrollment courses designed for underrepresented, low-income, and first-generation students at a Hispanic Serving Institution. As a first-generation student from a low-income family, I benefited from similar programs as an undergraduate. However, I am white, cis-gender, and straight—meaning I am not socially underrepresented and have not struggled to find mentors who share my identity.

Nora and Crisp's (2007) four major domains of mentoring have already been researched in two-year colleges (Nora and Crisp 2007), Hispanic Serving Institutions (Crisp and Cruz 2010), and four-year institutions with course-embedded mentors (Henry, Bruland, and Sano-Franchini 2011). Unlike the study for this chapter that includes faculty, mentor, and student perspectives of mentoring together, these studies mainly focus on student or mentor perspectives separately. While Henry, Bruland, and Omizo (2008) discuss embedded mentoring from mentor, instructor, and program director perspectives, they are interested in how roles were constructed by and for mentors, excluding a broader discussion of synthesized purposes and their relation to constructed roles. In Bruland's (2012, 47) dissertation, she discusses trinary teaching configurations (those with students, teachers, and third-classroom actors) to study a writing mentor program; however, despite her original goal to discuss all three trinary parties equally, her work emphasizes mentors' perspectives and performances. These studies do not investigate how everyone involved in a class supported by embedded mentors understands those mentors' purposes. As embedded mentors defy traditional teacher/student classroom dynamics and ideas about who mentors are, it is important for instructors, mentors, and students to understand why mentors are in the class space.

Mentoring students in the university is historically associated with dyadic relationships, where one experienced or skilled member in the university guides and supports a protégé—often in relationships where senior faculty or experienced scholars mentor students or less experienced faculty and teaching associates. This pattern of dyadic relationships between faculty and their mentees emphasizes the importance of mentoring in the university, but not for first-year students and students from systematically oppressed racial or cultural groups (Budge 2006; Okawa 2002). By being accessible to more students, untraditional models of mentoring that position students as mentors address these gaps in mentoring research, such as horizontal mentoring (VanHaitsma and Ceraso 2017), in-residence mentoring (Benjamin 2004; Chidister, Bell, and Earnest 2001), mentoring in service-learning projects within linked courses (Kincaid and Sotiriou 2004), and mentoring networks (Goerisch et al. 2019). Formal mentoring programs—which are organized with structures like training, planned meetings, and mentees being assigned to mentors (Budge 2006)—rarely account for perceptions of mentoring from oppressed groups (Pope 2002). By embedding mentors directly into required classes like first-year writing, it increases access to them by removing the need for formal appointments (Muraskin et al. 2004). While mentoring has been associated with dyadic relationships between experienced and new professionals, it should be made more accessible to undergraduate students through the polyadic, course-situated relationships of embedded mentorship.

The move toward course-embedded mentoring addresses the issue of voluntary mentoring models by offering support to more students—not just those who seek help. A popular early model of undergraduate course-embedded support is Keller's (1968) Personalized System of Instruction, which employed proctors to serve as relatable guides, support students by sharing expertise about a particular course and its tests, and assist the teaching staff with grading. Like proctors, writing fellows (Haring-Smith 2000) and classroom-based writing tutors (Spigelman and Grobman 2005) also work with groups of students in classes to increase academic success within courses. These models, however, tend to focus primarily on educational support and sometimes personal support. Similarly, by using Nora and Crisp's (2007) four major domains of mentoring to code their research, Henry, Bruland, and Sano-Franchini (2011, 6–7) explain how students see embedded mentors as offering academic subject knowledge support and psychological or emotional support. Henry, Bruland, and Sano-Franchini (2011, 9) also found a fifth domain they coined as "mentee willingness," which addresses the predispositions of mentees to being mentored. Since embedded mentoring is often involuntary, this fifth domain is important to consider for future mentoring programs.

Together, these studies show the importance and effectiveness of embedding mentors into classrooms; however, they do not investigate how *all* members within a classroom connect the purposes and roles of mentors. Since mentoring relationships are dynamic and individualized, it is necessary to include everyone involved in a mentoring context or program to understand what support is offered and how that support is taken up. This chapter offers a discussion of mentoring from all perspectives in a classroom with embedded mentors, utilizing a combination of interviews, surveys, and field notes. In particular, field notes are valuable to complement data from both surveys and interviews, as they provide context and an understanding of what embedded mentoring looks like in practice.

METHODOLOGY

Institutional Context

Following IRB approval, I collected data in fall 2018 from a rural four-year public Hispanic Serving Institution in northern California. One embedded-only mentoring model was analyzed for this study. An "embedded-only" model is one where mentors only meet with students during class time. This differs from models with workshops or breakout rooms accompanying the regular class, where mentors and students meet without faculty. The embedded-only model was used in a large-enrollment (over ninety students) "combined course," merging first-year composition (FYC) and lower-division anthropology (cultural diversity) courses. The researcher had experience as an embedded mentor in other similar programs and was enrolled in similar support programs as an undergraduate, giving him an insider's perspective. However, the researcher did not participate as a mentor in this particular class, meaning he was limited to an observer's role.

Faculty, mentors, and students in the class were invited to participate in the study based on the researcher's connection with one of the faculty members teaching the course. The combined course was taught by two tenured faculty members, each with over thirty years of teaching experience. While one faculty member worked with embedded mentors for several years, the other was working with mentors for the first time. Prior to the study, both faculty members knew and had co-taught with each other. There were also two graduate teaching assistants who facilitated some classroom activities and grading. Eight embedded mentors trained in promoting student success (both in the class and at the university) supported the course. All of the participating mentors were upper-level undergraduates themselves and were assigned randomly to a group of ten to thirteen students. To qualify for this position, mentors had to pass a peer-mentor training course and submit an application. While second-year students could mentor in the program, third- and fourth-year students are more regularly hired as mentors. This differs from Henry, Bruland, and Sano-Franchini's (2011) study, which mostly employed graduate students.

Embedded mentoring in the six-unit combined course is an established model through the campus's first-year experience program. The course focused on ethnography and global migration, encouraging students to take on ethnographer identities through collaboratively conducting primary ethnographic research to address issues for first-year college students. Students' research culminated in a co-authored ethnography paper and team presentation wherein they highlighted key findings and offered recommendations to campus stakeholders. The combined course was designed to be supported by embedded mentors. Primarily, the students in the course enrolled through campus support programs for underrepresented, low-income, and first-generation students.

Methods

There were three instruments used in this study: field notes, surveys, and semi-structured interviews. Wanting to gain a thorough understanding of the daily practices and roles of embedded mentors, the researcher prioritized going into the classroom and taking observational field notes. Course documents (assignment sheets, schedules, etc.) were also collected for context. Faculty, mentors, and students participated in end-of-semester surveys and volunteered to have field notes recorded during class meetings. Additionally, seven out of eight mentors were interviewed at the end of the semester, and roughly a third of students in the course completed a survey.

Field notes were recorded in a private Google Doc between August and December 2018 during twice-weekly three-hour class sessions, though the final fifty to sixty minutes of the second class each week were not recorded due to a schedule conflict. The researcher also kept field notes of meetings where faculty planned classes for the following week, though not all of these meetings were observed, based on the researcher's availability. Despite missing portions of class and meetings, five and one-half hours of field notes were typically recorded each week.

The field notes captured what embedded mentoring looked like, providing a more holistic understanding than what could be gleaned through interviews and surveys alone. In other words, the field notes provided context and examples of mentoring in practice. Only three days during weeks 2, 9, and 15 were coded. These three days represent mentoring at the beginning, middle, and end of the semester, accounting for differences in practices at different points in the class. To analyze the field notes, a coding glossary was created based on the major roles of mentors: teacher, tutor, peer, discussion facilitator, passive participant, and teammate. The following list defines each of the codes relating to mentor roles:

- **Teacher**: a mentor acts as a teacher or takes on teacherly responsibilities (e.g., managing the class, delivering course information to the class)
- **Tutor**: a mentor works with a student one-on-one
- **Peer**: a mentor acts as a student by responding to questions from faculty, chatting with other students about subjects unrelated to the course, and so on
- **Discussion facilitator**: a mentor structures discussions and works with multiple students at once
- **Passive participant**: a mentor is a passive or unresponsive observer in the course
- **Teammate**: a mentor works directly with the faculty during class, usually to coordinate an activity or direct students to see the faculty as a resource

While there are more roles that mentors enact, the above roles act as general categories. For each, a mentor would act "role-like" (e.g., peer-like, teacher-like), meaning they took on responsibilities or performed actions associated with being a peer, teacher, and so on. While "passive participant" might *appear* negative at first, it was a necessary role when students were working with each other for peer review or working alone during class. Descriptive coding based on roles was used to code field notes. A descriptive code is one summarizing a passage's "primary topic" (Saldaña 2016, 4). Sometimes, multiple descriptive codes were applied to a single passage if a mentor moved quickly between roles or enacted multiple roles in one instance. For example, a mentor might facilitate discussion about a subject unrelated to the course to build community.

Ascribing roles to mentors through these codes is only one way to understand the work mentors do. While the codes allowed the researcher to describe and record how mentors switch between approaches for working with students, they also characterized mentors by an amalgamation of roles. This approach to coding mentor roles emphasizes the unique role-switching ability of mentors, but also portrays mentors as having a stock of familiar roles that they deliberately enact in different situations. This is not true to life—the codes applied to mentors limit how they are understood and fail to accurately represent the responsive and complicated approaches that mentors practice. However, having a set of roles is one method of making mentoring more apparent and definable to faculty, mentors, and students, which is why they are useful in this study.

Within the last few weeks of the fall 2018 semester, Google Form surveys were sent out to faculty, mentors, and students. Around the same time, semi-structured interviews for the embedded mentors were created and conducted by the researcher. Each of the surveys differed in the exact questions asked but used the same categories: mentor purposes and goals, mentor roles, factors to positive or negative experiences, and effectiveness. Additionally, mentors and faculty were asked questions about training and preparation. For interviews with mentors, the questions asked were mostly open-ended, inviting mentors to reflect on their semester of mentoring through questions involving the same categories from the surveys, development of students and mentors, and practices or experiences of mentoring. All of the thirty-to-sixty-minute interviews were transcribed. Like field notes, interviews and the survey results were descriptively coded to locate patterns; unlike the field notes, in vivo codes were applied to some survey responses to capture exactly what students wrote, such as "help" when they mentioned their mentor being helpful (Saldaña 2016, 4).

Limitations

Writing field notes involved the researcher dividing attention between eight mentors. This meant field notes focused on only one mentor at a time. If a mentor was passive while students were working, that was documented in the field notes and the researcher would move to another group. Mentors were difficult to hear sometimes, especially when they were talking with small groups or individual students. When this happened, notes were taken on the actions or movement of mentors. In hindsight, asking mentors to keep self-reflective journals about their practices could have provided a richer understanding of mentoring throughout the semester.

The mentors and students were not asked about their race during data collection, so a robust discussion of how race may affect course-embedded mentoring and students' perceptions of mentoring in this program is not possible with the research gathered and analyzed for this study.

In spite of creating a coding glossary to apply codes consistently across the data, coding was done by one researcher instead of a team, making findings less triangulated. While both faculty members and all eight combined course mentors agreed to be observed for field notes, one mentor did not schedule an interview, five mentors did not complete the survey, and more than two-thirds of students did not complete the survey.

RESULTS AND DISCUSSION

Instead of being trained to respond to student writing, combined course mentors focused on mentoring for student success and support. In preparation for this work, prospective mentors either took a three-day crash course or completed a two-unit credit/no credit lower-division course for mentor training the semester prior to mentoring. The crash course was only offered when mentors were desperately needed. In both training options, mentors gained theoretical and practical knowledge, helping them act effectively, supportively, and intentionally. Training continued into the semester, as mentors met weekly for one hour with faculty and each other to prepare for upcoming class sessions. Additionally, mentors from different combined courses met with a mentor supervisor once every two or three weeks for two hours to discuss and (re)learn relevant theoretical and practical knowledge.

Table 11.1 summarizes experience and training for faculty and mentors. Not all mentors and faculty participated equally in this study, as faculty were only surveyed, one mentor opted out of the interview, and just three mentors completed the survey. These inconsistencies affect the findings, particularly the frequency at which data from some mentors appears more often than that of others. Grace, for example, is nearly absent in the data, since she could not schedule an interview and did not take the survey. For faculty, the "Experience" column identifies how long they have been teaching with, supervising, or training embedded mentors.

THE PURPOSES OF EMBEDDED MENTORING IN THE COMBINED COURSE

In this context, purposes refer to the intentions for mentoring that are predetermined by the instructor of the training course and reinforced by mentor practice, faculty feedback, and continued training with the mentor supervisor throughout the semester. The purposes are the *why*

Table 11.1. Experience and training of combined course faculty and mentors

Pseudonym	Position	Experience	Crash Course	2-Unit Course	Survey	Interview
Dr. Faye	Faculty	5 years*	N/A	N/A	Yes	No
Dr. Fennell	Faculty	1st semester*	N/A	N/A	Yes	No
Barbara	Mentor	3rd semester	Yes	No	No	Yes
Natalia	Mentor	1st semester	No	Yes	Yes	Yes
Grace	Mentor	1st semester	No	Yes	No	No
Rafael	Mentor	3rd semester	Yes	No	Yes	Yes
Kathleen	Mentor	3rd semester	Yes	No	Yes	Yes
Vergel	Mentor	1st semester	No	Yes	No	Yes
Isabella	Mentor	1st semester	Yes	No	No	Yes
Paige	Mentor	1st semester	Yes	No	No	Yes

* Faculty experience refers to their experience working with mentors, not their experience teaching.

behind mentor actions, relating to the reasons mentors perform some actions instead of others. Roles, however, name the work mentors perform. That is, they are the positions that mentors act within—whether they are acting as peers, discussion facilitators, co-teachers, and so on.

Both Dr. Faye and Dr. Fennell describe purposes that present embedded mentors as resources to students and faculty (especially faculty of large-enrollment courses), suggesting mentors prioritize attending to their students and helping with classroom management. Secondarily, mentors should focus on using mentoring to gain experience for their own professional development and success in college and beyond. Additionally, Dr. Faye explained that mentors personally benefited her and her approach to teaching: "Working with a faculty partner and working with a peer mentor team have improved my thinking about learning and about designing for learning." Dr. Fennell did not mention any personal benefits resulting from working with embedded mentors, instead he highlighted the benefits to the course and classroom management.

For mentors, purposes of mentoring were learned in training and practice (Natalia, Kathleen, Vergel, Isabella, and Paige) or past experience (Barbara, Rafael). Combined course mentors describe their purpose as encouraging student transition, supporting classroom management, being a means of support more approachable than faculty, and creating connections between faculty, mentors, and students. While mentors prioritized some purposes over others, there was overlap in how mentors described purposes overall. For example, Vergel talked about the importance of forming "a community where everyone feels comfortable" and encouraging students to "extend their relationships outside of class." Despite using different language and prioritizing different purposes, faculty and mentors shared purposes for mentoring.

All of the mentors who were uncertain about purposes reported that their experience during the semester of this study gave them a better sense of their purposes or reinforced what they knew about their purposes. This suggests that while purposes can be partially learned in training, they should be reinforced through practice and meetings throughout the semester.

CONNECTING PURPOSES AND ROLES

In this section, quotes from the surveys, interviews, and field notes are synthesized into a discussion about how mentors' purposes and roles are articulated and practiced. Theoretically, mentors' roles should fulfill particular purposes. For instance, if a purpose of mentoring is to help students with assignments, then a teacher role could be used to explain an assignment, a tutor role could be used to help students (re)consider their approach, and a discussion facilitator role could be used to share experiences, insights, and inquiries relevant to the assignment. However, in practice, this is not usually the case, as the purposes of mentoring constructed by faculty and mentors do not capture the roles that students see their mentors enacting most often. Additionally, while both faculty and mentors use training and meetings to create a shared understanding of mentoring, students do not have this experience and are less familiar with what mentors are for or how they are supposed to support students. This distance from the theory underpinning mentoring practices leads students to identify what mentors actually do in classrooms and for students, which differs from what faculty and mentors intend to do.

As the faculty co-teaching the course spent time discussing and planning for how mentors affect students and learning, both faculty members shared an understanding of mentor roles. While Dr. Fennell mixed roles with purposes, he still described roles that mentors performed. He notes that mentors were "highly conversant" with the campus's learning-management system, "modeled appropriate behavior," and showed "genuine concern for the success of their students." In these examples, mentors take on teacher roles when navigating the learning-management system, peer roles when modeling appropriate behavior, and a mix between teacher and peer roles when showing concern for their students' success. Dr. Fennell saw mentors as more professional than not, explaining that mentors "slipped a bit in their professional conduct . . . using cell phones inappropriately or joking around too much with their student groups. But these were exceptions." The emphasis on conduct positions mentors as role models. When discussing the purposes of mentors, Dr. Fennell suggested mentors act as translators (for assignments), informants (for classroom management), and insiders (into student struggles or confusion). While not named roles in the data analysis, these roles fall between those of peers and teachers. A mentor as a course-content translator, for example, must understand assignments from a teacher's perspective, then use that understanding to translate and describe assignments to other students as a peer. This was something mentors did often, as 50 percent of students who took the survey reported the purpose of mentors was to increase understanding of the course and its assignments.

Dr. Faye agrees that mentors serve as role models, saying they "modeled attentive focus on course work" and "guided/coached students through in-class work," showing friendliness and interest in their students and fostering "a community of practice where students had a sense of belonging, purpose and developing expertise." Role model, guide, and coach are roles existing between peer and teacher. Supporting this, Dr. Faye explained: "Mentors approximate [these roles], falling into 'teaching' or 'pal' roles at least some of the time." Both Dr. Fennell and Dr. Faye suggest mentors' roles vacillate between teacher and peer.

While purposes were discussed by mentors and faculty consistently, some of the roles discussed by mentors differed from the ones discussed by faculty. When this happened, roles were less likely to connect to purposes. Barbara explained her role as "a friendly like go-between, from faculty to student . . . a giver of like real-life advice to students because sometimes faculty like makes things seem like they're simpler than they are"; Natalia said her role was to support students, saying if students are "scared to ask like the professors or the teaching staff like a question, . . . I'm there to kind of help answer or if like I can't, I like encourage them to ask [the teaching team], I'm like 'hey, they're the ones that know [what] you want'"; Isabella described her role as a "motivator" and "informer" who did a lot of "student assisting," primarily informing students "of everything, like the purpose . . . [and helping them see] the finish line. Seeing the purpose of like getting to the end"; and Vergel said his role was to "facilitate [how] the day goes and I think it helps the students out . . . [faculty are] in charge of like the education stuff, and then we're in charge of like [students]"—which he noted was important in a large-enrollment class.

While Natalia and Barbara both describe their role as someone who is between students and faculty to help students form connections with faculty, Isabella saw her role as helping students individually by being a motivator and source of information. In spite of how she described her role, Barbara did not identify a main purpose of mentoring as helping students to form connections with faculty. While Natalia described her role as connecting students with faculty, for her the purpose of mentoring is to affect student-to-student connections. Isabella identified purposes of connecting students with faculty and herself, but characterized her role as support for students to understand and complete their work. Vergel described his role as a facilitator who took responsibility for students. While Vergel mentioned a purpose of mentors is helping faculty manage a large-enrollment course, he also talked about providing students support to "transition from high school." In other words, his role only captures a small and adjacent part of the purposes he described. While these four mentors indicate how purposes do not always decide roles, the other mentors named roles that were closer to their purposes.

Kathleen and Rafael both described roles that relate to the purposes they identified and the roles that faculty discussed. For Kathleen, she explained, she is a college student "just a little bit ahead of them . . . a role model of like 'hey, if you want to be successful in college, here's some things that you should do.'" This position as a more experienced student who imparts strategies that help students "feel more confident in their own abilities as a college student" relates to Kathleen's purposes of being approachable and guiding students in becoming independent. Being relatable to students was important to Rafael, who described his role as "someone that [students] can, you know, really relate to," specifically a "role model, making people feel comfortable, of course, but you know having that intimate interaction." He emphasizes that part of his role is being in a group with his students, though he still takes responsibility by trying "to include everyone within the team . . . and just really facilitating discussion." Rafael, who characterized a mentor's purpose as making students feel included and facilitating connections between students, describes a nearly perfect connection between purposes and roles. Further, both Kathleen and Rafael named one of the major roles identified by Dr. Fennell and Dr. Faye, which is to be role models who share practices and foster a sense of belonging at the university. While Kathleen saw her position as a role model, useful to making students independent, Rafael valued his influence as a role model and discussion facilitator in helping students feel included.

Paige, like Kathleen and Rafael, defined her role in relation to her purposes and the roles that faculty identified. While not claiming she is a role model, Paige compares mentoring to "big brother programs, in a way—but like, like more formal in the classroom, not like outside of the classroom type of thing," saying that she also helps students build "relationship[s] with the people around them because you can't really do that in a lot of classes." These roles align with Paige's purpose of sharing habits for students to be "the best college student they can be," as well as the roles Rafael described.

Barbara, Natalia, and Isabella scarcely connect roles with purposes; Vergel connects them only partially; and Kathleen, Rafael, and Paige connect them directly (though Paige's connection is less direct compared to Kathleen and Rafael). It is notable that both Kathleen and Rafael are third-semester combined-course mentors while Paige is new. While all mentors did not explicitly connect their roles with purposes, they always described roles relating to purposes valued in the combined-course mentoring program. For example, Barbara being a "friendly go-between" from faculty to student serves the purpose of creating connections between students and faculty, which were purposes discussed by Kathleen and Isabella; and a "friendly go-between" role involves translating assignments and desired outcomes, which Dr. Fennell identified as a purpose of mentoring.

In addition to talking about her role, Paige suggests she is clearer about her role than students are, suggesting students "sometimes see [mentors' roles] more as like 'oh, we're here to just help them get through the class.'" From the survey, students described the purpose of mentors as helping students get through the course and understand assignments, which is partially reflected by the roles they chose to describe mentors. Of the survey participants, 90 percent of students characterized mentors as co-teachers or faculty assistants, 80 percent said mentors were discussion facilitators, 47 percent said they were peers, 37 percent said they were passive group members, 33 percent said they were tutors, 13 percent said they were teachers, and 10 percent said they were friends (a response they wrote in). While mentors rarely connected their role to teaching, students overwhelmingly saw mentors acting in teacher-like roles. However, students understand that mentors are different than teachers, with only 13 percent of students equating mentors with teachers.

In spite of mentors being role models, motivators, classroom managers, and facilitators (of discussions or relationships), they are not being

Table 11.2. Frequency of roles used by combined course mentors in their classroom interactions

Role	Day 1 #	Day 1 %	Day 2 #	Day 2 %	Day 3 #	Day 3 %	Combined #	Combined %
Teacher	45	39%	44	43%	28	23%	117	35%
Discussion Facilitator	34	30%	9	9%	31	26%	74	22%
Peer	10	9%	22	22%	12	10%	44	13%
Teammate	9	8%	20	20%	13	11%	42	13%
Passive	13	11%	0	0%	25	21%	38	11%
Tutor	3	3%	7	7%	10	8%	20	6%
Total #	114		102		120		336	

Note: Day 1 is from week 2, day 2 is from week 9, and day 3 is from week 15.

perceived that way to students. While the majority of students also identified mentors as discussion facilitators, it is concerning that more students identified them as co-teachers or faculty assistants, considering none of the mentors ever described their role as teacherly. Paige, who has experience with student teaching, said mentoring was "like an opposite" to student teaching, which involved "more like teaching than supporting . . . it was really hard to like get the support in there . . . whereas like with mentoring, it's more of support and then teaching." While supporting students is a part of teaching, Paige names and values support over other aspects of teaching.

With this in mind, discussion facilitator and peer roles should be the most common ones applied to mentors, since they are the roles most associated with personal and educational support. However, as shown in table 11.2, these roles are not observed most frequently in the classroom. Referencing representational field notes from the beginning, middle, and end of the semester, the teacher role was used by mentors most frequently. Combined, the discussion facilitator and peer roles are roughly equal to the teacher role. Referring back to Dr. Faye's statement that mentors typically fall into "'teaching' or 'pal' roles at least some of the time," the data discussed in this section suggests mentors fall into peer roles far less often than they fall into teaching roles.

CONCLUSION

The findings from this empirical study show that individual mentor purposes and roles are only sometimes connected. While mentors and faculty generally described purposes and roles that were connected, students were far more likely than faculty and mentors to see their mentors in co-teacher or faculty assistant roles, connecting their mentors' purposes with course and assignment help. This indicates that even when faculty and mentors understand mentoring similarly, their understanding is not shared with students. If mentoring differs in its practices and purposes from other support roles, then more should be done to communicate the roles of mentors to students. Findings further suggest that while faculty and mentors indicated peer roles as valuable to creating connections and community, fewer than half of the students identified their mentors in peer roles (seeing mentors more often as discussion facilitators) and only 13 percent of interactions from the representational field notes recorded mentors taking on a peer role. Regardless of these results, embedded mentors were still successful, with faculty, mentors, and students being satisfied or very satisfied with mentors. Only a handful of students reported they were neither satisfied nor dissatisfied with their mentors, and no one reported any dissatisfaction.

Mentor roles are not concrete or static, and thus the methods we use to research with them must reflect this. Mentoring is perhaps best studied longitudinally and adaptively, where different moments of mentoring can be captured, and adjustments can be made based on who the mentors are and what they do in a context. If the researcher for this study did not go to the classroom and take field notes, then the insight from student participants could be less substantial. It is easy, for example, to suggest that students do not have the same language that faculty and mentors do when it comes to describing mentors; however, the field notes support student responses, showing that the top roles observed are the same as the top roles identified by students (teacher-like, discussion facilitator, and peer-like, respectively). While roles are attributable to embedded mentors, a list of roles will never exhaustively capture what mentors do. To define all the roles of mentors, then, should not be the goal for future research; instead, researchers might focus on categories of support offered by mentors (e.g., educational, personal, and professional) or how to communicate mentors' roles and purposes with students.

More important than creating a list of roles is understanding that mentoring is dynamic (for more on dynamic and relational mentoring from a mentor's perspective, see Sicari in this collection). Mentors' access to a range of roles based on educational history, personality, positionality, and developing expertise provide them with a responsive repertoire of roles for adapting to the learning and support preferences of individual students. Mentoring is not a single role that works across contexts and for all students; responsive practices make mentors meaningful to those with whom they work closely. How race and positionality influence course-embedded mentoring needs to be better understood too. If mentors and their students have different races, how does that affect a mentor's roles and purposes?

The benefits of embedded mentoring are not precise because of the number of ways that relationships manifest. Dr. Fennell said the combined course does not work without embedded mentors, and Dr. Faye said mentors improved her "thinking about learning and about designing for learning." Combined-course mentors benefited by learning about learning and working with students and faculty. Some mentors (Rafael, Kathleen, Isabella, and Paige) said they became more social and gained confidence through mentoring, while others (Vergel, Kathleen, and Natalia) said it will help them teach in the future. Mentors also helped students learn about the course and its assignments by answering questions and being approachable to students. Aside from one student who felt their mentor only repeated what faculty in the combined course said, all participants reported mentors as beneficial.

Undergraduate embedded-mentoring models show great potential because mentors are able to form personal connections with students and support them in becoming more intentional learners. Embedded mentors should see their role in a class as dynamic and negotiable, but their purposes (which are decided in training and reinforced or modified in conversations between faculty and mentors) should be more explicit to give mentors goals and ideas for how to approach student support.

REFERENCES

Benjamin, Maryanne. 2004. "Residential Learning Community Peer Mentors: A Qualitative Study of Role Construction/Enactment and Learning Outcomes." PhD diss., Iowa State University, Ames.

Bruland, Holly H. 2012. "Trinary Collaborations in First-Year Composition: A Mixed Methods Study of the University of Hawai'i Writing Mentors Program." PhD diss., University of Hawai'i at Mānoa.

Budge, Stephanie. 2006. "Peer Mentoring in Post-Secondary Education: Implications for Research and Practice." *Journal of College Reading and Learning* 37 (1): 73–87.

Chidister, Mark J., Frank H. Bell Jr., and Kurt M. Earnest. 2001. "Lessons from Peers: The Design Exchange." In *Student-Assisted Teaching*, edited by Judith E. Miller, James E. Groccia, and Marilyn S. Miller, 8–14. Bolton, MA: Anker Publishing Company.

Crisp, Gloria. 2009. "Conceptualization and Initial Validation of the College Student Mentoring Scale (CSMS)." *Journal of College Student Development* 50 (2): 177–194.

Crisp, Gloria, and Irene Cruz. 2010. "Confirmatory Factor Analysis of a Measure of 'Mentoring' among Undergraduate Students Attending a Hispanic Serving Institution." *Journal of Hispanic Higher Education* 9 (3): 232–244.

Goerisch, Denise, Jae Basiliere, Ashley Rosener, Kimberly McKee, Jodee Hunt, and Tonya M. Parker. 2019. "Mentoring *With*: Reimagining Mentoring across the University." *Gender, Place and Culture* 26 (12): 1740–1758.

Haring-Smith, Tori. 2000. "Changing Students' Attitudes: Writing Fellows Programs." In *Writing Across the Curriculum: A Guide to Developing Programs*, edited by Susan H. McLeod and Margot Soven, 123–131. Fort Collins, CO: WAC Clearinghouse.

Henry, Jim, Holly Bruland, and Jennifer Sano-Franchini. 2011. "Course-Embedded Mentoring for First-Year Students: Melding Academic Subject Support with Role Modeling, Psycho-Social Support, and Goal Setting." *International Journal for the Scholarship of Teaching and Learning* 5 (2): 1–22.

Henry, Jim, Holly Huff Bruland, and Ryan Omizo. 2008. "Mentoring First-Year Students in Composition: Tapping Role Construction to Teach." *Currents in Teaching and Learning* 1 (1): 17–28.

Keller, Fred S. 1968. "Good-Bye, Teacher." *Journal of Applied Behavior Analysis* 1 (1): 79–89.

Kincaid, Nita Moots, and Peter Sotiriou. 2004. "Service-Learning at an Urban Two-Year College." *Teaching English in the Two-Year College* 31 (3): 248–259.

Muraskin, Lana, John Lee, Abigail Wilner, and Watson Scott Swail. 2004. *Raising the Graduation Rates of Low-Income College Students*. Washington, DC: The Pell Institute for the Study of Opportunity in Higher Education.

Nora, Amaury, and Gloria Crisp. 2007. "Mentoring Students: Conceptualizing and Validating the Multi-Dimensions of a Support System." *Journal of College Student Retention* 9 (3): 337–356.

Okawa, Gail Y. 2002. "Diving for Pearls: Mentoring as Cultural and Activist Practice among Academics of Color." *College Composition and Communication* 53 (3): 507–532.

Pope, Myron L. 2002. "Community College Mentoring: Minority Student Perception." *Community College Review* 30 (3): 31–45.

Saldaña, Johnny. 2016. "An Introduction to Codes and Coding." In *The Coding Manual for Qualitative Researchers*, 1–42. London: Sage.

Sambunjak, Dario, and Ana Marušić. 2009. "Mentoring: What's in a Name?" *Journal of the Associated Medical Association* 302 (23): 2591–2592.

Speizer, Jeanne J. 1981. "Role Models, Mentors, and Sponsors: The Elusive Concepts." *Signs: Journal of Women in Culture and Society* 6 (4): 692–712.

Spigelman, Candace, and Laurie Grobman. 2005. *On Location: Theory and Practice in Classroom-Based Writing Tutoring*. Logan: Utah State University Press.

VanHaitsma, Pamela, and Steph Ceraso. 2017. " 'Making It' in the Academy through Horizontal Mentoring." *Peitho* 19 (2): 210–233.

PART 4

Complicating the Slash

Futures in Mentorship/Methodology

12
LEAKY BODIES AND CONNECTIVE TISSUES
A Cripped Metho-Epistemology of Mentoring

Leslie R. Anglesey and Melissa Nicolas

When searching for a mentor as a graduate student, Leslie knew she needed to work with someone she could, at some point, disclose parts of her body-mind that she would normally seek to hide and mask in academic and professional settings. As a person with mental health disabilities, Leslie was searching for a mentor who would insist on academic excellence without forgetting the other parts of her, those that often went undiscussed in Leslie's previous mentoring relationships yet needed to be recognized and accounted for. While Leslie didn't have the words to describe it then, what she needed was a mentoring relationship in which it would be safe to leak.

Throughout this chapter, we purposefully say that *we* were (are) engaged in a mentoring relationship, but not to pay lip service to the idea that everyone gets something out of these pairings. And we don't necessarily mean "horizontal mentoring" (VanHaitsma and Ceraso 2017), although there is definitely an exchange of teaching and learning between us, this chapter being a prime example. But it has always been clear—and we choose to acknowledge this rather than pretend it's not there—that Melissa is farther along the academic ladder. When Leslie was a graduate student, Melissa had the institutional power and authority as well as the disciplinary knowledge Leslie needed access to in order to complete her program. And even now, as collaborators, Leslie is pre-tenure faculty and Melissa is tenured faculty. We inhabit different institutional positions and play different institutional roles. From Leslie's perspective, however, Melissa wasn't simply a good choice because she had the institutional gravitas needed, or because we shared similar pedagogical approaches, or because she worked in the areas of our field that Leslie imagined moving in some day (though, of course, these factors were taken into account).

We say *we* were engaged in a mentoring relationship because we see our work together from a dis/ability[1] perspective that troubles normate assumptions about boundaries between bodies and institutional roles. The term "normate" was first used by Daryl P. Evans (then president of the Society for Disability Studies) to describe both the "burden" and the "unstable position" that disabled individuals must take on to try to pass as able-bodied—a term, Garland Thomson (2017) recollects, through which Evans "gathered the cumulative burden of stigma theory's hard truths and spewed it out with the force of an exorcism" (xiii). As later defined by Garland Thomson (1997), the normate is a "social figure" by which a person can "represent themselves as definite human beings" and is ascribed to "those who, by way of the bodily configurations and cultural capital they assume, can step into a position of authority and wield the power it grants them" (8). Leaky bodies, boundaries, and roles challenge normate assumptions and hold within them the possibility of dis-figuring traditional bodies of knowledge (epistemologies) and bodies of knowledge production (methodologies). Jay Dolmage (2014) suggests that "imperfect, extraordinary, nonnormative bodies [are] the origin and epistemological home of all meaning making" (19). By situating mentoring as a nonnormative function of imperfect (leaky) bodies, we contend that leaky mentoring creates a cripped *metho-epistemology*; that is, ways of knowing and ways of learning that are fluid, that leak into, around, and through each other. This cripped metho-epistemology is similar to the "methodological homeplace" that Eric House, Kelly Medina-López, and Kellie Sharp-Hoskins describe in this collection. What distinguishes this cripped metho-epistemology from more traditional forms of mentoring is that it is unabashedly embodied and assumes—even insists—on forms of embodiment that are permeable, interdependent, and messy.

For us, leaky bodies honor the fact that mentorship relationships have "connective tissues [that] flow through, across, and between always-already connected bodies" (Patsavas, 2014, 213). This idea of circulation among connected bodies is also rhetorical. Dolmage (2014) defines rhetoric as "the circulation of discourse through the body" (5). Our concept of leaky mentoring as a metho-epistemology, then, is ultimately rhetorical as it explains the way connective tissues link bodies of knowledge and knowledge production through a mucosity that stretches across and between mentoring and research. Several decades ago, Patricia Sullivan and James Porter (1997) made the argument that "methodologies are ... rhetorical constructions" and suggested that these constructions are "empowering" (Sullivan and Porter 1997, 10, 11). For Sullivan and Porter

(1997), methodology "is itself an act of rhetoric" (13), a form of invention. Putting together the ideas that methodologies are rhetorical and that rhetoric is the circulation of discourse through the body, we have the foundation for leaky mentoring as a rhetorical metho-epistemology.

In this chapter, we first discuss common models of mentoring in composition studies. We then provide a detailed explanation of how a leaky body practice of mentorship creates an embodied form of knowing (epistemology), after which we turn to the connective tissue between leaky bodies and leaky methodologies by drawing on critical dis/ability studies methodologies. We conclude by proposing a cripped vision of mentoring that not only enables us to rethink traditional mentoring roles but also creates space for a cripped metho-epistemology.

MENTORING

In composition studies, mentoring is often described for the way it "works." There are apprenticeship models where new TAs are assigned to more experienced teachers (Enos 1996; Rickly and Harrington 2002) or informal mentoring relationships that happen serendipitously (Clary-Lemon and Roen 2008; Horner 2008). Sometimes, mentoring is positioned as a solution to management problems (Reid 2010). Feminist scholars have further critiqued the "old-boys' network" (Enos 1996; Rickly and Harrington 2002) ethos of mentoring relationships that "grows out of a master/apprentice model, a model that invokes patriarchal and hierarchical power issues" (Rickly and Harrington 2002, 110).

In tracing the idea of mentoring back to ancient Greece, Jenn Fishman and Andrea Lunsford note that composition studies has a hard time talking about mentoring, and when it does, it "promotes a sense of imbalance by virtually erasing mentees" (Fishman and Lunsford 2008, 28). For example, Julie Nelson Christoph et al. (2010) name three models of mentorship: mentor as friend, mentor as guide, and mentor as diplomat. While all three models break away from the patriarchal models that Horner (2008) and Enos (1996) seek to disrupt, there is no linguistic signaling of the mentee in these models; the emphasis is on what the mentor as actor (subject) does to or for the unsignified mentee (object). Seeing mentors as subjects and mentees as objects simultaneously places impermeable boundaries around the institutional roles they inhabit and erases their individual embodiment. This erasure, however, is a semantic ruse. Mentors and mentees are always already embodied, whether scholarly models articulate or even acknowledge this fact.

The kind of mentoring we are proposing isn't radical per se. Indeed, what we hope to show is that leaky mentoring is simply hidden under layers of paint—paint that can be stripped.[2] Our model of leaky mentoring is born in permeability that is primordial. Fluidity (or mucosity, which we describe below) is essential to leaky mentoring. Because many mentor/mentee relationships are so closely aligned with academic success, and academic success is usually measured through scholarly production, there is a powerful, albeit undertheorized and crooked line between the way we are mentored and the way we approach knowledge production. If our relationships with our mentors reify a master/apprentice model that elides the embodiment of both participants, the implicit message is that research (methodology) should also remain at a remove from its "subjects." If a mentee only experiences discussions about research within the context of the institutional, disembodied role of mentor/mentee, there is little opportunity to critically examine the ways that fleshy presences (Price 2011) complicate the research process. Leaky mentoring, on the other hand, models a methodological stance that foregrounds interdependence, embodiment, and a dismantling of the researcher/subject binary through example (also see Bartlett et al. in this collection).

LEAKY BODIES

Margrit Shildrick (1997) proposes leaky bodies as an ethical concept that responds to the limitations of post-Enlightenment's "devaluation of bodies in general" and to the legacy of the Cartesian dualism, with its reliance on a false sense of fixed, impermeable boundaries between bodies (34); I am me, and you are you (34). Under the rule of such binary thinking, any two people (a mentor and a mentee, for example) interact as "gender-neutral, individual and autonomous actors [who] conduct their own lives and enter into contractual relations with other individuals on the basis of free will and rationality" (Shildrick 1997, 5).

While Shildrick's primary application of leaky bodies is to medical relationships, the concept has been applied to various kinds of identity-formation and ethical decision-making scenarios. Alyson Patsavas, for example, extends leaky bodies through a queercrip analysis that emphasizes our interdependence. When viewed from this standpoint, experiences and relationships have "connective tissues" that "flow through, across, and between always-already connected bodies" (Patsavas 2014, 213). Dan Goodley and Katherine Runswick-Cole (2013) further argue that while some dis/abled bodies are perceived to be more "leaky" than others, ultimately, all bodies leak. Drawing on psychoanalytical theories, Erin Manning (2009) argues for an expanded, leaky "sense of self" that rejects the "skin's capacity to serve as a container for experience" (33). Transnational feminist scholars Teija Rantala, Taru Leppänen, and Mirka Koro (2020) bring leaky bodies to bear on their experiences as women writing in academia in both Finland and Arizona. For these scholars, the "*viscosity* [of leaky bodies] *makes our corporeality* s t r e t c h y and to yield and bend without b*reaking*" (Rantala, Leppänen, and Koro 2020, 121; emphasis in original). The result of leaky bodies is a conceptualization of "leaky writing," which generates and exemplifies "leaky, embodied, and messy writing" that "inform[s] and facilitate[s] academic knowledge production and practices" (Rantala, Leppänen, and Koro 2020, 121, 123).

Applying leaky bodies to bodies in academia and writing reveals another characteristic of leaky bodies: mucosity. For Rantala, Leppänen, and Koro (2020), mucosity emphasizes movement as a central element of leakiness. Drawing on Luce Irigaray's work, they note that mucosity "has no solid permanence and no given form, yet it constitutes the primal material tissue or membrane upon which solidity and permanence ground their form" (Rantala, Leppänen, and Koro 2020, 121). Mucosity as a way of mentoring is a significant departure from traditional theories of mentoring, because it anticipates that the connections between mentor and mentee, and between them to other bodies on campus and in their profession, and between them as researchers to bodies of knowledge and knowledge production, may pulse, morph, and alter in their material constitutions. Such connections, then, are always in flux, always being negotiated and renegotiated, never monolithic, never permanently stabilized. Such an approach to relationships may sound risky. Our experiences tell us it is, and other contributors to this collection, including House et al. and Lesley Erin Bartlett, Jessica Rivera-Mueller, and Sandra L. Tarabochia, report on similar experiences.

LEAKY EPISTEMOLOGY

Citing Hans Keller, Jay Dolmage suggests that disability rhetoric is about "get[ting] the story crooked" (1). This sense of crookedness, of looking at something askance, of seeing dotted, wavy, or curvy lines, opens mentoring up to getting bent. When things are bent, we readjust our lenses to take in the imperfection. And this is how mentoring becomes an epistemology. Looking at the world sideways and upside down impacts the kinds of claims we can make about it (research). Seeing research through a bent lens opens up a plurality of methodologies, because there are myriad ways the lenses can be adjusted.

As we describe above, mentors are most often senior to mentees in terms of institutional role. Sometimes, these relationships are governed by departmental or programmatic guidelines: "Mentors will initiate contact with mentees within the first 3 weeks of the semester;" "mentors will observe mentees' teaching at least twice during their first semester," and so on. These guidelines serve the important function of laying out expectations as well as defining the nature of the relationship (coach, guide, evaluator). Embedded in these defined roles are assumptions about some of the caring labor of a mentoring relationship, such as mentors being available to answer mentee questions, mentors providing professional development advice, and the like.

Yet even these unwritten expectations are generic: *any* mentor is expected to provide these services to *any* mentee. In this sense, the fleshy presence of an individual is not a consideration as the role definition is predicated on normate (Garland Thomson 1997) expectations: abled, white, heterosexual, cis-gender, male bodies that are able to perform the role of mentor or mentee without calling attention to their own embodiment. We call this kind of mentoring "normate mentoring." Normate mentoring is a relationship that proceeds strictly by the book; it is formulaic in the sense that its expectations follow fairly standard paths, paths defined in handbooks or handed down through lore. In some ways, having clear expectations and formulas is comforting—there are no surprises if there is a well-followed script, and having a clear outline of when and how things will happen affords both mentors and mentees a kind of predictability that can ease anxiety and help with time management.

Ultimately, though, normate mentoring requires generic, institutional bodies. Leaky mentorship, on the other hand, is grounded in embodiment, meaning that it is predicated on *individuals'* relationships to each other. While it is certainly the case that all mentoring relationships are about two or more people interacting with each other, leaky mentoring is a kind of "full-contact" mentoring. We don't mean full-contact in the literal sense of bodies smashing up against each other, but we do consider leaky mentoring to be a case where fleshy presences (body-minds) come into full contact with each other. According to Rantala, Leppänen, and Koro (2020), these "leaky processes [bodies] are not obedient; hence, they do not solely remain within our bodies, encounters, and actions as they also leak to everything we do, as to the scientific knowledge we produce" (124). Leaky mentoring encourages different relationships overlapping and feeding each other and producing different relationships among different bodies of knowledge—knowledge as motion, in motion, emotion.

WHAT LEAKING LOOKS LIKE

We began our mentoring relationship during Leslie's doctoral program when Leslie asked Melissa to be her committee chair. At the time, even though not written down anywhere, we knew what our respective institutional roles were. Melissa knew them from her experience with mentoring other graduate students as well as learning from her own mentors and colleagues. Leslie internalized expectations based on her previous experiences as a mentee, through stories from other graduate students, and by observing other faculty-student relationships.

Because Melissa disclosed in class one night that she has had a lifelong struggle with depression, Leslie felt safe enough to disclose that she has social anxiety disorder and generalized anxiety disorder. Melissa's disclosures, as Ribero and Arellano (2019) explain, were important for beginning the relationship, because "a few words about family, hobbies, or even weekend plans can change the dynamic of the conversation so that the junior *comadre* feels safe in sharing some of her own experiences" (345). Indeed, we find many overlaps between our concept of leaky mentoring and the idea of a *comadre* or *comadrismo* that Ribero and Arellano (2019) advocate. A comadre is a "kind of kinship relationship [that] can be built through an effort to get to know and to mentor the whole person" (Ribero and Arellano 2019, 345).[3]

Getting to know each other as comadres made space for us to talk honestly about how our mental health affects our work. As life's inevitable ups and downs—and graduate school's mental and emotional demands—piled up, we were not afraid to openly discuss how our mental states were impacting our work. This honesty mattered because our mental health is part and parcel of who we all are as embodied individuals, and it allowed us to create a kind of shorthand between us wherein we didn't even need to necessarily talk about our struggle, but we could understand, care for, and support each other when needed.

It wasn't just our mental state that leaked into our work. During Leslie's graduate program, we both suffered from significant physical health issues that affected our energy, our ability to concentrate, and sometimes even our ability to just show up. Melissa was hospitalized more than a half a dozen times during Leslie's program and had both emergency and planned surgery. Leslie suffered from debilitating endometriosis and polycystic ovary syndrome, and underwent diagnostic testing for uterine cancer, for which she couldn't get adequate treatment because of the limitations of graduate school health insurance. Performing our institutional roles during these times was complicated, emotional, political, and messy: we missed deadlines, we pulled out of some commitments, we took unofficial[4] mental health days, we cried—yes, in front of each other!—we met off-campus. We hid (some of)[5] our conditions from the director of Graduate Studies and the department chair.

And yet, we leaked. What should not be surprising to anyone is that Leslie was not the only graduate student, nor Melissa the only faculty member, who was struggling with mental and physical health issues, and word quietly spread through the departmental grapevine that we were engaged in something supportive and mutually sustaining. Women scholars, particularly women of color,[6] often talk about the invisible labor of mentoring and, indeed, the leakiness of our relationship was invisible labor. There is no place on our CVs to put "helped mentor/ee schedule X around her cancer/bowel obstruction screening;" no category for "handed out tissues for thirty minutes as mentor/mentee cried about harassment/bullying/discrimination." But, somehow, word got out that we were engaged in something different from what was visible to us of other mentor/mentee relationships.

As one of approximately twenty graduate students in the department, Leslie listened to her peers occasionally talk about their mentoring relationships. Their descriptions seemingly revolved around the "business" of mentoring: meetings that centered students' academic work first and foremost.[7] Leslie's sharing with other graduate students what her mentoring relationship looked (and felt) like even led to some negative criticism from other graduate students, one of whom mentioned that Melissa was less rigorous. The implication seemed to be that, in attending to Leslie's needs holistically, and in allowing Melissa's needs to leak into the mentoring relationship, we somehow were not as disciplined as other mentors and mentees. Leslie sometimes felt that her decision to engage in our mentoring was perceived by other graduate students as a kind of cowardice—as a decision to "get out" of the kinds of mentoring that would prepare her for the "realities" of academia.

We were both struck by the implicit connections graduate students (and perhaps Melissa's colleagues?) might be making between academic "rigor" and embodiment. Why were the two mutually exclusive? Why was talking about and caring for ourselves and each other potentially seen as antithetical to being an academic success? How did being an embodied mentor and mentee become synonymous with having a weak research methodology and poor academic credentials?

These questions ultimately led to the creation of a group that affectionately called itself "Compsters." Compsters, an example of the "slow mentoring" Bartlett et al. (this collection) describe, began from a simple meeting Leslie organized for a group of graduate students, all being advised by Melissa, to discuss their exams and Melissa's expectations. While Melissa and each graduate student co-created their own mentoring space, the leakiness of those relationships seeped into Compsters, wherein those graduate students (led by Leslie) co-created their own mentoring spaces. Mentoring begets mentoring; leakiness begets leakiness. Leakiness generates knowledge.

The best example of the leakiness of the Compsters peer-mentoring group was their face-to-face meetings. When Leslie and the founding members of Compsters conceptualized the group, they called themselves Compsters because they were all at some stage of preparing for *comp*rehensive examinations. Leslie already had her reading lists finalized by the first meeting; others were working on creating reading lists.

In the beginning, Compsters meetings had a specific agenda that was planned ahead of time, such as reading an article or a book on all of their reading lists and then having the space to work through them together. But mentoring begets leakiness and leakiness begets mentoring. Compsters rarely stuck to those agendas, because, in time, Leslie and the other members found they needed a place to be whole—to leak—more than they needed another space to talk about theory. A conversation that might start off with a question like "How did you decide what to put on your reading list" often leaked to other concerns: Are these books available in the library or interlibrary loan? If not, how would we get ahold of them on our shoestring stipends? Was it the kind of book that was compact and could be taken to the park with kids? What seemed at the time like getting off-topic quickly became the topic of our meetings. The more time the group went off-track, the more time Compsters devoted to *choosing to get off-track*, the more Compsters went *sideways and crooked*, the more members were able to support one another through the various challenges they faced, by cripping what mentoring looked like.

And as Compsters' conversations went down these bendy roads, the members' methodologies changed as well. One member ultimately decided to pursue a creative-scholarly dissertation instead of the qualitative one he originally planned on; another member decided that teaching was his primary objective and left the doctoral program; another decided to do a theoretical dissertation instead of the pedagogical one she originally imagined. Arguably, these kinds of changes are part and parcel of the invention and revision of any research project. But we believe what catalyzed these changes—or at least authorized them—was the attention to embodiment in our mentoring relationships. Ultimately, the question of whether our mentoring relationship was academically rigorous enough shouldn't be assessed by traditional measures of "academic success" (tenure and promotion, awards, publications, etc.) but rather by whether Leslie and Melissa both achieved their goals while honoring the needs, desires, and will of our body-minds—and we did![8] (Also see House et al. in this collection.)

PUTTING THE METHO IN METHO-EPISTEMOLOGY

A methodology, in its simplest sense, is a theory about how research should proceed and the assumptions about knowledge-making embedded in such theories. Gesa Kirsch and Patricia A. Sullivan (1992) define methodology as "the underlying theory and analysis of how research does or should proceed" (2). Gesa Kirsch (1992) expands this definition by suggesting research methods are "specific research technique[s] . . . and methodology [means] the theory of knowledge making *implied* in a method or set of methods" (266–267; emphasis added). J. Blake Scott and Lisa Melonçon (2018) add that methodologies are "value-laden frameworks" (1). These definitions foreground methodology as a way of approaching our research subjects, topics, and practices. Taken in this light, it becomes impossible to escape the sinuous connective tissues between methodologies and epistemologies. How we make sense of the world will always inform how we choose to study the world around us. Epistemologies inform methodologies. Similarly, the way we study the world around us informs how we make sense of the world around us. Methodologies inform epistemologies.

Because the mentor/mentee relationship is so closely aligned with academic success, there is a bold, albeit undertheorized and crooked, line between the way we are mentored and the way we approach knowledge production. If our relationships with our mentors reify a master/apprentice model that elides the embodiment of both participants, the implicit message is that research (methodology) should also remain removed from its subjects. If a mentee only experiences discussions about research within the context of normate mentoring, there is little opportunity to critically examine the ways that fleshy presences complicate the research process. Leaky mentoring, on the other hand, models a methodological stance that foregrounds interdependence, embodiment, and a dismantling of the researcher/subject binary through example.

Our purpose in framing mentoring around a metho-epistemology framework is to honor and emphasize the connective tissues that primordially exist between bodies, human and nonhuman. In the previous section, we explored the connective tissues that exist among mentor bodies, mentee bodies, and bodies of knowledge (epistemologies). In this section, we build upon these connective networks by exploring the connective tissues among mentor and mentee bodies and bodies of knowledge production (methodologies) and argue that without attending to the connections among all these bodies, methodological innovation stalls. These constellations of bodies mirror Rantala, Leppänen, and Koro's (2020) image of mucosity. Leaky mentoring relationships must "expand and contract" as mentees' and mentors' needs change, to honor the fact that mentoring "is more fluid than solid, and even though it does not necessarily transform itself in terms of shape or in a quantifiable manner" (121). Likewise, as graduate student researchers move through the liminal space between student and scholar, graduate mentors aid in bridging the divide through mentoring students in research practices.

In many normate mentoring relationships, graduate students may generate their own research projects, but too often those projects look more and more like a pattern cut from the mentor's work. Aja Y. Martinez's (2014) story of a Chican@ graduate student who has failed her qualifying exams is illuminative here. In the story, graduate instructors and the graduate program director discuss the student's failures, in part because they reject her research project ("her work is difficult for us to wrap our minds around because it's unconventional, probably by and large due to the fact that she approaches it from a perspective we're not trained in or accustomed to") and because "her research interests are beyond our areas of expertise," which leads them to fear "that she has the potential to say things we're uncomfortable with" (Martinez 2014, 43–44). We add to Martinez's critique of the normalizing effects of traditional mentoring by calling for an approach to mentoring that makes space for graduate students to explore methodological questions by way of the leaks and flows they experience.

But meaning-making, when viewed through a leaky perspective, is not just a two-way street between epistemologies and methodologies. A leaky approach to meaning-making necessarily requires an understanding of how the human actors impinge upon (and are impinged upon by) methodologies and epistemologies. While many postmodern epistemologies recognize that bodies must be central to our theoretical work—standpoint theory, queer theories, critical race theories, crip theories—some of our methodologies do not yet fully account for how the researchers' bodies inform methodologies and vice versa. Put another way, many methodologies assume a normative body when conceptualizing who researchers are and what they do. Some methodologies, particularly those that insist on RADs (replicable, aggregable, data-driven approaches), assume that researchers are interchangeable; they can be replaced, and the research can continue.

Our experiences with Leslie's dissertation offer some insight into how a leaky-bodies metho-epistemology impacts research practices. Because of Leslie's ongoing health problems, we began having extended conversations about how to carry out the project Leslie had proposed in her prospectus. Some committee members felt strongly that to do the case study component of the project, Leslie should apply for a fellowship that would extend her funding by a year. Doing so would give Leslie the time needed to sink into the depth of a "proper" case study. If the fellowship could not be obtained, some committee members felt that delaying graduation, even without funding, would make for the best case studies and, therefore, was the best option for her dissertation and for her prospects as a job candidate.

From Leslie's perspective, the most pressing need was not an extensive case study; rather, it was securing employment that would provide her with health insurance to attend to her needs and the (relative) stability that would make caring for herself more manageable. As we worked together to find a path that would honor Leslie's needs and lead to successful case studies, we began to see this part of the research not as Leslie doing a case study but as *Leslie's Case Study*. The project began to take on an aspect of Rantala, Leppänen, and Koro's sense of mucosity: protocols were (re)set crookedly, timelines rewritten, all meant to flow between Leslie's needs (as a researcher, a graduate student, a first-generation college student, a human being) and accepted disciplinary expectations for this research method.

Margaret Price and Stephanie Kerschbaum (2016) challenge the idea of normative, institutional research by proposing a critical disability studies (CDS) methodology. A CDS methodology is about "studying broken systems, broken attitudes, broken gazes" and looks at research "sideways, crooked and crip (Price and Kerschbaum 2016, 23, 19)." One of the important foci of CDS is on *inter*dependence, or the idea that we are "collectively enabled and collectively limited" (Price and Kerschbaum

2016, 27). CDS methodology taps into the inherent connectedness of all bodies, thereby making it also a form of institutional embodiment. It is only with "fleshy presences" that research is conducted.

Price and Kerschbaum's work also demonstrates how a CDS methodology would alter disciplinary assumptions about objectivity and replicability in our research practices. Their CDS methodology emerges from their ongoing qualitative research on the experiences of dis/abled faculty members. Even within rhetoric and composition, we expect certain standards to inform research, to be implemented during research, and to be presented when research is reported. However, Price and Kerschbaum's (2016) work reveals the already existing cracks in the facade of scientific objectivity; their work illustrates how they function as both "actors and characters" within interviews (23). Leaky mentoring is a form of CDS methodology inasmuch as it challenges assumptions about what mentoring means, who participates in it, and in what contexts. Leaky mentoring's values-laden framework, like Price and Kerschbaum's, honors the sideways, the crooked, and the crip by presupposing that there are no normative mentoring relationships, no standard or typical mentors or mentees, no rigid rules for the place mentoring happens, no institutional bodies. Only and always institutional embodiment.

Leaky mentoring as a CDS methodology requires researchers to "ask difficult questions and accept provisional answers" (Garland Thomson 1997, 40) and to acknowledge—rather than obscure—how their (and their research subjects') evolving needs require that research methods remain in flux, always flowing, always leaky. And if our methods are leaky, then methodologies are ipso facto leaky as well. We have little doubt that there are links, relationships, and leakages between most—if not all—researchers and their subjects (or subject matters), or even that our research always already produces provisional answers rather than unqualified, absolute knowledge. However, what we have seen are research projects that have largely attempted to deemphasize these entanglements rather than celebrate and nurture them.

Like CDS, critical race theory offers us another example of methodological innovation by attending to leakages. As Aja Y. Martinez (2020) explains, methodologies of critical race theory (CRT) are premised on many of the same tenets we have advanced in leaky bodies; namely, a rejection of the idea that research is objective, or that the researcher's fleshy presence is irrelevant. Martinez (2020) adds that, "[importantly,] critical race methodology recognizes that experiential knowledge of people of color is legitimate and critical to understanding racism that is often well disguised in the rhetoric of normalized structural values and practices" (3). Just as Price and Kerschbaum arrive at a CDS methodology by attending to how positioning disability is central to their work as researchers and continually prioritizing access throughout the research process, Martinez (2020) likewise outlines how counterstory has emerged by prioritizing the needs of scholars of color: "POC have thus developed methods and methodologies that serve as coping mechanisms and navigation strategies, while also serving as ways to raise awareness of issues affecting people of color that are often overlooked, not considered, or otherwise invisible to whites" (10).

Another notable component of counterstory methodologies is the insistence on accessibility. Returning again to Martinez (2020), "a methodological consideration for counterstory should always envision a multiplicity of audiences beyond the ivory tower" and, in this regard, "if my work in counterstory is inaccessible to the very people who it is for—well, then what's the point" (18). We hear resonances between leaky bodies and Martinez's work in defining counterstory as a methodology. Both insist that who we are as researchers is always part of the complex web that exists between researchers, epistemologies, and epistemologies. But Martinez's work also highlights the value—not just the reality—of the leaks and flows that cross all bodies.

Taken together, what we see in recent methodological developments in rhetoric and composition is that new and innovative methodological innovations are coming from scholars and practices that foster leaks and flows between researchers, research practices, and research subjects. Centering leaky bodies from the beginning of mentoring relationships reveals specific ways that leaky bodies change the assumptions and outcomes that ordinarily characterize research situations. More specifically, leaky mentoring enables methodological innovation by breaking down myths of institutional bodies doing research and prioritizes researchers' fleshy presence and positionality as the starting points of research. We need mentoring relationships that prioritize leaky bodies in order to prepare graduate students, emergent researchers, for methodological practices that will require them to leak. Again, leaky mentoring begets leaky scholars who can engage in leaky research.

CONCLUSION

One final example. After Melissa left the university where Leslie was finishing her doctoral work, Leslie needed to lean on other committee members for day-to-day-type questions. Julie (not her real name) was a committee member and new assistant professor who specialized in research methods, so she became the go-to for most study-related questions. Unbeknownst to Leslie at the time, however, was that Melissa (associate professor) and Julie (assistant professor) were also engaged in an unofficial mentoring relationship, and as Julie took on a more proactive role of mentoring Leslie in Melissa's physical absence, Melissa was providing advice to Julie about how to mentor graduate students. We were leaking all over each other!

These connected mentoring relationships formed and reformed the ways in which Leslie thought about her research project and eventually collected data and analyzed it. Melissa's coaching about how to work with doctoral students helped shape and reshape Julie's mentoring of Leslie; Julie's mentoring of Leslie shaped and reshaped Melissa and Leslie's relationship; and Julie's emerging mentoring skills shaped and reshaped her relationships to other mentees. Additionally, all of these stretchy connections influenced the ways we individually and collectively interpreted Leslie's dissertation. The discourse of "the dissertation," of "mentoring," of "doing research" circulated among us individuals (re)forming consubstantial spaces for knowledge creation and production.

As this last example illustrates, the institutional roles the members of a mentoring relationship occupy are not of as much import as the inter- and intra-workings of the embodied individuals in those roles. Leaky mentoring offers composition studies a model of mentoring that de-emphasizes a mentoring formula (i.e., more experienced mentors and less experienced mentees) and instead reframes mentoring as a means of knowledge production and assembly that is primordially rooted in embodiment. Leaky mentoring starts with embodiment on full display. A cripped metho-epistemology that begins with leaky mentoring enables us to see knowledge production and assembly sideways and crooked within rhetorical consubstational spaces that are ever enfolding and s t r e t c h i n g.

NOTES

1. Throughout this chapter we use the term "dis/ability" to convey the different aspects of disabled lives. We follow dis/ability scholars before us (Goodley 2014; Goodley and Runswick-Cole 2016; Schalk 2017) in representing dis/ability with the forward slash to "designate the socially constructed system of norms which categorizes and values bodyminds based on concepts of ability and disability" (Schalk 2017). In so choosing, our goal is not to minimize the reclamation of "disabled" as an identity category or the use of other forms of representing dis/abled lives (crip, mad, disabled, [dis]abled, etc.) (cf. Kafer 2013; Price 2017).

2. This collection is an excellent example of the ways scholars are beginning to chip away at this topic.
3. *Comadrismo* is a specific kind of mentoring relationship that Ribero and Arellano (2019) suggest is necessary for Latinas to find the support and community they need and to be successful in the academy. While their model centers Latina experiences, they also suggest that "some or all of what we propose here may be useful to people of different positionalities" (Ribero and Arellano 2019, 336). We see our model of leaky mentoring and comadrismo as sharing the same concern for community (kinship) building.
4. We say *unofficial* mental health days, because most universities have no mechanism in place for graduate students or faculty to take a day or two off. We are usually expected to be on call, even when we should be resting, so many of us try to create our own sick days by rearranging meetings, canceling class, or "only" answering email for a few hours. However, even these work-arounds are problematic, because there is worry about being "caught" or anxiety about how much work is not getting done, or fear of having a body-mind that can't cut it in academia.
5. While we did not share our mental health issues with departmental administration, there were certain things that we needed to share, like Melissa's need to take six weeks of medical leave for surgery.
6. While it is beyond the scope of this article, we want to acknowledge the connections between leaky mentoring, invisible labor, race, gender, socioeconomic class, and other elements of intersectionality. For more detailed analysis, readers may wish to start with Buttorff (2020); June (2015); and Social Sciences Feminist Network (2017).
7. Given that neither of us were part of these other mentoring relationships, we can't guess at what was said in other people's meetings. We are only remarking on our perception, based on what we heard and how other graduate students responded (often surprise, sometimes a bit of incredulousness) when Leslie shared some of the leaky mentoring in which she engaged with Melissa.
8. By traditional measures, we have been successful as well.

REFERENCES

Buttorff, Gail. 2020. "Gender, Covid, and Faculty Service." *Inside Higher Ed*, December 18, 2020. https://www.insidehighered.com/advice/2020/12/18/increasingly-dispropor tionate-service-burden-female-faculty-bear-will-have.

Christoph, Julie, Rebecca Nowacek, Mary Lou Odom, and Bonnie Kathryn Smith. 2010. "Three Models of Mentorship: Feminist Leadership and the Graduate Student WPA." In *Performing Feminism and Administration in Rhetoric and Composition Studies*, edited by Krista Ratcliffe and Rebecca Rickly, 93–106. New York: Hampton Press.

Clary-Lemon, Jennifer, and Duane Roen. 2008. "Webs of Mentoring in Graduate School." In *Stories of Mentoring: Theory and Praxis*, edited by Michelle Eble and Lynée Lewis Gaillet, 178–192. West Lafayette, IN: Parlor Press.

Dolmage, Jay. 2014. *Disability Rhetoric*. Syracuse, NY: Syracuse University Press.

Enos, Theresa. 1996. "Mentoring—and (Wo)mentoring—in Composition Studies." In *Academic Advancement in Composition Studies: Scholarship, Publication, Promotion, Tenure*, edited by Richard Gebhardt and Barbara Genelle Smith Gebhardt. New York: Taylor and Francis.

Fishman, Jenn, and Andrea Lunsford. 2008. "Educating Jane." In *Stories of Mentoring: Theory and Praxis*, edited by Michelle Eble and Lynée Lewis Gaillet, 18–32. West Lafayette, IN: Parlor Press.

Garland Thomson, Rosemarie. 1997. *Extraordinary Bodies: Figuring Physical Disability in American Culture and Literature.* New York: Columbia University Press.

Garland Thomson, Rosemarie. 2017. "Preface to the Twentieth Anniversary Edition." In *Extraordinary Bodies: Figuring Physical Disability in American Culture and Literature.* Twentieth anniv. ed. New York: Columbia University Press.

Goodley, Daniel. 2014. *Dis/abilty Studies: Theorising Disablism and Ableism.* London: Taylor & Francis.

Goodley, Daniel, and Katherine Runswick-Cole. 2013. "The Body as Disability and Possability: Theorizing the 'Leaking, Lacking and Excessive' Bodies of Disabled Children." *Scandinavian Journal of Disability Research* 15 (1), 1–19. https://doi.org/10.1080/15017419.2011.640410.

Goodley, Daniel, and Katherine Runswick-Cole. 2016. "Becoming Dishuman: Thinking about the Human through Dis/Ability." *Discourse: Studies in the Cultural Politics of Education* 37 (1): 1–15.

Horner, Winifred Bryan. 2008. "On Mentoring." In *Stories of Mentoring: Theory and Praxis*, edited by Michelle Eble and Lynée Lewis Gaillet, 14–17. West Lafayette, IN: Parlor Press.

June, Audrey Williams. 2015. "The Invisible Labor of Minority Faculty." *Chronicle of Higher Education*, November 8, 2015. https://www.chronicle.com/article/the-invisible-labor-of-minority-professors/.

Kafer, Alison. 2013. *Feminist, Queer, Crip.* Bloomington: Indiana University Press.

Kirsch, Gesa. 1992. "Methodological Pluralism: Epistemological Issues." In *Methods and Methodologies in Composition Studies*, edited by Gesa Kirsch and Patricia Sullivan, 247–269. Carbondale: Southern Illinois University Press.

Kirsch, Gesa, and Patricia Sullivan. 1992. "Introduction." In *Methods and Methodologies in Composition Studies*, edited by Gesa Kirsch and Patricia Sullivan, 1–11. Carbondale: Southern Illinois University Press.

Manning, Erin. 2009. "What If It Didn't All Begin and End with Containment? Toward a Leaky Sense of Self." *Body and Society* 15 (3): 33–45. https://doi.org/10.1177/1357034X09337785.

Martinez, Aja Y. 2014. "A Plea for Critical Race Theory Counterstory: Stock Story versus Counterstory Dialogues Concerning Alejandra's 'Fit' in the Academy." *Composition Studies* 42 (2): 33–55.

Martinez, Aja Y. 2020. *Counterstory: The Rhetoric and Writing of Critical Race Theory.* Champaign, IL: National Council of Teachers of English.

Patsavas, Alyson. 2014. "Recovering a Cripistemology of Pain: Leaky Bodies, Connective Tissue, and Feeling Discourse." *Journal of Literary and Cultural Disability Studies* 8 (2): 203–218. https://doi.org/10.3828/jlcds.2014.16.

Price, Margaret. 2011. *Mad at School: Rhetorics of Mental Disability and Academic Life.* Ann Arbor: University of Michigan Press.

Price, Margaret. 2017. "Defining Mental Disability." In *The Disability Studies Reader*, edited by Lennard J. Davis, 333–342. 5th ed. New York: Routledge.

Price, Margaret, and Stephanie Kerschbaum. 2016. "Stories of Methodology: Interviewing Sideways, Crooked and Crip." *Canadian Journal of Disability Studies* 5 (3): 18–56.

Rantala, Teija, Tara, Leppänen, and Mirka Koro. 2020. "Mucous Bodies, Messy Affects, and Leaky-Writing in Academia." *Taboo: The Journal of Culture and Education* 19 (5): 120–132.

Reid, E. Shelley. 2010. "Managed Care: All Terrain Mentoring and the 'Good Enough' Feminist WPA." In *Performing Feminism and Administration in Rhetoric and Composition Studies*, edited by Krista Ratcliffe and Rebecca Rickly, 125–141. New York: Hampton Press.

Ribero, Ana Milena, and Sonia C. Arellano. 2019. "Advocating Comadrismo: A Feminist Mentoring Approach for Latinas in Rhetoric and Composition." *Peitho* 21 (2): 334–356.

Rickly, Rebecca, and Susanmarie Harrington. 2002. "Feminist Approaches to Mentoring Teaching Assistants: Conflict, Power, and Collaboration." In *Preparing College Teachers of Writing: Histories, Theories, Programs, Practices*, edited by Betty P. Pytlik and Sarah Liggett, 108–120. Oxford: Oxford University Press.

Schalk, Sami. 2017. "Critical Disability Studies as Methodology." *Lateral: Journal of the Cultural Studies Association* 6 (1). https://csalateral.org/issue/6-1/forum-alt-humanities-critical-disability-studies-methodology-schalk/.

Scott, J. Blake, and Lisa Melonçon. 2018. "Manifesting Methodologies for the Rhetoric of Health and Medicine." In *Methodologies for the Rhetoric of Health and Medicine*, edited by J. Blake Scott and Lisa Melonçon, 1–23. New York: Routledge.

Shildrick, Margrit. 1997. *Leaky Bodies and Boundaries: Feminism, Postmodernism, and (Bio)Ethics*. London: Routledge.

Social Sciences Feminist Network Research Interest Group. 2017. "The Burden of Invisible Work in Academia: Social Inequalities and Time Use in Five University Departments." *Humboldt Journal of Social Relations* 1 (39): 228–245.

Sullivan, Patricia, and James Porter. 1997. "Introducing Critical Research Practices." In *Opening Spaces: Writing Technologies and Critical Research Practices*, edited by Patricia Sullivan and James Porter, 1–14. Greenwich, CT: Ablex Publishing.

VanHaitsma, Pamela, and Steph Ceraso. 2017. " 'Making It' in the Academy through Horizontal Mentoring." *Peitho* 19 (2): 210–233.

13
TESTIMONIO AS A METHODOLOGY FOR EXAMINING MARGINALIZED EXPERIENCES WITH MENTORSHIP

Michelle Flahive

In this chapter, I present *testimonio* as a method and methodology for studying mentorship with women of color (WOC) in writing studies. Testimonio is a narrative method grounded in critical race theory (CRT) and Latino critical race theory. I propose testimonio as a way to address the need for equitable mentorship for marginalized graduate student instructors (GSIs) in writing studies.

Mentorship is a critical component of graduate student preparation. However, there remains a problem with access to mentorship for graduate students in rhetoric and composition (e.g., Okawa 2002; Ribero and Arellano 2019; VanHaitsma and Ceraso 2017). Research in writing studies has called attention to the fact that differences in race, gender, ethnicity, and language can affect mentorship for GSIs (e.g., Okawa 2002; Ribero and Arellano 2019; VanHaitsma and Ceraso 2017; Villanueva 1993). However, research on GSI mentorship in writing studies has yet to address *how* these differences affect access to mentorship for GSIs (e.g., see Reed 2020; Reid 2008; Restaino 2012; Stancliff and Goggin 2007; Stenberg and Lee 2002). Essentially, the histories of writing studies demonstrate how the problems marginalized GSIs face with mentorship remain unaddressed.

In what follows, I demonstrate how testimonio can be used to connect and present the experiences of WOC[1] with the purpose of developing strategies for improving mentorship in their particular context. To do this, I will first define testimonio as a method and methodology. Then, I will discuss how I initially approached testimonio by exploring my own experiences with mentorship as a Latina GSI in writing studies at a PWI, some lessons I learned about mentorship from my own individual testimonio, and how my initial individual approach to testimonio shaped the way that I approached my dissertation. Next, I discuss what

https://doi.org/10.7330/9781646425822.c013

I learned by applying collaborative testimonio—*testimoniando*, which is a collaborative methodology of dialogic research that I used to research mentorship with WOC GSIs in writing studies in my dissertation. I will also discuss the lessons I learned about using testimoniando to study mentorship with WOC, including the value and challenges of beginning with written critical reflection, the need for ample time and space to discuss experiences, and the capacity of testimonio to activate change. I conclude this chapter with further potential uses of testimonio in writing studies.

TESTIMONIO

To situate testimonio as a method and methodology for studying mentorship in writing studies, this section defines testimonio as a method of data collection, then discusses testimonio as a methodology. Next in this section, I present examples of how testimonio has been used to examine injustices in education. I then detail my own approaches to individual testimonio and collaborative testimonio. Finally, I discuss how my application of testimonio in my dissertation studies differs from traditional applications.

Testimonio is a method of articulating the lived experiences of marginalized people and connecting those experiences to social and political realities in order to identify and counter social and racial injustices. As a critical research practice in educational contexts, testimonio has been developed by Chicana and Latina feminist theorists who have drawn on Latin American social movements (e.g., Paulo Freire's process of *conscientization*) to develop a method for naming and resisting oppression and marginalization (Blackmer Reyes and Curry Rodríguez 2012, 527; Pérez Huber and Cueva 2012, 393). Testimonio can be applied to research to counter hegemonic norms from the perspective of marginalized people, thus transforming disciplinary knowledge by including perspectives that might be otherwise overlooked (Latina Feminist Group 2001, 19). Because of its foundation in CRT and LatCrit theory, testimonio provides a framework for eliciting and analyzing critical narratives from research participants.

As a method of data collection, testimonio engages participants in the research process by centering their experiences as knowledge through critical self-reflection. As a product, testimonio is a personal narrative that connects the oppressed storyteller's lived experiences to sociopolitical realities (Delgado Bernal, Burciaga, and Flores Carmona 2012, 364). As a process for the participant, testimonio involves critical reflection on personal experiences within particular sociopolitical realities (364). These stories respond to social and political injustices with the purpose of identifying injustices and raising awareness of oppression (Pérez Huber 2012, 379). Thus, the process of testimonio empowers the participant, and the product works to counter systemic structures of oppression by naming systems of oppression and identifying collective strategies for resisting and transforming those systems.

As a methodology, testimonio is guided by how and in which principles of CRT or LatCrit the researcher has framed their study and the research's purpose. However, this interpretation is guided by the collective goal of naming oppressive structures and stopping their actions (Blackmer Reyes and Curry Rodríguez 2012, 527). For example, J. Estrella Torrez (2015) analyzed her own testimonio, of how she experienced obstacles to enacting a "pedagogy of love," in her classroom through a Chicana feminist framework so that she could examine her classroom practices and understand how her experiences shaped those practices (127). While Torrez's methods for interpreting her testimonio are similar to autoethnographic methods, Lindsay Pérez Huber (2012) offers a syncretic, iterative approach of critical race–grounded theory for analyzing a collection of testimonios (383). While the motivations and purposes for engaging in testimonio may vary, they must be rooted in the desire to reveal how the marginalized and oppressed experience injustice, in order to empower the storyteller and reveal collective strategies for resisting and surviving oppression.

While I position testimonio as a method for examining mentorship in writing studies, testimonio has been commonly applied as a way to examine pedagogical practices in the field of education. For example, J. Estrella Torrez (2015) and Cruz Medina (2018) both highlight the value of testimonio as a CRT method in the writing classroom. Torrez offers testimonio as a strategy for BIPOC teachers who are engaging in antiracist pedagogy to critically reflect on how they encounter challenges to their pedagogy in their classroom in order to identify and adopt strategies for resisting the structures that create those challenges. Also, Medina identifies testimonio as a pedagogical practice by framing it in a multimodal framework of composition. Medina offers digital testimonio as an activity that can be used in writing courses to provide students from marginalized backgrounds the chance "to write for a public audience," which "works against the experience of feeling silenced as a so-called imposter, an affirmative action beneficiary, or a scholarship student who does not belong" (para. 1). Medina also points out that "digital testimonio exposes students who do not experience systemic or institutional oppression to experiences that inform them of their roles as allies" (para. 1). Together, Torrez's and Medina's work show how testimonio can support marginalized people to identify tools for resisting oppression through their experiences, and then share those tools with allies who seek to challenge oppression.

Lindsay Pérez Huber's (2009) research is also in the field of education; however, her application of testimonio focuses on student experiences of oppression. In her article "Disrupting an Apartheid of Knowledge: Testimonio as Methodology in Latina/o Critical Race Research in Education," Pérez Huber examined how students in primary and secondary public schools experience and counter microaggressions. Also, Pérez Huber (2012) describes her use of testimonio to study the differences between documented and undocumented Chicana undergraduate experiences. Pérez Huber also identifies a framework for testimonio, which shows where the goals of testimonio overlap with LatCrit theory (645):

1. Revealing injustices caused by oppression
2. Challenging dominant Eurocentric ideologies
3. Validating experiential knowledge
4. Acknowledging the power of human collectivity
5. Showing a commitment to racial and social justice

The collaborative testimonio approach that I followed for my dissertation was adapted from Lindsey Pérez Huber's (2012) approach to testimonio, which she calls testimoniando. Testimoniando is a process of doing research with WOC. This process requires the researcher to co-construct knowledge with the participants rather than tell their stories for them. Pérez Huber engaged in the process of testimoniando with both US-born and undocumented Chicana undergraduates in order to study their experiences with racism in their institution of study. In her study, Pérez Huber engaged her twenty participants in two audio-recorded testimonio interviews. She audio recorded and transcribed these interviews and began preliminary data analysis. Then, she conducted two focus groups with participants to collaboratively analyze the themes that she found in the data before she conducted her final data analysis.

Following the work of Pérez Huber's (2012), my analyses for my dissertation drew on Malagnón, Vélez, and Pérez Huber's (2009) approach to critical race–grounded theory and Thornberg and Charmaz's (2012) grounded theory. What a critical race–grounded methodology approach to grounded theory involves is the intentions of "illuminat[ing] the patterns of racialized inequality by recounting experiences of racism, both individual and shared, in order to reveal multiple perspectives that have long been silenced" (267). Malagón, Pérez Huber, and Vélez suggest that a critical race–grounded methodology is also defined by the use of

- theoretical sampling as a strategy to include participants and contexts capable of revealing categories around patterns of inequality.
- a conditional matrix (as introduced by Strauss and Corbin), used to "uncover the relationship between agency, structure, and critique" (267).
- a collaborative analysis process that includes participants in the construction of knowledge during the data-analysis process.

A major difference in my application of testimoniando in my dissertation is that I employ testimoniando to examine the experiences of WOC GSIs, rather than explicitly focusing on subaltern or Latinx experiences. This brings up the possible, and welcome, critique of the application of this methodology in this study. As mentioned by Delgado Bernal, Burciaga, and Flores Carmona (2012), testimonio as a methodology has been traditionally reserved to tell the stories of the subaltern—those whose voices would otherwise remain silent (366). Further, the history and use of testimonio has been traditionally and historically used to tell the stories of Latinx people. I wholly acknowledge that WOC in a graduate school setting cannot (or perhaps should not) be described as subaltern; however, I acknowledge their oppression by both global and national social and political structures, and within the context of the institution. In Pérez Huber's (2012) response to Tierney's warning of the possibility of the appropriation of testimonio by anyone who has struggled, regardless of their privilege, she states: "However, we must remember the original purpose of testimonio—to center the knowledge and experiences of the oppressed" (386). I agree with Pérez Huber on this front, and while I know that none of my participants need me to tell their story, I do believe testimonio is a valuable tool for studying those who are oppressed within my graduate program. Further, there are implications for empowering those participants through collectivity and developing inclusive practices for GSI training and mentorship in doing so.

While there is plenty of guidance on testimonio to be gleaned from the field of education, the researcher's flexibility within the methodology of testimonio reflects the principles of CRT in LatCrit theory that guide testimonio research.

USING TESTIMONIO INDIVIDUALLY: EXAMINING THE SELF

For my individual testimonio, I reflected on the question of how I, as a Latina GSI, was able to navigate bringing antiracist and decolonizing methods of teaching and research into my work as a GSI in a predominantly white program. I then analyzed my reflection using a CRT grounded theory approach from a Chicana feminist epistemological standpoint. From my individual testimonio, I found two major themes. First, I identified mentorship interactions as a key factor in how I was able to navigate my research and identity as a Latina in writing studies at a PWI. However, I was troubled that I had also noticed that, for the most part, the mentoring interactions that supported me in my trajectory were ones that I had specifically sought out. Considering my position and privileges in the context of my graduate program, I wondered how other marginalized GSIs were able to (or not able to) access mentorship to support their needs as teachers and scholars. These two findings are what eventually led me to my dissertation, which I discuss further in the next section. In this section, I discuss why I chose testimonio as an approach to my individual testimonio, and how a critical race-grounded theory approach was used in analysis. Then, I will present the lessons that I learned about mentorship and positionality from that individual testimonio. Finally, in this section, I explain how recognizing the relationship between my positionality and access to mentorship shaped my dissertation study.

Testimonio: How and Why

I first encountered testimonio as a methodology through the works of J. Estrella Torrez (2015) and Lindsey Pérez Huber (2012); both authors drew on Delgado Bernal et al.'s (2012) work to develop approaches to testimonio that could identify and counter places of oppression for Latinxs in education. I chose testimonio because, as a methodology, it not only accounts for but also leverages positionality as a research tool for examining experiences and connecting them to larger social and political contexts. Further, engaging in Chicana feminist theory in a PWI was empowering, because it made me feel connected to a larger community of Latinidad, which I felt isolated from in my graduate program. My goal for using testimonio was to analyze my experiences and find a way to discuss and learn from those experiences in a larger scholarly context. Of equal importance to me was to explore testimonio, Chicana feminist epistemologies, and critical race–grounded methodology to prepare for my dissertation.

Lessons from My Individual Testimonio: Positionality and Mentorship

From my analysis of my individual testimonio, two prominent findings informed my dissertation research: first, I uncovered the significance of my positionality as it related to the context in which I was working to bring decolonial and antiracist approaches into my work as a GSI. Second, I noted that the instances of mentorship that supported me in my endeavor were not ones built into my program but instead ones that I sought out. Below I discuss these findings further.

The most difficult part of bringing decolonial and antiracist approaches into my work as a GSI was negotiating how to discuss race, ethnicity, and linguistic justice in the context of a PWI as a Latina. The struggles, I found, were related to my positionality: first, I was navigating a new, predominantly white field that largely assumes heterogeneity in definitions of language and English; I did not see myself nor my perspectives in this field. Second, I was learning to navigate a predominantly white space in my program, where the topic of race was rarely mentioned and felt taboo. Next, I will discuss instances from my testimonio that demonstrate these struggles I faced.

First, learning how to incorporate conversations around racial justice in my work proved laborious in time and emotion. In my testimonio, I noted:

> Looking for scholarship entirely outside of my course readings, and outside of, and sometimes conflicting with the foundational theories that I had learned thus far, was exhausting. I also worried how pursuing this mode of inquiry would affect my chances of one day being able to join in "legitimate" scholarly conversations in rhetoric as a discipline.

The lack of representation in the field also brought on anxieties—feelings of not belonging in the discipline—and caused me to view the centering of marginalized voices in my classroom as an act of vulnerability. I noted in my testimonio, "I was worried that bringing in Chicana scholarship might seem like I was centering the beliefs of my own subjectivity." The scarcity of the voices and knowledges of Black, Indigenous, and people of color (BIPOC), in both my graduate classroom and writing program also compounded feelings of being an imposter as a new PhD student and GSI, and the lack of comfortability that I had with incorporating antiracist theory into my teaching and research. For example, as I worked through my research ideas in a discussion with a white professor and mentor, I noted that "I did not have discomfort with the term white, what I had, and still have, is discomfort presenting ideas that are critical of whiteness to White people." This discomfort points to the importance of white faculty's willingness to discuss whiteness and white supremacy in

PWIs. Especially for marginalized scholars, who may already be hesitant to challenge or offend faculty in their program by discussing race, white faculty, who maintain more power than GSIs of color in both their institutional and social positions. The silence around race in the context that I was navigating as a GSI proved difficult for me to breach because of my anxieties around my lack of knowledge and power.

Ultimately, it was mentoring interactions and relationships that supported me in overcoming these challenges. However, I noticed in my analysis that these instances were largely ones that I sought out purposefully with the intention of finding support in my research goals. For example, the mentorship relationship that pushed me to pursue antiracist and decolonial approaches was one with a Latinx scholar whom I met through a Facebook group, with a mentor who shared my cultural values and understood my research goal was valuable and demonstrated the value of representation for minorities. In my testimonio, I noted about this mentor:

> While she will listen to my struggles, she never lets me wallow. Feeling disoriented is a good thing, she reminds me, it means you are thinking critically. She reminds me that my very position in this struggle is what made my place to challenge what is known about mentorship with new ways of knowing. "Be radical!" she told me.

It was this initial interaction that motivated me to approach the professors in my program who helped me think through research and approaches in antiracist and decolonial studies.

In regard to the professors who I approached about my research and teaching ideas, my testimonio revealed that it was their willingness to listen or how they revealed themselves as allies that led me to approach them with my ideas. For example, I wrote about my first experience approaching a professor with my research idea as follows:

> I sprawled a question on my white board: "How can decolonizing approaches in FYW be taught by TAs?" This grammatically and semantically passive sentence came from my fear of including the words "white" or "Latina" in a potential paper addressed to my professors, or maybe even composition scholars. Nevertheless, I mapped out my idea on that white board, took a picture of it, and then scheduled an office appointment request to the only professor in my program that I knew at that time who would both be able to hear my idea and make the time to listen.

Without a professor who had shown the willingness to listen patiently without judgment, I may not have pursued my research question.

I also discovered in my testimonio how a professor's course syllabus and readings can demonstrate their willingness to act as an ally in the pursuit of racial equity in research and pedagogy. My testimonio states how

> the theme and readings in the course, and the readings and discussion that I had encountered in that professor's course the previous semester, led me to a place where I trusted her to be able to hear and understand my ideas and offer feedback. . . . Her classes, by offering readings, ideas, and discussion that centered around (not just mentioned) marginalized scholars and theories of difference and oppression, also provided a way for me to more clearly see my way into the field—to identify places where I fit.

By demonstrating, through her work, her commitment to justice and equity, this professor created space for conversations around racial equity and demonstrated her willingness to collaborate in these efforts.

After analyzing my testimonio, I found that many of my struggles came from my own anxieties around my positionality; specifically, how critiquing whiteness to a white audience of gatekeepers risked my position as a GSI (or at least felt as such). This realization had a direct impact on how I approached my dissertation. While I learned valuable lessons about my own experiences with mentorship at a PWI, the process of testimonio required me to critically reflect on my positionality in a way that brought not just my lack of power and oppression to the forefront of my research trajectory but also my privileges as a GSI in my predominantly white program and field of study. It was my consideration of those privileges that prompted me to move forward with testimonio as a methodology for my dissertation and motivated the research questions that my dissertation addressed.

In my case, I found that my privileges were connected to my finding that the mentorship I received was mentorship that I intentionally sought. For me, these privileges were connected to my race, class, nationality, language, gender, and sexuality. While I am an ethnic minority and a Chicana with mixed European and Indigenous ancestry, I have an advantage in a PWI as a light-skinned, non-Black Hispanic; I also have a European last name. In terms of class, my privileges lie in an established career in higher education and a large network of family who would be more than able and happy to support me emotionally and financially should I fail or get pushed out of my program. Indeed, while I may have felt like I risked my position in my graduate program as I sought out mentorship, I never risked my livelihood. I also was born in the United States and spoke US English as a first language, meaning that I had some implicit understandings of the structures and rules of navigating whiteness in the institution. I am also a cis-gender female who does not present with any visible disabilities. Considering the ways that I benefit from whiteness, I wanted to extend my research to be able to understand how BIWOC GSIs in my program navigate mentorship. For my dissertation, this meant shifting from the question of how marginalized GSIs bring antiracist and decolonial approaches into their practices and shifting my primary question to ask how BIWOC experience mentorship at PWIs.

APPLYING TESTIMONIANDO TO MY DISSERTATION

While I will not discuss findings from my dissertation in detail here, I do want to bring forward lessons that I learned about using testimoniando—Pérez Huber's (2012) collaborative method of testimonio—to study mentorship. To contextualize these lessons, I will first describe my dissertation study design. Then I will consider these three lessons that I learned about using testimonio to study mentorship: the value and challenges of beginning with written critical reflection, the need for ample time and space to discuss experiences, and the capacity of testimonio to activate change and empower participants.

Before I detail the lessons that I learned about using testimoniando to study the experiences of BIWOC with mentorship, I will describe my dissertation study design. The dissertation seeks to understand BIWOC GSIs' knowledge and experiences with mentorship through their critical reflections and interviews and through a focus group and debriefing interview. These methods were designed to include participants in analyzing, categorizing, and bringing meaning to the data collected from them in the study. Through these methods, my dissertation theorizes inclusive practices for mentoring GSIs in English departments.

For my dissertation study I used an intake survey designed to recruit four to six GSIs from Texas Tech's English Department who identify as Black, Indigenous, or WOC. The choice of sample size was largely based on limiting participants to those who meet the study criteria: GSIs in the English Department at Texas Tech and are predominantly white.[2] However, six was an ideal sample size for the focus groups; as Mary Sue MacNealy (1999) suggests, keeping focus groups to no more than eight to ten participants allows for open conversation (loc. 4096). After the intake survey, participants who met study criteria were asked to participate in a critical reflection.

Once participants were recruited, the study took place in four phases:

> **Phase 1.** Participants were asked to provide their testimonio on mentorship through a critical reflection.

Phase 2. Participants were asked to participate in an open-ended semistructured interview, which followed up on and expanded on the critical reflection.

Phase 3. Participants took part in a focus group, purposed to collectively discuss and determine themes from the data and determine how those themes should be categorized.

Phase 4. Participants were asked to participate in a debriefing interview to discuss their experiences being in the study, discuss what they learned, and inquire about their feelings of safety and comfort during the study process.

Participants were compensated up to one hundred dollars, through a gift card of their choice, for their participation in the study, twenty-five dollars for each phase they participated in. In total, six participants were recruited for the study, two Mexican American women, three East Asian women, and one Middle Eastern woman. One participant only participated in the critical reflection and the initial interview and was not able to be in the focus group or debriefing interview. Due to a happy accident during recruitment, one participant from outside of the English Department completed the intake survey, and I adjusted the IRB to include her valuable perspectives (she took part in all four stages of the study),

The study aimed to answer the following research questions:

1. How do BIWOC graduate student instructors at predominantly white institutions experience formal and informal mentorship?
2. How can the perspectives and experiences of BIWOC contribute to methods and approaches to addressing the need for inclusive processes of construction and assessment of GSI preparation in rhetoric and composition at the departmental, programmatic, and classroom levels?
3. How will engaging in collaborative participant research models impact participant practices?

THE VALUE AND CHALLENGES OF BEGINNING WITH WRITTEN CRITICAL REFLECTION

In this section, I would like to focus on lessons I learned about applying testimoniando to study mentorship with WOC, rather than explicitly discussing my findings; however, the third of these lessons does respond, in part, to research question three. The lessons that I will focus on are the value and challenges of beginning with written critical reflection, the need for ample time and space to discuss experiences, and the capacity of testimonio to activate change and empower participants.

What I found using a written critical reflection to collect initial testimonios was that this asynchronous method created space for participants to contribute their own definitions of mentorship to the study. However, I also noted some anxieties from participants around writing the critical reflection and initially questioned my decision to begin that way. Because the critical reflections were the point of entry into the study for participants—I emailed them the prompt and instructions for uploading the reflection once they qualified through the intake survey—I was not able to influence their responses to the question I asked about participant definitions of and experiences with mentorship. Therefore, I was able to consider forms of mentorship and types of mentoring relationships outside of my own definitions, which I derived from literature on mentorship. For example, one participant discussed how her professor taught and gave feedback as mentorship for her as a teacher: "I took the amalgamation of my favorite professors and adapted their style to fit mine." Another discussed how her experiences as an international student have impacted how she provides mentorship to her students:

> I admit that I do not know a lot of things and I am not ashamed of it. This might seem to undermine my authority, but it creates an atmosphere of goodwill and modesty, which puts the students at ease. Now since I am in a much better place in my life (in compare to my first semester), I am willing to speak the unspoken and help other people like me.

I found the value of understanding and incorporating participant definitions of mentorship to be greater than the risk; however, I do have a suggestion on how to mitigate some of the anxieties of beginning with a written critical reflection.

The majority of my participants reported feeling anxious or hesitant to write the reflection because they were not sure if they were defining mentorship correctly, if they had written enough, or if they had overall provided what I needed for the study. While my prompt did anticipate and address these concerns, I do recognize that, especially for participants who didn't know me, there must have been anxiety around sharing personal stories in an asynchronous, written context. To counter this anxiety and support, I would begin a study like this with a brief orientation for participants. A brief fifteen-to-thirty-minute meeting with participants to verbally discuss the study process and deliver the prompt and field questions could ease participants' anxieties while limiting the amount of time I, as the researcher, would have to influence participants' initial definitions of mentorships.

The Need for Ample Time and Space to Discuss Experiences

While the focus group component of the study was crucial to the critical race–grounded approach to analysis—the focus group provided the opportunity to collaboratively analyze data with participants—the topic and context of this study required more time and space for participants to connect and share experiences. As previously mentioned, this study took place at a PWI in a predominantly white program. Also, discussions of race are not common in the classroom. Instead, instructors often do not acknowledge issues of structural racism, because they themselves are not explicitly racist. Ignoring structural racism while perpetuating and upholding racist structures is what Eduardo Bonilla-Silva (2006) and Aja Martinez (2009) call colorblind racism (585). Another thing to note about the context where the focus group took place was that it was during the summer of 2022, and while our campus was transitioning back to an in-person setting during that time, we had spent the majority of the past two years disconnected in either remote or socially distanced settings.

These factors, contextual of the study, meant that seven women of color (six participants and myself) being in the same space to discuss race was not common, to say the least. Thus, during the ninety-minute focus group, participants needed time to greet and catch up with each other, and participants wanted the time and benefited from sharing experiences with racism and validating those experiences. This was not something I planned for, and in the future, I might either schedule two focus groups or schedule a meeting before the focus group to check in with participants as a group. This meeting could serve as an opportunity for participants to get to know each other, share experiences, and prepare for the focus group. However it's done, especially at a PWI, a collaborative study with WOC should provide time to build community and support each other.

The Capacity of Testimonio to Activate Change and Empower Participants

It is important to acknowledge the emotional labor that this research requires from participants, and I constantly look for ways to improve participant experiences. However, I also want to point to the capacity of testimoniando research around mentorship to activate change and empower participants. First, participants noted how the study impacted their understanding of mentorship and how they provide mentorship to their students. In terms of understanding mentorship, one participant said,

> This project has made me think [about] what is more effective for us, and as we are also mentoring our students, my students, . . . and in our future career, right? What we can do to help our mentees more effectively.

This participant also mentioned that during the study, she came to think of mentorship as more than simply an expert guiding a novice into a new practice, and, instead, "it's like a connection . . . the mentors and mentees are closely interconnected and interrelated, and the it's like a mutual relationship." Another participant discussed how reflecting on her own experiences and connecting with the experiences of other WOC made her realize how alone she had felt as a new graduate student, and "that maybe other students think in the same way that they're alone, and they don't know there are other people here that are . . . experiencing the same things." This participant also discussed how these realizations shaped the way she related to a struggling student of hers during the study. Along with impacting how participants sought and provided mentorship, the study also worked as a way to empower participants.

In regard to empowerment, participants reported feeling supported by a sense of community, validity around their experiences with racism or discrimination, and understanding of their own experiences and capacity to impact change. For example, one participant said her experience was "eye-opening mostly because it's finding out that I wasn't alone in my experience so that gives a sense of community." That same participant discussed how that realization helped her understand her struggles during her graduate program from a new perspective. These experiences demonstrate empowerment through community. Another participant discussed how the process helped validate her experience and motivate her to support others:

> I think [about] how powerful I was that I went through all these things, and how things happened to me, and I was just surviving, and no one was here to help me. I feel that it would be useful [for me] to help other graduate students. Maybe these experiences will help them as well so that's the main reason that I'm here, and so far that was the effect of this study.

This participant's reflection demonstrates how empowerment can lead to social action—the participant felt empowered through reflecting on her experiences and decided to intentionally mentor and support other graduate students.

Thus far from my dissertation I have identified quite a few opportunities for improving the application of collaborative testimonio methods. The two areas of improvement in the application of these methods I brought forward in this chapter are the value and challenges of using a written critical reflection to collect initial testimonios from participants and the need for planning ample time and space for participants to connect with each other and share experiences. Despite the challenges of implementing testimonio, I hope that I have demonstrated its value for studying mentorship with WOC through examples of impacting positive change in how participants practice mentorship and empowering participants.

CONCLUSION AND DISCUSSION

Testimonio is valuable as a research methodology for gathering WOC to collaboratively research mentorship in PWIs; it also provides a research context that can positively impact participants by providing a supportive and empowering space. While there are many ways for people of color to approach testimonio research, the research should seek to illuminate injustices caused by oppression, challenge dominant ideologies, validate experiences, acknowledge the power of collectivity, and show a commitment to racial justice (Pérez Huber 2009). In my case, using individual testimonio—focused on myself—helped me to examine how my positionality shaped my experiences with mentorship and develop questions to investigate mentorship with other WOC. A collaborative testimonio approach to studying mentorship with WOC has taught me the value and challenges of beginning with written critical reflection, the need for ample time and space to discuss experiences, and the capacity of testimonio to activate change and empower participants. For the field of composition and rhetoric, testimonio offers a way for people of color to collectively address disparities in mentorship and representation in the field while receiving community and support.

NOTES

1. While my dissertation study was designed to recruit Black, Indigenous, and women of color (BIWOC), the participants who ultimately signed up and participated in the study were all women of color; that is, none of the participants were Black or Indigenous. In this chapter, I refer to my study design and research interests as including BIWOC, however, when referring to my research, I use WOC in order to be precise about how these methods were used.
2. I do not have exact data on race and ethnicity for graduate students in the English Department at Texas Tech University, but according to the university's Institutional Research factbook's data, within the College of Arts and Sciences, where the English Department is situated, 0.42% of graduate students identity as Native American, 4.02 % as Asian, 2.89% as Black or African American, 14.1% as Hispanic, 0.14% as Native Hawaiian or Pacific Islander, 2.96% as two or more races, and 26.45% as

non-resident international students. While the university's data reports that 49% of graduate students in English are white, according to information from Peterson's and College Factual, who collect demographic data from universities annually, approximately 70% of graduate students in the English Department at Texas Tech University identify as white (Peterson's reported 72%, and College Factual, 68.14% in 2021).

REFERENCES

Blackmer Reyes, Kathryn, and Julia E. Curry Rodríguez. 2012. "Testimonio: Origins, Terms, and Resources." *Equity and Excellence in Education* 45 (3): 525–538. https://doi.org/10.1080/10665684.2012.698571.

Bonilla-Silva, Eduardo. 2006. *Racism without Racists: Color-Blind Racism and the Persistence of Racial Inequality in the United States.* 2nd ed. Lanham, MD: Rowman & Littlefield.

Delgado Bernal, Delores, Rebecca Burciaga, and Judith Flores Carmona. 2012. "Chicana/Latina Testimonios: Mapping the Methodological, Pedagogical, and Political." *Equity and Excellence in Education* 45 (3): 363–372. https://doi.org/10.1080/10665684.2012.698149.

Latina Feminist Group. 2001. *Telling to Live: Latina Feminist Testimonios.* Durham, NC: Duke University Press.

MacNealy, Mary Sue. 1999. *Strategies for Empirical Research in Writing.* Boston: Allyn and Bacon.

Malagon, Maria C., Lindsay Pérez Huber, and Verónica N. Vélez. 2009. "Our Experiences, Our Methods: Using Grounded Theory to Inform a Critical Race Theory Methodology." *Seattle Journal for Social Justice* 8 (1): 253–272. https://digitalcommons.law.seattleu.edu/sjsj/vol8/iss1/10.

Martinez, Aja Y. 2009. "'The American Way': Resisting the Empire of Force and Color-Blind Racism." *College English* 71 (6): 584–595.

Medina, Cruz. 2018. "Digital Latin@ Storytelling: Testimonio as Multi-Modal Resistance." In *Racial Shorthand: Coded Discrimination Contested in Social Media,* edited by Cruz Medina and Octavio Pimental. Computers and Composition Digital Press. http://ccdigitalpress.org/book/shorthand/chapter_medina.html.

Okawa, Gail Y. 2002. "Diving for Pearls: Mentoring as Cultural and Activist Practice among Academics of Color." *College Composition and Communication* 53 (3): 507–532.

Pérez Huber, Lindsay. 2009. "Disrupting Apartheid of Knowledge: Testimonio as Methodology in Latina/o Critical Race Research in Education." *International Journal of Qualitative Studies in Education* 22 (6): 639–654. https://doi.org/10.1080/09518390903333863.

Pérez Huber, Lindsay. 2012. "Testimonio as LatCrit Methodology in Education." In *Handbook of Qualitative Research in Education,* edited by Sara Delamont and Angela Jones, 377–390. Cheltenham, UK: Edward Elgar Publishing.

Pérez Huber, Lindsay, and Bert Maria Cueva. 2012. "Chicana/Latina Testimonios on Effects and Responses to Microaggressions." *Equity and Excellence in Education* 45 (3): 392–410. https://doi.org/10.1080/10665684.2012.698193.

Reed, Meredith. 2020. "Enacting Bricolage: Theorizing the Teaching Practices of Graduate Writing Instructors." *WPA: Writing Program Administration* 44 (1): 107–128. https://wpacouncil.org/aws/CWPA/asset_manager/get_file/555794?ver=3.

Reid, E. Shelley. 2008. "Mentoring Peer Mentors: Mentor Education and Support in the Composition Program." *Composition Studies* 36 (2): 51–79.

Restaino, Jessica. 2012. *First Semester: Graduate Students, Teaching Writing, and the Challenge of the Middle Ground.* Carbondale, IL: Conference on College Composition and Communication; National Council of Teachers of English.

Ribero, Ana Milena, and Sonia C. Arellano. 2019. "Advocating Comadrismo: A Feminist Mentoring Approach for Latinas in Rhetoric and Composition." *Peitho* 21 (2): 34–356. https://cfshrc.org/wp-content/uploads/2019/03/RiberoArellano_IV_Advocating-Comadrismo-2.pdf.

Stancliff, Michael, and Maureen Daly Goggin. 2007. "What's Theorizing Got to Do with It? Teaching Theory as Resourceful Conflict and Reflection in TA Preparation." *WPA: Writing Program Administration* 30 (3): 11–28. http://associationdatabase.co/archives/30n3/30n3stancliff-goggin.pdf.

Stenberg, Sheri, and Amy Lee. 2002. "Developing Pedagogies: Learning the Teaching of English." *College English* 64 (3): 326–347.

Thornberg, Robert, and Kathy Charmaz. 2012. "Grounded Theory." In *Qualitative Research: An Introduction to Methods and Designs*, edited by S. D. Lapan, MaryLynn T. Quartaroli, and Frances J. Riemer, 41–67. Hoboken, NJ: Jossey-Bass.

Torrez, J. Estrella. (2015). "Translating Chicana Testimonios into Pedagogy for a White Midwestern Classroom." *Chicana/Latina Studies* 14 (2): 101–130. https://thisbridgecalledcyberspace.net/FILES/3713.pdf.

VanHaitsma, Pamela, and Steph Ceraso. 2017. "'Making It' in the Academy through Horizontal Mentoring." *Peitho* 19 (2): 210–233.

Villanueva, Victor. 1993. *Bootstraps: From an American Academic of Color*. Champagne, IL: National Council of Teachers of English.

14
A POST-ARRIVAL MENTORSHIP THAT'S NOT A MENTORSHIP
Mediated Discourse Theory and the Ecological Approach to Learning over Time and Place

Aurora Matzke and John Paul Tassoni

PART WHERE WE DO AN INTRODUCTION

Unlike many mentorship stories, this one begins and dwells in present action; pretty much with an email. In the email, Aurora sends this collection's call for papers to John, and she frames it with a single line: "Wanna try together?" The fact that John once served as the WPA at Aurora's graduate institution, on her dissertation committee, and as instructor in five of her courses certainly does fuel our "round and round" (Bateson 2015, 99), as Gregory Bateson might say; we begin, however, in the here and now, with the email.

We begin here (even though we've since moved on) to foreground what theorists of mediated discourse would call a "site of engagement" in our field's "nexus of practice." Aurora's email represents an all-too-common time/space station (de Saint-Georges 2005, 156–157), one where the field of rhetoric and composition's (rhet/comp's) social practices, materials, discourses, values, and expectations can "come together to form action in real time" (Scollon 2001, 28). Although mentorship studies in rhet/comp compel us to start somewhere else—start maybe with Aurora, a dozen-plus years ago, struggling to locate the classroom where we'd first meet, or with John carefully crafting the syllabus for that seminar—we have decided to resist this compulsion, to let "introductory Aurora and John" wander those halls a bit longer. We have decided instead to "try together," to dwell right here, where we are now, in a practice that bonds members of our field and continually opens us/it to diverse perspectives.

Mentorship stories in rhet/comp typically focus on relationships between mentors and mentees at sites of protégés' training, and the tales more or less culminate at events that signal protégés' arrivals at landmark events—dissertation defended, job secured, or tenure granted (Cole and Hassel 2017; Flynn and Bourelle 2018; Goodburn, Lecourt, and Leverenz 2013). The charting of these relationships and culminatory events marks important nodes, because although we resist dwelling in our introductory selves, we still mention them, still have them. The narrative pattern representing such endeavors generates recommendations regarding practices and goals of mentorships based on those past interactions. Yet the pattern by its very focus on these culminating events (and whatever interactions that lead to them) may undervalue ways mentorships generate insights (often reshaping old insights) post-arrival. After all, narratives from perspectives of former mentees (Cain 1994; Welch 1993) and collaborative projects composed by former mentees and mentors (Miles and Burnett 2008; Mullin and Braun 2008; Sharer, Enoch, and Glenn 2008) indicate how memories of past mentorships and ongoing interactions among (former) mentees/mentors continually inform their present (here, in the future).

While they tend not to dwell in presents, the very existence of these stories—the fact that people use their memories of mentorships *now* to think about them then—suggests the degree to which post-arrival mentorships permeate the field and should be approached with intentionality (Tassoni 2022, 63). We hope to address this permeation more fully by explaining a methodology of post-arrival mentorships that are not mentorships. Our post-arrival site of engagement marks, we think, the limitation of mentorship stories–en-scène, the ways their "narrow curricular imaginings" (Prior 2018) preclude the broader textual landscapes in which teachers resemiotize their (past) mentoring and their (past) menteeing (Roozen and Erickson 2017, 2.01). Rather than consider these post-arrival reflections as shadows of finalized institutional arrangements, we (Aurora and John) chart our ecological, cognitive embodiment using mediated discourse theory to explicate the persistence of (past) mentorships in rhet/comp's "nexus of praxis" (Scollon 2001, 28). In this nexus, the relationships among (former) mentors and mentees may inform more egalitarian relationships—ones in which history exists in relation to the now, in the continual becoming of the various parties. These interactions may reflect communication unrelated to reward (Downs and Goldstein 2008, 149) or fear of punishment (Brock and Ellerby 1997, 127), at least in ways not as tangibly or lethally related to reward/punishment as might be experienced in a graduate program or in the probationary period prior to tenure (Tassoni 2022, 72).

As such, post-arrival mentorships that are not mentorships necessitate a new narrative pattern we seek to develop here (see Tassoni 2022, 65).

In this space, in this activity that is our collaborative response to Aurora's email, we theorize but, in doing so, remember and reconstruct memory, attune our past to our current conditions, and vice versa. Round and round. At various times, we step aside to share new insights, to individually crawl through windows that our collaboration opens for us, and we share these asides in ways that, at times, blur identities, entangle the activities of mentoring and being mentored. These asides (in italics) mark places where we draw on what Paul Prior (2018) describes as "multiple semiotic resources . . . so deeply entangled that distinct modes simply don't make sense," where we "try together," even where and when it might appear we step out alone. Throughout this chapter, we attune insights derived from our past interactions to our current nexuses (and vice versa), augmenting/transforming those insights in the process. This process and attention to mediated discourse as ecological cognitive practice marks, we think, the limitation of mentorship stories–en-scène.

In short, we consider this post-arrival space as much more than what Kathy Kram (1983), writing about mentorships in the field of business, would describe as a "redefinition phase." We practice not a phase so much as we relocate and resemiotize the thread(s) of our mentorship. What distinguishes the post-arrival mentorships-that-are-not-mentorships we discuss here from other ongoing collaborations is the self-reflexivity mediated through post-arrival, the ways in which we evoke our mentorship (as opposed to just key concepts in our field) as we make meaning of our field, particularly in regard to how we become teachers and teachers of teachers in this field. As Kram describes her redefinition phase, we (John and Aurora) would now reflect on our (past) mentorship with sensations of gratitude, pride, appreciation, and friendship rather than generate new insights about and from within our mentorship (620). However, as we existed, do exist, and will exist as part of rhet/comp's nexus of practice, the post-arrival stage we are now in remains useful to our continued becoming as teachers and as teachers of teachers. Here, then, we dwell.

THE PART WHERE WE DO THEORY AND SOME OTHER STUFF

By pinpointing action, instead of discourse (Jones 2014, 39), as it is both chronologically and kairotically motivated, mediated discourse theory underscores how discourse and other cultural tools and historical trajectories function to get things done, to, in cases such as ours, keep us learning about life in the field and, particularly, how this learning uptakes and transforms past learning. Our action in this place/time signals a desirable function of mentorship at any point in time, but the practice is perhaps more achievable in post-arrival space, where more equitable ground might exist, and more experiences can be brought into dialogue. Mentorship for mentees/mentors in post-arrival space functions as a simultaneous happened, is happening, and will happen occurrence. This responsiveness cannot occur within any narrow curricular imagining (Prior 2018); mediated discourse theory provides a longer, wider view on those actions that comprise our becoming in the field.

It occurs to me as we write that this approach is not unlike how the concept of bricolage might be applied in the enactment of mentorship—where, through uptake, we understand individuals in real time manipulating and working through memories and experiences to make sense of the now-world, not the historical world or future world they may inhabit, but as we are right now. By placing these resemiotized patterns next to the process of becoming in mentorship, a kairotic opening is created in what might be otherwise a chronologically driven landscape. This attention toward kairotic openings provides insight regarding the always-already-experiencing cognitive pathways utilized through mediation, through the embodiment of the current subjects.

Imagine the chronotopic landscape—via Prior and Shipka (2003, 183), the "dispersed and fluid chains of places, times, people, and artifacts that come to be tied together in trajectories of literate action, the ways multiple activity footings are simultaneously held and managed"—and then apply that to instances of connection and reconnection marked by mentorship—marked by the desire to learn some thing(s) from some one(s). Mentorship that is not mentorship assumes the individuals involved are both mentor and mentee simultaneously, both more and less than those classic designations of learner and teacher, actively existing in and resisting patterns of being as they already are and will become. Mentorship that is not mentorship is simultaneously chronotopically laminated and kairotopically laminated—it is chron(kair)otopic. The dispersed and fluid chains, when triggered by action or reaction, then tie together to form new anchors. These anchors may persist and change over chronological and kairological time, as we no longer consciously call it, or consciously re-call it, or consciously shift its recalling as new embodiment, ambient ties, or both are formed.

Privileging action, mediated discourse theory accounts for the array of tools/factors implicated in an action (Jones 2014, 41). In our case, Aurora's inviting John to collaborate on this chapter represents a "site of engagement," which Ron Scollon (2001) defines as a "window that is opened up through the intersection of social practices and meditational means (cultural tools) that make that action the focal point of attention of the relevant participants" (2001, 4). The focus on action helps us to distinguish significant patterns among all those other discourses that compete for our attention. This email now draws our attention in ways it would not others. As Rodney H. Jones points out,

> "sites of engagement" are created not just through the physical presence of tools, actions and people at a particular place at a particular time, but rather through the "attention" or "engagement" of the people involved. The same configurations of tools at the same moments in time and the same points in space may for some people function as sites of engagement for particular actions, whereas for others they may not. (2014, 41)

The discursive moment at which we begin this essay—"Wanna try . . . ?"—functions through an array of trajectories, of fluid chains, not just discourse, or even email, but through conditions that develop and maintain what we have come to call our "post-arrival mentorship that is not a mentorship." The email becomes *a* tool through which attention functions as *the* tool for the mentee and mentor. The action reflected in Aurora's email, Jones might say, marks our enduring mentorship, our post-arrival mentorship that is not a mentorship, which is what makes the action, this action, possible to begin with (2014, 41).

THE PART WHERE WE EXAMINE POWER RELATIONS IN THIS FIELD'S NEXUS OF PRACTICE

While academics honor / trouble each other with emails every day, the one Aurora sends here engages us in ways unique to post-arrival mentors who are not mentors. Paying attention to who initiates contact, as well as the frequency and content of that contact are guideposts for determining if post-arrival mentorships that are not mentorships may be in effect. Much of our own interactions are characterized by invitational play—moments in time, this moment in time, where one asks the other if they want to come along. The embodiment of the open and easy yes marks one of the first methods in our mentorship that is not mentorship.

Mentees often say yes to mentor requests, maybe even when they don't want to, but mentors rarely agree to be led—to "come play," as it were. Or perhaps they intentionally play in well-established patterns of high reward, low risk—co-authoring an article fits here, perhaps, and so it is both traditional mentorship and not. Post-arrival assumes either or both individuals may not know the pattern. At the same time, this sense of play does come with its own boundaries. Post-arrival is not devoid of purpose. Rather, purpose is something framed in-action and not al-

ways in alignment with classic understandings. We aren't writing this chapter because either of us "need it" for professional reasons. We just like thinking together.

I think the questions of who's saying yes and why, and who's asking whom, are crucial issues to consider in post-arrival space, just as they are en scène. I can see where a post-arrival mentor's requests might still carry with them an unfair power imbalance, at least until the post-arrival mentorship that's not a mentorship is well underway, where there's been enough time for the (former) mentee to get in a few requests as well. "Just like thinking together" and "the easy yes" do help mark our post-arrival mentorship that's not a mentorship, it could be useful to think of forms "just like thinking together" and "easy yes" might take elsewhere.

The "easy yes" is not marked by feelings of anxiety or stress. Joy, delight, challenges to known patterns of thought that are not bound to risk or reward characterize "just like thinking together." Conformity and duty do not, in our experience, motivate post-arrival mentorships. I believe it's characterized by the psychosocial elements of mentoring relationships much more so than career advancement. The motivation is intrinsic rather than extrinsic.

Paulo Freire (1997) writes that anyone seeking "to be an authentic mentor" must "not be a mentor" (1997, 324). Like the Freirean classroom, where teachers teach but are also taught (*Pedagogy* [1970] 1990, 67), the Freirean mentor mentors but is also mentored (by the mentee). While it is clear that Freire would like mentorships all along to be democratic and dialogic sites, post-arrival space provides not only more equitable but also more heterogeneous ground (Tassoni 2022, 69)—and frankly, more realistic ground, as higher education in the United States is clearly built on whiteness in such a way as to make a truly democratic mentor/mentee relationship improbable if not outright impossible. As such, post-arrival provides a space for Freirean concepts to exist alongside what we must acknowledge as the largely hetero-, hegemonically normative, and racist spaces of much of higher education. In post-arrival space, a mentorship that is not a mentorship draws on many points in time and on many places that are not necessarily housed in a particular program or school or even within the mentor/mentee relation itself. This long and wide view of mentorship challenges unidirectional stories of teacher development, particularly those that confine teacher training to a specific time and place along "a sequentially graded curricular path" (Prior 2018).

Some people might experience manipulated yeses or forced thinking; these feelings I'd be wary of. I can see where they might stem from mentorships that fall more along the cloning than bilateral models, but they might also arise through a sense of desperation someone might feel in terms of job security or even professional reputation. For me, I think, a sense of continuity and trust helps deliver to me invitations that are especially poignant. I don't ever think you would be inviting me to do anything unless you felt I might already be interested in the project or might just have something to contribute. There's no need for you to do otherwise.

The best thing, though, is that in a lot of your requests, I question why you are even asking me, which is an aspect of that "invitational play" we describe. These invitations pique my sense of curiosity, because they usually don't align explicitly with things I think I know. They don't, in other words, situate me as knower in the sense that I'm some authority you've come to consult. These types of requests could be key to disrupting any hierarchical arrangement. "I don't know anything about bricolage," I recall saying that time you asked me to join you on a panel about bricolage; "Oh, you know more than you think you do," you said. Anybody on the outside could quite reasonably ask who is mentoring whom.

While it is certainly feasible to understand Aurora's "Wanna try . . . ?" as a request for collaboration among colleagues or peers (Fishman and Lunsford 2008, 29), our response to this collection's call for papers, especially in addition to previous discussions in which we have reflected on our past exchanges (reciting our encounters-en-scène at the site of Aurora's graduate training and John's role as WPA), marks our mentorship's persistence into post-arrival space. Along this line of action, John continues to mentor Aurora by virtue of her memory / embodying of his (past) mentoring. Aurora, in turn, mentors John through her accounting of ways these memories attune to Aurora's subsequent nexuses. Post-arrival space mediates our action. So, while we would not altogether extract our practice here from what might be considered knowledge-sharing among colleagues, our activity nevertheless extends our mentorship.

Regarding people looking in from the outside, there's probably something to keep an eye on in terms of frequency as well, right? You and I have already seen (via online video-chat platforms) each other more this year than most years because of this project, but I can guess there are other post-arrival relationships that entail more frequent meetings. Maybe these are the ones that mark the development of a peer relationship, where the mentor / mentee are now colleagues? And while we are friends, we don't send one another gifts, or chat on the phone about our lives, or do most of the things that would mark a friendship outside of professional engagements. What we're focusing on here are those aspects of the relationship in which the mentorship persists, where en-scène memories are summoned or at least take the form now of common understanding (in other words, concepts / approaches agreed upon years ago maintain sway in the here and now, even though they might no longer receive explicit attention).

Someone might look at collaborations between junior faculty and their former supervisors as marks of dependency. I think there would be a kind of dependency evident if we were asking (bugging?) the other all the time to help with all our projects and even our administrative work at our universities, but this couldn't be further from the case. Also, if I were the one inviting you more frequently, there might even be some indication that I'm not honoring your input so much as I am afraid that I or you might fail if left to my or your own devices. This also couldn't be further from the truth, and conversely, I hope I never get to the point where you feel I am someone who must be carried. I think the fact that most (just about all, really) of our research and university work happens independently of each other is what keeps the post-arrival relationship vital, keeps diverse ideas flowing through.

At the site of graduate or similar on-the-job training, uneven power relationships can be especially impactful, not always in good ways (Matzke, Rankins-Robertson, and Garrett 2019). The trust that develops in effective mentorships can often seem to override the fact that the more established community member can disrupt a protégé's aspirations—make sure a practicum is not passed, a dissertation fails, or a job opportunity dematerializes. Nonetheless, these possibilities remain; it sometimes takes the time and distance of post-arrival space to facilitate more honest dialogue (Tassoni 2022, 77). As such, post-arrival mentorships that are not mentorships provide what Edwin Hutchins might describe as "patterns in the density of interconnectivity" that shape activity in our field (2010, 711). The reciprocation facilitated in post-arrival space allows for participants to revisit, amend, revise, and even in some cases abort "cognitive properties" that (re)shape our actions in rhet/comp and, perhaps, (re)shape rhet/comp itself (Hutchins 2010, 711). Aurora's email, in this sense, represents a thread that courses through the dense nexuses of practices that constitute our lives in rhet/comp, a thread that marks a point of departure, all the while gathering new ports of entry.

THE PART WHERE WE WRITE ABOUT WRITING AND WRITING TEACHERS AND WRITING ABOUT WRITING TEACHERS

This chapter is our first attempt to create together, not in parallel (like you might do for a conference panel, which we've done plenty of), and was my attempt to link up an idea I knew you had but hadn't yet found a place for. And then, because you write more, are currently writing more than me, I am constantly struck by first authorship—right now, as I write. The first time I mentioned it, you laughed, "I can't be first author on a chapter about reciprocal mentorship!"

I laughed, too. "Our field," I said, "values production more than ideas. So while I might have encouraged us to work with these ideas and theories, you are producing." I actually hate this about higher ed at large, but that's neither here nor there. The fact of the matter is that first author writes more, and you will always write more than me. It's how you think. It is not how I think. So, due to our embodiment, if I work with you in ways the field can hold (i.e., publication) I will always be the mentee. I will be the mentee from a pre-arrival perspective and a post-arrival perspective. Our relationship will always be uneven. What is it that has value in the relationship? And who is defining that value? And really, at the end and beginning of it, who really is the first author of this chapter? And do we actually both care?

Most likely, mentorships along the wide and long spectrum of post-arrival will find participants share at least some markers. Where our mentorship that is not a mentorship is marked intergenerationally (John is older than Aurora), across gendered lines (Aurora identifies as female and John identifies as male), socioeconomically (John hails from a lower socioeconomic background, Aurora from the low middle), and more, we are also both cis-gender, white, first-generation scholars with concerted interest and attention to open-access pathways in writing education. Consistent through these similarities and differences is the mentorship that we return to and that is returned to us. Subjectivities, and the performances of such, provide several threads to interrogate in post-arrival space, as we mark and remark on how our current subjectivities both do and don't affect our historical, current, or future selves.

The more prolonged and heterogeneous the trajectory of a mentorship, the more experiences and insights mentors / mentees are able to bring to bear on their (past) interactions and the subsequent patterns that help guide them within the field's (present) dense interconnectivity, and the more likely post-arrival has room to be enacted (future). Post-arrival spaces create room for mentors' / mentees' subsequent experiences to come into play, to not only resemiotize everyday practices but also ("round and round") the common ground of that mentorship itself and the memories it is comprised of. While on some plane in our relationship, Aurora still seeks the classroom where John and she will meet, she has since earned her PhD and secured university positions in California (miles and miles away from the site where John and she first worked together). There she has served first as a novice and then experienced WPA, and she has since moved on to a senior associate provost position and back down where, along the way, Aurora has overseen and led in such sites as writing centers, centers for teaching and learning, general education programming, strategic planning, and university budgeting. On another plane, John is just now deciding to include Geller et al.'s (2006) *Everyday Writing Center* among the readings that Aurora's cohort will discuss in their summer seminar on the theories and teaching of composition. Meanwhile, John has left the WPA position at his and Aurora's Ohio school, served as university director of liberal education there, and now lives life again as a "civilian" teacher, focusing on basic writing programming at the university's open-access regional campuses. Our mentorship that is not a mentorship endures, accruing what Jones would call "new meditational means which allow [us] to take future actions, and through this process [our] selves ('historical bodies') are created, social identities are claimed and imputed, and societies and cultures are produced and reproduced" (2014, 43). So, while our historical selves may have at one time been rooted in unidirectional meditational means—teach the class, turn in the paper, perform teacher, perform student, and so on—post-arrival mentorship that is not mentorship encourages understanding through a cognitive ecology where risk and reward may change hands, may heighten or lower based upon "attention" we pay to the interaction in relation to the other happenings we have experienced or will experience.

Locating our post-arrival mentorship in rhet/comp's nexus of practice "illuminates," Roozen and Erickson (2017) might say, "the historical trajectory a practice traces as it comes to be linked across a series of nexus throughout the life of the person" (2.03.2). They write,

> As they interact with each nexus, people move from setting to setting, from institution to institution, from activity to activity, and from genre to genre. And, even though each nexus offers different discourses with different expectations and affordances, they are not disconnected; rather, they are experienced with some degree of continuity. Part of that continuity is the re-use of practice along this history. (2.03.2)

It's ecology. Centralized principles and practices in our en-scène mentorship impress upon our post-arrival selves, providing continuity and all the while gathering new inflections and possibilities, or dropping away. Other instances, while perhaps important en scène, lose emphasis—perhaps remembered by the body, but not consciously by the mind. These new accentuations and abatements offer us ways to speak back to our (past) en-scène selves as well as generate future action. This thinking back, while being and being or speaking forward, is what we encourage for ourselves and our students in our writing classes: embodying the ecosocial, stable-yet-reaching self. It establishes the importance of a growth mindset at all stages in an educational journey, including the never-ending stage of teacher-learner. Approaching post-arrival space with intentionality, our mentoring culture can better reflect the dynamics we wish to see among students and their own approaches to writing.

What I find related to mentorship here, particularly to the enduring, bilateral kind, is Joshua Cruz's (2020) article on bullshit in a recent issue of Composition Studies. *He underscores good aspects of bullshit: the benefits of people pretending to know more than they actually do. I know I've talked about this with students—the ways bullshitting in the writing process might take you into creative territories. The idea is to afterward find out the degree to which what you wrote can actually be true. As Cruz (2020) says, "Those who pretend to know more than they do may be self-conscious enough to educate themselves in the future on certain topics" (121). Mentorships, especially post-arrival ones, can provide us with comfort zones at the same time they still cast lines (trajectories) out ahead of us, ones that we can chase with a degree of uncertainty and then later make these ideas more part of ourselves, live up to them.*

I don't think "living up to" would help me mentor without being a mentor if not for my feeling invited to "not know." Maybe this sort of invitation is more readily available and more readily received post-arrival? A couple of years ago, when you invited me to join your panel on bricolage, you told me I knew more than I thought, but you were also inviting me to not know. From that point, I felt compelled to know, to be at least as smart a bricoleur as you were remembering me to be.

This whole project (stemming from another invitation you'd extended to me, to present with you on a panel about the rhetorical making of teachers) has really forced me into some self-conscious reflection on the role of mentor. Sort of like those cases where someone, usually a therapist, tells someone that they have to consciously stop thinking about something that they're always thinking about; I'm in a similar conundrum here, where I have to think about being a mentor without being a mentor. I hadn't actually thought of myself in these terms, as mentor, but now that I do, I'm more aware of the ways I might perform that role and also find that I am stretching to live up to it, on both my en-scène and post-arrival stages, including the one that is this chapter.

I think "living up" to mentorship is one of the potential dangers. I'm actually not convinced the pressures and expectations are healthy for any party. From my experience, they so easily slide into co-dependence and jockeying for position among both mentors and mentees—a constant cyclical contest that we replay at conferences, in publications, and the work in the field. At the same time, expressing care and help to others should always (most-ways) be tempered by the knowledge of constant becoming and embodiment. Perhaps "living up" both is and is not the "bullshit" of Joshua Cruz's (2020) work. Perhaps, also, the embodiment of humility—through timely and sincere expressions of "not knowing"—frames another method of the methodology of post-arrival.

I honestly remember nothing of what should have been the "important" parts of our relationship. Those "culminating" moments—the dissertation, the job, the first panel, or whatever. I have more vibrant memories of that one restaurant in Kansas City where we were with friends, and was it German food? I have a million of these tiny moments. Interacting with you in casual settings, where we perhaps discuss work obliquely, where you demonstrate not knowing. I know we are both first-gen, and I think we both often have those weird, out-of-body experiences when we're around "the field"—the imposter syndrome—but I also think it's rooted in not believing too much of what Cruz (2020) would call our own "bullshit." Post-arrival, it seems to me, is an awful lot of deciding that not knowing is safe, that answers won't necessarily be found in full in any one instance or time, narratives will be stumbling and heroic (in real time and in the chrono[kairo]topic ecology that is continually becoming, being, dying, and becoming). The performance of not knowing is as integral, if not more integral, to post-arrival as the performance of knowing.

Basically, experiencing mentorship in post-arrival space mimics more holistically the way people write and learn to write (Prior and Shipka 2003). By enacting post-arrival more concretely—not knowing, demonstrating curiosity, viewing time and return to time as ecologically driven, forefronting attention as a tool for meaning-making—we create openings for the teaching of writing and the creation of writing as a communal already-always-becoming art. We understand these openings of time, space, and pace to be critical not only in mentorship but in the teaching of writing, and in the teaching of teachers of writing. Viewing post-arrival interactions as cognitively embodied nexuses of practice, our chapter shows how mediated discourse theory provides a framework through which to view interstitial ecological tracings that form our continued becoming. A pattern "in the density of [the field's] interconnectivity," our post-arrival mentorship that is not a mentorship keys our methodologies of becoming. It deepens our understanding of how to participate as citizens in communities of practice, how to teach writing, and how to teach other people how to be teachers of writing.

THE PART WHERE WE DISCUSS HOW POST-ARRIVAL HELPS RECONFIGURE HISTORY

Our dwelling here in the action of Aurora's email marks a site of engagement in what Prior would describe as "a trajectory of semiotic becoming" (2018). In this perspective, we view our ongoing mentorship as a vehicle for our continued becoming, and that becoming as

> embodied, dispersed, mediated, laminated, and deeply dialogic. Becoming happens not inside domains, but across the many moments of a life. Becoming happens in spaces that are never pure or settled, where discourses and knowledge are necessarily heterogeneous, and where multiple semiotic resources are so deeply entangled that distinct modes simply don't make sense. (Prior 2018)

Contrarily, mentorships focused on interactions en scène (in the past) often confine their density/trajectory to what Prior would describe as "narrow curricular imaginings" (2018). Focused primarily on arrivals, the dominant narrative pattern in mentorship stories matches what Prior calls a (singular) "tale of learning" (2018). He writes,

> A tale of learning says that learning happens inside specific territorial communities, each of which owns its own space of knowledge and discourse. Novices must enter these magic circles as individuals and make their way to the centers (or fail to do so) by moving step-by-step along a sequentially graded curricular path.

A focus on territorial communities inadvertently privileges white and potentially male ways of making meaning and knowing. Connected to ownership, separation, and inculcation, such a focus is boundaried and potentially malicious. It is not a neutral space. In our teachings, in our embodiments, we must actively work for different opportunities of meaning-making and knowing. We also acknowledge that differing opportunities present themselves in different ways due to individuals' embodiments. This individuated work is of imminent importance to those that wish to work in post-arrival space. It is both deeply individual and always already shaped by established and becoming communities of practice.

Mediated discourse theorists Roozen and Erickson (2017) have us focus on actions, as they are "dynamic, continually in-the-making heterogeneous nexus[es] of practice" tempered by "historical trajectories stretching across multiple nexus[es]" (2.03). Consequently, while we have thus far resisted representations of our relationship as individual moments in time that have built toward particular actions or ways of being in a linear fashion, culminating in accomplishment, we must also acknowledge that our continual re-finding of one another forms instantiations of mentorship bound by rhizomatic return to a co-created complex cognitive ecology. This ecology is often marked by points of entry understood as more or less significant and resemiotized differently by different actors—Aurora (cis-gender woman, white, rhet/comp scholar by training, now administrator) or John (cis-gender man, white, literature scholar / creative writer by training, now faculty member). We would also argue entry points within the joint ecology also determine potentialities for various actors, in various times, at various places. It is also not beyond us that there are several embodied elements we share with one another, and that embodied recognition is an integral part of post-arrival space, in that it provides space for shared understanding on which "not knowing" can rest.

In the paper I wrote for the panel we did on the rhetorical making of teachers, I found myself rehearsing a few moments in your graduate studies that you've reminded me of. Notably, they are predominantly memories of things I might have just mentioned in passing and recognize now only in light of your reflections. You mentioned, for instance, that I pointed out when people seemed to be using "but" when an "and" might be more useful to a particular dialogue. You'd also mentioned that you recall my speaking of first-year composition as a service course that should be considered in terms of Serena Williams service rather than butler service.

I use this all the time in my work. All. The. Time.

It's almost like my WPA self has gone traveling through time and place; your recollections are like parts of myself returning with passport stamps all over it (which remind me where I've been—or better yet, where I've not been) and with the passport itself now up for renewal. Given what I know about your experiences both before and after we worked together in the graduate program, I see your stamps now on these stories, begin to see them now as your *stories. They represent points of departure but also ports of entry for new inflections.*

In a way, they have become mine more than they ever were yours. And, they've returned to us to teach us both something we needed to learn. Aurora is still searching for that room; John is more aware now of the implications of his making that room so hard to find.

I think of these introductory moments now more in terms of gender and race—what it must have been like for that cohort to finally find that white man (at once the cause and destiny of that design) at the end of that high-anxiety search. I think also of the ways the conversations you've recounted for me might apply to your own life as a WPA and the gender politics you likely encountered there—older male colleagues all full of "but," colleagues across the curriculum who view WPAs (especially those who are women with newly minted PhDs) and the field itself as something along the lines of academia's two-legged stool. At this point, I don't think I can even begin to see any of the moments we've brought up here through my eyes alone.

In post-arrival, we share stories of our introductory selves, the maps of ourselves that we understand to have been at play in the world, and rarely do our recollections match. So, then, what actually happened and is happening? We share, through words and deeds, accountings of accountings. Herein lies the danger of romanticizing the past. If a memory is recalled of a past interaction, both parties aren't necessarily experiencing that at the same time in the same ways. The memory is simultaneously true and not true. "Introductory Aurora" exists in John's cognitive pathways in different ways than she exists in Aurora's, even though they both share the chron(kair)ological lamination. Memory as a distinct and measured thing does and does not exist when they are both in the "there."

When bringing memories forward, both parties jointly create a version of history in the now that also influences the future of the interaction. Once again, the value of post-arrival comes into play; distance facilitates new insights, which sustain and reshape the continuity of mentorships. What separates our actions in this chapter from a knowledge-sharing among peers (although it is also that) is that we are attuning these insights in ways that help us to (re)consider our mentorship across time and place. We consciously step into the cognitive ecology of learning. Our subject is the mentorship itself, not locked into any narrow tale of learning, not a propulsion of the past into the present, but as a "round and round." We could not have had this conversation back then, fifteen years ago, but the one we are having now does nonetheless speak to "Introductory Aurora" and "WPA John," and our guess is they/we are listening.

THE PART WHERE WE CONCLUDE—FOR NOW

By interrogating sites of engagement, histories of the field that make these sites possible, and how the practices in and of themselves form the frameworks for our continued action, the mentor and mentee might more easily understand themselves as participating in relationships where post-arrival is understood as a root experience for both, instead of a relationship methodologically chartered through linear, chronotopic experience that culminates in achievement. Methods of post-arrival, then, might be seen as the following:

- Open acknowledgment of embodiment and affordance
- Evaluation of attunement
- Uptake of play

- Resistance to understanding as a single point of entry
- Resistance to accomplishment as the impetus for mentoring
- Charting of cognitive ecology informed by both the self and complex educational communities
- Understanding collaboration as a finding ritual enacted by mentors and mentees
- Resistance to closure

Instead of a post-mortem dissection focused on clarifying the "true" event, circumstance, or conversation with all the politeness and professionalism of a block of wood, we argue for interchange, interplay, and understanding, for time as a chronotopic *and* kairotopic—time connected to both physical passage *and* critical moments for action or inaction as they are connected to embodiment.

We've conjectured at times what personal markers have provided for our mentorship's persistence: first-gen scholars, the imposter syndrome, race, memories of unofficial events and those persisting from our work together in a graduate program, open-access education. In terms of the impact of post-arrival mentorship that's not mentorship on the field, Roman Krznaric's (2020) work on long-term thinking broadens our own senses of connection and legacy. In *The Good Ancestor*, Krznaric writes about the notion of intergenerational justice in a way that can take rhet/comp's notions of mentorship beyond the legacy mindset that might more readily shape mentorship stories, especially those that extend beyond points of arrival. A legacy mindset, Krznaric says, "can foster a sense of personal connection with future holders," while "intergenerational justice encourages a sense of collective responsibility" (72). Potentially, a focus on post-arrival space might not only foster the continued becoming of the persons (mentors who are not mentors) involved but also that of the field itself. It may help us extend our personal legacies toward a sense of responsibility for the future of the field and its stake in social justice efforts.

As we think more in terms of the field's continued growth and transformation, we can approach with more intentionality the chron(kair)otopes through which reciprocal becomings happen—any time/place where opportunity exists for cross-generational and other cross-cultural contact and reflection. Perhaps together, we (rhet/comp) might find ways to recognize and value our moments/dynamics of attunement and not knowing as much as, if not more than, our achievements/productions. This recognizing/valuing *does* happen in personal correspondence. However, there might also be value in en-scène mentorship at professional venues—places where more concerted attention can be paid to the "interstitial ecologic tracings" that we find in post-arrival spaces. Where exactly are we performing not knowing with one another? Where are we performing in ways that mark us in advance and in the wake of achievement?

How, for instance, might we examine the chron(kair)otopic laminations available to attendees and presenters at our professional conferences, and those available to dissertation directors and dissertation writers in faculty offices, and to authors and editors, and to students and teachers in classrooms, and to colleagues reminiscing over cups of coffee? How much has a culture of whiteness, of whitely behavior tied to "politeness," shut down opportunities to critique hegemonic structures within spaces we want to design to dismantle? How many intergenerational sites of engagement open for us every day across time and space, chron(kair)otopic opportunities in which cross-cultural exchanges might reshape our field's past, present, future? Like any discipline, we'll constitute ourselves in relation to our ancestors, but we have multiple opportunities now in post-arrival (and maybe en scène?) spaces to be good ancestors without being ancestors, to generate and prepare a "round and round" that can reshape power and power relations, that can meet in today's institutions the needs of future comp/rhet teachers and their students (Krznaric 2020, 72).

Our chapter enacts (right now!) ways mentorships exceed simple "tales of learning" and represents more of what Prior (2018) would describe as "a trajectory of semiotic becoming"—extending beyond locality, production, or tactical interaction. As such, throughout the chapter, we attempt to frame history as it is happening currently, as we experience it through the writing of this article in real time. We do so to ground post-arrival in the here and now, to demonstrate how post-arrival does not ignore prior pathways but elucidates how these pathways shape continual becomings (and vice versa). Focusing on practices that maintain and develop our mentorship that is not a mentorship, we "try together" here to extend scholarly work on mentorships, and with that, mentorships themselves into practices that bond members of our field and the field itself, round and round, to diverse perspectives.

REFERENCES

Bateson, Gregory. 2015. "Form, Substance and Difference." *ETC: A Review of General Semantics* 72 (1): 90–104.

Brock, Mary Anne Browder, and Janet Ellerby. 1997. "Out of Control: TA Training and Liberation Pedagogy." In *Sharing Pedagogies: Students and Teachers Write about Dialogic Pedagogies*, edited by Gail Tayko and John Paul Tassoni, 114–128. Portsmouth, NH: Boynton/Cook.

Cain, Mary Ann. 1994. "Mentoring as Identity Exchange: Conflicts and Connections." *Feminist Teacher* 8 (3): 112–118.
Cole, Kirsti, and Holly Hassel, eds. 2017. *Surviving Sexism in Academia: Strategies for Feminist Leadership*. Oxfordshire: Routledge Press.
Cruz, Joshua. 2020. "An Ethics of Bullshit: The Good, the Bad, and the Ugly." *Composition Studies* 48 (3): 120–124.
de Saint-Georges, Ingrid. 2005. "From Anticipation to Performance: Sites of Engagement as Process." In *Discourse in Action: Introducing Mediated Discourse Analysis*, edited by Sigrid Norris and Rodney H. Jones, 155–165. Oxfordshire: Routledge Press.
Downs, Doug, and Dayna Goldstein. 2008. "Chancing into Altruistic Mentoring." In *Stories of Mentoring: Theory and Praxis*, edited by Michelle F. Eble and Lynée Lewis Gaillet, 149–152. Anderson, SC: Parlor Press.
Fishman, Jenn, and Andrea Lunsford. 2008. "Educating Jane." In *Stories of Mentoring: Theory and Praxis*, edited by Michelle F. Eble and Lynée Lewis Gaillet, 18–32. Anderson, SC: Parlor Press.
Flynn, A. Elizabeth, and Tiffany Bourelle, eds. 2018. *Women's Professional Lives in Rhetoric and Composition: Choice, Chance, and Serendipity*. Columbus: Ohio State University Press.
Freire, Paulo. (1970) 1990. *Pedagogy of the Oppressed*. Translated by Myra Bergman Ramos. New York: Continuum.
Freire, Paulo. 1997. "A Response." *Mentoring the Mentor: A Critical Dialogue with Paulo Freire*, edited by Paulo Freire, James W. Fraser, Donaldo Macedo, and Tanya McKinnon, 303–329. Lausanne: Peter Lang.
Geller, Anne Ellen, Michele Eodice, Frankie Condon, Meg Carroll, and Elizabeth Boquet. 2006. *The Everyday Writing Center: A Community of Practice*. Logan: Utah State University Press.
Goodburn, Amy, Donna Lecourt, and Carrie Leverenz, eds. 2013. *Rewriting Success in Rhetoric and Composition Careers*. Anderson, SC: Parlor Press.
Hutchins, Edwin. 2010. "Cognitive Ecology." *Topics in Cognitive Science* 2 (4): 705–715.
Jones, Rodney H. 2014. "Mediated Discourse Analysis." In *Interactions, Images and Texts: A Reader in Multimodality*, edited by Sigrid Norris and Carmen Daniela Maier, 39–52. New York: Mouton de Gruyter.
Kram, Kathy E. 1983. "Phases of the Mentor Relationship." *Academy of Management* 26 (4): 608–625.
Krznaric, Roman. 2020. *The Good Ancestor: A Radical Prescription for Long-Term Thinking*. New York: The Experiment.
Matzke, Aurora, Sherry Rankins-Robertson, and Bre Garrett. 2019. " 'Nevertheless, She Persisted': Strategies to Counteract the Time, Place, and Structure for Academic Bullying of WPAs." In *Defining, Locating, and Addressing Bullying in the WPA Workplace*, edited by Christyn L. Elder and Bethany Davila, 49–68. Logan: Utah State University Press.
Miles, Katherine S., and Rebecca E. Burnett. 2008. "The Minutia of Mentorships: Reflections about Professional Development." In *Stories of Mentoring: Theory and Praxis*, edited by Michelle F. Eble and Lynée Lewis Gaillet, 113–128. Anderson, SC: Parlor Press.
Mullin, Joan, and Paula Braun. 2008. "The Reciprocal Nature of Successful Mentoring Relationships: Changing the Academic Culture." In *Stories of Mentoring: Theory and Praxis*, edited by Michelle F. Eble and Lynée Lewis Gaillet, 262–275. Anderson, SC: Parlor Press.
Prior, Paul. 2018. "How Do Moments Add Up to Lives: Trajectories of Semiotic Becoming vs. Tales of School Learning in Four Modes." In *Making Future Matters*, edited by Rick Wysocki and Mary P. Sheriden. Logan, UT: Computers and Composition Digital Press. https://ccdigitalpress.org/book/makingfuturematters/prior-intro.html.
Prior, Paul, and Jody Shipka. 2003. "Chronotopic Lamination: Tracing the Contours of Literate Activity." *Writing Selves / Writing Societies: Research from Activity Perspectives*, edited

by Charles Bazerman and David Russell. Mind, Culture, and Activity. Fort Collins, CO: WAC Clearinghouse.

Roozen, Kevin, and Joe Erickson. 2017. *Expanding Literate Landscapes: Persons, Practices, and Sociohistoric Perspectives of Disciplinary Development*. Logan, UT: Computer and Composition Digital Press. https://ccdigitalpress.org/expanding.

Scollon, Ron. 2001. *Mediated Discourse: The Nexus of Practice*. Oxfordshire: Routledge.

Sharer, Wendy, Jessica Enoch, and Cheryl Glenn. 2008. "Performing Professionalism: On Mentoring and Being Mentored." In *Stories of Mentoring: Theory and Praxis*, edited by Michelle F. Eble and Lynée Lewis Gaillet, 129–144. Anderson, SC: Parlor Press.

Tassoni, John Paul. 2022. "Post-Arrival Mentorships That Are Not Mentorships: Cross-Gender and Cross-Generational Trajectories in Rhet/Comp's Nexus of Practice." *College Composition and Communication* 74 (1): 58–83.

Welch, Nancy. 1993. "Resisting the Faith: Conversion, Resistance, and the Training of Teachers." *College English* 55 (4): 387–401.

ACKNOWLEDGMENTS

We begin these acknowledgments by thanking our contributors, who have made this collection what it is. We couldn't be more excited to share their excellent work with our readers. We are grateful to have learned from these scholars, and we thank them for trusting us with their work.

Because this collection works to explore how mentorship and methodology inform each other, we want to highlight the (often invisible) work that makes any publication possible. Rachael and the team at Utah State University Press guided us through every step of this messy, delightful process. Thank you as well to the two anonymous reviewers whose feedback helped us better highlight and situate our contributors' work. The labor that goes into this work is essential, and we are grateful for your time and energy.

We also want to thank the English Department at Auburn University, which provided summer funding so that we could begin this project. We are fortunate to work alongside vibrant, energizing students and colleagues both in our department and beyond, and are so appreciative of their many gifts. Finally, we wish to thank the broader disciplinary community of writing studies, where we have found a home. Our friends and colleagues in the field challenge us in the best possible ways.

LEIGH

It would be a mistake to not name those mentors who have profoundly shaped the work that I do. During my time at Florida State University, and then at Miami University, I was fortunate to have studied with Kristie Fleckenstein, Heidi McKee, Jason Palmeri, and the late, very great, Kate Ronald. I thank them for showing me how much good mentorship matters. I've been mentored by countless others in my personal and professional life, but here I want to offer a special thanks to my friend and collaborator, Charlie. You've made me a better teacher, writer, and thinker. Finally, any work that I do is only possible because I receive unending love, support, and joy from my favorite people: my family. Veikko, Mikko, and Evie are the best parts of me. I am lucky to love you, and even luckier to be loved by you.

CHARLIE

My life has been filled with remarkable, selfless mentors, all of whom taught me what it means to build strong bonds with others. At the University at Buffalo, Jim Holstun taught me what a commitment to student learning looks like when he would meet me on lunch breaks at my job to work on my senior thesis. In graduate school and in my first job, Chris Gallagher, Beth Britt, Mya Poe, Steve Parks, and others—including many graffiti writers—taught me that camaraderie and mutual respect can be the soil out of which good research grows. My co-editor, Leigh, has taught me that mentorship-friendship is the only way to thrive in academic spaces. And finally, my family—Allie, Jack, and Graham—taught me to make life fun, even when it's hard. In terms of mentorship, to say I've been lucky would be the understatement of this book.

INDEX

Locators followed by *n* indicate an endnote; locators followed by *t* indicate a table.

ableism: higher education, 193; knowledge-making, 148–49; writing center administrators (WCAs), 165
academia: administrative roles, 74, 75; belonging, sense of, 131, 136–38, 142, 208, 209; decoloniality/coloniality, 31, 32; dominant narratives, 46, 47, 151, 152, 168–69, 186, 190, 191; feminist scholars, 11; fitting in, 154, 155; gatekeeping, 29, 243; hierarchy, 93, 147; institutional processes, 18*n1*, 93, 94; learning-management system, 206; linguistic diversity, 95–96; quality enhancement plans (QEPs), 85; rigor, 224; structures, 11, 186; systemic inequities, 7, 9, 58, 68, 119, 189, 193, 237, 238, 247; un/becoming, 150, 153; whiteness, 12, 58, 66, 72*n1*, 130, 141, 257; writing centers, 178
academic publishing: call for proposals (CFP), 8–9, 252; diversity and inclusion, 136–37, 141, 142, 193; editing practices, 7; faculty writers, 98, 129–30, 156–57; imposter syndrome, 130, 135; journal articles, 127, 192; manuscript-writing process, 127, 139–40; peer review, 128–30, 134–38, 139, 171; professional development, 133, 138, 140, 142, 169; publish or perish, 43–44, 131, 132, 190, 191, 193; Reviewer 2, 128–31; revise-and-resubmit status, 138; scaffolded writing support, 130; scholarly voice, 45, 53, 132. *See also* dissertation-writing process
academic subject knowledge support, 197, 199
access. *See* gatekeeping
accomplices. *See* allies
accomplishment, post-arrival space, 267
accountability of researchers, 36
action, sites of engagement, 254–56, 264–65
administrative roles, 74, 75, 78, 79, 110, 113, 120

advanced faculty, 96, 104
Advanced Writing in the Disciplines, 96
advisor-advisee relationship, 29–30, 44, 45, 46, 188, 189–92
advocacy, writing centers, 85
affordance, post-arrival space, 266
After Whiteness, 131
agency, 149, 155–58, 169, 177, 239
Ahmed, Sara, 189–90
Ahrens, Marieke, 61
allies: antiracist work, 184; faculty, 242–43; social justice work, 184; testimonio, 237–38
Alm, Mary, 94
already-always-becoming, 263
analytics data, 93
Anglesey, Leslie R., 17, 59, 151
anonymous review process. *See* peer review
Anson, Chris M., 94
Anti-Racist Scholarly Reviewing Practices: A Heuristic for Editors, Reviewers, and Authors, 137
antiracist work: allies, 184; dissertation-writing process, 190, 241; mentorships, 244; pedagogy, 237; publishing practices, 141; research, 189, 240, 241, 242; white privilege, 176; writing centers, 181, 189, 190
Anzaldúa, Gloria, 59
apprenticeship models, 219
appropriation, testimonio, 239
archival research, 25, 26, 50
Arellano, Sonia C., 146, 153, 223, 232*n3*
Art of Fertility organization, 35
Asher, William, 42, 50
Asian students, 249–50*n2*
assessments, writing, 16, 85, 91, 92, 93, 94, 96–99
assimilation, linguistic diversity, 99, 103, 156
assumptions, research methodologies, 47
atmosphere, writing centers, 76
Auburn University, 18*n2*
autoethnography, 53, 54, 75

274   INDEX

Babcock, Rebecca Day, 172
Balester, Valerie M., 77
Ball, Cheryl, 140
Banks, William P., 132–33
barrio epistemologies, 63, 64, 65
Bartlett, Lesley Erin, 16, 80, 221, 225
Bateson, Gregory, 252
Bawarshi, Anis, 174–75
becoming, process of, 46, 150, 153, 158, 253–55, 262–64, 267–68
belonging, sense of: academic publishing, 131, 136–37, 138, 142, 208, 209; marginalized students, 12, 58, 237; mentoring, 131, 154, 155, 156
benefits of mentoring, 121, 165–66, 197, 205, 212
Berg, Maggie, 147
Berlant, Lauren, 83
best practices of writing program administrators (WPAs), 92
Beyond Conversation, 166
BIPGM (Black, Indigenous, and People of the Global Majority), 61–63, 64–65, 66, 67, 69–70, 71, 72*n1*
BIPOC (Black, Indigenous, and People of Color). *See* faculty of color
Bivens, Kristin, Marie, 147
BIWGM (Black, Indigenous and Women of the Global Majority), 15, 57–59
Bizzell, Patricia, 50*t*
Blankenship, Lisa, 154
Blewett, Kelly, 8, 193
Bloom, Lynn Z., 6, 18
Boehm, Beth, 49
Bolker, Joan, 46–47
Bonilla-Silva, Eduardo, 42, 247
Boquet, Elizabeth, 75
boss text, 187–89, 190, 191, 193–94
boundaries, post-arrival space, 39, 256–57
Braddock Report, 49
Brooks-Gillies, Marilee, 35
Brown, Brené, 154
Bruffee, Kenneth A., 166
Bruland, Holly H., 198, 199, 201
"bullshitting" in the writing process, 262
Bunch, Charlotte, 53
Burciaga, Rebecca, 239
Burke, Kenneth, pentad, 27
business field, mentorships, 224, 254
Buttorff, Gail, 232*n6*

Cagle, Lauren E., 137, 141, 193–94
Calafell, Bernadette, 58, 59, 60, 64, 67
call for proposals (CFP), 8–9, 95, 185, 252
Campbell, Karlyn Kohrs, 81
Campbell, Marie, 182

care and support, writing centers students, 76, 77
career paths, 197, 199
Cargile Cook, Kelli, 41
caring, slow mentoring, 152–53
Carino, Peter, 75
Cartesian dualism, 220
case studies, qualitative research, 173
Castillo, Jennifer, 13
Caswell, Nicole I., 79, 81, 177
CCCC Statement on Professional Guidance for Mentoring Graduate Students, 191
CDS (critical disability studies), 228–30
Cedillo, Christina V., 7, 9, 12
Ceraso, Steph, 146
Certeau, Michel de, 31
CFP (call for proposals), 8–9, 95, 185, 252
Charmaz, Kathy, 238
Chi-squared Automatic Interaction Detection (CHAID), 172
Chicana scholars, 59, 236, 238, 240, 241
Chilisa, Bagele, 51
Choffele, Ezekiel, 174
Chomsky, Noam, 41
chronotopic experiences, 255, 256, 266, 267–68
CIMP (Cross-Institutional Mentoring Program), 16, 109–11, 112–16, 121, 122, 125*n1*
Cisneros, Sandra, 59, 65
citation practices, journal editing, 193
Clary-Lemon, Jennifer, 13
Classical scholarship, 30, 32
classism, 6–7, 85, 140, 148–49, 167, 173, 175
classroom practices: antiracist pedagogy, 237; mentoring roles, 205, 207, 209, 210*t*; racial justice, 241, 242, 243, 247; rhetoric and composition, 245; writing tutors, 73, 199
Clements, Jessica, 16
closure, resistance to, post-arrival space, 267
co-authoring, 128, 166, 172, 173
co-constructs, 238
co-mentoring, 146, 157–58
co-teaching, 202, 206, 209, 210, 211
Coalition of Feminist Scholars in the History of Rhetoric & Composition, 139–40
coding field notes, 98, 103, 104, 202–4
cognitive ecology, 261–63, 264–66, 267
collaborative learning: co-authoring, 166; conference presentations, 168; critical race–grounded methodology, 239; digital humanities, 101; disciplinary boundary work, 106; diverse perspectives, 245, 249, 252; E2K, 57; fellowship programs,

140; idea-sharing sessions, 167; insights, 254; interdisciplinary research, 98–100; journal editing, 192; linguistic identities, 123; mentorships, 115, 148–50, 164, 172, 254; multigenerational, 92, 96, 102; peer review, 136; post-arrival space, 267; process-oriented, 94; publications, 168, 173; sites of engagement, 255–56; testimonio, 236, 248, 244–46; virtual, 96–97, 99, 113, 116; writing centers, 82, 84, 163, 176, 177, 181, 183; writing, 73–74
colleague/peer, 39, 46
collective cultural history, 59, 267
College Factual, 250n2
coloniality: frameworks, 31; grand narratives, 168–69; knowledge-making, 148–49; mentorships, 185; modernity narrative, 29–30; research methods, 52; writing centers, 175
colorblind racism, 247
combined-course mentoring, 200, 204, 205t, 206, 209, 212
comfort zones, 262
common ground, 260
community-building: decoloniality, 28; differing perspectives, 69; ethos, 81; field knowledge, 130; homeplace, 70; listening, 183; making as world-making, 25–26; marginalized groups, 54; meaning-making, 27; mentorships, 140, 160, 166; outside theoretical lens, 35; practices, 32, 85; storying, 34–35, 37; women of color, 248; writing centers, 175, 176–77
compensation, research participants, 245
Composition-Rhetoric, 47
Compsters, 225
comradismo, 146, 153, 232n3
conditional matrix, 239
conditions, mediated discourse theory, 256
Condon, Frankie, 42, 176
Conference on College Composition and Communication (CCCC), 3, 43
conferences, professional development, 168, 171
conflicts, storying, 35, 37
Connecting Writing Centers Across Borders, 138
connectivity: experiences, 220; faculty-to student, 205, 208, 209; mentors/mentees, 218, 254, 255; research participants, 244, 249
Connors, Robert J., 47, 50t
concientización, 236
constellations, 139
constructive criticism, 137–38

continuity, nexus of practice, 261
contributors, publishing process, 8–9
conventions, academic, 190, 191
CoPI, multilingual research, 100
coping mechanisms, faculty of color, 230
Corbin, Juliet, 239
Cordell, Ryan, 104
core writing courses, 83
counselor roles, 205, 207, 208
Counterstories from the Writing Center, 85
counterstorytelling, 7, 53–54, 230
course-content translator, 207, 208, 209
course-embedded mentoring. *See* embedded-only mentoring
COVID-19 pandemic, 92, 100, 104, 105, 117
Cox, Matt, 37
creative writing, 18n2
Crenshaw, Kimberlé, 175–76
crip theories, researchers, 228
Crisp, Gloria, 197, 198
Cristoph, Julie Nelson, 219
critical autoethnography, 189–91
critical disability studies (CDS), 228–30
critical race theory (CRT), 228, 229–30, 235, 236, 237, 238–39, 240, 247
critical reflection, 47, 220, 236–37, 240, 244, 245–46, 249
critical resistance, 69
critique, disciplinary structures, 54, 239, 268
crookedness, 221
cross-cultural reciprocal becoming, 267–68
cross-disciplinary collaboration, 16–17, 93–94, 101–2, 168, 169
cross-generational reciprocal becoming, 93, 267–68
cross-institutional mentoring, 113, 114, 115–18, 121, 163, 173
Cross-Institutional Mentoring Program (CIMP), 16, 109–11, 112–16, 121, 122, 125n1
Cruel Optimism, 83
Cruz, Joshua, 262–63
cultural rhetorics: academic publishing, 139; boundaries, 39; decoloniality, 29–32; differing perspectives, 33, 47; dissertation-writing process, 26–27, 35, 38; institutional resistance, 28; knowledge-making, 30, 174; lived experiences, 28; making, process of, 40; meaning-making, 27, 59–60; principles, 15; qualitative research, 34–35; storying, 26, 34–36, 37–39; teaching, 139; writing centers, 174
Cultural Rhetorics Theory Lab (CTRL), 28–29

culturally-relevant mentoring, 71
culture of transparency, 134
culture of writing center studies, 81
current conditions, past mentorships, 254
curriculum development, 91

data analysis/data collection: coding, 98, 103, 104; critical race theory (CRT), 228, 240, 247; digital humanities, 101, 104; Google Docs, 201; knowledge constructs, 239; multigenerational assessment, 102, 105, 122–23; objectivity/subjectivity, 12, 13, 14, 229; split-apply-combine, 102; testimonio, 236–37, 244; transformation, 102; writing assessment research, 94, 98. *See also* research methods; research participants
Day, Michael, 11
debriefing interview, research participants, 245
decision-making, writing center pedagogy, 94, 168, 181, 183
decoloniality: communities of practice, 28, 32; cultural rhetorics, 26, 31–34; dissertation-writing process, 33, 241; graduate student instructors (GSIs), 244; knowledge-making, 28–30; mentorships, 185, 186; methodologies, 42; research methods, 50–51, 174, 240, 242; rhetoric and composition, 30, 31, 32; writing centers, 77, 174–75
Decolonizing Educational Research: From Ownership to Answerability, 51
Decolonizing Methodologies: Research and Indigenous Peoples, 51
Delgado Bernal, Dolores, 239, 240
deliberate mentoring practices, 85, 86*t*
democratic mentorships, 257
demographics, graduate students, 92, 173, 250*n*2
Denny, Harry C., 79, 85
departmental protocols, 85, 192, 245
dependency, mentors/mentees, 259
descriptive survey research method, 96
design research, 14
Detweiler, Jane, 41, 45, 46, 47, 48, 49, 54
developing mentorships, 32, 49, 121, 268
Di Pressi, Haley, 102
dialogue, mentorships, 39, 255
differing perspectives, mentorships, 34, 35, 57, 69, 70, 111, 186
digital futures method, 50
digital humanities, 98, 100, 101–2, 104
digital testimonio, 237–38
Directors of Writing Centers Facebook group, 171

disability (dis/ability) rhetoric, 17, 85, 114, 218, 221, 229, 231*n1*
disciplinary communities: academic publishing, 132; boundary work, 92, 101, 106; knowledge-making, 93; mentors/mentees, 7, 192; peers, 142; rhetoric and composition, 49; structures, 53, 54; sustainability, 62, 121; writing assessment research, 96
discourse analysis, 43, 49, 67, 173, 231, 254–56
discrimination 29, 248
"Disculpe las molestias, esto es una revolución," 63, 64*t*, 65
discussion facilitator role, 202, 206, 208, 209, 210*t*
displacement methodologies, 58, 71
disruption of academic norms: academic communities, 189; dominant narratives, 151, 152, 186; institutional ethnography (IE), 192; mentoring models, 147, 185–86, 258; methodologies, 66, 67; neoliberal institutional structures, 156; power structures, 164, 182
dissertation-writing process: advisor-advisee, 45, 46: antiracism, 190, 241; autoethnography, 189–90; committees, 26, 38, 43, 223; critical race theory (CRT), 240; cultural rhetorics, 26–27, 35, 38, 39; decoloniality, 33, 241; discourse, 231; feedback, 151; graduate students, 16, 235–36; mentoring, 37, 114, 149, 151, 221, 223, 225–26, 231; positionality, 241; qualifying defense, 189, 190; research practices, 25, 48–49, 228; ruling texts, 193–94, 190; storying, 36; testimonio, 243–46; white privilege, 189, 190; writing centers, 138, 170, 173; zero draft, 46, 47. *See also* academic publishing
distance, research, 32
diversity and inclusion: academia, 62, 103; call for proposals (CFP), 8–9; collaborative learning, 252; college campuses, 95; knowledge-making practices, 175; lack of, 165; mentorships, 11–12, 14–16, 121–22, 253; methodologies, 17, 42, 53; peer reviews, 140–41; students, 169; white privilege, 194; writing studies, 6–7, 91, 105, 111–12, 127, 141, 239. *See also* gatekeeping
Dixon, Elise, 15, 35, 54
doctoral advising, 167, 171
doctoral students, 33–34, 37–38, 41, 230–31
documented students, 238
Dolmage, Jay, 218, 221

dominant narrative: academic culture, 47; disruption, 186; grand narratives, 168–69; ideologies, 249; legacy, 46; located agency, 155–57; majoritarian storytelling, 47; mentorships, 151, 152, 191, 264; neoliberalism, 151, 155, 157; research methods, 51; rhetoric and composition, 49; scholarship legitimacy, 190, 191; writing centers, 174
double-blind peer review, 129, 139
Driscoll, Dana Lynn, 170, 171, 172
Duffy, William, 166
dyadic relationships, 198–99

E2K collaboration, 57
early-career faculty researchers, 96, 98–101, 104, 122–23, 135–36, 192
"easy yes" requests, 257
Eble, Michelle, 82
ecological cognitive practice, 254, 263
editing practices, 7, 8, 128, 136–37
educational support in mentorships, 105, 169–70, 197, 198, 210, 211
effects of white supremacy in academia, 67, 68
Ejército Zapatista de Liberación Nacional (EZLN), 63, 64t
Elements of Academic Style, The, 131
elitism in academia, 9
Ellsworth, Elizabeth, 150
email, tools/factors, 256
embedded-only mentoring: combined-course, 204–6; field notes, 201–2; models, 212; Personalized System of Instruction, 199; race, 203, 211; research methods, 17, 201, 203–6; students, 200, 205, 212
embodied experiences: cultural rhetorics, 26; homeplaces, 62; mentoring, 28, 225, 226, 227, 231; metho-epistemology, 218; methodologies, 58, 59; people of color, 69–71; post-arrival space, 258, 264, 265, 266; rhetoric and composition, 61
emerging methodological perspectives, 178
Emig, Janet, 44
emotional labor, 77, 79, 81, 84, 85, 148, 149, 248
empathy, lived experiences, 154, 178
empirical research methods, 74, 104, 163, 172
employable skills, 86
empowerment, people of color, 237, 240, 244, 247, 248, 249
en scene memories, 258, 261
English Departments: demographics, 250n2; knowledge-making practices, 101; undergraduate students, 95; women of color, 244; writing centers, 170
Enlightenment philosophies, 32
Enoch, Jessica, 111
Enos, Theresa, 45, 82, 219
epistemologies: barrio, 63, 64, 65; BIPGM, 71; leaky bodies, 218; meaning-making, 227–28; mentoring, 221–22; methodologies, 58, 226; racism, 14
equitable approaches to research: collections, 7, 8; disciplinary communities, 62; mentorships, 7, 9, 62, 71, 94, 156, 235; pedagogy, 243; post-arrival space, 255; research, 243; writing centers, 164, 176
Erickson, Joe, 261, 264
ethical research practices, 9, 35, 37, 122, 166, 188
ethnicity, students, 11–12, 186, 235, 241, 243, 249–50n2
ethnographic research, 50
ethos: academic publishing, 136; collaboration, 94; feminist praxis, 80, 82; mentoring, 80, 86t, 138–41; professional development, 133; writing centers, 81, 83, 84
etymology of methodology, 48
Eurocentrism in academia, 131, 238
evaluation of attunement, 266
Evans, Daryl P., 218
Everyday Writing Center, The, 85, 261
evidence, subjectivity, 12, 13, 14
excess, slow mentoring, 150–53
exclusion. *See* diversity and inclusion; gatekeeping
expectations, writing centers, 76, 79, 86, 177, 222
experiential knowledge. *See* lived experiences; testimonio

Facing the Center, 79, 85
faculty: administrative roles, 74, 75; allies, 242–43; assistants, 209, 210, 211; collaborative learning, 94; early-career, 96, 98, 99–101, 104; ghost advising, 95; identity, 79; junior faculty, 190, 195n1; mental health days, 223–24, 232n4, 232n5; mentoring, 15, 96, 104, 200, 201, 204, 205t, 206, 208, 209; peer review, 156–57; professional development, 97, 133; publishing opportunities, 98, 192; self-perception, 133, 134; senior faculty, 190, 195n1; tenure, 122–23
faculty of color: allies, 9; coloniality, 29; compensation, 245; connectivity, 248,

249; coping mechanisms, 230; critical reflections, 240, 244, 245, 246; debriefing interview, 245; discourse, 67; discrimination, 247, 248; focus groups, 245; ghost advising, 95; graduate students, 237, 244, 249–50*n*2; homeplaces, 58–59, 69; inclusion, 7, 11–12; invisible labor, 148, 224; journal editing, 192; lived experiences, 229–30, 235–36, 238, 247; mentors/mentees, 68, 118, 119, 175, 188; predominantly white institutions (PWIs), 243–44, 245; representation, lack of, 130, 241; research participants, 249*nr*; social injustices, 70; survival in academia, 184, 241; tutors, 85, 187; writing centers, 79, 85, 175
failure, cross-institutional mentoring, 117–18
Faison, Wonderful, 175
Faye, Dr., 205*t*, 207, 208, 212
feedback, peer review, 137–38, 151, 153, 192
fellowship programs, 140, 167
feminist scholarship: agency, 149; co-mentoring, 11; collaborative learning, 94; comadrismo, 153; ethos, 80, 82; excess, 150–51, 236, 237; fellowship programs, 140; hierarchy, 176, 185; inclusion, 149; institutional ethnography (IE), 184; leaky bodies, 221; located agency, 155–57; mentorships, 7, 11, 80, 82, 146, 167, 185, 219; multigenerational, 105; peer review, 136, 137; positionality, 165; reciprocity, 12–13; research methods, 33, 54; survival in academia, 59, 184; un/becoming, 147–48; values, 4; writing centers, 77, 175–76
field notes research, 201, 202–4, 206
fields of study, sustainability, 111, 112
first authorship, reciprocal mentorships, 259–60
first-generation students, 119, 166, 177, 186, 198, 201, 267
first-year writing programs, 113–14, 131, 199, 200
Fishman, Jenn, 219
Fiske, John, 150
fit (in) spaces, 57, 58
fitting in to academia, 154, 155
Fitzgerald, Lauren, 74
Flahive, Michelle, 17, 43
Flanders, Julia, 94
flexibility, cultural rhetorics, 15, 26, 27, 28
Flinchbaugh, Kerri, 132–33
Flores Carmona, Judith, 239
Flores, Lisa, 59, 60, 64
fluidity, leaky mentoring, 218, 220

focus groups. *See* research participants
forced thinking, mentors/mentees, 257–58
formal mentorships, 109–11, 171, 172
formation story research method, 44
Foucault, Michel, 80, 82
frameworks, 48, 62, 226, 263
Freire, Paulo, 29, 257
functions, post-arrival space, 255
funding, writing centers, 170, 171

Gagnon, John T., 36–37
Garcia, Romeo, 175
gatekeeping: academic publishing, 128, 136–37, 141, 142; counterstory, 230; graduate student instructors (GSIs), 240; higher education, 11, 29, 243; mentorships, 7, 46, 82, 121–22, 175, 235; methodologies, 14; writing across the curriculum (WAC), 109, 110, 111; writing center administrators (WCAs), 174. *See also* diversity and inclusion
Geib Chavin, Elizabeth, 17, 74, 77
Geller, Anne Ellen, 85, 176, 261
gender: academic publishing, 140; identity, 76–77; inequities, 6–7; language, 175; lived experiences, 85; mentorships, 232*n*6, 235, 243, 260; writing center patrons, 167
general education outcomes assessment, 105
generational differences, writing assessment research, 98
generative friction, 92
genre, 44, 105
gentefying, 15, 58, 61, 69–70
gentrifying, 71
ghost advising, 95
Gilyard, Keith, 175
Ginsburg, Shiphra, 130
Glenn, Cheryl, 111, 191
global mobility, 95
goal-setting/career paths, 197, 199
Godbee, Beth, 14–15, 128, 145–46
Goggin, Maureen Daly, 50*t*
Gold, Penny, 44, 46
Goldsmith, John, 44
Good Ancestor, The, 267
Goodburn, Amy, 147
Goodley, Dan, 220
Google suite of tools, 97, 201, 203
Grabill, Jeff, 4
graduate students: critical resistance practice, 69; cultural rhetorics, 26; demographics, 243, 246, 249–50*n*2; discussion groups, 45; dissertation-writing

process, 15, 48–49, 131, 191; health issues, 217, 223–24, 228, 232n4, 232n5; instructors, 46, 235, 239, 240, 241, 243; mentoring, 10, 41, 91, 122–23, 201, 227, 232n7; methodology courses, 3, 41; positionality, 167; pre-tenure, 18n1; research assistants, 96, 97, 101–2, 104; students of color, 11–12, 62, 71, 235–37, 244, 247–48; training, 15, 16; tutors, 187–89; writing center administrators (WCAs), 177; writing program assessment, 91, 93, 94
grand narratives, 168–69
grant applications, 167
Grant-Davie, Keith, 18n3
Green, Neisha-Anne, 85, 175
Greenfield, Laura, 183, 194–95
Gregor, Frances, 182
Grobman, Laurie, 95, 104
grounded theory, 173, 238–39
growth mindsets, writing classes, 261–62
Grutsch McKinney, Jackie, 76, 77, 79, 81, 163, 177
Gruwell, Leigh, 185
guidelines, ruling texts, 193–94
Gumbs, Alexis Pauline, 184

Halberstam, Jack, 148
Hallman, Rebecca, 174
Halloran, Michael, 81
Harris, Muriel, 75, 76
Haswell, Richard, 170
Hayot, Eric, 131, 132
HBCUs. *See* Historically Black Colleges and Universities
health issues, 217, 223–24, 228, 232n4, 232n5
Healy, Dave, 74
Henry, Jim, 198, 199, 201
Herzberg, Bruce, 50t
heuristic mentoring practices, 85, 86
hierarchical constructions of mentoring: academic publishing, 131; disruption, 258; feminist theory, 176, 185; institutional positions, 18n1; journal editing, 193; knowledge-making, 29, 30; language use, 195n1; mentoring spaces, 7, 16, 82, 93, 94, 125n1, 219; problematic terminology, 18n1; white privilege, 190, 193; writing center administrators (WCAs), 169
higher education. *See* academia
Hinsdale, Mary Jo, 186, 188, 192
Hispanic students, 198, 249–50n2
historical periods, rhetoric and composition, 50t

historical selves, post-arrival space, 261
Historically Black Colleges and Universities (HBCUs), 175
historiographic methods, 49, 50
history of research methodologies, 41, 47
history of writing centers, 75, 169
holding space, storying, 33, 34
holistic identity work, 150, 153–55
home languages, 15
homeplace: community-building, 70; creating, 60; methodologies, 62; safe space, 61, 63–65, 67–68; E2K, 57; embodied knowledges, 62; methodologies, 60–61; scholars of color, 58–59, 69; space, 68
homogenization, mentoring, 71
homophobia, knowledge-making, 148–49, 165
hooks, bell, 7, 59, 67–68
horizontal mentoring, 11, 146, 153–54, 157–58, 199, 217
Horner, Winifred Bryan, 219
House, Eric A., 15, 218
Hughes, Bradley, 128
human collectivity, 238
human constructs, 32
humanities, data analysis, 101–2, 104
humanity, BIPGM mentees, 67, 69–70
Hutchins, Edwin, 259

Ianetta, Melissa, 74
IWCA (International Writing Centers Association), 166, 171
idea-sharing sessions, collaborative learning, 167
identity: academic publishing, 140; faculty, 79, 154; inequities, 6–7; intersectionality, 101, 175–76; intrapersonal characteristics, 117–18; linguistic, 123; mentorships, 117–19; politics, 79; slow mentoring, 150, 153–55, 156, 157, 158; students, 79, 169; testimonios, 240; writing centers, 73, 79, 80, 83, 86, 174
importance of mentoring, 10, 43, 200
imposter syndrome, 130, 135, 237, 241, 267
in-residence mentoring, 199
individualize mentoring, 198, 200
inclusion in mentorships, 62, 71, 112, 121–22, 138–39, 149, 193, 194, 208, 209, 245
Indigenous perspectives, 33, 36, 42, 51, 52, 148, 241, 244, 249n1, 249–50n2
Indigenous Research Methodologies, 51
individual education plan (IEP), 103
individualize mentoring, 198, 200
influence of mentoring relationships, 119–21, 253
informal mentorships, 171, 172

injustices of oppression, 238
insights, mentors/mentees, 253, 254, 255, 260, 265–66
institutional critique methods, 50
institutional ethnography (IE): interactions, 181–84; lived experiences, 184, 188–89; local discourse, 191; mentoring practices, 17, 181, 185–86, 193, 229; peer reviewers, 194; positionality, 173, 182; power dynamics, 182, 189, 192; radicalism, 195; resistance, 28; scholarship, 190, 191
Institutional Ethnography, 173
IRBs (institutional review boards), 167, 200
institutional space. *See* space
institutional structures, 10, 16, 18*n1*, 86, 93, 94, 157, 171, 194
institutionalized whiteness, 72*n1*
intellectual labor, scholars of color, 148
interaction: cognitive pathways, 262, 265–66; graduate student instructors (GSIs), 241–42; mentorships, 209, 210*t*, 240, 254; narrow curricular imaginings, 264; post-arrival space, 256, 263; tutors with writers, 75
interchanging roles of mentors/mentees, 228, 255
interconnection in mentorships, 247–48, 259–60
interdisciplinary research, 96, 99–100
international students: academia, 95; graduate students, 246, 249–50*n2*; higher education, 95; lived experiences, 98, 100–101; mentoring work, 16; program assessments, 92, 106; super-diversity, 98, 100; writing centers, 16, 138–39
International Writing Centers Association (IWCA), 166
intersectionality, 3–4, 5, 6, 7, 101, 175–76, 232*n6*
interstitial ecological tracings, 263
interventions, peer reviewers, 134
interviews. *See* research methods; semistructured interviews
intrapersonal characteristics, 117–18
introductory methods course, 41
invisible labor, 10–11, 224, 232*n6*
invitational play, 258
IRBs (institutional review boards), 167, 200
Irigaray, Luce, 221
isolation, feelings of, 67
IWCA (International Writing Centers Association), 166, 171

Jackson, Rebecca, 79, 81, 177
Jarratt, Susan C., 80
Jennings, Willie James, 131, 132
job security, 257–58
Johnson, W. Brad, 112
Jones, Rodney H., 256, 261
journal articles. *See* academic publishing
Journet, Debra, 49
June, Audrey Williams, 232*n6*
junior faculty, 190, 195*n1*
justice-oriented research, 7, 8, 93, 102, 104

Kairos, 140, 141
kairotopic experiences, 255, 267
Keller, Elizabeth, 18*n3*
Keller, Fred S., 199
Keller, Hans, 221
Kerschbaum, Stephanie, 228–30
King, Thomas, 34
Kinkead, Joyce, 76, 95, 104
kinship, mentorships, 146, 224
Kirkpatrick, Keaton, 17
Kirsch, Gesa, 42, 50, 226
knowing, becoming, process of, 262–64
knowledge-making: collaborative learning, 166; cultural rhetorics, 174; decoloniality, 28–31; disciplinary, 93; diversity and inclusion, 175; experiential, 13, 238, 239; institutional ethnography (IE), 186; leaky mentoring, 222–23; mentoring practices, 80, 149–50; methodologies, 12, 226; post-arrival space, 258; practices, 11, 101, 172; production, 218, 220; testimonio, 17; un/becoming, 147–48; writing center pedagogy, 168, 186; writing studies, 52
Kohrs Campbell, Karlyn, 81
Komlos, John, 44
Kopelson, Karen, 151
Koro, Mirka, 221, 222, 227
Kram, Kathy, 254
Krznaric, Roman, 267
Kynard, Carmen, 7, 12, 53, 188

L1/L2/L3 linguistic labels, 98, 100
labor practices, writing center studies, 17, 173
labs. *See* writing centers
Ladson-Billings, Gloria, 71
LaFrance, Michelle, 93, 173, 183, 184, 190, 191
land-grant universities, 31
language, 15, 18*n1*, 101, 175, 178, 235, 243
LatCrit theory, 236, 237, 238
Latino/a/x scholars: barrio epistemologies, 63, 64, 65; comadrismo, 232*n3*;

Index   281

critical race theory (CRT), 235; mentoring, 62, 242; predominantly white institutions (PWIs), 17; rhetoric and composition, 146, 148; testimonio, 236, 237, 239, 240
Lauer, Janice, 42, 44, 50, 82
Leahy, Elizabeth, 110
leaky mentoring: comadrismo, 223, 232n3; critical race theory (CRT), 229–30; embodiment, 231; fluidity, 218, 220; graduate students, 232n7; health issues, 223–24; meaning-making, 227–28; mentoring relationships, 217, 219; peer-mentoring, 225; research methods, 227, 229; self, sense of, 221. *See also* mentoring; slow mentoring
Learning from the Lived Experiences of Graduate Student Writers, 12, 185
learning stages, 27, 265–66
learning-management systema, 206
LeCourt, Donna, 147
legacy mindset, 42, 267
legacy of care, 84
legitimacy of scholarship, 190, 191
Leppänen, Taru, 221, 222, 227
Lerner, Neal, 172, 173
Lesbian Avengers, 25–26, 35
Lesh, Charles, 185
Leverenz, Carrie, 147
Lewis Gaillet, Lynée, 82
LGBTQA narrative, 25, 26, 33, 42, 52, 54, 79, 82, 83, 148, 220, 228
linear experiences, 264, 266
Lingard, Lorelei, 130
linguistic background, lived experiences, 85
linguistic diversity: academia, 95–96; assimilation, 99, 103; identities, 123; justice, 241; L1/L2/L3 linguistic labels, 98, 100; marginalized perspectives, 103; super-diversity, 100, 105
listening to learn, 183
listservs, 74
literature studies, 18n2, 44, 49, 104
Little Traverse Bay Band, 35
Liu, Lu, 111
lived experiences: cultural rhetorics, 28; connectivity, 220; dialogue, 255; empathy, 154; faculty of color, 61–62, 64–66, 70, 229–30, 235–36; institutional ethnography (IE), 186, 188–89; international students, 98, 100–101; mentorships, 60, 82–83, 86t, 145, 182, 184, 185, 205t; peer review, 128; writing center administrators (WCAs), 85, 163, 165, 176. *See also* testimonio

local discourse, institutional ethnography (IE), 191
located agency, slow mentorship, 157, 158
Lockett, Alexandria, 14
Lorde, Audre, 184
lore, writing center scholarship, 74
low-income students, 201
Lucas, Brad, 15
Lunsford, Andrea, 219

Mackiewicz, Jo, 172
MacNealy, Mary Sue, 42, 50, 244
Madden, Shannon, 12, 185
maintaining mentorships, 268
majoritarian storytelling, 42, 44–45, 47, 53–54
making, process of, 25–26, 40
Malagón, Maria C., 238, 239
male perspective, territorial communities, 264
managing editors, 135
manipulated yeses, 257–58
Manning, Erin, 221
manuscript-writing process. *See* academic publishing; dissertation-writing process
Mapping Social Relations: A Primer in Doing Institutional Ethnography, 182
mapping, knowledge-making, 51
marginalized narratives: classroom discussion, 243; counterstorytelling, 53–54; faculty of color, 71; institutional ethnography (IE), 17; knowledge-making, 12; linguistic diversity, 103; lived experiences, 70; positionalities, 194; power dynamics, 189; research projects, 227; rhetoric and composition, 47; students, 52, 53, 199, 237; support framework, 62; testimonio, 236; writing assessment research, 97; writing centers, 163, 173
Martinez, Aja Y., 54, 227, 229, 230, 247
Marušić, Ana, 197
master narratives, 47
master-apprenticeship mentoring, 82
Matheson, Breeanne, 18n3
Matzke, Aurora, 17, 148
McDonald, James, 77
meaning-making: communities, 27, 149, 263; cultural rhetorics, 59–60; decoloniality, 28–31; graduate students, 91; male perspective, 264; mentoring, 148, 227–28
mediated discourse theory: actions, 255–56; frameworks, 263; mentors/mentees, 253; past learning, 254–55; points of entry, 264–65; traditional narratives, 18; Medina-López, Kelly, 15, 27, 60, 218

Medina, Cruz, 237–38
meditational means, 255–56
Mejía, Jaime Armin 43, 44
Melonçon, Lisa, 226
memories, cognitive pathways, 258, 262–63, 265–66
mental health issues, 223
mentoring: cross-institutional, 109–12, 116, 121; deliberate, 86*t*; differing perspectives, 70, 218, 253; discussion facilitator, 45, 202, 206, 209, 210*t*; dyadic relationships, 198–200; ethos, 80, 81, 86*t*, 138–41; faculty, 44, 96, 99–101, 104, 209–11, 241–42; fellowship programs, 140; feminist rhetorical approach, 7, 11, 68, 149, 175–76; graduate students, 10, 15, 26, 41, 235–36, 240, 243; institutional initiatives, 86, 191, 229; knowledge-making, 11, 204, 220, 221, 222–23; lived experiences, 86*t*, 145, 184, 185; metho-epistemology, 227; multigenerational, 91, 92, 105; normate, 218, 222; professional support, 128, 146, 197–99, 205, 207, 210, 211; research participants, 27–28, 117–18, 227, 244, 246; spatial practices, 58, 61; students, 91, 96, 101–4; teaching duties, 10–11, 202, 206, 209, 210*t*, 212; teammate, 202, 210*t*; unofficial, 230–31; visibility, 73, 85, 86*t*; welcoming practices, 59–61. *See also* leaky mentoring; slow mentoring
mentoring models: agreements, 64; apprenticeships, 219; conservative, 12; decoloniality, 185; disrupt, 147; equity-oriented, 7; feminist-centered, 80; field notes research, 201–2; invention, 53; leaky, 220; pairing program, 171; paradigms, 178, 185–86; progressive, 12; research, 201, 203–4; roles, 37, 82, 125*n1*, 202–4; subject/object, 219; traditional, 12; voluntary, 199; writing centers, 178. *See also* embedded-only mentoring
mentors/mentees: allies, 242–43; becoming, 253, 255, 263–64, 267; belonging, sense of, 131; boundaries, 218, 219, 220; checking in, 65, 69–70; chronotopic experience, 266, 267; co-teachers, 202, 209–11; collaborative learning, 10, 115, 164, 166, 172, 254; faculty of color, 9, 12, 46, 67–70, 118–19, 188, 244, 245, 247–49; first authorship, 259–60; forced thinking, 257–58; hierarchy, 6, 93, 94, 147, 176, 219; insights, 254, 260; interconnection, 227, 247–48; linear experience, 264, 266; mediated discourse, 253; peer-relationships, 115–17, 185, 202, 206–7, 209, 210*t*; power dynamics, 29–30, 158, 164, 219, 241–42, 257, 259; reciprocity, 38, 120, 186, 259–60; relationships, 1, 26, 43, 63–66, 121, 192, 253; requests, 256–58; resistance, 69, 70; role models, 125*n1*, 205, 207, 208, 211, 222; self-reflection, 203, 262; support, 197, 198, 205, 207–8, 210, 211, 248; tutors, 202, 206, 209, 210*t*; un/becoming, 147–48; writing across the curriculum (WAC), 121–24, 135
mentorship: academic culture, 134, 224; cognitive ecology, 264–65; connectivity, 218, 254, 255; cultural rhetorics, 26–28, 38, 39, 40; decoloniality, 29–30, 33–34, 186; diversity and inclusion, 7–11, 12, 14–17, 62, 71, 83, 121–22, 138–39, 162, 175, 199, 232*n6*; doctoral research, 33–34, 41, 171, 167; dominant narrative, 18, 26, 168–69; embodiment, 28, 225, 226, 227; epistemologies, 221–22; first-generation status, 166, 186; formal/informal, 109–11, 171, 172; gentefying, 69–70; gentrification, 71; institutional ethnography (IE), 181–82; intersectionality, 3–4, 51, 232*n6*; legacy narratives, 42, 267; neoliberal ideology, 16, 145–47, 148; post-arrival insights, 253, 254, 255, 257; privilege, 243–44; rhetoric and composition, 231, 252–53; sexism, 119, 186; site of engagement, 252–53; trajectories in research, 115, 260, 262; writing centers, 77, 79, 97–99, 165, 173–74, 177
methodology: critical disability studies (CDS), 228–29; critical race theory (CRT), 229–30, 235–37; cultural rhetorics, 59–60; decoloniality, 42; development, 32, 62; dominant narratives, 190, 191; epistemologies, 14, 58, 226; faculty of color, 42, 59, 60–62, 71, 230; fit (in) spaces, 57, 58, 61; frameworks, 62, 164, 226; importance to mentoring, 73, 188; institutional ethnography, 17; journal article publication, 127; knowledge-making, 226; legitimacy of scholarship, 190, 191; meaning-making, 227–28; positionality, 4, 9–10, 12–13, 37, 42, 57, 58, 173, 241–43, 249; racial justice, 7; reciprocity, 62; rhetoric and composition, 168; surveys, 52; transdisciplinary, 101; values, 29, 32; writing across the curriculum (WAC), 121. *See also* methods; testimonio
methods: challenges to existing models, 15, 66, 67; etymology, 48; generative friction, 92; introductory methods

course, 41; negotiations, 98; outcomes assessments, 92; post-arrival space, 266–67; qualitative/quantitative research, 49–50; white perspective, 42; writing centers, 75, 177, 178. *See also* methodology; research methods; testimonio
metho-epistemology, 218, 227, 228
Micchiche, Laura, 156
Michigan State University 31
microaggressions, 187–88, 238
micro narratives, 128
Mid-Atlantic Writing Centers Association (MAWCA), 175
Mignolo, Walter, 29, 30
Miley, Michelle, 173, 181, 183
Miller, Janet L., 150
Miller, Susan, 44
minorities. *See* faculty of color
mixed-methods study, 17
MLWRP survey instrument, 98
models. *See* mentoring models
modernity narrative, 29–31
mood, writing centers, 76
Moraga, Cherríe, 59
mosaic metaphor, 6
motivation, mentorships, 117–18, 257
Mountz, Alison, 151
movement/mucosity, mentoring, 221
Mukavetz, Andrea Riley, 35, 36
multiethnic mentoring networks, 185
multigenerational mentoring: collaborative learning, 96; faculty, 94, 122–23; generational differences, 98; graduate students, 91; Multilingual Assessment Outcomes Project, 97; multilingualism, 105; outcome assessments, 92, 105; transversal interjections, 102; undergraduate students, 95; writing assessments, 94, 97, 99–100
Multi-Generational Research Teams, 96
multilingual research, 96, 98, 99, 100, 100–101, 105
Multilingual Writers Research Project (MWRP), 95
Multiplicity, feminist approach, 149
multiracial students, 154
mutual mentoring, 97
mystery in mentorships, 186, 187

naming excess, feminist theories, 150–51
narrative patterns, 42, 44, 174, 176, 253–54, 264
narrow curricular imaginings, 264
Native Hawaiian/Pacific Islander students, 249–50*n*2
navigation strategies, people of color, 230

neoliberal ideology, 16, 145–47, 148, 149, 151, 152, 155, 156, 157
networking, 68, 94, 111, 164, 171, 173, 185, 199
neutrality in research, 32
nexus of practice, 254, 261, 263, 264–65
Nichols, Amy McCleese, 181
Nicolas, Melissa, 17, 59, 183, 184, 190
non-equitable mentoring spaces, 167
nonnormative function, 218
non-Western perspective, 29–31
Nora, Amaury, 197, 198
Nordstrom, Georganne, 166
normate mentoring, 182, 218, 222
North, Stephen, 44, 49, 50*t*, 51, 75
Northeastern University College, 92, 96, 105
not-knowing, becoming, process of, 262–63
Novotny, Maria, 35, 36–37, 146
now-world, 255

objectivity in research, 32, 142, 229
observational researcher role, 200–204
Okawa, Gail Y., 11–12, 46, 185
Omizo, Ryan, 198
one-on-one interaction, 195
online double-blind peer review publishing space, 139
online journals, 140, 142
online webinars, professional development, 138
Open Doors report, 95
open-access pathways, 141, 260, 267
open-ended inquiry, 147
oppression in higher education, 148–49, 237, 238, 243
oral traditions, meaning-making, 31, 174
Ore, Ersula, 7, 9, 12
orientation in research methodologies, 48
Orner, Mimi, 150
Ortiz, Jennifer, Dr., 127
outcome assessments, 96, 105–6
outside theoretical lens, 35
Oxford Guide for Writing Tutors, 74

pairing surveys, 109–10, 118–19
Palermo, Gregory J., 16, 101–2, 122
Pantelides, Kate, 18*n*3
paradigms, mentoring, 178, 185–86
passive group members, 202, 209, 210*t*
past mentorships, 253–55, 260
Patel, Leigh, 51, 190
pathways, post-arrival, 268
patriarchal narrative, 30, 47, 219
patrons of writing centers, 167

284 INDEX

Patsavas, Alyson, 220
patterns, post-arrival space, 239, 256–57
pay it forward mentoring, 138
PEAK. *See* Project-Based Exploration for the Advancement of Knowledge
pedagogy, racial equity, 237, 243
peer mentoring: appropriate behavior, 202, 206–7; benefits, 205; face-to-face meetings, 225; graduate students, 201; mentors/mentees, 185, 209, 210*t*, 211, 258; relationships, 46, 115, 116, 117; writing program administrators, 135
peer review: academic publishing, 136, 171; anonymous reviews, 129; diversity and inclusion, 140–41; double-blind, 139; faculty writers, 156–57; feedback, 129, 134–35, 137–38, 192; institutional ethnography, 194; journal articles, 127; lived experiences, 128; people of color, 130; publish or perish, 193; reader reports, 193, 194; standards, 129–30
Peer Review, The, 175
Peitho, 139–40
Pelkowski, Stephanie, 174–75
Pell, John, 16
Pencheva, Denny, 128
people of color. *See* faculty of color
Perdue, Sherry Wynn, 170, 171, 172
Pérez Huber, Lindsey, 237, 238, 239, 240, 244
permeability/impermeability of boundaries, 218, 219, 220
personal lives, 121, 153
personal support, 197, 198, 210, 211
personality of mentors, 211–12
Personalized System of Instruction, 199
perspectives, differing, 34, 35
Peterson's, 250*n*2
Phelan, Molly, 135, 138
physical space, writing centers, 75, 76
place/time, 61, 254–55
Poe, Mya, 16, 97–99
point of entry, territorial communities, 246, 264–65
policies of writing centers, 84, 91, 187–88
politics, identity, 79
Polk, Thomas, 16
Porter, James, 218–19
positionality: dissertation-writing process, 241; feminist scholars, 165, 176; graduate students, 167; institutional ethnography (IE), 173, 182; mentoring, 164, 211–12, 223, 232*n*3, 246; methodologies, 9–10; research, 13, 230, 240–43, 249; white privilege, 194
positivity, lack of, 62

post-arrival space: becoming, process of, 267; boundaries, 256–57; common ground, 260; embodiment, 258, 264; equitable dialogue, 255; evaluation of attunement, 266; heterogeneous ground, 257; historical selves, 261; insights, 253, 265–66; methods, 266–67; pathways, 268; patterns, 253–54, 256–57; rhetoric and composition, 259; sites of engagement, 255–56, 266; teacher development, 257, 263
post-structuralist perspectives, 45
postmodern perspectives, 45
Powell, Malea, 15, 54
power dynamics: disruption, 164, 182, 192; intersectionality, 101; marginalized positions, 189; mentors/mentees, 26, 158, 219, 241–42, 257, 259; modernity/coloniality, 29–30; power dynamics, 195*n*1; research participants, 27; ruling relations, 188; slow mentorship, 158; writing center pedagogy, 181
practical knowledge, 204
Praxis, 74
praxis, mentoring, 80, 85, 86, 104, 164, 177, 195, 253
pre-tenure faculty, 18*n*1, 113–14
predominantly white institutions (PWIs): decoloniality, 240; graduate student instructors (GSIs), 17, 235–36, 241, 243–45; institutional change, 182, 186; methodologies, 58; research participants, 245, 247; whiteness, 43, 241–42; writing centers, 167
present interconnectivity, 260
Present Tense, 128, 136, 137–38, 139, 140, 142
Price, Margaret, 228–30
principles, cultural rhetorics, 15
Prior, Paul, 254, 255, 263–64, 268
privilege: acknowledgement of, 186; mentorships, 243–44; modernity, 31; storying, 42
process-oriented intimate collaboration, 94
process. *See* methodology
professional development: academic publishing, 131–32; faculty, 91, 133; interdisciplinary research, 99–100; mentoring practices, 85–86, 128, 146, 205; online webinars, 138, 142; support, 197, 198, 210, 211; tutors, 74; writing center administrators (WCAs), 85, 164
professional reputation, 44, 117–18, 257–58
program assessments: critique, 54; justice-oriented goals, 104; multilingualism, 100–101; outcomes assessment, 105–6;

rhetoric and composition, 245; students, 94, 106; writing programs, 91, 92
progressive mentoring, 12
Project-Based Exploration for the Advancement of Knowledge (PEAK), 96
psychological/emotional support, 197, 199
public-facing mentoring, 140–41
publish or perish, 43–44, 131, 132, 190, 191, 193
publishing. *See* academic publishing
Purdue Writing Center, 76
purpose of mentoring, 75, 204–6, 207, 208, 209, 210

qualifying defense, 189–92
qualitative research: antiracism, 189; cross-disciplinary mentoring, 93–94; cultural rhetorics, 34–35; dis/ability, 229; objectivity, 32; rhetoric and composition, 45, 50; writing studies, 44, 173
quality enhancement plans (QEPs), 85
quantitative research, 32, 49, 71, 93–94, 173
Queen City Writers, 95
queer rhetoric, 25, 26, 33, 42, 52, 54, 79, 82, 83, 148, 220, 228
queercrip analysis, 220
Queerly Centered, 79

R coding, 98, 104
race: academic publishing, 140; embedded-only mentoring, 203; equity/inequity, 6–7, 243; graduate student instructors (GSIs), 235, 243, 249–50n2; intersectionality, 101; knowledge-making, 12; language, 175; lived experiences, 42, 85; mentorships, 11–12, 212, 232n6; personal marker, 267; wellness, 85; writing center patrons, 167
Race, Rhetoric, and Research Methods, 14
racial justice, 72n1, 236, 238, 241, 242, 243, 249
racism, 9, 14, 119, 148–49, 165, 175, 187–89, 193, 230, 247, 248
radical relationally, 183
radicalism, institutional ethnography (IE), 195
RADs (replicable, aggregable, data-driven approaches), 170–71, 172, 174, 228
Ralston, Devon Fitzgerald, 15
Rantala, Teija, 221, 222, 227
reader reports, 193, 194
reciprocity: cross-cultural, 267–68; cultural rhetorics, 37–39; feminist methodologies, 13; first authorship, 259–60; mentors/mentees, 38, 115–17, 120, 186;

methodologies, 62; multigenerational research, 94; research participants, 35, 36, 37–38; writing across the curriculum (WAC), 122; writing centers, 177, 181
reconnection, mentorships, 255
redefinition phase, 254
reenactment, mentorship practices, 182
reflective survey research method, 96
Regan, Devon Skyler, 16, 102–4
Reid, E. Shelley, 185
relatable knowledge, 168, 208
relational labor, 77, 181
relationality, 26, 30, 36–38
relationships: advisor/advisee, 188; building, 38, 147; cultural rhetorics, 39; disciplinary norms, 192; dyadic, 198–99; embodiment, 225, 226; experiences, 220; hierarchy, 82; identities, 118–19; knowledge production, 29; leaky, 222; mentors/mentees, 43, 63, 64, 65, 66, 115, 116, 117, 121, 224; methodologies, 9–10, 13; peer roles, 202, 211; positivity, lack of, 62; power dynamics, 26; tutors, 81, 83
religion, 140, 167
re-making, storying, 35
renegotiation, disciplinary boundary work, 92
Re/Orienting Writing Studies: Queer Methods, Queer Projects, 52
replicable, aggregable, and data-driven approaches (RAD/RADs), 170–71, 228
replication in research methods, 52, 229
repositioning excess, 150–51
representation, lack of, faculty of color, 52, 53, 58, 136, 237, 241
requests, mentors/mentees, 257–58
research assistants, 44, 95, 96, 97
Research Is Ceremony: Indigenous Research Methods, 36
research methods: autoethnography, 53, 54; collaborative learning, 10, 114; cultural rhetorics, 25, 26, 27, 33; decoloniality/coloniality, 5, 14, 50–52, 174, 242, 243; disciplinary/interdisciplinary, 53, 92, 99–100; disruption, 189; faculty, 96, 98, 99–101, 104, 242–43; field notes, 201–4; justice-oriented, 102; lens, 32–33; lived experiences, 184; methodologies, 28, 47, 48, 58, 68, 75, 173; observational role, 200–204; positionality, 13, 230, 194, 240, 249; qualitative/quantitative, 93–94; rhetoric and composition, 44, 48–49, 74, 93; semi-structured interviews, 201, 203–4; subject binary, 227;

surveys, 96, 201, 203–4, 123, 124; writing across the curriculum (WAC), 110, 112, 113, 119–21; writing centers, 85, 173, 174, 177. *See also* data analysis/data collection; research participants

research participants: connectivity, 244, 249; critical self-reflection, 236–37, 240, 244–46, 249; cross-institutions, 114; differing perspectives, 28, 33, 44, 45, 54, 97, 227, 238–39, 241; ethical checkpoints, 35, 37; focus groups, 52, 238, 244, 245, 247; mentorships, 85, 117–18, 185, 200, 201, 246; needs, 28; pairing surveys, 118–19; power dynamics, 27; queer rhetoric, 25–26; reciprocity, 35, 36, 37–38; recruiting, 172; relationality, 36; researcher perspective, 32–33; storying, 27–28, 34, 35; transparency, 33; women of color, 239*n1*, 240, 244, 245, 246, 247, 248, 249*n1*. *See also* data analysis/data collection; research methods

research trajectories, 115, 148–49, 151, 163, 240, 243, 255–56, 260–64

resemiotize, 254, 260

resistance in mentorships, 69, 70

responsive mentorship, 185–86, 188, 191, 194

Restaino, Jessica, 148

Reviewer 2, 128–31

reviewing practices. *See* peer review

reviews, academic publishing, 134–35

revise-and-resubmit status, 138

reward/punishment: graduate programs, 253

Rewriting Success in Rhetoric and Composition Careers, 147

Reynolds, Nedra, 50*t*, 61, 80, 81

rhetoric and composition: chron(kair)otopes, 267–68; cross-institutional mentoring, 113, 115; dissertation-writing process, 48–49; diversity and inclusion, 25, 31, 32, 47, 49, 245, 252; dominant narratives, 49, 51; ethos, 81; faculty of color, 58–59, 71, 146, 241; hierarchical constructions, 147; histories of research, 28, 41, 47, 49, 50*t*; literature studies, 44, 49; lived experiences, 61; mentoring, 10, 59–61, 219, 231, 235, 252–53, 267; metho-epistemology, 218–19; nexus of praxis, 253, 254; predominantly white institutions (PWIs), 43; qualitative/quantitative research, 44, 45, 48–50, 229; Standard Academic English, 30–31; storying, 34–35; writing pedagogy, 43. *See also* writing studies

Rhetoric Review, 7

Rhetorical Tradition, The, 52
Ribero, Ana Milena, 146, 153, 223, 232*n3*
Rickly, Rebecca, 18*n3*, 41, 50
rights and responsibilities of tutors, 187–88
Rivera-Mueller, Jessica, 16, 221
role models, 73, 197–98, 202–3, 206, 207–9, 210–12, 222
Ronald, Kate, 80
Roozen, Kevin, 261, 264
Rosner, Mary, 49
Royster, Jacqueline Jones, 13, 14, 60, 64
Ruiz, Iris D., 14
ruling texts, 184, 187–89, 190, 191, 193–94
Runswick-Cole, Katherine, 220
Rupp, Leila, 176
Russell, Alisa, 16, 93
Rutz, Carol, 94

safe space, faculty of color, 59, 61, 63, 64, 65, 66
Salem, Lori, 172
Sambunjak, Dario, 197
Sanchez, James Chase, 52
Sano-Franchini, Jennifer, 199, 201
scaffolded writing support, 130
scholarship: collaborative learning, 10; diverse perspectives, 8–9; dominant academic narratives, 190, 191; empirical research, 74; extension of mentorship, 11, 12; publications, 45; rhetoric and composition, 30, 74; voice, 132
science and engineering methodologies, 168
Scollon, Ron, 255–56
Scott, J. Blake, 226
Seeber, Barbara K., 147
self-awareness, 221, 262
self-commodification, 156
self-expression, 81
self-perception, 133, 134, 203, 236–37, 254
semi-structured interviews, 201, 203–4, 206, 245
semiotic becoming, 263–64
senior faculty, 195*n1*
sense of self, 221
service-learning projects mentoring, 199
sexism, 7, 119, 148–49, 193
sexual orientation, 85, 167, 186
Shakur, Assata, 103
shaming, peer review, 129
shared ownership, 37
Sharer, Wendy, 111
Sharp-Hoskins, Kellie, 15, 27, 218
Shildrick, Margrit, 220
Shipka, Jody, 255
Sicari, Anna, 17

single-authored research articles, 172
sites of engagement, 252–53, 255–56, 263–64
Slack communication tool, 84
Slaughter, Jerel, 112
slow mentoring: belonging, sense of, 154, 155, 156, 158; caring, 152–53; Compsters, 225; dominant narratives, 147, 151, 152; faculty writers, 156–57; fitting in to academia, 155; horizontal, 146, 153–54, 157–58, 199, 217; informal reading groups, 16; kinship, 146; knowledge-making, 148–50; meaning-making, 148; relationship-building, 147; un/becoming, 147–48, 150, 153. *See also* leaky mentoring; mentoring
Slow Movement, 147
Small, Nancy, 18*n*3
Smith, Dorothy, 184, 186, 187, 188
Smith, Linda Tuhiwai, 32, 51
Smith, Trixie, 15, 54, 174
Smitherman, Geneva, 175
social action, women of color, 244, 247, 248
social justice initiatives, 13, 53–54, 70, 174–75, 178, 181, 184, 236, 238
social media, 130, 138, 142, 171
social practices, 255–56
Social Sciences Feminist Network, 232*n*6
social-material identity, 117
socioeconomics, 232*n*6, 260
sociopolitical realities, 236–37
Southern Discourse in the Center, 74
space: ethos, 81; gentefying, 69; home-place, 61, 63–65, 67–68; mentoring, 9; racial equity, 243; storying, 33, 34, 35; underrepresented voices, 58, 85; writing centers, 183
spatial practices, 58, 61
split-apply-combine, 102
staffing, writing centers, 169, 170
Standard Academic English, 30–31
standards, peer review, 129–30, 228, 229
standpoint theory. *See* lived experiences
statistical analysis, 94
Stenberg, Shari J., 145, 156, 157
Stephens, Eric, 18*n*3
storying: cultural rhetorics, 26, 34–36, 39; data analysis, 27–28; differing perspectives, 31, 34, 35; privilege, 42; relationality, 37
storytelling, 34, 42, 44–45, 53–54, 174
Strauss, Anselm, 239
structural racism in academia, 52, 66, 247
students: allies, 9; discrimination, 29, 238; diversity and inclusion, 169, 205, 208, 209; identity, 79, 169; mentoring, 46, 200, 201, 204, 206, 207, 210; peer roles, 202, 211; productivity, 92; writing center, use of, 76, 77, 84, 173
subaltern, 239
subdisciplines, 171
subject/object model, 219
subjectivity in research, 12, 13, 14, 229, 260
Sullivan, Patricia A., 42, 50, 218–19, 226
super-diversity, 100–101, 102, 105
support systems: critical resistance practice, 69; dissertation-writing process, 139, 191; marginalized graduate students, 11, 62, 248; mentorships, 115–16, 117, 205, 207–8, 210; students, 92, 168–69, 204; writing centers, 76, 77, 177
surfacing excess, feminist theories, 150–51
survey research methods, 96, 112, 118–19, 123, 124, 201, 203–4, 206
sustainability, writing programs, 16, 62, 110, 111, 112, 121, 122, 177
systemic inequities, 66, 68, 134, 148–49, 158, 237

Takayoshi, Pamela, 13
tale of learning, 264, 268
Tarabochia, Sandra L., 16, 221
Tassoni, John Paul, 17, 148
Taylor, Verta, 176
Teaching English to Speakers of Other Languages (TESOL), 99
teaching practices: cross-disciplinary, 93–94; decoloniality, 240; learning-management system, 206; mentor role, 7, 10–11, 202, 209, 210*t*, 212; post-arrival space, 257, 263; professional development, 91, 254; teacher-learner, 262; writing across the curriculum (WAC), 110, 113, 120
teammate mentor role, 202, 210*t*
technical and professional communication. *See* rhetoric and composition; writing studies
Technologies of Text (ToT), 104
tenure, 122–23, 142, 165, 166, 170, 193, 253
terminology, academic hierarchy, 18*n1*
terms and methods, disciplinary boundary work, 92
territorial communities, 264
testimoniando, 236, 238–39, 244–47
testimonio: allies, 237–38, 242–43; appropriation, 239; collaborative learning, 96, 236, 245, 248; data collection, 236–37; dissertation-writing process, 243; graduate students, 3, 15, 42, 235; identity, 240; marginalized scholars,

236; mentors, 242–43; research methods, 236, 237, 244, 246; social justice, 236–38, 249; subaltern, 239; women of color, 17, 239, 240, 241, 245, 249. *See also* lived experiences; methodology; research methods
Texas Tech University, 244, 249–50n2
text types surveys, 96
textual analysis, 31, 44, 49, 184
theoretical research, 27, 29–30, 61, 74, 204, 239
theory and body, 59
Thomson, Garland, 218
Thornberg, Robert, 238
time and space, 244, 246, 247, 249, 256
tokenism, master-apprenticeship mentoring model, 82
Tomlinson, Elizabeth, 13
top-down hierarchy, knowledge production, 29
Torrez, J. Estrella, 237, 238, 240
Towle, Beth A., 17, 74, 77
traditional academic conventions, 12, 28, 171, 190, 191
training, mentoring, 78, 201, 204, 205t; tutors, 82, 167–69, 171
trajectories in research, 115, 148–49, 151, 163, 240, 243, 255–56, 260–64
transdisciplinary methodologies, 101
translingual orientations, 93
transnational writing across the curriculum, 114–15
transparency in mentoring, 33, 41, 142
transversal interjections, 102
trinary teaching configurations, 198
Troutman Robbins, Stephanie (Dr.), 69, 70, 71
trust in post-arrival space, 259
tutors: classroom-based, 86, 199; discrimination, 187–88; emotional labor, 81, 85; graduate students, 189; identity, 79; interaction with writing students, 75; lived experiences, 85; mentoring, 74, 202, 206, 209, 210t; networking, 173; practices, 76; professional development, 74; rights and responsibilities, 84, 187–88; training courses, 82, 167–69; writing centers, 81, 83, 86t, 173
Twale, Darla J., 110

un/becoming, 147–48, 150, 153
unconventional writing, dissertation-writing process, 189
undergraduate student researchers: academic publishing, 138; agency, 169; mentoring, 17, 96, 102–4; programmatic research, 92; research opportunities, 91, 95, 96, 97; support, 167–69; writing collaboration, 173
underrepresented voices, 85, 201
undocumented students, 238
university space. *See* space
upper-level administration, 171
uptake of play, 266

validation, experiential knowledge, 238
value, leaky bodies, 230
values: feminist methodologies, 4; mentorships, 4, 153, 155–56, 191; methodologies, 32; program assessment, 105; researchers, 12–13; writing center directors, 86
VanHaitsma, Pamela, 146
Vélez, Verónica N., 238, 239
Vicino, Thomas, 106n1
Villanueva, Victor, 60, 175
virtual collaboration, 96–97, 99, 113, 116
visibility, mentoring, 73, 85, 86t
voice of the discipline, 132
voluntary mentoring models, 199

WAC. *See* writing across the curriculum (WAC)
WAC Graduate Organization (WAC-GO), 109
Watling, Chris, 130
WCRP (Writing Centers Research Project), 170
Weber, Jessica, 135, 138
Webster, Travis, 79
Weidman, John C., 110, 111
welcoming practices in mentoring, 59–61, 70
wellness, writing center administrators, 84–85
Western dominant narratives, 14, 26, 28–32, 49, 51, 142
white perspective: academic publishing, 130, 131, 141, 190, 193; acknowledgment of, 186; allies, 184; antiracist work, 176; coloniality, 49; dissertation-writing process, 189, 190; graduate students, 244, 250n2; institutionalization, 58, 72n1; patriarchy, 52, 53; positionality, 194; predominantly white institutions (PWIs), 241–42, 257; research, 44, 45; territorial communities, 264; white supremacist legacy structures, 42, 43, 47, 66, 67, 68; writing center studies, 165
WID (writing in the disciplines), 123, 124
Wieser, Kim, 7, 9, 12
Williams, Bronwyn, T., 181

Wilson, Shawn, 36, 37
WLN: A Journal of Writing Center Scholarship, 84–85, 138, 139
women of color (WOC). *See* faculty of color
Women's Ways of Making It in Rhetoric and Composition, 147
Working Lives of New Writing Center Directors, The, 79, 177
working-class students, 154, 177
writerly development, 131, 132
writing across the curriculum (WAC): administration, 110, 113, 120; diversity and inclusion, 111–12; identity, 109, 119; influence, 119–21; mentoring practices, 121, 122, 135; multigenerational research, 94; pairing surveys, 123, 124; research, 110, 112, 113, 120; transnational, 114–15
writing assessment research, 91, 92, 93, 94, 96–99
writing center administrators (WCAs): antiracist work, 165, 189, 190; collaborative learning, 177; educational backgrounds, 169–70; International Writing Centers Association (IWCA), 171; lived experiences, 85, 163, 165, 176; mentoring, 73, 178; networking, 173; people of color, 175; professional development, 85, 164; research, 75, 85, 174; role models, 73; tenure-track positions, 170; tutors, 74; wellness, 84–85
writing center directors (WCDs): autonomy, 75; collaborative learning, 168; educational background, 169–70; ethos, 81, 83, 84; faculty, 166; identity, 76–77, 79, 80, 83, 86; institutional ethnography (IE), 183; responsibilities, 78–80
Writing Center Journal (WCJ), 74, 163, 172
A Writing Center Practitioner's Inquiry into Collaboration, 166
writing centers: academic publishing, 138, 170, 175, 193; classroom labs, 73; collaborative learning, 168, 176, 177, 181, 183; core writing courses, 83; cross-disciplinary writing, 169; decision-making, 181, 183; diversity and inclusion, 163–65, 173–76, 178, 181, 188, 189, 194; early-career contributors, 135–36;

feminist mentoring, 77, 140, 165, 175–76; funding, 170, 171; international students, 138–39; knowledge-making, 186; mentorships, 85, 164; narrative inquiry, 174; physical space, 75, 76; policies, 84, 187–88; predominantly white institutions (PWIs), 165, 167; research, 74, 163, 170–71, 172; subdisciplines, 171; support for students, 76, 167, 169, 183; tutors, 74, 78, 81, 82, 86t, 169, 187–88
Writing Centers in Context, 76
Writing Centers Research Project (WCRP), 170
writing in the disciplines (WID), 123, 124
Writing Lab Newsletter, 74, 172
writing program administrators (WPAs), 16, 91, 92, 94, 135, 166
Writing Program Administrators—Graduate Organization (WPA-GO), 91
Writing Program Assessment Project, 104
writing studies: academic publishing, 127, 132, 135, 139–40, 142; Auburn University, 18n2; belonging, sense of, 142; collaborative learning, 73–74, 168, 169; digital humanities, 101; diversity and inclusion, 6–7, 91, 105, 235, 236, 237, 240; growth mindsets, 261–62; knowledge-making, 52; listservs, 74; literary studies, 104; methodology, 3, 230; multilingualism, 99, 100; open-access pathways, 260; post-arrival space, 259, 263; process of "bullshitting," 262; professional development, 86, 138; program directors, 113; research, 13, 44; tutors, 75, 86, 199; *See also* rhetoric and composition

XChanges, 95

Yamada, Mitsuye, 59
Yosso, Tara J., 42, 54

Zebroski, James Thomas, 50t
Zeleznik, Julie M., 93
zero draft, 46, 47
Zhang-Wu, Qianqian, 16, 99–101
Zickar, Michael J., 112
zine-making, 25
Zoom, 96–97, 116, 117
Zuberi, Tukufu, 42

ABOUT THE AUTHORS

Leslie R. Anglesey (she/her) is assistant professor of rhetoric and composition in the Department of English at Sam Houston State University, where she co-directs the first-year writing program. Her research interests focus on disability studies, composition pedagogy, mentorship, and rhetorics of health and medicine. She is a co-editor of *Standing at the Threshold: Liminality and the Rhetoric and Composition TAship* and *Threshold Conscripts: Rhetoric and Composition Teaching Assistantships*. Her work has also appeared in *College Composition and Communication, Prompt: A Journal of Academic Writing Assignments*, and *The Peer Review* and in multiple edited collections on rhetorics of health and medicine.

Lesley Erin Bartlett is assistant professor of English at Iowa State University, where she directs ISUComm foundation courses. Her scholarship and teaching focus on composition theories and pedagogies, feminist rhetorics, and rhetorical performance. Her work has appeared in *English Leadership Quarterly, Feminist Teacher, Teaching/Writing: The Journal of Writing Teacher Education*, and other venues. She is a co-editor of *Diverse Approaches to Teaching, Learning, and Writing Across the Curriculum: IWAC at 25* (2020).

Jessica Clements is associate professor of English and composition commons director at Whitworth University in Spokane, Washington. She has served as style editor for *Present Tense: A Journal of Rhetoric in Society* since 2012 and stepped into the role of co-managing editor in fall 2020. Her scholarship centers on *ethos* and the role of human and object-oriented actors in contemporary multimodal communication. She has co-written an interdisciplinary book evaluating the influence of social media networks in shaping binary-bound parenting decisions, called *Optimal Motherhood and Other Lies Facebook Told Us*. She has published in *WLN: A Journal of Writing Center Scholarship* an article titled "The Role of New Media Expertise in Shaping Writing Consultations" and in edited collections on using game studies ethnography to raise tutors' intersectional awareness as well as pedagogical performance of neutrality at faith-based institutions.

Elise Dixon is the director of the Writing Center at the University of North Carolina at Pembroke, where she is assistant professor in the English, Theatre, and World Languages Department. Her teaching and research focus on queer, cultural, and multimodal rhetorics, as well as writing center studies. Much of her work is focused on how marginalized communities and organizations empower themselves through collaborative writing and making. Her scholarship has appeared in *The Writing Lab Newsletter, The Peer Review Journal, The Journal of Veterans Studies*, and in multiple book chapters.

Michelle Flahive is assistant teaching professor of writing and rhetoric in the Notre Dame University Writing Program. She received her PhD in technical communication and rhetoric at Texas Tech University in 2023. Michelle's research interests include translingual theory, writing program assessment, mentorship, and teacher development. Her current research is focused on how to improve mentorship for women of color graduate student instructors through antiracist writing program design, implementation, and assessment. She is co-author of "Integrating the Marginalized and the Mainstream: Women of Color Graduate Instructors' Experience with Identity, Difference, and Belonging," published in 2023 by the WAC Clearing House and University Press of Colorado in William J. Macauley et al.'s *Threshold Conscripts: Rhetoric and Composition Teaching Assistantships*.

ABOUT THE AUTHORS

Elizabeth Geib Chavin is assistant professor of English and director of the Writing Center at Slippery Rock University. Her research focuses on community writing centers, writing center tutor-training, community engagement, and public literacy. Elizabeth is the co-author of "Writing Centers as Intersections for Controversy and Change" (University Press of Colorado and Utah State University Press) and a forthcoming article for *The Peer Review* titled "Accessing Community Writing Support beyond Writing Center Spaces: Institutional Barriers to Sustainable Engagement." She received her PhD in rhetoric and composition from Purdue University in 2022.

Leigh Gruwell is associate professor of English at Auburn University, where she teaches undergraduate and graduate courses in writing and rhetoric. Her research centers on digital, feminist, and new materialist rhetorics as well as composition pedagogy and research methodologies. Leigh's work has appeared in *Computers and Composition, Peitho,* and *Present Tense,* among other venues. Her book, *Making Matters: Craft, Ethics, and New Materialist Rhetorics,* was published in 2022.

Eric A. House is assistant professor of critical composition and writing studies at New Mexico State University, where he researches Black rhetorics and writing, cultural rhetorics, and composition theory and pedagogy.

Keaton Kirkpatrick (he/him/his) is a PhD candidate in Michigan State University's Rhetoric and Writing program. Drawing on experiences as a first-year writing educator and student WPA, he primarily researches student and teacher support within first-year writing programs. While he plans to continue studying embedded models of support and mentorship in higher education, he is broadly interested in literacies, pedagogies, teacher education, and writing program administration.

Charles N. Lesh is associate professor of English at Auburn University. Charlie regularly researches and teaches on community and public writing, subculture, space and place, and rhetorical theory. He is the author most recently of *The Writing of Where: Graffiti and the Production of Writing Spaces.*

Brad Lucas is associate professor of English at Texas Christian University, where he has served as department chair, director of both undergraduate and graduate programs, pre-law advisor, and a member of thirty-three thesis and dissertation committees. He is the former editor of *Composition Studies,* the author of *Radicals, Rhetoric, and the War: The University of Nevada in the Wake of Kent State,* and the recipient of his college's Graduate Faculty Mentor Award in 2021.

Aurora Matzke's work largely focuses on systems theories, feminist leadership principles, and open-access education initiatives. She has served as an assistant and associate professor, WPA, core (liberal arts) director, and senior associate provost. She currently serves as the Writing Center director at Chapman University. She has publications in journals and edited collections around feminist leadership, digital education, and open-access education.

Kelly Medina-López is assistant professor of composition studies at California State–Monterey Bay. She researches Latinx and Indigenous rhetorics and writing, border studies, language politics, and myths, monsters, and ghost stories. You can find her projects in *Constellations, Latinx Rhetoric and Writing Studies,* and a co-edited collection, *Monsters and Saints: LatIndigenous Landscapes and Spectral Storytelling.*

Melissa Nicolas is professor of English at Washington State University. Her research interests include disability studies, the rhetoric of health and medicine, and feminist studies.

Most recently she published the co-edited collection *Our Body of Work* with Anna Sicari. Her work has appeared in numerous collections and journals, but her greatest joy is watching her graduate students go out and change the world.

Gregory J. Palermo is assistant teaching professor in the Writing Program at Emory University. His research and teaching focus on the rhetorics of data, algorithms, and disciplinary formation. He has worked as a research associate and project manager for the Digital Scholarship Group in Northeastern University Library and a Graduate Fellow of the NULab for Texts, Maps, and Networks. His work has appeared in the *Journal of Writing Analytics* and *Digital Humanities Quarterly (DHQ)*, and he has been a managing editor of *DHQ*. He currently serves as co-editor of reviews for *The Journal of Interactive Technology and Pedagogy*.

John Pell is associate professor of English and the director of Whitworth University's Writing Program. His scholarship focuses on rhetoric and human rights, composition pedagogy, public discourse, and collaboration. His work has appeared in a number of edited collections, as well as in *Present Tense, Literacy in Composition Studies,* and *Teaching English in the Two-Year College*. This fall John joined Dr. Jess Clements as a co-managing editor of *Present Tense: A Journal of Rhetoric in Society*.

Mya Poe is associate professor of English at Northeastern University. Her research focuses on writing assessment and writing development, with particular attention to equity and fairness. She has published four books, including her latest book, *Writing Placement in Two-Year Colleges: The Pursuit of Equity in Postsecondary Education*. She is co-editor of *Written Communication*.

Thomas Polk serves as director of Writing Across the Curriculum at George Mason University, where he also teaches academic and professional writing in the Department of English. He has published on assignment design, mentoring, and research methodologies in writing studies, and his scholarship appears in *College Composition and Communication, WAC Journal, Across the Disciplines,* and other venues. His current research project focuses on authenticity, access, and holistic writing development.

Malea Powell is professor in the College of Arts and Letters at Michigan State University as well as a faculty member in American Indian and Indigenous Studies. She is the editor of *College Composition and Communication*, director of the Cultural Rhetorics Consortium, founding editor of *Constellations: A Journal of Cultural Rhetorics,* past chair of the CCCC, and editor emerita of *SAIL: Studies in American Indian Literatures*. A widely published scholar and poet, her current book project, *The Medicine Path*, examines the continuum of Indigenous rhetorical production in North America, from beadwork to alphabetic writing to traditional medicine practices. In her spare time, Powell does beadwork, reads tarot, and hangs out with other aunties, artists, poets, and healers.

Devon Fitzgerald Ralston directs the University Writing Center and teaches writing and rhetoric courses at Winthrop University. Her research interests include intellectual property, identity, and online communities.

Devon Skyler Regan is an undergraduate student majoring in English at Northeastern University. She is an advocate of the illuminative and transformative power of language and has worked with Mya since 2019 on the Multilingual Writing Assessment Project. In her spare time, she thinks a lot about human and animal rights, and currently serves as curation manager at WRBB 104.9 FM.

ABOUT THE AUTHORS

Jessica Rivera-Mueller is assistant professor of English at Utah State University. At USU, she directs the Department of English's concurrent enrollment program and teaches courses in English education and writing studies. Her scholarship focuses on facilitating teacher-learning for middle school, high school, and college English teachers. Her work has appeared in *Teaching/Writing: The Journal of Writing Teacher Education*, *Journal on Empowering Teaching Excellence*, *Prompt: A Journal of Academic Writing Assignments*, *Utah English Journal*, and edited collections in the fields of writing studies and education. Jessica also serves as the current president for the Utah Council of Teachers of English.

Alisa Russell is assistant professor in the Writing Program at Wake Forest University, where she also researches and facilitates Writing Across the Curriculum initiatives. Her most recent projects explore genre access in government writing, and her articles have appeared in publications such as *Written Communication*, *Pedagogy*, and *The WAC Journal*.

Kellie Sharp-Hoskins is professor at New Mexico State University, where she specializes in critical rhetoric and writing studies and directs the Writing Program. Emphasizing the complex relations among language and bodies in pedagogies and public rhetorics, her research and collaborations have appeared in *Enculturation*, *Peitho*, and *Rhetoric Review*, as well as a number of edited collections. Her monograph, *Rhetoric in Debt*, was published by the Penn State University Press Series in Transdisciplinary Rhetorics in 2023.

Anna Sicari is assistant professor at Southern Illinois University. Her research interests include feminist theories, research methodologies, and rhetorics; writing program administration; writing center theory and pedagogy; and community work.

Trixie Smith is director of the Writing Center and the Red Cedar Writing Project at Michigan State University, where she is associate professor in the Department of Writing, Rhetoric, and Cultures and assistant director of the graduate program. Her teaching and research are infused with issues of gender and activism even as they revolve around writing center theory and practice, Writing Across the Curriculum and across the globe, and teacher / tutor training. Likewise, these areas often intersect with her interests in pop culture, community engagement, and the idea that we're just humans learning with / from other humans (you know, with bodies, feelings, lives outside the academy).

Sandra (Sandy) L. Tarabochia is associate professor of English at the University of Oklahoma. Her research and teaching interests include holistic writerhuman development, critical and artistic writing research methods, and rhetoric and sexuality. She is the author of "Reframing the Relational: A Pedagogical Ethic for Cross-Curricular Literacy Work" (2017), part of the NCTE series Studies in Writing and Rhetoric, and co-editor of *Diverse Approaches to Teaching, Learning, and Writing Across the Curriculum: IWAC at 25* (2020), part of the WAC Clearinghouse Perspectives on Writing series. Sandy is a founding co-editor of *Writers: Craft and Context*, an open-access, interdisciplinary journal committed to inclusive publication and equitable representation.

John Paul Tassoni is professor of English / languages, literatures, and writing at Miami University. Among publications in basic writing, open-access education, and teacher education, he has co-edited three collections on English pedagogy and co-founded and served as editor for two scholarly journals, *Open Words: Access and English Studies* and *Journal on Centers for Teaching and Learning*. John has also served as a WPA, co-coordinator of his campus's Center for Teaching and Learning, and university director of Liberal Education.

Beth A. Towle is an assistant professor of English and associate director of the Writing Center at Salisbury University. Her work on institutional relationships, first-generation and working-class students, and writing center administration has been published or is forthcoming in the *Writing Center Journal, The Peer Review, WLN,* and several edited collections.

Qianqian Zhang-Wu assistant professor of English and director of Multilingual Writing at Northeastern University. Her research and teaching focuses on language, race, and power. Zhang-Wu is author of the award-winning book *Languaging Myths and Realities: Journeys of Chinese International Students.* She is the recipient of the 2023 CCCC Outstanding Teaching Award, 2022 CIES Best Book Award, 2023 CCCC Research Impact Award, and 2023 CCCC Advancement of Knowledge Award Honorable Mention.

www.ingramcontent.com/pod-product-compliance
Lightning Source LLC
Chambersburg PA
CBHW060551080526
44585CB00013B/528